T0235329

Lecture Notes in Computer Science　　9409

Commenced Publication in 1973
Founding and Former Series Editors:
Gerhard Goos, Juris Hartmanis, and Jan van Leeuwen

More information about this series at http://www.springer.com/series/7408

Xuandong Li · Zhiming Liu · Wang Yi (Eds.)

Dependable Software Engineering

Theories, Tools, and Applications

First International Symposium, SETTA 2015
Nanjing, China, November 4–6, 2015
Proceedings

 Springer

Editors
Xuandong Li
Nanjing University
Nanjing
China

Wang Yi
Uppsala University
Uppsala
Sweden

Zhiming Liu
Birmingham City University
Birmingham
UK

ISSN 0302-9743   ISSN 1611-3349   (electronic)
Lecture Notes in Computer Science
ISBN 978-3-319-25941-3   ISBN 978-3-319-25942-0   (eBook)
DOI 10.1007/978-3-319-25942-0

Library of Congress Control Number: 2015952753

LNCS Sublibrary: SL2 – Programming and Software Engineering

Springer Cham Heidelberg New York Dordrecht London
© Springer International Publishing Switzerland 2015

Printed on acid-free paper

Springer International Publishing AG Switzerland is part of Springer Science+Business Media
(www.springer.com)

Preface

This volume contains the papers presented at the inaugural conference of SETTA — The Symposium on Dependable Software Engineering: Theories, Tools and Applications — held during November 4–6, 2015 in Nanjing, China.

Formal methods emerged as an discipline area of computer science and software engineering half a century ago. An international community has been formed researching, developing, and teaching formal theories, techniques, and tools for software modeling, specification, design, and verification. However, its impact upon commonly used software systems is still far from convincing to software engineering practitioners. The gap between the development of formal methods and the advances in software technologies is not getting narrower. More precisely, the relation between formal methods and software technologies is not well understood. This is clearly reflected by the challenges in their applications in engineering large-scale systems, including cyber-physical systems (CPS), networks of things, and cloud-based systems, which have multi-dimensional complexities. This background is the motivation for this new symposium series on the foundations, practice, and trends in formal software engineering methods, with the mission and vision to build a high-quality forum for computer scientists from the Chinese and international communities to exchange academic ideas, and to strengthen collaboration between the formal methods communities inside and outside China. SETTA has been established with a long-term view in expectation that younger scientists will play an ever greater role.

SETTA 2015 received over 70 submissions of abstracts, and among them 60 materialized as full-paper submissions with authors from 22 countries. Each full-paper submission was reviewed by at least three Program Committee members. After two weeks of online discussions, the committee decided to accept 20 papers for presentation at the conference.

We would like to express our gratitude to all the researchers who submitted their work to the symposium. We are particular thankful to all colleagues who served on the Program Committee, as well as the external reviewers, whose professional and hard work in the review process helped us to prepare a high-quality conference program. Special thanks go to the invited speakers, Sanjoy Baruah from the University of North Carolina at Chapel Hill, David Harel from the Weizmann Institute of Science, and Huimin Lin from the Software Institute of Chinese Academy of Sciences, for their willingness to talk about their research to and share their perspective about formal methods in software engineering. The abstracts of the invited talks are included in this volume.

The inaugural edition of a conference series is always more challenging, thus it received more support. Martin Fräenzle and Cliff Jones made a great start to the organization of the event in 2013 and put in a lot of work ever since. Organizing Chair Xin Chen, Publication Chair Martin Fräenzle, and Publicity Chairs Jonathan Bowen and Lijun Zhang worked very hard to make the conference possible. We are very grateful for their support. The Steering Committee, led by Naijun Zhan, and the Advisory Board gave their enthusiastic support and advice on all aspects of the conference. Finally, we enjoyed great support from Nanjing University, with the support of General Chair Professor Jian Lv and the local organisers in particular, without which the conference could not have happened

In addition to the main conference program of the presentations included in this volume, the first Young Researchers Workshop on Formal Methods (YR-SETTA 2015) organized by Xinyu Feng and Zhilin Wu was held on November 3, 2015. We would like to offer our thanks to all the organizers for their work, which led to a successful workshop.

September 2015   Xuandong Li
                                                                        Zhiming Liu
                                                                         Wang Yi

Organization

Program Co-chairs

Xuandong Li   Nanjing University, China
Zhiming Liu   Birmingham City University, UK
Wang Yi   Uppsala University, Sweden

Program Committee

Farhad Arbab	CWI and Leiden University, The Netherlands
Luis Barbosa	Universidade do Minho, Portugal
Nikolaj Bjorner	Microsoft Research, USA
Jonathan P. Bowen	Birmingham City University, UK
Michael Butler	University of Southampton, UK
Martin Fräenzle	University of Oldenburg, Germany
Goran Frehse	Université Joseph Fourier Grenoble 1–Verimag, France
Lindsay Groves	Victoria University of Wellington, New Zealand
Ian J. Hayes	University of Queensland, Australia
Holger Hermanns	Saarland University, Germany
Gerwin Klein	NICTA and UNSW, Australia
Tei-Wei Kuo	National Taiwan University, China
Insup Lee	University of Pennsylvania, USA
Xuandong Li	Nanjing University, China
Shaoying Liu	Hosei University, Japan
Zhiming Liu	Birmingham City University, UK
Xiaoguang Mao	National University of Defense Technology, China
Paritosh Pandya	TIFR, India
Jun Pang	University of Luxembourg, Luxembourg
Paul Pettersson	Mälardalen University, Sweden
Shengchao Qin	Teesside University, UK
Zongyan Qiu	Peking University, China
Jean-Francois Raskin	Université Libre de Bruxelles, Belgium
Stefan Ratschan	Czech Academy of Sciences, Czech Republic
Martin Steffen	University of Oslo, Norway
Cesare Tinelli	The University of Iowa, USA
Tarmo Uustalu	Tallinn University of Technology, Estonia
Hung Dang Van	UET, Vietnam National University, Vientam
Irina Virbitskaite	A.P. Ershov Institute of Informatics Systems, Russian Academy of Sciences, Russia
Farn Wang	National Taiwan University, China

Qixin Wang	The Hong Kong Polytechnic University, SAR China
Yi Wang	Uppsala University, Sweden
Lijun Zhang	Institute of Software, Chinese Academy of Sciences, China
Jianhua Zhao	Nanjing University, China
Huibiao Zhu	East China Normal University, China

Additional Reviewers

Attie, Paul	Hofner, Peter	Salehi Fathabadi, Asieh
Bannister, Callum	Ivanov, Radoslav	Sankur, Ocan
Chang, Hsin Yu	Jansen, David N.	Sewell, Thomas
Chen, Sanjian	Jhawar, Ravi	Sokolsky, Oleg
Chen, Wei Ming	King, Andrew	Su, Wen
Chipara, Octav	Korovina, Margarita	Truong, Hoang
Colley, John	Li, Qin	Tseng, Chien Chih
Enoiu, Eduard Paul	Lin, Han-Yi	Wang, Tse Yuan
Fang, Huixing	Lindsay, Peter	Wildman, Luke
Feng, Lu	Marinescu, Raluca	Wilkinson, Toby
Gallagher, Marcus	Monmege, Benjamin	Winter, Kirsten
Gribovskaya, Nataliya	Moszkowski, Ben	Xu, Zhiwu
Hahn, Ernst Moritz	Murray, Toby	Yin, Hang
Hoang, Thai Son	Neves, Renato	Yuan, Qixia
Hu, Tingting	Park, Junkil	Zhu, Longfei

Invited Talks

Criticality-Cognizant Modeling and Analysis of Mixed-Criticality Systems (Extended Abstract)

Sanjoy Baruah

The University of North Carolina
Chapel Hill, NC 27599, USA
baruah@cs.unc.edu
http://www.cs.unc.edu/~baruah

Abstract. Driven by cost and related considerations, there is an increasing trend in embedded systems towards implementing functionalities of different degrees of importance (or criticality) upon a shared platform. The real-time scheduling community has been developing a theory of mixed-criticality scheduling that seeks to solve resource allocation problems for such systems; this theory, used in conjunction with appropriate software engineering methodologies, has the potential to significantly enhance our ability to design and implement large, complex, real-time systems in a manner that is both provably correct and resource-efficient.

Many safety-critical systems must have their correctness established at very high levels of assurance, sometimes to the satisfaction of statutory Certification Authorities. In earlier times, such correctness was ensured by keeping things very simple: safety-critical computer systems were restricted to being very simple, responsible for very simple, highly repetitive, functionalities. They were commonly implemented as carefully hand-crafted code executing upon very simple and predictable processors. Run-time behavior was therefore highly predictable, and correctness could hence be demonstrated in a fairly straightforward manner.

Over time, safety-critical system requirements have increased significantly in size and complexity, and continue to increase at a very rapid pace. It has consequently become necessary to implement such systems upon more powerful computing platforms. Cost and availability considerations dictate that such platforms be built using commercial off-the-shelf (COTS) processors and other components. But COTS components are generally developed with the objective of providing improved "typical" or average-case performance rather than better worst-case guarantees; they therefore incorporate advanced features that do indeed significantly improve average performance but may also lead to very large *variances* in run-time behavior. In order to predict the precise behavior that will be experienced during run-time by any particular process executing upon such a platform, extensive knowledge of the precise context during run-time – the inputs that are provided to the process during a specific run; the states of the other processes that are executing concurrently; etc.– must be known; since such knowledge is not usually obtainable during system design time, the precise run-time behavior is essentially unpredictable during the system's design process.

Since the systems are so complex and the run-time behavior essentially unpredictable at design time, system correctness at the required high levels of assurance is demonstrated during the system design process by tremendous over-provisioning of computational and other platform resources. That is, very conservative and pessimistic assumptions are made regarding run-time system behavior, and correctness is demonstrated to hold in the face of such conservative assumptions. However, these very conservative assumptions are highly unlikely to occur during the typical run; hence, much of the over-provisioned resources are unlikely to actually be used during run-time. As a consequence, such conservative system implementations based upon making very pessimistic resource-allocation design decisions will tend to experience very low resource utilization during run-time. SWaP considerations (the Size, and Weight of the implementation platform, and the Power, or more accurately, the energy, that is consumed by it) make such resource under-utilization increasingly unacceptable. This has motivated a move towards *mixed-criticality* implementations, in which highly safety-critical functionalities share an implementation platform with less critical functionalities. Informally speaking, the idea behind such mixed-criticality implementations is that the resources that are provisioned to highly critical functionalities during design time, but are likely to remain unused by these functionalities at run-time, can be "re-claimed" and used to make performance guarantees, albeit at lower levels of assurance, to the less critical functionalities.

Mixed-criticality scheduling theory. The recently emergent field of mixed-criticality scheduling theory is concerned with the study of resource-allocation, scheduling, and synchronization in such mixed-criticality systems. Two related but distinct approaches have been widely investigated: one focused primarily on run-time robustness, and the other on verification.

Run-time robustness is a form of fault tolerance that allows graceful degradation to occur in a criticality-cognizant manner: if all functionalities implemented upon a shared platform cannot be serviced satisfactorily the goal is to ensure that less critical functionalities are denied their requested levels of service before more critical functionalities are. Approaches in mixed-criticality scheduling theory that seek to ensure such run-time robustness are centered upon identifying, during run-time, when cumulative resource demand exceeds the available supply, and triggering a *mode change* when this happens. Real-time scheduling theory has a rich history of results towards obtaining resource-efficient implementations of mode changes; these techniques may be adapted to ensure run-time robust mixed-criticality systems.

Static verification of mixed-criticality systems is closely related to the problem of certification. The increasing trend towards computerized control of an ever-increasing range of functionalities, both safety-critical and non-critical, means that even in highly safety-critical systems, typically only a relatively small fraction of the overall system is actually of critical functionality and needs to be certified. In order to certify a system as being correct, the certification authority (CA) may mandate that certain assumptions be made about the worst-case behavior of the system during run-time. It is often the case that these assumptions that are mandated by the CA are far more conservative than those the system designer would typically use during the system design process if certification was not required. However, while the CA is only concerned with the correctness of the safety-critical part of the system the system designer wishes to ensure that the entire system is correct, including the non-critical parts. Vestal[1] first identified the challenge of obtaining certification for integrated system implementations in which different functionalities need to have their correctness validated to different levels of assurance, while simultaneously ensuring efficient resource-utilization. The real-time scheduling community has since produced a vast amount of work that builds upon Vestal's seminal idea.

A call for participation by the SETTA community. Mixed-criticality scheduling theory offers a promising approach towards efficient implementations of provably correct safety-critical systems. However, much of this work is based upon relatively low-level and simple workload models, such as collections of independent jobs, or systems represented as a finite collection of recurrent (e.g., periodic and sporadic) tasks. Prior experience has shown that such simple models are inadequate for building truly complex systems; instead, the concepts and ideas revealed by the exploration of such simple models must be integrated into the software engineering design flow used in safety-critical systems development. There is therefore a pressing need for the dependable software engineering community to take a closer look at mixed-criticality systems, to integrate the latest results and insights from mixed-criticality scheduling theory into the tools and theories that are the focus of this community.

Acknowledgements. The ideas discussed in this extended abstract are based upon discussions with a number of colleagues and research collaborators, Alan Burns in particular. This research was supported in part by NSF grants CNS 1115284, CNS 1218693, CNS 1409175, and CPS 1446631, AFOSR grant FA9550-14-1-0161, ARO grant W911NF-14-1-0499, and a grant from General Motors Corp.

S. Vestal. Preemptive scheduling of multi-criticality systems with varying degrees of execution time assurance. In *Proceedings of the Real-Time Systems Symposium*, pages 239–243, Tucson, AZ, December 2007. IEEE Computer Society Press.

Wise Computing
(Abstract of Invited Lecture)

David Harel

The Weizmann Institute of Science, Rehovot, Israel

Major advances in languages, tools and methodologies have improved our ability to develop reactive systems, but the task remains difficult, expensive and error prone. One of the key reasons is the growing complexity of many kinds of reactive systems, which increasingly prevents the human mind from managing a comprehensive picture of all their relevant elements and behaviors. We present a vision that calls for a major change in the way complex software and systems are developed, by shifting the power balance between the human engineers and the development environment. In our computing paradigm, which we term *Wise Computing*, the development environment is turned into a much smarter, proactive, creative and interactive stakeholder in the development and maintenance processes. Ideally, the computer will join the development team as an equal partner−knowledgeable, concerned, and active.

The *wise development suite* (WDS) would interact with us wisely, like a colleague. It would respond to our needs with knowledge, and, utilizing extensive computing power "under its hood", will proactively help in the variety of tasks that constitute the development process of the desired system. It should thus become a creative and proactive stakeholder, perhaps even a leader, in the development process. This will be manifested in it initiating discourse and actions based on deep insights into the system's structure and behavior, its overarching goals and rationale, and the environment in which it operates. It will use relevant knowledge (both general and domain-specific) to participate in the elicitation, formalization, validation and iterative enrichment of requirements, thus helping to increase confidence in the requirements, and establishing their consistency. And in the spirit of almost 30 years of model-driven development, the WDS will also be central to the ability to directly execute/simulate those requirements and/or translate them into running code.

The WDS will be able to explore, on its own, functionality and behavior both exhaustively and under various "what-if" conditions, communicating on multiple levels. Throughout development and maintenance, the computer will be constantly investigating itself, in a sort of self-aware fashion. It will detect problems, including bad and conflicting behaviors, goals and requirements that are not met, inefficiency in execution, and unneeded complexities in specification and implementation. The WDS will then initiate and propose changes and enhancements.

This represents joint work with Guy Katz, Rami Marelly and Assaf Marron.

The WDS vision calls also for runtime enhancements, where the system will be able to interact with users and with other systems in order to explain past behavior and allow the user to influence future behaviors. For example, a door in a chemical plant or an airplane will be able to explain to a human why it is presently closed, what will happen if it is manually opened, and discuss in detail sensor information and alternative sequences of manual and automated actions associated with opening and closing it.

The two-way interactions of the WDS will employ visual representations, examples, pseudo and conventional code. A key capability will be the use of natural language in both directions. Indeed, despite much work on natural languages for requirements and program specification, we are still far from the point where we can automatically read and parse requirements specified in a way that is natural and accessible to humans, and from them create a correct formal specification.

The most immediate benefit of a wise computing suite will be, of course, a significant reduction in the development time and cost of complex systems, and will result in much improved system quality. Run-time wisdom will increase user and regulator confidence in systems, further expanding development and adoption. And over and above all of this, we believe that in the farther future we will experience new dimensions of innovation, as rich new capabilities and new ranges of safety will be initiated (and often invented!) by wise systems, rather than only by humans.

How will the WDS do all this? Well, this is a vision, and for many facets thereof much research is required even to figure out they can be achieved. However, we have already done some work, and our ideas are explained in a paper we recently submitted for publication. A preliminary version can be found at: http://arxiv.org/abs/1501.05924. Also, we have built a modest and preliminary wise development suite, which we view as a promising proof-of-concept. The current version of the tool, as well as prerecorded video clips demonstrating its main principles on two examples, can be found at: http://www.wisdom.weizmann.ac.il/ ~ harel/CACM.wisecomputing.

The Myth of Linearization Points

Huimin Lin

State Key Laboratory of Computer Science
Institute of Software, Chinese Academy of Sciences
lhm@ios.ac.cn

Abstract. Linearizability has been established as a widely accepted criterion for the correctness of concurrent data structures. Intuitively, an implementation of a concurrent object is *linearizable* with respect to a sequential specification if every method call has a *linearization point* at some instant between its invocation and return, such that every method call appears "to take effect" instantly at its linearization point, behaving as defined by the specification. However, despite more than two decades of intensive studies, the notion of linearization points still remains informal. This has caused confusions in the verification of Linearizability.

To formulate a formal definition of linearization points we work in a behavioral formwork in which the semantics of an object system is represented as a labeled transition system. Our characterization of linearization points is based on a refined notion of trace equivalence, termed *max-trace equivalence*, which equites two states if they have not only the same set of (ordinary) traces but also the same branching potentials of the states on their traces. With max-trace equivalence two kinds of internal transitions can be distinguished: those change the object's states, and those do not. The former corresponds to linearization points.

It turns out that max-trace equivalence coincides with branching bisimulation, a refinement of Milner's weak bisimulation by requiring two related states should respect not only their own branching structures but also the branching potentials of all intermediate states that are passed through. This allows, for finite state systems, to efficiently compute the equivalence class under max-trace equivalence, from which a quotient system can be constructed. Since most internal transitions in the original object system are not linearization points and have been abstracted away in the quotient construction, the size of the quotient system is significantly smaller than the original system, which results in huge state space reductions when verifying linearizability. The advantages of our approach have been confirmed by experiments on benchmark problems.

(Based on joint work with Xiaoxiao Yang, Joost-Pieter Katoen and Hao Wu)

Contents

Probabilistic Systems

Fault Trees on a Diet
— Automated Reduction by Graph Rewriting —

Sebastian Junges[1]([⊠]), Dennis Guck[2], Joost-Pieter Katoen[1,2], Arend Rensink[2], and Mariëlle Stoelinga[2]

[1] Software Modeling and Verification, RWTH Aachen University, Aachen, Germany
`sebastian.junges@cs.rwth-aachen.de`
[2] Formal Methods and Tools, University of Twente, Enschede, The Netherlands

Abstract. Fault trees are a popular industrial technique for reliability modelling and analysis. Their extension with common reliability patterns, such as spare management, functional dependencies, and sequencing — known as *dynamic* fault trees (DFTs) — has an adverse effect on scalability, prohibiting the analysis of complex, industrial cases by, e.g., probabilistic model checkers. This paper presents a novel, fully automated reduction technique for DFTs. The key idea is to interpret DFTs as directed graphs and exploit graph rewriting to simplify them. We present a collection of rewrite rules, address their correctness, and give a simple heuristic to determine the order of rewriting. Experiments on a large set of benchmarks show substantial DFT simplifications, yielding state space reductions and timing gains of up to two orders of magnitude.

1 Introduction

Probabilistic safety assessment is common practice in the design and monitoring of safety-critical systems, and often required by law. Typical measures of interest are the system reliability (what is the probability that the system is operational up to time t?) and availability (what is the expected up time?).

Fault tree analysis [38] is one of the most prominent safety assessment technique. It is standardized by the IEC [21], and deployed by many companies and institutions, like FAA, NASA, ESA, Airbus, Honeywell, etc. Fault trees (FTs) model how failures propagate through the system: FT leaves model component failures and are equipped with continuous probability distributions; FT gates model how component failures lead to system failures. Due to, e.g., redundancy, not every single component failure leads to a system failure.

Dynamic fault trees (DFTs) [13,38] are a well-known extension to standard fault trees that cater for common dependability patterns, such as spare management, functional dependency, and sequencing. Analysis of DFTs relies on extracting an underlying stochastic model, such as Bayesian networks [3,6], continuous-time Markov chains (CTMCs) [14], stochastic Petri nets [32,2], and interactive Markov chains [4]. Stochastic model checking is an efficient technique to analyse these models [25,33]. Since the order in which the DFT components fail matters, these approaches severely suffer from the state space explosion problem.

ⓒ Springer International Publishing Switzerland 2015
X. Li et al. (Eds.): SETTA 2015, LNCS 9409, pp. 3–18, 2015.
DOI: 10.1007/978-3-319-25942-0_1

This paper presents a novel technique to reduce the state space of DFTs prior to their analysis. The key idea is to consider DFTs as (typed) directed graphs and manipulate them by *graph transformation* [15], a powerful technique to rewrite graphs via pattern matching. We present a catalogue of 28 (families of) rules that rewrite a given DFT into a smaller, equivalent DFT, having the same system reliability and availability. Various rewrite rules are context sensitive.

We have implemented our techniques on top of the graph transformation tool GROOVE [17] and the DFT analysis tool DFTCalc [1], yielding a fully automated tool chain for graph-based DFT reduction and analysis. A simple heuristic determines the order to apply the rewrite rules. We have analysed several variations of seven benchmarks, comprised of over 170 fault trees in total, originating from standard examples from the literature as well as industrial case studies from aerospace and railway engineering. Rewriting enabled to cope with 49 DFTs that could not be handled before. For the other fault trees rewriting pays off, being much faster and more memory efficient, up to two orders of magnitude. This applies to both the peak memory footprint and the size of the resulting Markov chain (see Figures 9(b) and 9(c), page 15). This comes at no run-time penalty: graph rewriting is very fast and the stochastic model generation is significantly accelerated due to the DFT reduction.

Related Work. Reduction of fault trees is well-investigated. An important technique is to identify independent static sub-trees [31,26,19,39,35]. These static sub-trees are analysed using efficient techniques (such as BDDs), whereas the dynamic parts require more complex methods, as mentioned above. While such modular approaches yield significant speed ups, they largely depend on the DFT shape. Shared sub-trees, or a dynamic top-node, inhibits the application of these techniques. Merle *et al.* [28,29] map DFTs onto boolean algebra extended with temporal operators. The resulting expressions can then be minimised via syntactic manipulation. This approach imposes several restrictions on the DFTs. Parametric fault trees [32,2] exploit the symmetry in replicated sub-trees while translating DFTs (using graph transformation) to generalized stochastic Petri nets. Finally, DFTCalc exploits compositional aggregation, of (interactive) Markov chains using bisimulation [4].

2   Dynamic Fault Trees

A dynamic fault tree (DFT) is a tree (or more generally, a directed acyclic graph) that describes how component failures propagate through the system. DFT leaves represent component failures, called basic events (BEs; drawn as ellipses).

Fail-safe components and components that have failed already, are denoted respectively by CONST($\perp$) and CONST($\top$).

Gates, depicted in Figure 1, model failure propagation. The static gates OR, AND, VOT(k) fail if respectively one, all or k of their inputs fail. The PAND, SPARE and FDEP are dynamic gates. A PAND-gate fails if the inputs fail from left to right; if the components fail in any other order, then no failure occurs.

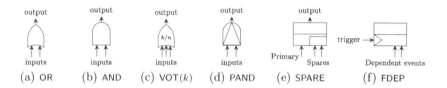

(a) OR   (b) AND   (c) VOT(k)   (d) PAND   (e) SPARE   (f) FDEP

Fig. 1. Dynamic fault tree gates.

A SPARE-gate contains one primary, and one or more spare inputs. If the primary input fails, then a spare takes over its functionality, putting the spare from dormant into active mode. If all spares have failed as well, then the SPARE-gate fails. Note that (1) primary and spares can be subsystems; and (2) spares can be shared among several components. An FDEP-gate contains a trigger input, which triggers the failure of all its dependent events.

We follow the standard approach and model component failure by exponential probability distributions. Since dormant spare components fail less frequently, we equip each leaf node with a failure rate $\lambda \in \mathbb{R}^+$ and a dormancy factor $\alpha \in [0,1]$, reducing the failure rate of a dormant component. Thus, the probability for an active component to fail with time t equals $1 - e^{-\lambda t}$; for a dormant component this is $1 - e^{-\alpha \lambda t}$.

Example 1. The DFT in Figure 2 represents the (simplified) failure behaviour of a railway level crossing [18], consisting of three subsystems: the sensors, the barriers and the controller. The crossing fails if either of these subsystems fails. The sensor system fails if at least two out of the four redundant sensors fail Furthermore, there can be a detection problem due to a disconnection of the cables, making all sensors unavailable, modelled by the FDEP-gate No detection specifying that the trigger Disconnection causes the failure of its dependent events Sensor$_1$–Sensor$_4$. Finally, the barriers fail if either the main and spare motor fail, modelled by the SPARE-gate Motors, or if the switch and then a motor fails.

Well-Formedness. As usual, DFTs must be *well-formed*, meaning: (a) the DFT is acyclic; (b) leaves have leaf-types, other nodes have gate-types; (c) VOT(k)-gates

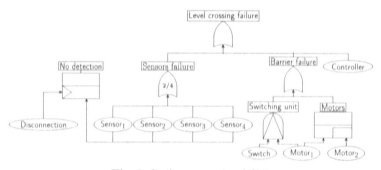

Fig. 2. Railway crossing DFT.

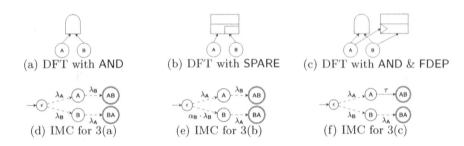

(a) DFT with AND   (b) DFT with SPARE   (c) DFT with AND & FDEP

(d) IMC for 3(a)   (e) IMC for 3(b)   (f) IMC for 3(c)

Fig. 3. Example DFT to IMC transformations

have at least k inputs; (d) the top level event is not an FDEP; (e) FDEPs have no parents; (f) all dependent events of an FDEP are BEs; (g) spare modules, i.e., sub-trees under a SPARE-gate, are independent; (h) primary spare modules, i.e., sub-trees under the primary input of a SPARE-gate, do not contain CONST($\top$)-nodes; (i) primary spare modules are never shared between SPARE-gates.

DFT Semantics. The semantics of a DFT F is — like in [10] — expressed using a transition system $\mathcal{C}_F$, where transitions correspond to the failure of a BE and states to sequences of distinct BEs. As the properties of interest are stochastic in nature, $\mathcal{C}_F$ is an interactive Markov chain (IMC) [20]. This IMC has two types of transitions: interactive (here: immediate τ-transitions) and Markovian (labelled with a rate λ, being the parameter of an exponential distributed delay).

The formal definitions and the construction of $\mathcal{C}_F$ are given in [22]. Here, we illustrate the principle by three small examples, depicted in Figure 3. For ease of reference, we have labelled each state with the sequence of failed BEs. The DFT in Figure 3(a) fails if BE A and then B (upper path in 3(d)) fails, or if first B and then A fails (lower path in 3(d)). The DFT in Figure 3(b) fails if BEs A and B fail, as above. However, if A has not yet failed, then the failure rate of B is reduced by factor α_B. Thus, B is initially dormant, and failes with rate $\lambda_B \cdot \alpha_B$ (see 3(e)). The DFT in Figure 3(c) also fails if BEs A and B fail. However, the failure of A causes B to fail immediately afterwards, as realized by the τ-transition in Figure 3(f).

DFT Analysis. A wide variety of qualitative and quantitative DFT analysis techniques are available, see [36] for an overview. We concentrate on two of the most common quantitative measures: the *reliability until a given mission time t*, i.e., the probability that no failure occurs within time t, and the *mean time to failure* (MTTF), i.e., the expected time until the first system failure. Example measures for the DFT in Figure 2 are: "what is the reliability of the level crossing for a time frame of 10 years after deployment?", or "what is the mean time until a first failure of the level crossing occurs?".

We define the probability measures on a DFT F in terms of $\mathcal{C}_F$. Let Fail be the set of states in IMC $\mathcal{C}_F$ in which the top event in F has failed. If a state has multiple dependent events, their order is non-deterministically resolved. This is formalised using a policy (or scheduler) $\mathcal{P}$ on $\mathcal{C}_F$, resulting in a continuous-time Markov chain $\mathcal{C}_F[\mathcal{P}]$.

Definition 1 (Relevant measures). *Given a DFT F, a policy $\mathcal{P}$ on F, and a mission time $t \in \mathbb{R}$, the* reliability *of F under $\mathcal{P}$ given t, $\mathsf{RELY}^t_{F[\mathcal{P}]}$, is given by $\mathrm{Pr}_{\mathcal{C}_F[\mathcal{P}]}(\lozenge^{\leq t}\mathsf{Fail})$. The* mean time to failure *in F under $\mathcal{P}$ $\mathsf{MTTF}_{F[\mathcal{P}]}$ is given by $\mathsf{ET}_{\mathcal{C}_F[\mathcal{P}]}(\lozenge\mathsf{Fail})$, where ET is defined as the expected time.*

3 Rewrite Rules for Dynamic Fault Trees

DFTs tend to be verbose. They are often based on the system architecture, therefore reflecting their sub-system structure [38]. Moreover, modern techniques automatically generate DFTs from architectural description languages [7], also yielding rather verbose DFTs. Given that state-of-the-art algorithms construct the underlying IMC by a parallel composition of IMCs corresponding to gates, it is a natural idea to shrink DFTs prior to their analysis. Observe that simplifying *static* fault trees (SFTs) can be done by simple Boolean manipulations [38]. This remains true for FDEPs, but no longer holds in the presence of dynamic gates such as SPARE- and PAND-gates.

We have identified a set of 28 rewrite rules valid for DFTs, which include the (now context-sensitive) rules for SFTs originating from the bounded lattice axioms. Other rules consider combination of dynamic gates which can be simplified. Each rule contains a left-hand (lhs) and a right-hand (rhs) sub-DFT; they are applied by matching the lhs in a given DFT and replacing it by the rhs. Rule application fails if it results in a non-well-formed DFT: in particular, if deletion of a node produces a dangling edge, then the rule cannot be applied. Technically, the mappings between the nodes are defined by a few graph morphisms and context restrictions. For details, see Section 4.

All rules can be used in both directions, i.e., from left to right or from right to left. Below, we present a few key rules and discuss the main issues involved, including the correctness of the rules. Please, notice that the application of some rules might cause an intermediate growth in the number of elements of the DFT, but makes other rules applicable. In this paper, we display rules only graphically. The complete set of formally defined rules can be found in [22].

Left-Flattening. The first rewrite rule is rather simple and indicates how a DFT with root A (lhs) can be flattened into a DFT with root A' (rhs). In fact, we define a family of rules here, as A can be an AND-, OR-, or PAND-gate. The rule asserts that if A's first successor B has the same type as A, the DFT can be flattened such that B's successors become A's successors (instead of its grandchildren). The rule's correctness in case A is an AND- or OR-gate is obvious; in fact, it can then be applied to any successor of A, not just the first. If A is a PAND-gate, the correctness follows from the fact that the ordering of B's successors is maintained. In this case, the restriction to the first successor is essential.

Rewrite rule 1 Left-flattening of AND-/OR-/PAND-gates

Flattening of PAND-gates. If a PAND-gate has a PAND-successor which is not necessarily its first successor, then the following rule applies. The ordering of C_1 and C_2 is ensured by C' (rhs) whereas the fact that B should fail prior to C_1 and C_2 (in that order) is guaranteed by the PAND-gate A_2 (rhs). This PAND-gate also ensures that B and C_2 should fail before D_1–D_k fail. (Note that successor B is optional.)

Rewrite rule 2 PAND-gate with a PAND-gate as successor

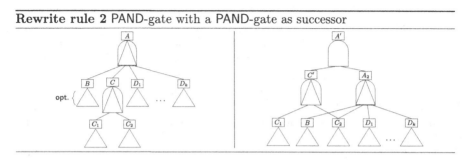

PAND-gates with a First OR-successor. This rewrite rule illustrates a distribution rule for PAND-gates. If the first successor C is an OR-gate with successors C_1 and C_2, then the DFT can be rewritten into a disjunction of two PAND-gates where the first one takes care of the failure of C_1 whereas the second PAND considers the failure of C_2. Although this rule does not give rise to a reduction of the number of DFT elements, it may enable other rewrite rules.

Rewrite rule 3 PAND-gate with an OR-gate as first successor

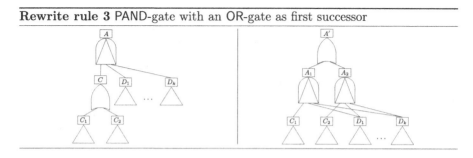

The rules so far are context-free: they can be applied to any sub-DFT matching the lhs. We now give an example of a context-sensitive rewrite rule.

Conflicting PAND-gates. Consider a DFT rooted by an AND-gate which has two PAND-successors whose ordering requirements conflict: D_1 requires B to fail before C, whereas D_2 requires the opposite. In contrast to the rule above, the rewrite rule for this case is context-sensitive: under the assumption that the successors never fail simultaneously (indicated as B and C having independent inputs), the PAND-gates D_1 and D_2 can never both fail. Therefore, the AND-root cannot fail, and the entire DFT is reduced to the DFT on the right. Note that nodes B and C are not eliminated, as they may be connected to other elements of the DFT. However, elimination of the edges may prevent the activation of elements in the sub-tree. Therefore, the rule may only be applied if, e.g., the sub-trees are activated via another path or if the sub-trees were never activated in the original DFT, as required by the context restriction ActivationConnection.

Rewrite rule 4 Conflicting PAND-gates with independent children

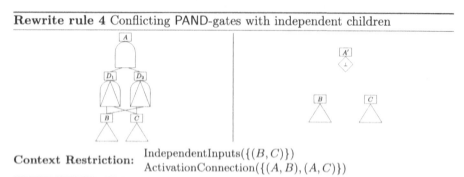

Context Restriction: IndependentInputs($\{(B,C)\}$)
ActivationConnection($\{(A,B),(A,C)\}$)

Simplifying of FDEP-gates. If the trigger event C of the FDEP occurs, then the dependent events B_1– B_m all fail, yielding a failure of the AND A. The right DFT emulates this behaviour by adding X – which only fails once trigger C occurs. The root thus fails if either all basic elements B_i fail, or trigger C occurs. This rule is context-sensitive, as its correctness depends on the fact that the successors B_1 through B_m do not have other predecessors besides the AND-gate A. Further rule allow us to get rid of both the FDEP and X in subsequent steps.

Rewrite rule 5 Simplifying FDEP in context of an AND.

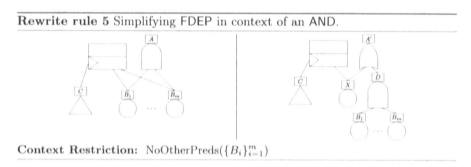

Context Restriction: NoOtherPreds($\{B_i\}_{i=1}^m$)

Rewriting Order. A DFT is rewritten by applying a series of rules, with the intention to end up with a simpler, equivalent model. We first consider an example.

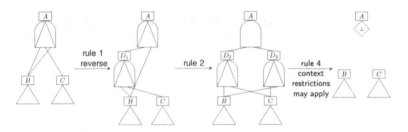

Fig. 4. Steps for rewriting PAND with a duplicate successor.

Example 2. Consider the DFT in Figure 4 (left). The second DFT results from applying rewrite rule 1 in the reverse direction. Note that this DFT is larger than the first, but enables the application of rule 2, which yields a DFT with a conflicting PAND with independent successors. Applying rule 4 finally allows us to remove the two PAND-gates.

Typically, for a given DFT many different rules are applicable, some of which may be conflicting (in the general sense of rewriting theory [12], meaning that the application of one rule makes the other inapplicable). For instance, in Figure 4, instead of applying rule 2 as a second step, we could also have applied rule 1, thereby returning to the original DFT. Our overall aim of rewriting any given DFT to a structurally simpler one can in fact be seen as a search problem in the space of DFTs, where the search steps are rule applications. In this paper, we have chosen a fixed, deterministic search strategy. We classified the rewrite rules in three groups, roughly corresponding to the notions of cleaning (e.g., removal of disconnected elements), elimination (e.g., rule 1), and rewriting (e.g., rule 2). Our heuristic is to apply rules from these groups as long as possible, with descending priority.

Correctness. In [22] it is shown that the all 28 rule families are correct, in the sense of preserving the measures-of-interest (see Definition 1).

Theorem 1. *All rewrite rules in [22] preserve all RELY- and MTTF-properties.*

The proof (cf. [22]) amounts to showing that local equivalence of lhs and rhs, consisting of a number of local conditions and context restrictions, implies global equivalence with respect to RELY and MTTF of the source and target DFT of any rule application. These local conditions are then proven to be fulfilled by the rule under consideration — much like the explanations given above.

Theorem 1 means that after rewriting a DFT F into DFT F' using our heuristic strategy (or, indeed, any sequence of rewrite rules whatsoever), we may establish F's properties by analysing the — generally smaller — F'. We notice that these results remain true even if the set of used rules is incomplete (in the sense that not all equivalent DFTs can be transformed into each other).

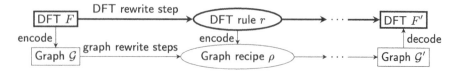

Fig. 5. Operationalising DFT rewriting via graph rewriting.

4 Rewriting DFTs via Graph Transformation

Operationalising our rewrite rules is a non-trivial step. Essentially, we need to ensure that the implementation correctly reflects the rules as formally defined. Ideally, one would like to be able to use the rule definitions themselves as executable specifications. In this paper, we have approached that ideal by using *graph transformation* (GT) as a framework in which to encode the rules, and GROOVE [17] as rule engine. Therefore, we encode the DFTs as graphs and encode rewrite rules by a *sequence* of GT rules (called *recipes* in GROOVE). The operational framework is depicted in Figure 5.

DFTs as Simple Graphs. DFTs are directed acyclic node-typed graphs with an ordering imposed on the successors (children) of every node. The graphs in our graph transformation framework, commonly called *simple graphs*, are slightly different: on the one hand they are more basic, since they do not directly support node ordering. Thus, to represent the ordering of dynamic gate successors, we use auxiliary intermediate nodes connected by next-edges. On the other hand, simple graphs are edge-labelled, offering opportunities for compact encodings. In particular, functional dependencies can be encoded as (sets of) edges rather than as nodes, leading from trigger to dependent events.

We have to omit the formal definition of simple graphs and of the DFT encoding. Instead, Figure 6 (slightly simplified for presentation purposes) shows the types of nodes and edges that may occur in a graph-encoded DFT. The italic node types are abstract (in the programming language sense, meaning that only their subtypes can be concretely instantiated). **BE**-typed nodes represent basic events, with corresponding failure rate and dormancy factor, whereas

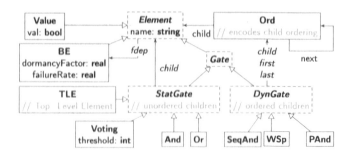

Fig. 6. Type graph for encoded DFTs (slightly simplified)

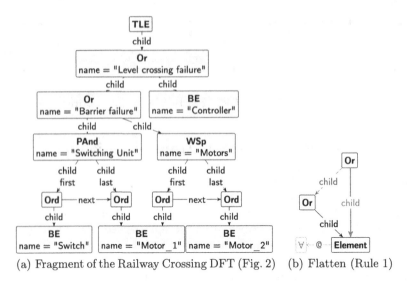

(a) Fragment of the Railway Crossing DFT (Fig. 2)   (b) Flatten (Rule 1)

Fig. 7. Example DFT and rewrite rule encodings.

Value-typed nodes represent CONST($\top$) or CONST($\bot$), depending on the val flag. **Ord**-nodes encode the child ordering of a dynamic gate, and the fdep-edges the functional dependencies, as discussed above. Figure 7(a) shows the encoding of a fragment of the Railway Crossing DFT of Figure 2.

Rewriting Through GT Rules. Our GT rules have a structure very similar to the DFT rewrite rules they encode. Each rule consists of a left hand side (lhs) and a right hand side (rhs); the difference between them specifies which nodes or edges should be deleted and which should be created upon application of the rule. GROOVE uses a graphical syntax in which lhs and rhs are combined into a single graph and color coding is used to indicate deletions and creations. In particuar, dashed blue nodes/edges should be deleted, whereas fat green nodes/edges are created upon rule application. For example, Figure 7(b) shows the encoding of the left-flattening of **Or**-gates in rule 1. A feature of GROOVE that is very convenient in this context is the ability to universally quantify over substructures [34]: in the case of left-flattening, *all* successors of the redundant **Or**-gate should be added to the root **Or**. The context-sensitive side conditions of, for instance, rules 4 and 5 are directly encoded as part of the GT rules (which are themselves context sensitive in general). The heuristic search strategy described in Section 3 is implemented in GROOVE using a control program, which is a mechanism to specify a dedicated schedule of rule applications.

Implementation. We have developed prototypical tool-support[1] exploiting the tools GROOVE [17] for graph rewriting, and DFTCalc [1] for the analysis of DFTs. As shown in Figure 8, our tool chain takes as input a DFT and a measure, i.e.,

---

[1] Available online at http://moves.rwth-aachen.de/ft-diet/.

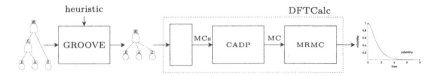

Fig. 8. Tool chain for rewriting and model checking dynamic fault trees.

the reliability up to time t, or the MTTF. We translate the DFT into the input format of GROOVE and the output of GROOVE, i.e., the rewritten graph, back into a DFT that then is analysed by DFTCalc. DFTCalc exploits CADP [16] for compositional state space generation and reduction (using bisimulation minimisation) of the underlying IMC of the DFT. Finally, the resulting Markov chain is analysed for the user-specified measure by the probabilistic model checker MRMC [24].

5   Experiments

We have selected a set of benchmarks for DFTs from the literature and from industrial case studies. We have considered four sets of benchmarks that are scalable in a natural manner, to show the scalability of the approach. Several variations of these four benchmarks have been considered, yielding in total 163 cases. We have considered another three industrial cases, yielding an additional 20 cases. All benchmarks are shortly described below; Fig. 9(d) shows, in brackets after the acronym, for each case how many instances were analysed. Full details and DFTs of the case studies, as well as all statistics can be found at http://moves.rwth-aachen.de/ft-diet/.

For each benchmark, we compared the performance of *base* and *rewriting* (rw) executions, the difference being whether or not the GROOVE component of Figure 8 was invoked before DFTCalc was run. We investigated the influence of rewriting on (1) the number of nodes in the DFT, (2) the peak memory consumption, (3) the total analysis time (including model generation, rewriting, and analysis), as well as (4) the size of the resulting Markov chain. As can be seen in Figure 9(a)-(c), rewriting DFTs improves the performance for all these criteria in almost all cases. In particular, 49 cases could be analysed that yielded a time-out or out-of-memory in the base setting.

HECS. The *Hypothetical Example Computer System (HECS)* stems from the NASA handbook on fault trees [38]. It features a computer system consisting of a processing unit (PU), a memory unit (MU) and an operator interface consisting of hardware and software. These subsystems are connected via a 2-redundant bus. The PU consists of two processors and an additional spare processor which can replace either of the two processors, and requires one working processor. The MU contains 5 memory slots, with the first three slots connected via a memory interface (MI) and the last three connected via another MI. Memory slots either fail by themselves, or if all connected interfaces have failed. The MU requires three working memory slots. We consider a system which consists of multiple (m) (identical) computer systems of which $k \leq m$ are required to be operational in order for the system to be operational. Furthermore, we vary the MI configuration, and consider variants in which all computers have a power supply which is functionally dependent on the power grid.

MCS. The *Multiprocessor Computing System (MCS)* contains computing modules (CMs) consisting of a processor, a MU and two disks. A CM fails if either the processor, the MU or both disks fail. All CMs are connected via a bus. An additional MU is connected to each pair of CMs, which can be used by both CMs in case the original memory module fails. The MCS fails, if all CMs fail or the bus fails. The original MCS model was given as a Petri net [27], a DFT has been given in [30]. The latter includes a power supply (whose failure causes all processors to fail) and assumes the usage of the spare memory component to be exclusive. This is the case we consider. Variations of this model have been given in [1,32]. Based upon these variations we consider several cases. Therefore, we consider a farm of m MCSs of which k are required to be operational. Each MCS contains n CMs (for n uneven, one spare MU is connected to three CMs). Each system has its own power supply. Which is either single power (sp, no redundancy) or double power (dp, one redundant supply for each computer).

RC. The *Railway Crossing (RC)* is an industrial case modelling failures at level crossing [18] (cf. Figure 2). We consider an RC that fails whenever any of the sensor-sets fail, or any of the barriers fail, or the controller fails. We obtain scalable versions with b identical barriers and s sets of sensors (each with their own cable which can cause a disconnect). Either the controller failure is represented by a single basic event or by a computer modeled as in HECS.

SF. The *Sensor Filter (SF)* benchmark is a DFT that is automatically generated from an AADL (Architecture Analysis & Design Language) system model [7]. The DFT is obtained by searching for combinations of basic faults which lead to the predefined configurations in the given system. The SF benchmark is a synthetic example which contains a number of sensors that are connected to some filters. The set contains a varying number of sensors and filters.

Other Case Studies. In addition to these scalable benchmarks we have considered other industrial cases such as a *Section of an Alkylate Plant (SAP)* [9], a *Hypothetical Cardiac Assist System (HCAS)* [5], and some DFTs (MOV) of railway systems from the Dutch company Movares.

Experimental Results. All experiments were run on an Intel i7 860 CPU with 8GB RAM under Debian GNU/Linux 8.0. Figure 9(a) indicates the run time for all 163 benchmarks comparing the case with rewriting (x-axis) and without rewriting (y-axis). Note that both dimensions are in log-scale. The dashed line indicates a speed-up of a factor ten. The topmost lines indicate an out-of-memory (MO, 8000 MB) and a time-out (TO, two hours), respectively. Figure 9(b) indicates the peak memory footprint (in MB) for the benchmarks using a similar plot. The dashed line indicates a reduction in peak memory usage of a factor 10. Finally, Figure 9(c) shows the size of the resulting Markov chain (in terms of

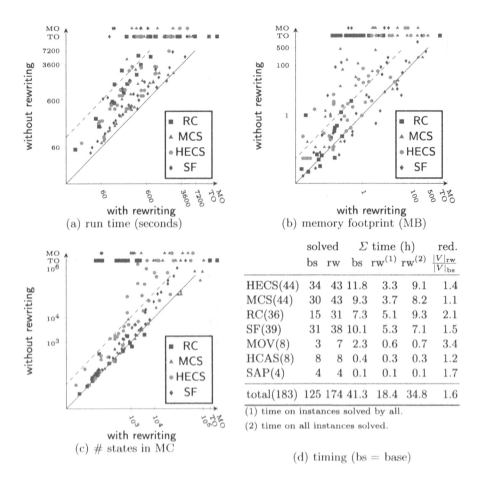

Fig. 9. Overview of the experimental results on four different benchmark sets.

the number of states), i.e., the model obtained by DFTCalc after bisimulation minimisation. The dashed line indicates a reduction of the Markov chain size by one order of magnitude.

Fig. 9(d) indicates for all 7 case studies how many instances could be handled in the base setting (second column), with rewriting (third column), the total time (in hours) in the base (fourth column), the total time with rewriting for those cases that also could be handled in the base (fifth column), and the total time for the cases that could be only dealt with rewriting (sixth column), and the average reduction in number of nodes of the DFTs (last column).

Analysis of the Results. In most cases, the reduction of the peak memory footprint as well as the size of the resulting Markov chain is quite substantial, where reductions of up to a factor ten are common with peaks of up to several orders of magnitude. Rewriting enabled to cope with 49 out of 183 cases that yielded

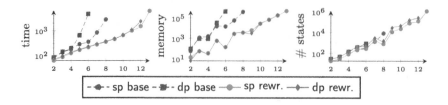

Fig. 10. Effect of rewriting on MCS (n = # CMs, sp/dp = single/double power).

a time-out or out-of-memory in the standard setting. For a few cases, rewriting does not give a memory or model reduction, see the points below the diagonal in Figures 9(b) and 9(c). This is mainly due to the fact that CADP exploits *compositional* bisimulation minimisation, where the order in which sub-Markov chains are composed and minimised is determined heuristically [11]. It may thus occur that equivalent, but structurally different DFTs yield different minimisation orders (and thus peak memory consumption) and distinct minimal Markov chains. In terms of run time, rewriting comes almost for free. In more than 99% of the cases, rewriting speeds up the model construction and analysis, see Figure 9(a). A more detailed analysis reveals that the graph rewriting with GROOVE is very fast, typically between 7 and 12 sec. Most time is devoted to the Markov chain construction and bisimulation minimisation (using CADP). The verification time of the resulting Markov chain with the probabilistic model checker MRMC is negligible. The results summarised in Fig. 9(d) underline these trends. The scalability of our approach becomes clear in Figure 10 that shows, for two variants of the MCS benchmark, the time, peak memory usage, and size of the resulting Markov chain (y-axis) versus the number of CMs (x-axis). The left plot shows that analysis time is decreased drastically, whereas the right plot shows that the size of the Markov chain is always very close. Plots for the other case studies show similar improvements. The results indicate that systems with two to four times more components become feasible for analysis.

6   Conclusions and Future Work

This paper presented a novel reduction technique to minimise DFTs using graph rewriting. Application to a large number of benchmarks showed that the savings in terms of time and memory consumption can be drastic, up to two orders of magnitude. Our rewriting approach is applicable too for alternative DFT analysis techniques (rather than DFTCalc). We firmly believe that rewriting can further improve techniques [31,26,19,39,35] that isolate static sub-trees and is applicable to trees similar to DFTs, e.g., dynamic event/fault trees [23], extended FTs [8] and attack trees [37]. Future work is needed to substantiate these claims, as well as to study completeness of the rewrite rules.

Acknowledgments. This work has been supported by the STW-ProRail partnership program ExploRail under the project ArRangeer (12238) and the EU FP7 grant agreements no. 318490 (SENSATION) and 318003 (TREsPASS). We acknowledge our cooperation with Movares in the ArRangeer project.

References

1. Arnold, F., Belinfante, A., Van der Berg, F., Guck, D., Stoelinga, M.: DFTCALC: a tool for efficient fault tree analysis. In: Bitsch, F., Guiochet, J., Kaâniche, M. (eds.) SAFECOMP. LNCS, vol. 8153, pp. 293–301. Springer, Heidelberg (2013)
2. Bobbio, A., Franceschinis, G., Gaeta, R., Portinale, L.: Parametric fault tree for the dependability analysis of redundant systems and its high-level Petri net semantics. IEEE Trans. on Softw. Eng. **29**(3), 270–287 (2003)
3. Bobbio, A., Portinale, L., Minichino, M., Ciancamerla, E.: Improving the analysis of dependable systems by mapping fault trees into Bayesian networks. Rel. Eng. & Sys. Safety **71**(3), 249–260 (2001)
4. Boudali, H., Crouzen, P., Stoelinga, M.I.A.: A rigorous, compositional, and extensible framework for dynamic fault tree analysis. IEEE Trans. Dependable Secure Comput. **7**(2), 128–143 (2010)
5. Boudali, H., Dugan, J.B.: A discrete-time Bayesian network reliability modeling and analysis framework. Rel. Eng. & Sys. Safety **87**(3), 337–349 (2005)
6. Boudali, H., Dugan, J.B.: A continuous-time Bayesian network reliability modeling and analysis framework. IEEE Trans. on Reliability **55**(1), 86–97 (2006)
7. Bozzano, M., Cimatti, A., Katoen, J.-P., Nguyen, V.Y., Noll, T., Roveri, M.: Safety, dependability and performance analysis of extended AADL models. The Computer Journal **54**, 754–775 (2011)
8. Buchacker, K.: Modeling with extended fault trees. In: Proceedings of HASE, pp. 238–246 (2000)
9. Chiacchio, F., Compagno, L., D'Urso, D., Manno, G., Trapani, N.: Dynamic fault trees resolution: A conscious trade-off between analytical and simulative approaches. Rel. Eng. & Sys. Safety **96**(11), 1515–1526 (2011)
10. Coppit, D., Sullivan, K.J., Dugan, J.B.: Formal semantics of models for computational engineering: a case study on dynamic fault trees. In: Proceedings of ISSRE, pp. 270–282 (2000)
11. Crouzen, P., Hermanns, H., Zhang, L.: On the minimisation of acyclic models. In: van Breugel, F., Chechik, M. (eds.) CONCUR 2008. LNCS, vol. 5201, pp. 295–309. Springer, Heidelberg (2008)
12. Dershowitz, N., Jouannaud, J.-P.: Rewrite systems. In: Handbook of Theoretical Computer Science, pp. 243–320. MIT Press (1991)
13. Dugan, J.B., Bavuso, S.J., Boyd, M.A.: Dynamic fault-tree models for fault-tolerant computer systems. IEEE Trans. Rel., pp. 363–377 (1992)
14. Dugan, J.B., Venkataraman, B., Gulati, R.: DIFtree: a software package for the analysis of dynamic fault tree models. In: Proceedings of RAMS, pp. 64–70. IEEE (1997)
15. Ehrig, H., Ehrig, K., Prange, U., Taentzer, G.: Fundamentals of Algebraic Graph Transformation, Monographs in Th. Comp. Science. Springer (2006)
16. Garavel, H., Lang, F., Mateescu, R., Serwe, W.: CADP 2011: a toolbox for the construction and analysis of distributed processes. STTT **15**(2), 89–107 (2013)
17. Ghamarian, A.H., de Mol, M., Rensink, A., Zambon, E., Zimakova, M.: Modelling and analysis using GROOVE. STTT **14**(1), 15–40 (2012)

18. Guck, D., Katoen, J.-P., Stoelinga, M.I.A., Luiten, T., Romijn, J.M.T.: Smart railroad maintenance engineering with stochastic model checking. In: Proceedings of RAILWAYS. Saxe-Coburg Publications (2014)

19. Han, W., Guo, W., Hou, Z.: Research on the method of dynamic fault tree analysis. In: Proceedings of ICRMS, pp. 950–953 (2011)

20. Hermanns, H.: Interactive Markov Chains: the Quest for Quantified Quality. Springer-Verlag, Berlin (2002)

21. Fault tree analysis (FTA). Norm IEC 60050:2006 (2007)

22. Junges, S.: Simplifying dynamic fault trees by graph rewriting. Master thesis, RWTH Aachen University (2015)

23. Kaiser, B.: Extending the expressive power of fault trees. In: Proceedings of RAMS, pp. 468–474. IEEE, January 2005

24. Katoen, J.-P., Zapreev, I.S., Hahn, E.M., Hermanns, H., Jansen, D.N.: The ins and outs of the probabilistic model checker MRMC. Perf. Ev. **68**(2), 90–104 (2011)

25. Kwiatkowska, M., Norman, G., Parker, D.: Stochastic model checking. In: Bernardo, M., Hillston, J. (eds.) SFM 2007. LNCS, vol. 4486, pp. 220–270. Springer, Heidelberg (2007)

26. Liu, D., Xiong, L., Li, Z., Wang, P., Zhang, H.: The simplification of cut sequence set analysis for dynamic systems. Proc. of ICCAE **3**, 140–144 (2010)

27. Malhotra, M., Trivedi, K.S.: Dependability modeling using Petri-nets. IEEE Trans. Rel. **44**(3), 428–440 (1995)

28. Merle, G., Roussel, J.-M.: Algebraic modelling of fault trees with priority AND gates. In: Proceedings of DCDS, pp. 175–180 (2007)

29. Merle, G., Roussel, J.-M., Lesage, J.-J., Bobbio, A.: Probabilistic algebraic analysis of fault trees with priority dynamic gates and repeated events. IEEE Trans. Rel. **59**(1), 250–261 (2010)

30. Montani, S., Portinale, L., Bobbio, A., Codetta-Raiteri, D.: Automatically translating dynamic fault trees into dynamic Bayesian networks by means of a software tool. In: Proceedings of ARES, p. 6 (2006)

31. Pullum, L.L., Dugan, J.B.: Fault tree models for the analysis of complex computer-based systems. In: Proceedings of RAMS, pp. 200–207. IEEE (1996)

32. Raiteri, D.C.: The conversion of dynamic fault trees to stochastic Petri nets, as a case of graph transformation. ENTCS **127**(2), 45–60 (2005)

33. Remke, A., Stoelinga, M. (eds.): Stochastic Model Checking. LNCS, vol. 8453. Springer, Heidelberg (2014)

34. Rensink, A., Kuperus, J.-H.: Repotting the geraniums: on nested graph transformation rules, ECEASST, vol. 18 (2009)

35. Rongxing, D., Guochun, W., Decun, D.: A new assessment method for system reliability based on dynamic fault tree. In: Proceedings of ICICTA, pp. 219–222. IEEE (2010)

36. Ruijters, E., Stoelinga, M.I.A.: Fault tree analysis: A survey of the state-of-the-art in modeling, analysis and tools. Computer Science Review **15–16**, 29–62 (2015)

37. Schneier, B.: Attack trees: Modeling security threats. Dr. Dobb's J., 24(12) (1999)

38. Stamatelatos, M., Vesely, W., Dugan, J.B., Fragola, J., Minarick, J., Railsback, J.: Fault Tree Handbook with Aerospace Applications. NASA Headquarters (2002)

39. Yevkin, O.: An improved modular approach for dynamic fault tree analysis. In: Proceedings of RAMS, pp. 1–5 (2011)

Cost vs. Time in Stochastic Games and Markov Automata

Hassan Hatefi[1], Bettina Braitling[2(✉)], Ralf Wimmer[2],
Luis María Ferrer Fioriti[1], Holger Hermanns[1], and Bernd Becker[2]

[1] Saarland University, Saarbrücken, Germany
{hhatefi,ferrer,hermanns}@cs.uni-saarland.de
[2] Albert-Ludwigs-Universität Freiburg, Freiburg im Breisgau, Germany
{becker,braitlin,wimmer}@informatik.uni-freiburg.de

Abstract. Costs and rewards are important tools for analysing quantitative aspects of models like energy consumption and costs of maintenance and repair. Under the assumption of transient costs, this paper considers the computation of expected cost-bounded rewards and cost-bounded reachability for Markov automata and stochastic games. We give a transformation of this class of properties to expected time-bounded rewards and time-bounded reachability, which can be computed by available algorithms. We prove the correctness of the transformation and show its effectiveness on a number of case studies.

1 Introduction

Markov automata (MA) [13] constitute a compositional modelling formalism for concurrent stochastic systems. They generalise discrete-time Markov chains (DTMCs), Markov decision processes (MDPs), probabilistic automata (PA [28]), continuous-time Markov chains (CTMCs), and interactive Markov chains (IMCs [22]). Markov automata form the semantic foundation of, among others, dynamic fault trees [6], stochastic activity networks, and generalised stochastic Petri nets (GSPNs) [12]. Compositional modelling for MA [31] is supported by the MAMA tool set [17,18], also providing access to effective model analysis via the IMCA tool [16]. That analysis follows the principles of model checking [5]. Concretely speaking, algorithms for model checking time-bounded reachability and continuous stochastic logic (CSL) [21], as well as long-run average and expected reachability times [17,18] are supported.

Apart from timing-related properties, there is an immensely large spectrum of potential applications that ask for integration of cost-related modelling and analysis. Costs, or dually rewards, are especially convenient to reflect economical implications, power consumption, wear and abrasion, or other quantitative

This work was partly supported by the German Research Council (DFG) as part of the Transregional Collaborative Research Center AVACS (SFB/TR 14), by the EU 7th Framework Programme under grant agreement no. 295261 (MEALS) and 318490 (SENSATION), by the CDZ project CAP (GZ 1023), and by the CAS/SAFEA International Partnership Program for Creative Research Teams.

© Springer International Publishing Switzerland 2015
X. Li et al. (Eds.): SETTA 2015, LNCS 9409, pp. 19–34, 2015.
DOI: 10.1007/978-3-319-25942-0_2

information. Therefore MA have lately been extended to MRA, Markov reward automata. In MRA, states and transitions can be equipped with rewards or costs, accumulated as time advances and as transitions are taken. Algorithms for computing the long-run average reward, for the expected cumulative reward until reaching a goal, and for the expected cumulative reward until a certain time bound are known and implemented [19]. Effective abstraction and refinement strategies for MRA have also been introduced [7], working on stochastic reward game abstractions of MRA.

In this paper, we turn our attention to properties that relate multiple dimensions of cost or rewards. In particular, we enable the computation of expected cumulative rewards until exceeding a cost bound, both for Markov reward automata and stochastic reward games. This can, for instance, answer questions of central importance for energy-harvesting battery-powered missions: *Under a given initial budget, what is the maximum probability of the battery running dry, or how many tasks can maximally be expected to be carried out by the battery?*

To answer such questions we give a fixed point characterisation of expected cost-bounded rewards and a transformation for stochastic games from cost- to time-bounded rewards. This transformation supports arbitrary non-negative transient costs. Markov automata are closed under this transformation. After the transformation, arbitrary algorithms for expected time-bounded rewards like [7,19] can be applied to compute expected cost-bounded rewards.

In order to develop our contribution, we take inspiration from various sources, especially from the domain of continuous-time Markov decision processes (CTMDPs). This encompasses works on necessary and sufficient criteria for optimality with respect to time-bounded rewards [24], and algorithms to compute optimal time-bounded rewards using uniformisation [10]. Instantaneous transition rewards have been added to the CTMC setting as well [11].

Our work is strongly influenced by the study of the duality between time and costs in CTMDPs under time-abstract strategies [4], built up on the earlier work in the setting of CTMCs [3]. We extend it in various dimensions: Our technique supports zero-cost states, where previously only strictly positive costs were allowed. We optimise over time-dependent strategies, which are a superclass of time-abstract ones. We extend the setting to expected reward analysis on two-player games with discrete and continuous locations, which is also an improvement over [14,15]. And finally our analysis technique works for any kind of models, not only uniform ones.

Structure of the Paper. In the following section, we introduce the necessary foundations. Sec. 3 describes the fixed point characterisation of optimal expected cost-bounded rewards and the transformation from cost to time bounds. We report on experimental results in Sec. 4 and conclude the paper in Sec. 5. An extended version of this paper with proofs of the main propositions is available at [20].

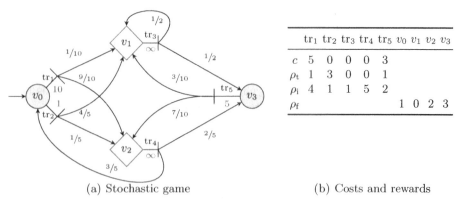

	tr$_1$	tr$_2$	tr$_3$	tr$_4$	tr$_5$	v_0	v_1	v_2	v_3
c	5	0	0	0	3				
ρ_t	1	3	0	0	1				
ρ_i	4	1	1	5	2				
ρ_f						1	0	2	3

(a) Stochastic game   (b) Costs and rewards

Fig. 1. An example of a stochastic game with costs and rewards

2   Foundations

Let V be a finite (or countably infinite) set. A probability distribution over V is a function $\mu : V \to [0,1]$ such that $\sum_{v \in V} \mu(v) = 1$. We denote the set of probability distributions over V by $\mathrm{Distr}(V)$. The real numbers are denoted by $\mathbb{R}$, $\mathbb{R}_{\geq 0}$ is the set of non-negative real numbers, and $\mathbb{R}_{\geq 0}^{\infty} := \mathbb{R}_{\geq 0} \cup \{\infty\}$. Accordingly $\mathbb{R}_{>0}$, $\mathbb{R}_{>0}^{\infty}$ etc. are used.

Definition 1 (Stochastic game). *A stochastic (continuous-time two-player) game (SG) is a tuple $\mathcal{G} = \big(V, (V_1, V_2), v_{\mathrm{init}}, T\big)$ such that $V = V_1 \uplus V_2$ is the finite set of states, $v_{\mathrm{init}} \in V$ is the initial state, and $T \subseteq V \times \mathbb{R}_{>0}^{\infty} \times \mathrm{Distr}(V)$ is the transition relation.*

V_1 and V_2 are the states of player 1 and player 2, respectively; we also denote them as V_1- and V_2-states. Transitions $(v, \lambda, \mu) \in T$ with rate $\lambda < \infty$ are called *Markovian*, transitions with infinite rate *probabilistic*. We denote the set of Markovian and probabilistic transitions by T_M and T_P, respectively. We use $T_M(v)$ and $T_P(v)$ to refer to the set of Markovian and probabilistic transitions available at state v. Then, $T(v) = T_M(v) \uplus T_P(v)$ is the set of all available transitions of v. We assume that $T(v) \neq \emptyset$ for all $v \in V$.

The game starts in state v_{init}. If the current state is $v \in V_1$, then it is player 1's turn, otherwise player 2's. The current player chooses a transition $(v, \lambda, \mu) \in T(v)$ for leaving state v. The rate $\theta_{\mathrm{rate}}\big((v, \lambda, \mu)\big) = \lambda \in \mathbb{R}_{>0}^{\infty}$ determines how long we stay at v, whereas $\theta_{\mathrm{distr}}\big((v, \lambda, \mu)\big) = \mu \in \mathrm{Distr}(V)$ gives us the distribution which leads to the successor states. If $\lambda = \infty$, the transition is taken instantaneously. Otherwise, λ is taken as the parameter of an exponential distribution. In this case, the probability that a transition to state $v' \in V$ happens within $t \geq 0$ time units, is given by $\mu(v') \cdot (1 - e^{-\lambda \cdot t})$. For conciseness, we write λ_{tr} instead of $\theta_{\mathrm{rate}}(\mathrm{tr})$ and μ_{tr} instead of $\theta_{\mathrm{distr}}(\mathrm{tr})$ for $\mathrm{tr} \in T$.

Example 1. Fig. 1(a) shows an example of a stochastic game. It consists of two player 1 states (drawn as circles) and two player 2 states (drawn as diamonds).

The exit rates of the transitions $tr_1, \ldots, tr_5$ are written in red. The game starts in v_0. Player 1 chooses one of the outgoing transitions $\{tr_1, tr_2\}$, say tr_1. The probability to stay in v_0 for at most t time units is then given by $1 - e^{-10 \cdot t}$. When the transition fires, we move to v_1 with probability 0.1 and to v_2 with probability 0.9; say v_1 is the successor state. There it is player 2's turn. As only one outgoing transition is available, namely tr_3, and its exit rate is ∞, it is left immediately, either to v_1, again, or to v_3, both with probability 0.5.   □

Markov automata (MA) [13] are a special type of stochastic games with a single player and without a nondeterministic choice between different Markovian transitions at one state. The reason for this restriction is that Markov automata are designed to be a compositional formalism, i.e. the MA for a system consisting of several components can be constructed from the MA of the individual components.

Definition 2 (Markov automaton). *A* Markov automaton *(MA) is a stochastic game* $\mathcal{M} = \big(V, (V, \emptyset), v_{\mathrm{init}}, T\big)$ *such that* $|T_{\mathrm{M}}(v)| \leq 1$ *holds for all* $v \in V$. *We simply write* $\mathcal{M} = (V, v_{\mathrm{init}}, T)$ *for a Markov automaton* $\mathcal{M}$.

In this paper we only consider *closed* Markov automata which are not subject to further composition operations. In this case, it is standard for Markov automata to make an *urgency assumption*: Since nothing prevents probabilistic transitions from happening instantaneously and the probability that a Markovian transition is taken without delay is zero, probabilistic transitions take precedence over Markovian transitions. Therefore we assume for MA that Markovian transitions have been removed from all states which also exhibit an outgoing probabilistic transition.

Paths Through Stochastic Games. The dynamics of an SG is specified by paths. An infinite path $\pi \in (V \times \mathbb{R}_{\geq 0} \times T)^\omega$ is an infinite sequence of states, sojourn times, and transitions. A finite path is such a sequence which is finite and ends in a state, i.e. $\pi \in (V \times \mathbb{R}_{\geq 0} \times T)^\star \times V$. We usually write $v \xrightarrow{t, tr}$ instead of $(v, t, tr) \in (V \times \mathbb{R}_{\geq 0} \times T)$. We use $\mathrm{Paths}^{\mathrm{fin}}$ and $\mathrm{Paths}^{\mathrm{inf}}$ to denote the set of finite and infinite paths, respectively. The length $|\pi|$ of a path π is ∞ if π is infinite, and equal to the number of transitions on π if π is finite. The last state of a finite path π is denoted by $\mathrm{last}(\pi)$. Given a finite or infinite path $\pi = v_0 \xrightarrow{t_0, tr_0} v_1 \xrightarrow{t_1, tr_1} \cdots$ and $0 \leq i < |\pi|$, v_i is the $(i+1)$-th state of π, denoted by $\pi[i]$; t_i is the time of staying at v_i, denoted by $\mathrm{time}(\pi[i])$; and $\mathrm{trans}(\pi[i]) = tr_i$ is the executed transition at v_i. Note that v_i is left instantaneously, i.e. $\mathrm{time}(\pi[i]) = 0$, if $\mathrm{trans}(\pi[i])$ has an infinite rate. For $0 \leq i \leq j \leq |\pi|$, the sub-path $v_i \xrightarrow{t_i, tr_i} \cdots v_j$ is denoted by $\pi[i \cdots j]$.

Strategies. The nondeterminism that may occur at a state is resolved by functions, which are called *strategies* (or policies or schedulers). Each player follows her own strategy in order to accomplish her goal. A strategy of player i $(i = 1, 2)$ is a function $\sigma_i : V_i \times \mathbb{R}_{\geq 0} \to T$ such that $\sigma_i(v, t) \in T(v)$ for all $v \in V$

and $t \in \mathbb{R}_{\geq 0}$. This strategy class is called *early total-time dependent positional deterministic* (ETTPD), since it uses the total time which has passed since the start of the system and the current state to make its choice, and returns a fixed outgoing transition. Early (in contrast to late) [26] means that the decision which transition to take has to be made when entering a state and may not be changed while residing in the state. ETTPD strategies can be easily extended to the more general *early total-cost dependent positional deterministic* (ETCPD) strategies, where the role of time is taken by costs. There are yet more general classes of early strategies whose decision may depend, e.g. on the whole history since the start of the system, and they may return a probability distribution over the available transitions instead of a fixed transition. However, one can show for the property classes we consider in this paper, that the supremum (and infimum) over ETCPD strategies coincides with the supremum (infimum, respectively) over this more general strategy class [14,15,25]. We denote the set of all ETCPD strategies of player i that are measurable in cost by Σ_i.

Probability Measure. Given strategies σ_1, σ_2 for both players and a state $v \in V$, a probability space on the set of infinite paths starting in v can be constructed. The set of measurable events is thereby the σ-algebra that is induced by a standard cylinder set construction [2] together with a unique probability measure $\Pr_{v,\sigma_1,\sigma_2}$ on the events. $\Pr_{v,\sigma_1,\sigma_2}(\Pi)$ is the probability of the set of paths Π, starting from state v, given that player 1 and player 2 play with strategies σ_1 and σ_2, respectively. Both the σ-algebra and the probability measure are constructed by extending the existing techniques used for MA and IMCs. We omit the details here; for more information see, e.g. [21,23,25].

Zenoness. It may happen that an SG contains an end component [5, Def. 10.117] consisting of probabilistic transitions only. Such an end component leads to the existence of sets of infinite paths π with finite sojourn times and non-zero probability, i.e. $\lim_{n \to \infty} \sum_{i=0}^{n} \mathrm{time}(\pi[i]) < \infty$. This phenomenon is known as *Zenoness*. Since such behaviour has to be considered unrealistic, we assume that the SGs under consideration are non-Zeno, i.e. that they do not contain such end components. Formally, an SG is non-Zeno iff

$$\Pr_{v,\sigma_1,\sigma_2}\left(\{\pi \in \mathrm{Paths}^{\mathrm{inf}} : \lim_{n \to \infty} \sum_{i=0}^{n} \mathrm{time}(\pi[i]) < \infty\}\right) = 0$$

holds for all states $v \in V$ and all strategies $\sigma_1 \in \Sigma_1$ and $\sigma_2 \in \Sigma_2$.

For more on strategies and on SGs in general we refer to [8,29].

Costs and Rewards. We now extend stochastic games by costs and rewards to analyse properties like "What is the maximal reward one can earn when the accumulated cost is bounded by b?"

Definition 3 (Cost and reward structures). *Let $\mathcal{G}$ be a stochastic game as above. A cost function $c : T \to \mathbb{R}_{\geq 0}$ assigns a non-negative cost rate to* *each transition. A reward structure ρ is a triple $\rho = (\rho_t, \rho_i, \rho_f)$ of functions $\rho_t, \rho_i : T \to \mathbb{R}_{\geq 0}$, and $\rho_f : V \to \mathbb{R}_{\geq 0}$; ρ_t is the transient reward rate, ρ_i the instantaneous reward, and ρ_f the final reward.*

For a transition $\mathrm{tr} = (v, \lambda, \mu) \in T$, costs and transient rewards are granted per time unit, i. e. residing in v for t time units before taking transition tr causes a cost of $t \cdot c(\mathrm{tr})$, and a transient reward of $t \cdot \rho_t(\mathrm{tr})$ is granted. In contrast, the instantaneous reward $\rho_i(\mathrm{tr})$ is granted for taking the transition tr. The final reward is granted for the state reached when the maximal cost has been spent. This allows, e. g. to consider cost-bounded reachability probabilities as a special case of expected cost-bounded rewards (for more details, see below).

Please note that we do not consider instantaneous costs in this paper. They would render the transformation in Sec. 3 impossible, since there is no instantaneous time. In principle, adapting the analysis algorithm for time-bounded rewards [7,19] to cost bounds should be possible. That algorithm is based on discretising the time interval, yielding a discrete-time probabilistic game. However, analysing cost-bounded properties for discrete-time models is expensive, even more so as we have to support non-integer costs [1].

Cost and Reward of Paths. Given a finite path $\pi^{\mathrm{fin}} = v_0 \xrightarrow{t_0, \mathrm{tr}_0} v_1 \xrightarrow{t_1, \mathrm{tr}_1} \cdots v_{n-1} \xrightarrow{t_{n-1}, \mathrm{tr}_{n-1}} v_n$, its cost is defined as $\mathrm{cost}(\pi^{\mathrm{fin}}) := \sum_{i=0}^{n-1} c(\mathrm{tr}_i) \cdot t_i$. The cost can be extended for an infinite path $\pi = v_0 \xrightarrow{t_0, \mathrm{tr}_0} v_1 \xrightarrow{t_1, \mathrm{tr}_1} \cdots$ by $\mathrm{cost}(\pi) := \lim_{n \to \infty} \mathrm{cost}(\pi[0 \cdots n])$. The cumulative reward of a finite and an infinite path can be defined in a similar way, i. e. $\mathrm{crew}(\pi^{\mathrm{fin}}) := \sum_{i=0}^{n-1} \left(\rho_t(\mathrm{tr}_i) \cdot t_i + \rho_i(\mathrm{tr}_i) \right)$ and $\mathrm{crew}(\pi) := \lim_{n \to \infty} \mathrm{crew}(\pi[0 \cdots n])$. Furthermore we define the *cost-bounded reward* of π by

$$
\mathrm{cbr}_{\rho,c}^{\mathcal{G}}(\pi, b) := \begin{cases} \mathrm{crew}(\pi), & \text{if } \mathrm{cost}(\pi) \leq b, \\ \mathrm{crew}(\pi[0 \cdots n^*]) + \frac{b - \mathrm{cost}(\pi[0 \cdots n^*])}{c(\mathrm{tr}_{n^*})} \cdot \rho_t(\mathrm{tr}_{n^*}) \\ \quad + \rho_f(\pi[n^*]), & \text{otherwise,} \end{cases}
$$

where $n^* \in \mathbb{N}$ is the index of the state along path π such that $\mathrm{cost}(\pi[0 \cdots n^*]) \leq b$ and $\mathrm{cost}(\pi[0 \cdots n^* + 1]) > b$. More precisely, the cost exceeds b after residing $\frac{b - \mathrm{cost}(\pi[0 \cdots n^*])}{c(\mathrm{tr}_{n^*})}$ time units in the n^*-th state of the path, and thereby the state is subject to the final reward. Note that such an index exists, provided that $\mathrm{cost}(\pi) > b$.

Example 2. Consider again the stochastic game in Fig. 1(a). We extend it by the cost function and reward structure shown in Fig. 1(b). Now consider the path $\pi = v_0 \xrightarrow{3, \mathrm{tr}_1} v_1 \xrightarrow{0, \mathrm{tr}_3} v_3 \xrightarrow{2, \mathrm{tr}_5} v_2 \xrightarrow{0, \mathrm{tr}_4} v_0 \to \cdots$ and assume the cost bound $b = 20$. The cost incurring in v_0 before taking tr_1 is $5 \cdot 3 = 15$. Since tr_3 is probabilistic, no cost incurs in v_1. In v_3 we have costs $3 \cdot 2 = 6$. Therefore the cost bound is reached while staying in v_3, after $1/3 \cdot (20 - 15) = 5/3$ time units. We then have $n^* = 2$. Since v_3 is the state in which the cost bound is reached, we additionally get its final reward $\rho_f(v_3) = 3$. The cost-bounded reward for this path is accordingly $\mathrm{cbr}_{\rho,c}^{\mathcal{G}}(\pi, 20) = (3 \cdot 1 + 4) + (0 \cdot 0 + 1) + (5/3 \cdot 1) + 3 = 12\,2/3$. $\square$

Given strategies $\sigma_1 \in \Sigma_1$ and $\sigma_2 \in \Sigma_2$ we can define the *expected cost-bounded reward* (ECR) as the expectation of cbr:

$$\mathbb{E}\mathrm{cbr}_{\mathcal{G},\rho,c}^{\sigma_1,\sigma_2}(v,b) := \int_{\pi \in \mathrm{Paths}^{\inf}(v)} \mathrm{cbr}_{\rho,c}^{\mathcal{G}}(\pi,b)\, \mathrm{dPr}_{v,\sigma_1,\sigma_2}(\pi) \,.$$

The two players can independently try to maximise or minimise the reward earned until the cost bound is reached. Hence, for $\mathrm{opt}_1, \mathrm{opt}_2 \in \{\inf, \sup\}$ we define the *optimal* expected cost-bounded reward by

$$\mathbb{E}\mathrm{cbr}_{\mathcal{G},\rho,c}^{\mathrm{opt}_1,\mathrm{opt}_2}(v,b) := \mathop{\mathrm{opt}_1}_{\sigma_1 \in \Sigma_1} \mathop{\mathrm{opt}_2}_{\sigma_2 \in \Sigma_2} \mathbb{E}\mathrm{cbr}_{\mathcal{G},\rho,c}^{\sigma_1,\sigma_2}(v,b) \,.$$

Two important classes of properties can be considered as special cases of expected cost-bounded rewards:

For *time-bounded rewards*, denoted by random variable tbr, the time is limited during which reward is collected. This corresponds to using the constant 1-function as cost. We therefor define $\mathbb{E}\mathrm{tbr}_{\mathcal{G},\rho}^{\sigma_1,\sigma_2}(v,b) := \mathbb{E}\mathrm{cbr}_{\mathcal{G},\rho,1}^{\sigma_1,\sigma_2}(v,b)$.

The second class encompasses *cost-bounded reachability probabilities*, i.e. questions like "What is the maximal probability to reach a set $V_{\mathrm{goal}} \subseteq V$ of states with cost $\leq b$?". We first make the states in V_{goal} absorbing and add a Markovian self-loop $\mathrm{tr}_v = (v, \lambda, \{v \mapsto 1\})$ with arbitrary finite rate $0 < \lambda < \infty$ to each state $v \in V_{\mathrm{goal}}$ and define the final reward by $\rho_{\mathrm{f}}(v) = 1$ if $v \in V_{\mathrm{goal}}$, and $\rho_{\mathrm{f}}(v) = 0$ otherwise. The transient and instantaneous rewards are constantly 0. Then the expected reward until cost b is reached corresponds to the probability of reaching V_{goal} with costs $\leq b$.

Algorithms to compute optimal expected time-bounded rewards are available both for Markov automata [19] and stochastic games [7]. To the best of our knowledge, up to now there are no algorithms available to compute the optimal expected cost-bounded rewards for MA and SG.

3   Transformation of Stochastic Games

In this section, we first give a fixed point characterisation of expected cost-bounded rewards for stochastic games and prove its correctness. Similar to time-bounded properties [7], this fixed point characterisation is not amenable to an efficient solution. Therefore we transform the stochastic game so that the optimal expected cost-bounded reward coincides with the optimal expected time-bounded reward in the transformed game. This allows us to apply arbitrary algorithms like [7,19] for expected time-bounded rewards to compute optimal expected cost-bounded rewards.

Theorem 1 (Fixed point characterisation).   *Let $\mathcal{G}$ be a stochastic game with cost function c and reward structure $\rho = (\rho_t, \rho_i, \rho_f)$. Let $b \in \mathbb{R}_{>0}$ be a cost bound, $\mathrm{opt}_1, \mathrm{opt}_2 \in \{\inf, \sup\}$, and $\mathrm{opt}_{[v]} = \mathrm{opt}_i$ if $v \in \bar{V}_i$.*

Then, $\mathbb{Ecbr}_{\mathcal{G},\rho,c}^{\mathrm{opt}_1,\mathrm{opt}_2}(v,b)$ *is the least fixed point of the higher-order operator*
$\Omega_{\mathrm{opt}_1,\mathrm{opt}_2} : (V \times \mathbb{R}_{\geq 0} \to \mathbb{R}_{\geq 0}) \to (V \times \mathbb{R}_{\geq 0} \to \mathbb{R}_{\geq 0})$, *such that*

$$\Omega_{\mathrm{opt}_1,\mathrm{opt}_2}(F)(v,b) =$$

$$
\underset{\mathrm{tr}\in T(v)}{\mathrm{opt}_{[v]}}
\begin{cases}
\displaystyle\int_0^{b/c(\mathrm{tr})} \lambda_{\mathrm{tr}} \cdot e^{-\lambda_{\mathrm{tr}}\cdot t} \cdot \sum_{v'\in V} \mu_{\mathrm{tr}}(v') \cdot F\big(v', b - c(\mathrm{tr})\cdot t\big)\, dt \\
\quad + \left(\frac{\rho_{\mathrm{t}}(\mathrm{tr})}{\lambda_{\mathrm{tr}}} + \rho_{\mathrm{i}}(\mathrm{tr})\right) \cdot \left(1 - e^{-\frac{\lambda_{\mathrm{tr}}\cdot b}{c(\mathrm{tr})}}\right) + \rho_{\mathrm{f}}(v) \cdot e^{-\frac{\lambda_{\mathrm{tr}}\cdot b}{c(\mathrm{tr})}}, \\
\qquad\qquad\qquad\qquad\qquad\qquad\quad \textit{if } \mathrm{tr}\in T_{\mathrm{M}}(v) \wedge c(\mathrm{tr}) > 0 \wedge b > 0, \\[4pt]
\frac{\rho_{\mathrm{t}}(\mathrm{tr})}{\lambda_{\mathrm{tr}}} + \rho_{\mathrm{i}}(\mathrm{tr}) + \displaystyle\sum_{v'\in V} \mu_{\mathrm{tr}}(v') \cdot F(v',b), \quad \textit{if } \mathrm{tr}\in T_{\mathrm{M}}(v) \wedge c(\mathrm{tr}) = 0, \\[4pt]
\rho_{\mathrm{i}}(\mathrm{tr}) + \displaystyle\sum_{v'\in V} \mu_{\mathrm{tr}}(v') \cdot F(v',b), \qquad\quad \textit{if } \mathrm{tr}\in T_{\mathrm{P}}(v), \\[4pt]
\rho_{\mathrm{f}}(v), \qquad\qquad\qquad\qquad\qquad\qquad \textit{otherwise.}
\end{cases}
$$

"Least" means in this context that $\forall v \in V, b \in \mathbb{R}_{\geq 0} : \mathbb{Ecbr}_{\mathcal{G},\rho,c}^{\mathrm{opt}_1,\mathrm{opt}_2}(v,b) \leq F(v,b)$, with F being another fixed point of $\Omega_{\mathrm{opt}_1,\mathrm{opt}_2}$.

The fixed point characterisation of expected cost-bounded rewards yields a system of integral equations, which are typically hard to solve. Instead, the following transformation turns cost-bounded rewards into time-bounded rewards. For the latter, not only a fixed point characterisation is available [7], but also a more efficient algorithm, based on discretisation [7,19].

Definition 4 (Cost-to-time transformation). *Let* $\mathcal{G} = \big(V, (V_1, V_2), v_{\mathrm{init}}, T\big)$ *be a stochastic game with cost function* $c : T \to \mathbb{R}_{\geq 0}$ *and reward structure* $\rho = (\rho_{\mathrm{t}}, \rho_{\mathrm{i}}, \rho_{\mathrm{f}})$. *We define the cost-transformed game* $\mathcal{G}^c = \big(V, (V_1, V_2), v_{\mathrm{init}}, T^c\big)$ *with*

$$
\begin{aligned}
T^c = \big\{ \mathrm{tr}\in T \,\big|\, \lambda_{\mathrm{tr}} = \infty \big\} \\
\cup \big\{ (v, \infty, \mu) \,\big|\, \exists \lambda \in \mathbb{R}_{\geq 0} : \mathrm{tr} = (v, \lambda, \mu) \in T \wedge c(\mathrm{tr}) = 0 \big\} \\
\cup \big\{ (v, \lambda/c(\mathrm{tr}), \mu) \,\big|\, \mathrm{tr} = (v, \lambda, \mu) \in T \wedge c(\mathrm{tr}) \neq 0 \big\}.
\end{aligned}
$$

and reward structure $\rho^c = (\rho_{\mathrm{t}}^c, \rho_{\mathrm{i}}^c, \rho_{\mathrm{f}}^c)$ *such that* $\rho_{\mathrm{f}}^c = \rho_{\mathrm{f}}$,

$$
\rho_{\mathrm{t}}^c(\mathrm{tr}) = \begin{cases}
\rho_{\mathrm{t}}(\mathrm{tr})/c(\mathrm{tr}), & \textit{if } c(\mathrm{tr}) \neq 0, \\
0, & \textit{if } c(\mathrm{tr}) = 0, \textit{ and}
\end{cases}
$$

$$
\rho_{\mathrm{i}}^c(\mathrm{tr}) = \begin{cases}
\rho_{\mathrm{i}}(\mathrm{tr}) + \rho_{\mathrm{t}}(\mathrm{tr})/\lambda_{\mathrm{tr}}, & \textit{if } c(\mathrm{tr}) = 0 \wedge \lambda_{\mathrm{tr}} < \infty, \\
\rho_{\mathrm{i}}(\mathrm{tr}), & \textit{otherwise.}
\end{cases}
$$

The motivation behind this transformation is as follows: Since we want to transform the cost bound b into a time bound we have to divide b through the cost gained per time unit. This is done by dividing the rate λ of a Markovian transition $\mathrm{tr} \in T_{\mathrm{M}}$ through its cost $c(\mathrm{tr})$. The same has to be done with the transient reward $\rho_{\mathrm{t}}(\mathrm{tr})$. If tr has no cost, i.e. $c(\mathrm{tr}) = 0$, the transition is transformed

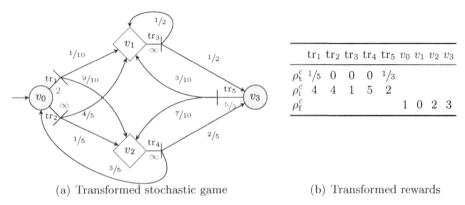

(a) Transformed stochastic game   (b) Transformed rewards

Fig. 2. Fig. 1 after transformation

into a probabilistic transition. The expected transient reward $\rho_t(\mathrm{tr})/\lambda_{\mathrm{tr}}$ has to be added to the instantaneous reward of the transition in this case.

The transformation does not change the structure or size of the SG, and the transformed system is an SG as well. Additionally, Markov automata are closed under this transformation, i.e. if the original SG is actually an MA, so is the transformed system.

Example 3. Consider again the stochastic game in Fig. 1(a) with the costs and rewards in Fig. 1(b). We assume a cost bound of $b = 20$. Then the rewards of the five transitions after transformation are shown in Fig. 2(b). The Markovian transitions tr_1, tr_2, and tr_5 are modified as follows. Transitions tr_3 and tr_4 remain unchanged as they are probabilistic. The expected residence time before taking tr_1 is scaled such that it matches the expected cost in the original game, i.e. the new exit rate becomes $\lambda_{\mathrm{tr}_1}/c(\mathrm{tr}_1) = {}^{10}/5 = 2$. The transient reward rate is adjusted accordingly and becomes $\rho_t(\mathrm{tr}_1)/c(\mathrm{tr}_1) = {}^{1}/5$. The instantaneous reward does not change. The transition tr_5 is modified in the same way. As the cost of tr_2 is zero, tr_2 becomes probabilistic and the expected reward $\rho_t(\mathrm{tr}_2)/\lambda_{\mathrm{tr}_2}$ earned in v_1 until tr_2 being taken is added to the instantaneous reward of tr_2. The stochastic game after the transformation is shown in Fig. 2(a).   □

Theorem 2 (Measure preservation). *Let $\mathcal{G}$ be a stochastic game with reward structure ρ, cost function c, cost bound $b \in \mathbb{R}_{\geq 0}$, $v \in V$, and $\mathrm{opt}_1, \mathrm{opt}_2 \in \{\inf, \sup\}$. Then we have*

$$\mathbb{E}\mathrm{cbr}_{\mathcal{G},\rho,c}^{\mathrm{opt}_1,\mathrm{opt}_2}(v,b) = \mathbb{E}\mathrm{tbr}_{\mathcal{G}',\rho'}^{\mathrm{opt}_1,\mathrm{opt}_2}(v,b).$$

Proof. Here we sketch the proof of the theorem. It is done by showing that the original and the transformed games have indeed the same fixed point characterisation for the respective objectives. For this, on the one hand, we construct the fixed point characterisation of the transformed game using Theorem 1 by assigning the constant cost of one to all Markovian transitions. On the other hand, we reinterpret the representation of the fixed point characterisation of the original model by a series of sound variable substitutions, partly inspired by the transformation. At the end we conclude that both of the fixed point characterisations are the same, and thereby their least fixed points are exactly equal. For more details, see the complete proof in [20].   □

Zero-cost transitions[1] in the original game can introduce Zenoness in the transformed game. It happens if a set of such transitions constitutes an end component in the transformed game. This will be problematic for the analysis, in particular if the end component contains positive rewards. Therefore the strategy that keeps the control of the game inside the end component delivers infinite expected rewards, since staying there gains reward without any cost. Nevertheless the analysis may ignore such a strategy in some cases, for instance in analysis of MA against minimal expected ECR. By any means and for simplicity we exclude such models from our analysis technique.

4   Case Studies and Experimental Results

For our experiments we used the following case studies:

(1) The *Dynamic Power Management System* (DPMS) [27] describes the following scenario: A service requester generates tasks which are stored within a queue until they are handled by a processor. This processor (P) can either be "busy" with processing a job, "idle" while the queue is empty, in a "standby" mode, or in a "sleep" mode. In the latter two modes P is inactive and cannot handle tasks. The change between "busy" and "idle" occurs automatically, depending on whether there are tasks in the queue or not. If P has been "idle" for some time, it is switched into "standby" or "sleep" by a power manager. The power manager is also responsible for switching from these two modes back to "idle". P consumes the least power in "standby" and "sleep" (0.35 W and 0.13 W, respectively), whereas it consumes more power while "idle" (0.95 W) and the most if it is "busy" (2.15 W) [27,30]. We model the DPMS as an MRA with the costs representing the power consumption of P. The reward corresponds to the number of served tasks. For our experiments we varied the number of different task types (T) and the size of the queue (Q). We explore the expected cost-bounded reward. The model instances are denoted as "DPMS-T-Q".

(2) The *Queueing System* (QS) [21] stores requests of T different types into two queues of size Q each. A server is attached to each queue, which fetches requests from its corresponding queue, and then processes them. One of the servers might insert, with probability 0.1, the already served request into the other queue to be reprocessed by the other server. Power is consumed by both servers when they are processing. We compute the minimum and the maximum number of processed requests under different energy budgets. The model instances are denoted as "QS-T-Q".

---

[1] Note that the cost of probabilistic transitions is implicitly zero as the delay until taking such transitions is zero.

(3) The *Polling System* (PS) [17,32] consists of S station(s) and one server. Each station comes with a queue of size Q, and buffers incoming jobs of T different types. The jobs are then polled and processed by the server. There is a probability of 0.1 for a job to be processed while erroneously remaining in the queue. Each job brings an instantaneous reward when it is completely processed by the server. Whenever processing, the server consumes energy. The model is subject to two kinds of analysis: First we compute the minimum and the maximum probability of encountering the error under some energy budget. The second analysis is on the computation of the minimum and the maximum expected energy bounded reward of the model. The instances of the polling system are denoted as "PS-S-T-Q".

(4) The *Stochastic Job Scheduling* benchmark (SJS) [9] originally stems from economy. In this setting, a number of jobs with different service rates are distributed between processors. Each processor consumes resources, e.g. energy which has to be paid for. The costs in our model represent these expenses. The goal is to have all jobs processed within a certain cost budget. In our experiments we explore the reachability of this goal with homogeneous costs ("all processors have the same costs") and heterogeneous costs ("all processors have different costs"), while varying the number of jobs (M) and the number of processors (N). Since the system degenerates to a CTMC if the service rates are homogeneous, we do not consider this case. The model instances are denoted as "SJS-N-M".

We used SCOOP [31] to create the model files. The transformation from cost to time was done with a python script; the computation time for this was negligible. We then employed the tool IMCA [16,17,19] to determine the minimum and maximum expected cost-bounded reward or the minimum and maximum cost-bounded reachability of the models. It would be possible to use any other analyser for MA, e.g. MeGARA, the prototype from [7].

All experiments were run on an Intel Xeon quad-core processor with 3.3 GHz per core and 64 GB of memory. We set a time limit of 12 hours. The memory consumption was negligible; all experiments needed less than 300 MB.

We will not give detailed time measurements due to space restrictions, nevertheless we want to briefly discuss the computation times. The shortest computations took only fractions of a second, e.g. the computation of the minimum reachability for SJS-2-4 with cost budget 5 took 0.06 seconds, whereas the longer computations needed several hours, e.g. for DPMS-4-10 the computation of the minimum reachability with cost budget 50 took almost 11 hours, which was the longest computation time of all our experiments. In general it can be said that larger systems need more time to analyse than smaller systems. The computation time is also influenced by the size of the cost budget. For example, for cost budget 10 the computation of the minimum reachability for DPMS-4-10 took less than 6 min. This is due to the fact that IMCA uses discretisation [17–19] to compute the values; for a larger bound more discretisation steps are needed. There is also an interesting connection between the costs within the system, its maximum rate, and the computation time: The size of a discretisation step depends on the maximum rate of the transformed system. The higher the maximum rate is, the smaller the discretisation step must be chosen in order to satisfy the given accuracy level. For the computation of cost-bounded rewards, this means that the computation time is strongly influenced by the value of $\max\{\lambda_{tr}/c(tr) \mid tr \in T_M : c(tr) > 0\}$. For details on the discretisation, see [7,19].

Tables 1 to 4 show the results of our experiments. The first two columns of each table contain the name of the respective model instance and its number of states.

In case of DPMS (Table 1) and QS (Table 2) we explore the minimum and maximum expected reward under different cost budgets. For DPMS we used cost budgets of 10, 20, and 50, whereas for QS we used cost budgets of 1, 5, and 10 (see the respective blocks in Table 1 and Table 2). It holds for both DPMS and QS that the expected reward grows with the budget, as does the difference between minimum and maximum reward, as to be expected. Another interesting fact is that the size of the queues in the models – while having a big influence on the size of the system – has practically no impact on the expected reward. It is completely determined by the number of different task types. This observation can be explained as follows: For the processing unit of DPMS (or of QS) it is not important how many jobs exactly can be stored in the queue(s), as long as there *are* jobs in the queue(s).

For PS (Table 3) we studied both minimum and maximum reachability and minimum and maximum expected reward (see the respective blocks in the table) under a cost budget of 5. If we increase the queue size, the minimum and maximum probability for encountering the error decreases, while the expected minimum and maximum reward increases. At the same time we can observe that the reachability increases with the number of stations, e. g. for PS-2-2-2, containing two stations, the maximum probability is 0.773, whereas for PS-5-2-2, containing 5 stations, it is 0.992. This makes sense, since the error is caused by the stations and the probability to encounter the error therefore increases with having more stations.

For SJS (Table 4) we also used a cost budget of 5. Here we studied the minimum and maximum reachability while assuming homogeneous or heterogeneous costs for the different processors of the system (see the respective blocks

Table 1. Expected reward in the dynamic power managment system

name	#states	budget = 10		budget = 20		budget = 50	
		min	max	min	max	min	max
DPMS-2-5	508	0.759	0.859	1.557	1.924	3.910	5.150
DPMS-2-10	1,588	0.759	0.859	1.557	1.924	3.910	5.150
DPMS-2-20	5,548	0.759	0.859	1.557	1.924	3.910	5.150
DPMS-3-5	5,190	0.785	0.883	1.617	1.930	4.129	5.088
DPMS-3-10	29,530	0.785	0.883	1.617	1.930	4.129	5.088
DPMS-3-20	195,810	0.785	0.883	1.617	1.930	4.129	5.088
DPMS-4-5	47,528	0.784	0.877	1.617	1.889	4.143	4.936
DPMS-4-10	492,478	0.784	0.877	1.617	1.889	4.143	4.936

Table 2. Expected reward of the queueing system

name	#states	budget = 1		budget = 5		budget = 10	
		min	max	min	max	min	max
QS-2-4	46,234	0.249	0.857	1.294	4.078	2.634	7.975
QS-2-5	191,258	0.249	0.857	1.294	4.078	2.634	7.975
QS-2-6	777,754	0.249	0.857	1.294	4.078	2.634	7.975
QS-3-3	117,532	0.125	0.857	0.649	4.078	1.332	7.972
QS-3-4	1,080,865	0.125	0.857	0.649	4.078	1.332	7.972
QS-4-2	42,616	0.125	1.287	0.649	6.127	1.333	12.075
QS-4-3	708,088	0.125	1.287	0.649	6.127	1.333	12.075
QS-6-2	266,974	0.084	1.713	0.433	8.187	0.892	16.201

Table 3. Results for the polling system

name	#states	rechability		reward	
		min	max	min	max
PS-2-2-2	455	0.743	0.773	3.128	3.219
PS-2-2-3	2,055	0.483	0.551	3.980	4.117
PS-2-3-2	2,392	0.995	0.996	1.209	1.253
PS-2-3-3	22,480	0.973	0.983	1.730	1.848
PS-3-2-2	3,577	0.888	0.917	2.549	2.685
PS-3-2-3	34,425	0.665	0.760	3.493	3.732
PS-3-3-2	35,659	1.000	1.000	0.918	0.965
PS-4-2-2	27,783	0.955	0.973	2.166	2.307
PS-4-2-3	570,375	0.793	0.879	3.116	3.403
PS-5-2-2	213,689	0.983	0.992	1.908	2.039

Table 4. Rechability in the stochastic job scheduling benchmark

name	#states	homogeneous costs		heterogeneous costs	
		min	max	min	max
SJS-2-4	464	0.241	0.241	0.186	0.243
SJS-2-6	4,144	0.041	0.041	0.021	0.029
SJS-2-8	29,344	0.004	0.004	0.001	0.002
SJS-4-4	3,168	0.241	0.241	0.120	0.610
SJS-4-6	71,644	0.041	0.041	0.013	0.130
SJS-4-8	1,032,272	0.004	0.004	0.001	0.012
SJS-6-4	13,924	0.241	0.241	0.059	0.945
SJS-6-6	685,774	0.041	0.041	0.005	0.374
SJS-8-4	41,552	0.241	0.241	0.033	0.999
SJS-10-4	98,436	0.241	0.241	0.019	1.000

in Table 4). For homogeneous costs we can observe a similar effect as for DPMS and PS: The number of processors influences the number of states in the system, but has a negligible impact on the reachability. The latter is completely determined by the number of jobs. What's more, the minimum and the maximum reachability are the same in this case. These effects vanish if we assume heterogeneous costs. In this case, the distance between minimum and maximum reachability increases, especially the maximum reachability becomes higher. These observations make sense: In case of a homogeneous system it does not matter, which processor handles which job. However, in a heterogeneous system there is a choice between more and less expensive processors which can handle the jobs, which in turn leads to a higher (lower) maximum (minimum) reachability.

5   Conclusion

We studied the computation of Markov automata and stochastic games against cost-bounded reward objectives. In this regard, we provided a fixed point characterisation for the optimal expected cost-bounded reward. Moreover, we proposed an efficient measure-preserving transformation from cost-bounded to time-bounded objectives. For the latter, an analysis technique based on discretisation with strict error bound exists. Our experiments demonstrate the effectiveness of the approach.

In the future, we plan to improve the efficiency of the proposed approach, e.g. via an abstraction/refinement technique on very large games and automata.

References

1. Andova, S., Hermanns, H., Katoen, J.-P.: Discrete-time rewards model-checked. In: Larsen, K.G., Niebert, P. (eds.) FORMATS 2003. LNCS, vol. 2791, pp. 88–104. Springer, Heidelberg (2004)
2. Ash, R.B., Doléans-Dade, C.A.: Probability & Measure Theory. Academic Press, 2nd edn. (1999)
3. Baier, C., Haverkort, B.R., Hermanns, H., Katoen, J.-P.: On the logical characterisation of performability properties. In: Welzl, E., Montanari, U., Rolim, J.D.P. (eds.) ICALP 2000. LNCS, vol. 1853, p. 780. Springer, Heidelberg (2000)
4. Baier, C., Haverkort, B.R., Hermanns, H., Katoen, J.: Reachability in continuous-time Markov reward decision processes. In: Logic and Automata: History and Perspectives [in Honor of Wolfgang Thomas]. Texts in Logic and Games, vol. 2, pp. 53–72. Amsterdam University Press (2008)
5. Baier, C., Katoen, J.P.: Principles of Model Checking. The MIT Press (2008)
6. Boudali, H., Crouzen, P., Stoelinga, M.: A rigorous, compositional, and extensible framework for dynamic fault tree analysis. IEEE Trans. Dependable Sec. Comput. 7(2), 128–143 (2010)
7. Braitling, B., Ferrer Fioriti, L.M., Hatefi, H., Wimmer, R., Becker, B., Hermanns, H.: Abstraction-based computation of reward measures for markov automata. In: D'Souza, D., Lal, A., Larsen, K.G. (eds.) VMCAI 2015. LNCS, vol. 8931, pp. 172–189. Springer, Heidelberg (2015)
8. Brázdil, T., Forejt, V., Krcál, J., Kretínský, J., Kucera, A.: Continuous-time stochastic games with time-bounded reachability. Information and Computation 224, 46–70 (2013)
9. Bruno, J.L., Downey, P.J., Frederickson, G.N.: Sequencing tasks with exponential service times to minimize the expected flow time or makespan. Journal of the ACM 28(1), 100–113 (1981)

10. Buchholz, P., Schulz, I.: Numerical analysis of continuous time Markov decision processes over finite horizons. Computers & Operations Research **38**(3), 651–659 (2011)
11. Cloth, L., Katoen, J., Khattri, M., Pulungan, R.: Model checking Markov reward models with impulse rewards. In: Proceedings of DSN, pp. 722–731. IEEE CS (2005)
12. Eisentraut, C., Hermanns, H., Katoen, J.-P., Zhang, L.: A semantics for every GSPN. In: Colom, J.-M., Desel, J. (eds.) PETRI NETS 2013. LNCS, vol. 7927, pp. 90–109. Springer, Heidelberg (2013)
13. Eisentraut, C., Hermanns, H., Zhang, L.: On probabilistic automata in continuous time. In: Proceedings of LICS, pp. 342–351. IEEE CS (2010)
14. Fu, H.: Maximal cost-bounded reachability probability on continuous-time markov decision processes. In: Muscholl, A. (ed.) FOSSACS 2014 (ETAPS). LNCS, vol. 8412, pp. 73–87. Springer, Heidelberg (2014)
15. Fu, H.: Verifying Probabilistic Systems: New Algorithms and Complexity Results. Ph.D. thesis, RWTH Aachen University (2014)
16. Guck, D., Han, T., Katoen, J.-P., Neuhäußer, M.R.: Quantitative timed analysis of interactive markov chains. In: Goodloe, A.E., Person, S. (eds.) NFM 2012. LNCS, vol. 7226, pp. 8–23. Springer, Heidelberg (2012)
17. Guck, D., Hatefi, H., Hermanns, H., Katoen, J.-P., Timmer, M.: Modelling, reduction and analysis of markov automata. In: Joshi, K., Siegle, M., Stoelinga, M., D'Argenio, P.R. (eds.) QEST 2013. LNCS, vol. 8054, pp. 55–71. Springer, Heidelberg (2013)
18. Guck, D., Hatefi, H., Hermanns, H., Katoen, J., Timmer, M.: Analysis of timed and long-run objectives for Markov automata. Logical Methods in Computer Science 10(3) (2014). http://dx.doi.org/10.2168/LMCS-10(3:17)2014
19. Guck, D., Timmer, M., Hatefi, H., Ruijters, E., Stoelinga, M.: Modelling and analysis of markov reward automata. In: Cassez, F., Raskin, J.-F. (eds.) ATVA 2014. LNCS, vol. 8837, pp. 168–184. Springer, Heidelberg (2014)
20. Hatefi, H., Braitling, B., Wimmer, R., Ferrer Fioriti, L.M., Hermanns, H., Becker, B.: Cost vs. time in stochastic games and Markov automata (extended version). Reports of SFB/TR 14 AVACS 113, SFB/TR 14 AVACS (2015). http://www.avacs.org
21. Hatefi, H., Hermanns, H.: Model checking algorithms for Markov automata. ECE-ASST 53 (2012)
22. Hermanns, H. (ed.): Interactive Markov Chains. LNCS, vol. 2428. Springer, Heidelberg (2002)
23. Johr, S.: Model checking compositional Markov systems. Ph.D. thesis, Saarland University, Germany (2008)
24. Miller, B.L.: Finite state continuous time Markov decision processes with a finite planning horizon. SIAM Journal on Control **6**(2), 266–280 (1968)
25. Neuhäußer, M.R.: Model checking nondeterministic and randomly timed systems. Ph.D. thesis, RWTH Aachen University and University of Twente (2010)
26. Neuhäußer, M.R., Zhang, L.: Time-bounded reachability probabilities in continuous-time Markov decision processes. In: Proceedings of QEST, pp. 209–218. IEEE CS (2010)
27. Qiu, Q., Qu, Q., Pedram, M.: Stochastic modeling of a power-managed system-construction and optimization. IEEE Transactions on CAD of Integrated Circuits and Systems **20**(10), 1200–1217 (2001)

28. Segala, R.: A compositional trace-based semantics for probabilistic automata. In: Lee, I., Smolka, S.A. (eds.) CONCUR 1995. LNCS, vol. 962, pp. 234–248. Springer, Heidelberg (1995)

29. Shapley, L.S.: Stochastic games. Proc. of the National Academy of Sciences of the United States of America **39**(10), 1095 (1953)

30. Simunic, T., Benini, L., Glynn, P.W., Micheli, G.D.: Dynamic power management for portable systems. In: Proc. of MOBICOM, pp. 11–19 (2000)

31. Timmer, M., Katoen, J.-P., van de Pol, J., Stoelinga, M.I.A.: Efficient modelling and generation of markov automata. In: Koutny, M., Ulidowski, I. (eds.) CONCUR 2012. LNCS, vol. 7454, pp. 364–379. Springer, Heidelberg (2012)

32. Timmer, M., van de Pol, J., Stoelinga, M.I.A.: Confluence reduction for markov automata. In: Braberman, V., Fribourg, L. (eds.) FORMATS 2013. LNCS, vol. 8053, pp. 243–257. Springer, Heidelberg (2013)

A Comparative Study of BDD Packages for Probabilistic Symbolic Model Checking

Tom van Dijk[1], Ernst Moritz Hahn[2], David N. Jansen[3], Yong Li[2], Thomas Neele[1], Mariëlle Stoelinga[1], Andrea Turrini[2(✉)], and Lijun Zhang[2]

[1] Formal Methods and Tools, University of Twente, Enschede, The Netherlands
[2] State Key Laboratory of Computer Science,
Institute of Software, Chinese Academy of Sciences, Beijing, China
turrini@ios.ac.cn
[3] Model-Based System Development,
Radboud Universiteit, Nijmegen, The Netherlands

Abstract. Symbolic data structures using Binary Decision Diagrams (BDDs) have been successfully used in the last decades to analyse large systems. While various BDD and MTBDD packages have been developed in the community, the CUDD package remains the default choice of most of the symbolic (probabilistic) model checkers. In this paper, we provide the first comparative study of the performance of various BDD/MTBDD packages for this purpose. We provide experimental results for several well-known probabilistic benchmarks and study the effect of several optimisations. Our experiments show that no BDD package dominates on a single core, but that parallelisation yields significant speedups.

1 Introduction

Probabilities play a central role in many areas such as distributed systems, sensor networks, and robotics. They are used to break symmetries, e.g., to elect a leader [21], to resolve conflicts in a network, like the exponential backoff in CSMA/CD [20], or to model unreliable components, such as sensors.

Model checking [7] is an important approach to assess the correctness of such systems, by exploring the state space of a model and checking whether a probabilistic property is satisfied. Model checking faces the so-called *state space explosion* problem: a combinatorial blowup of the number of states in the number of system components and variables. For real-world models, it is therefore infeasible to traverse all states explicitly, since they often contain billions of states [10]. To obtain a more compact representation of the state space, Burch *et al.* proposed Binary Decision Diagrams (BDDs) [10,27]. These have now become a standard technique to tackle large systems, with successful applications in the analysis of many systems.

BDDs are a heuristic method to represent a large set of states or a transition matrix. They are typically small if the state space contains symmetries, for example in a system containing multiple similar modules. Standard BDDs store state spaces (denoted by $S \subseteq \mathbb{B}^N$) and transition relations according to their

© Springer International Publishing Switzerland 2015
X. Li et al. (Eds.): SETTA 2015, LNCS 9409, pp. 35–51, 2015.
DOI: 10.1007/978-3-319-25942-0_3

characteristic function $\mathbb{B}^N \to \mathbb{B}$. To store functions with any codomain, multi-terminal BDDs (MTBDDs) have been proposed [12,16]. In this way, functions $\mathbb{B}^N \to \mathbb{N}$ and $\mathbb{B}^N \to \mathbb{R}$ can be represented.

In [5], MTBDDs were first applied in probabilistic symbolic model checking to represent the transition probabilities. They play a central role in the leading probabilistic model checker PRISM [23], which exploits the well-known MTBDD package CUDD [33].

Many parts of probabilistic model checking can be carried out using BDD operations only, and these are often the computationally most expensive steps of the process. In particular, the computation of the set of reachable states and the qualitative precomputation step, which finds the set of states satisfying a formula with probability 0 or 1, are computationally heavy, since they operate on the initial, large model.

In fact, MTBDDs may not be most efficient in probabilistic model checking. The reduced state space obtained after the above operations already contains the information required to compute the probability of the formula by means of numerical approaches, such as linear equation systems or linear programming. MTBDDs may be disadvantageous in such cases, as their regularity is destroyed [4,19]. A major advantage of avoiding MTBDDs is that the probabilistic model checking process could be accelerated by choosing a suitable BDD package.

In this paper, we provide a comparative study of the model checking process using several BDD packages, together with different settings that influence the performance of these packages. In our model checker IsCASMC [17], we have integrated the packages CUDD [33], BuDDy [13], CacBDD [26], JDD [35], Sylvan [36], and BeeDeeDee [25]. As case studies, we use various well-known probabilistic examples from the PRISM website [31]. We observe that there is no clear winner for the single-core BDD packages while computing BDD operations in parallel may improve the runtime considerably, in particular for large models. We observe moreover that native BDD features offered by the package to atomically perform a sequence of BDD operations on average improve both time and memory consumption, but there are cases where such a feature slightly degrades the performance. Our results suggest it is indeed useful to be able to choose among several BDD packages and optimisations when performing probabilistic model checking, since different BDD packages perform very differently on different models.

2   Probabilistic Model Checking

In this section, we first recall the formal definitions of Markov chains and Markov decision processes. To specify probabilistic properties, we then employ the temporal logic PCTL. Moreover, we sketch some techniques of model checking based on (MT)BDDs.

2.1   Markov Decision Processes

A Markov Chain (MC) can be used to describe a fully probabilistic model; a Markov Decision Process (MDP) serves to describe a system containing both probabilistic and nondeterministic choices. Such a system typically arises from the parallel composition of multiple probabilistic models.

Definition 1. *A* Markov decision process *is a tuple* $\mathcal{M} = (S, s_0, AP, L, Act, \mathrm{P})$ *where S is a countable, nonempty set of states, $s_0 \in S$ is the initial state, AP is a set of atomic propositions, $L \colon S \to 2^{AP}$ a labelling function, Act is a countable, nonempty set of actions, and $\mathrm{P} \colon S \times Act \times S \to [0,1]$ is the transition probability function such that for all states $s \in S$ and actions $\alpha \in Act$ it holds that $\sum_{s' \in S} \mathrm{P}(s, \alpha, s') \in \{0, 1\}$.*
    A (discrete-time) Markov chain *can be seen as an MDP where $|Act| = 1$.*

2.2   PCTL Model Checking

Now we introduce the probabilistic logic PCTL, which we use in our case studies.

Definition 2. *A* PCTL formula *is a state formula ϕ defined by the following grammar, where $a \in AP$ is an atomic proposition, $\bowtie \in \{<, >, \geq, \leq\}$, $p \in [0,1] \cap \mathbb{Q}$, $n \in \mathbb{N}$, and ψ is a path formula.*

$$\phi ::= a \mid \phi \wedge \phi \mid \neg\phi \mid \mathcal{P}_{\bowtie p}[\psi]$$
$$\psi ::= \mathbf{X}\phi \mid \phi \, \mathbf{U} \, \phi \mid \phi \, \mathbf{U}_{\leq n} \, \phi$$

A qualitative *formula is a formula where each p in $\mathcal{P}_{\bowtie p}[\cdot]$ is either 0 or 1.*

We use standard derived operators such as $\phi_1 \vee \phi_2 = \neg(\neg\phi_1 \wedge \neg\phi_2)$, $false = a \wedge \neg a$, $true = \neg false$, $\mathbf{F}\phi = true \, \mathbf{U} \, \phi$, $\mathbf{G}\phi = \neg\mathbf{F}\neg\phi$ and their bounded counterparts.
    PCTL model checking is performed by a recursive descent into the formula under consideration. For model checking the PCTL formula $\mathcal{P}_{\bowtie p}[\psi]$ over a MC $\mathcal{M}$, we first need to compute the probability that a path starting from each state s satisfies the path formula ψ, which is denoted $p_s(\psi)$. We divide all states into three disjoint sets: S^{no}, S^{yes}, and $S^?$; we call this operation the *precomputation*. The sets S^{no} and S^{yes} contain the states s such that $p_s(\psi)$ is trivially 0 and 1, respectively. The remaining states belong to $S^?$. In order to compute $p_s(\psi)$ for $s \in S^?$, we reduce it to solving a linear equation system iteratively. The remaining work is straightforward: we just compare the results with $\bowtie p$. Model checking PCTL over MDPs is similar, but it should deal with adversaries (schedulers, policies) and fairness because MDPs are non-deterministic models, see [7].

2.3   BDD-Based Probabilistic Symbolic Model Checking

In this section, we recall BDDs and MTBDDs. Then, we briefly discuss symbolic model checking using BDDs.

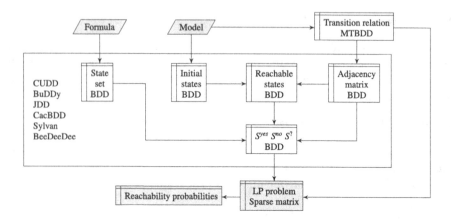

Fig. 1. Overview of the data structures used by the model checking algorithm

The concept of (reduced ordered) binary decision diagrams (BDDs) was proposed by Bryant [9], based on early works in [1,24]. A BDD represents a Boolean function $f(x_1, x_2, \ldots, x_n)$. It is a rooted directed acyclic graph [2] where terminal nodes (leaves) are labelled with either 0 or 1. Non-terminal nodes contain a variable label x_i and two edges labelled 0 and 1, typically called the low and the high edge. Each non-terminal node represents the Boolean expression $(\neg x_i \wedge f_{x_i=0}) \vee (x_i \wedge f_{x_i=1})$, where the cofactors $f_{x_i=0}$ and $f_{x_i=1}$ are represented by the target nodes of the low and the high edge, respectively. Furthermore, variable labels x_i appear along paths in the BDD according to an ordering. Finding a good variable ordering is critical for the performance of symbolic model checking; good heuristics exist, which are beyond the scope of this paper. Reduction rules that remove redundant and duplicate nodes ensure that BDDs represent Boolean functions canonically.

Some BDD packages use *complement edges* as further edge labels to denote negation of a Boolean function, which results in efficient negation and allows optimisations that are beyond the scope of this paper. To construct and manipulate BDDs efficiently, BDD packages usually have a unique node table to store all the BDD nodes and provide a way to access nodes in constant time. They also have a cache that stores previously computed results to avoid duplicate computations. The *initial node size* and *initial cache size* are the initial numbers of entries in the unique node table and the cache, respectively.

MTBDDs. The papers [12,16] use a variant of BDDs to represent general matrices. It is claimed that MTBDDs are the space-optimal representation of both dense and sparse matrices, and of permutation matrices [16]. Unlike BDDs, the terminal nodes in MTBDDs are not restricted to be 0 or 1. (MT)BDDs enable storing and manipulating very large matrices in a symbolic manner due to their shared structures. Symbolic encoding of MDPs with (MT)BDDs can be then applied directly, see [5].

BDD-Based Probabilistic Symbolic Model Checking. Figure 1 gives an overview of the data flow during model checking for PCTL formulas. The data structures with white background are symbolically stored as (MT)BDDs while the data structures with grey background are stored explicitly. Given a PCTL formula $\mathcal{P}_{\bowtie p}[\psi]$ and a description of the model, the common procedure is to first encode the transition relation of the model as MTBDDs and the formula and initial states as BDDs. Moreover, a BDD copy of the transition relation is constructed by abstracting the probabilities between the states. The resulting transition relation is the adjacency matrix of the underlying graph. Then the reachability analysis identifies the reachable states of the model. By employing the *reachE* and *prob1E* iterations proposed in [14], the reachable states are divided into the three sets we mentioned before, namely S^{no}, S^{yes}, and $S^{?}$.

In the next step, one computes the probability of ψ by solving a linear equation system for MCs, or a Linear Programming (LP) problem for MDPs. First, the transition relation MTBDD is transformed to a probability sparse matrix, which is used to encode the corresponding LP problem to compute the probabilities. In practice, approximate value iteration is often used. The resulting reachability probability is then compared with $\bowtie p$ to decide whether $\mathcal{P}_{\bowtie p}[\psi]$ is satisfied. For nested PCTL formulas, the smallest state subformula is handled first, and then the above procedure is recursively applied while traversing through the abstract syntax tree of the formula in a bottom up order.

And-Exist Optimisation. One of the first steps in the PCTL model checking algorithm is the computation of the states that are reachable from the initial states. These are obtained by a fix-point computation of the transition probability matrix for MCs or of the transition probability function for MDPs starting from the set of initial states. For simplicity, consider the MC case and define the function $Post: 2^S \rightarrow 2^S$ as $Post(X) = \{\, s' \in S \mid \exists s \in X.P(s, s') > 0 \,\}$. Symbolically, we can represent this operation as $\exists V.R \wedge T$ where R is the BDD encoding the set of states X, T the BDD encoding the adjacency matrix, and V are the variables representing the current states. The resulting BDD encodes the set of next states (using variables $\widehat{V}$); by means of a variable renaming from $\widehat{V}$ to V, we convert it to represent the states in $Post(X)$.

A similar construction underlies the computation of the predecessor states; this operation is the base of the precomputation step that, even for general PCTL properties, may be performed very frequently and it is quite time consuming.

In the above two computations, we first have to build the conjunction of two BDDs encoding the current states and the adjacency matrix and afterwards to remove a number of variables from this conjunction by existential quantification such as $\exists v.bdd_1 \wedge bdd_2$. It is often the case that the BDD representing the conjunction is quite large. Therefore, building $bdd_1 \wedge bdd_2$ and afterwards applying the existential quantification is often very slow. On the other hand, the BDD obtained after the existential quantification is often quite small. To improve this operation, many BDD packages support a so-called And-Exist (relational product) operator, in which these two steps are performed at once. This means that the construction of the intermediate BDD $bdd_1 \wedge bdd_2$ can be avoided, so as to reduce computation time and memory consumption.

2.4 BDD Packages

In this paper, we study the performance of six different BDD packages: CUDD [33], BuDDy [13], CacBDD [26], JDD [35], Sylvan [36], and BeeDeeDee [25]. CUDD is a well-known BDD implementation used in several model checkers. BuDDy has been integrated in several theorem provers and provides many efficient BDD operations. As for CacBDD, experiments in [26] show that it outperforms CUDD in many benchmarks. JDD is a BDD package implemented in Java. Sylvan is a novel parallel decision diagram implementation that parallelises the BDD operations [36]. BeeDeeDee is a recent Java thread-safe implementation of a BDD package. We remark that we are aware of other BDD packages including ABCD [8], PBF [37], Janssen's BDD [22], Carnegie Mellon's BDD [30], BDDNOW [29], and CAL BDD [32]: they are not included in our tool as these packages are outdated and no longer maintained since 2000. Two recently updated packages are BiDDy [28] and MEDDLY [3], however they lack certain basic operations and can therefore not be compared to the other packages.

CUDD is a C implementation of BDDs and MTBDDs developed by Fabio Somenzi, University of Colorado at Boulder. It provides support for operating with ordinary BDDs, Algebraic Decision Diagrams (ADDs), and Zero-suppressed Binary Decision Diagrams (ZDDs). ADDs are a special implementation of MTBDDs that are used, for instance, by PRISM as its MTBDD implementation. The three types of decision diagrams provide essentially the same set of operations; this means, for instance, that an operation available when operating with BDDs is also available for ADDs. A notable exception is the And-Exist operation that is not yet available for ADDs. Besides its several operations on BDDs, ADDs, and ZDDs, CUDD also supports the conversion of BDDs into ADDs or ZDDs and vice versa. In addition, it also provides a large assortment of variable reordering methods. Though written in C, it provides a C++ interface that provides overloaded operators and that offers to free the decision diagrams that are no longer used by the application.

BuDDy is a BDD package implemented in C by Jørn Lind-Nielsen as a Ph. D. project on model checking finite state machines. It supplies most useful operations for the manipulation of BDDs as well as functions for integer arithmetic like addition and relational operations like And-Exist. It provides also several highly efficient vectorised BDD operations and it supports dynamic variable reordering and garbage collection.

CacBDD is a BDD package written in C++ by Guanfeng Lv. It supports common BDD operations as well as other useful operations like the multiple-operand And-Exist. An interesting aspect of CacBDD is its dynamic cache management

Table 1. Overview of the features of the BDD packages used.

BDD engine	implementation language	MTBDDs/ ADDs	ZDDs	And-Exist	dynamic var reordering	remarks
CUDD	C	✔	✔	✔(✗)	✔	
BuDDy	C	✗	✗	✔	✔	
CacBDD	C++	✗	✗	✔	✗	dyn. cache mgmt.
JDD	Java	✗	✔	✔	✗	
Sylvan	C	✗	✗	✔	✗	supports multi-core
BeeDeeDee	Java	✗	✗	✗	✗	thread-safe

algorithm and lazy garbage collection that offer remarkable improvements in the performance of the BDD operations at the expense of free physical memory.

JDD is, unlike the previous BDD packages, a pure Java BDD package developed by Arash Vahidi. JDD supports BDDs as well as ZDDs and it has been originally inspired by BuDDy. Though it is implemented purely by Java, it is still an efficient BDD package and, thanks to its new cache scheme, JDD's memory usage per node is less than BuDDy, which is the major advantage of JDD.

Sylvan is a parallel decision diagram package implemented in C by Tom van Dijk as a Ph. D. project on multi-core decision diagrams. It uses work-stealing and scalable parallel data structures to provide parallelisation of algorithms on decision diagrams. Sylvan currently supports BDDs and list decision diagrams, which are a variation of multi-valued decision diagrams. Among the implemented parallel BDD operations, Sylvan provides other useful operations for model checking such as And-Exist and the Relnext operation that combines And-Exist with variable renaming. It has been designed as an extensible framework with custom BDD operations in mind and features parallel garbage collection.

BeeDeeDee is a thread-safe BDD package implemented in Java developed by Juliasoft, a spin-off company from the University of Verona. It supports the most common BDD operations. Thread-safety allows for sharing BDD nodes between threads, thus reducing the memory footprint when used in multi-threaded model checking. To improve its performance, BeeDeeDee uses the most modern techniques for multi-threading in Java such as the split locks that are used to control the concurrent garbage collection and the concurrent accesses to the node table.

An overview of the features of the considered BDD packages is given in Table 1.

3   Experimental Results

In order to compare the different BDD packages, we have implemented the BDD-based probabilistic model checking methods in our tool IscasMC [17].

In IscasMC, we provide a common high level Java interface to interact with the specific BDD packages, each of them wrapped into a dedicated Java class.

This separates the BDD implementations from the model checking algorithms and enables extending the tool with new or updated BDD packages, without having to change other parts of the tool. IsCASMC is mainly implemented in Java and it uses Java Native Access (JNA)[1] to call BDD libraries written in C or C++. JNA is a library decreasing the programmer's effort to call native methods from Java. JNA introduces a small overhead compared to using Java Native Interface (JNI). The overhead turned out to be negligible compared to the total runtimes.

Since we use some features that are not provided natively by all BDD packages, like the And-Exist operation, we have implemented IsCASMC such that it falls back to use ordinary BDD operations when these features are not available. The BDD package to use in the model checking process can be chosen by setting the corresponding IsCASMC command line option. We do not use dynamic variable reordering, since it is not supported by all BDD packages we compare. Also, the reorder algorithm typically has a high performance cost and good static orders were available for the models under consideration.

Experimental Setting and Models. We have performed several experiments on the BDD packages by tuning their settings. All experiments have been performed on a Linux machine with an Intel Core i7-4790 processor at 3.6GHz with 16GB of RAM of which only 8GB are usable by IsCASMC. The time-out for the experiments is 30 minutes.

Table 2. Models and properties.

model	path property ψ
firewire-impl	$\mathbf{F}((\text{s1}{=}8 \ \& \ \text{s2}{=}7) \mid (\text{s1}{=}7 \ \& \ \text{s2}{=}8))$
leader	$\mathbf{F}$ ("elected")
dining-crypt	$\mathbf{F}$ ("done" & parity=func(mod, N, 2))
phil-nofair	$\mathbf{F}$ ("eat")
cluster	$\mathbf{F}$ ("premium")
google	$\mathbf{F}$ ("light_hardware_disaster")

Table 2 shows the models and the path properties taken from the PRISM website [31] we used for the experiments: the IEEE 1394 FireWire protocol (implementation) [34] ("firewire-impl"), the Google File System model [6] ("google"), the Asynchronous Leader Election protocol [21] ("leader"), the Dining Cryptographers protocol [11] ("dining-crypt"), the Dining Philosophers protocol with no fairness assumption [15] ("phil-nofair"), and the Workstation cluster [18] ("cluster"). Except for the "cluster" and "google" models that are Continuous Time Markov Chains (CTMCs)[2], other models are MDPs. The actual formula we checked is $\mathcal{P}_{\geq 1}[\psi]$ for the firewire-impl, leader, cluster, and google models while it is of the form *filter(forall, cond $\Rightarrow \mathcal{P}_{\geq 1}[\psi]$)* for the remaining dining-crypt (where *cond* is

---

[1] https://github.com/twall/jna#readme

[2] As we consider qualitative unbounded properties, they can be checked by transforming the CTMCs to the corresponding embedded Markov chains.

"*hungry*") and phil-nofair (where *cond* is *pay* = 0) models. The keyword *filter* allows us to analyse the property in a given set of states we are interested in: *filter*(*forall*, (*cond*) ⇒ $\mathcal{P}_{\geq 1}[\psi]$) is satisfied whenever for all states satisfying *cond* the property $\mathcal{P}_{\geq 1}[\psi]$ holds. Note that the initial state may or may not be considered in the analysis, depending on whether it satisfies *cond*.

Remark 1. All the properties we consider here are qualitative properties, so they can be decided by using the information from the sets S^{yes}, S^{no}, and $S^?$ obtained from the precomputation step on BDDs. This allows us to measure the time spent by IsCASMC working with only (MT)BDDs, so we get a better understanding of the effects of the different packages and options on the time spent for checking the formulas. We do use MTBDDs to construct the transition relation, as doing so is easier than just using BDDs. The construction never took a significant amount of time.

We further emphasise that our tool can handle quantitative properties. For quantitative properties, various BDD packages will produce the same problem instance but –mostly– in different orders. This will further influence performance of the linear programming problem solvers in a way that is loosely connected to the BDD packages.

Running Time. Table 3 shows the running time in seconds for the six different engines CUDD, BuDDy, CacBDD, JDD, BeeDeeDee, and Sylvan. We repeated each experiment 10 times and report the rounded average time of the 10 runs. We used CUDD as a pure BDD package (cudd-bdd) or as a pure MTBDD package (cudd-mtbdd) while for Sylvan we considered the sequential computation with 1 worker (sylvan-1) or the parallel computation with 7 workers (sylvan-7); we use 7 workers instead of 8 to reserve a processor core for other threads in Java and the operating system, as explained at the end of the section. We kept the default values for the BDD packages except for the initial cache size that we set to 2 612 440 entries and the initial node size to 1 250 000 entries, for packages supporting such options. Moreover, we enabled the And-Exist optimisation for all packages whenever supported natively (see further below). For each model, we considered several instances corresponding to different parameter choices. For example, for the model "firewire-impl", we considered the values 36, 45, 54, and 63 for the parameter "delay". We marked by '–TO–' the cases where the computation took more than 30 minutes and by '–MO–' the computations using more than 8GB of RAM. We highlighted the best runtimes among all packages in bold font; we marked also the best runtimes excluding sylvan-7 so to consider only sequential computations.

By looking at the results in Table 3, we can immediately see that no BDD package outperforms the others in all case studies. The first thing we note is that Sylvan-7 takes a large advantage from its parallel operations for the high time-consuming models, but the overhead induced by the synchronisation on the parallel operations penalise it on small cases. If we focus on Sylvan-1 and the other sequential BDD packages, we note that for the CTMC models "cluster"

Table 3. IsCasMC performances with different BDD packages where the values are the rounded average running time of 10 executions.

BDD engine	time (secs)											
	cluster / N				firewire-impl / delay				leader / N			
	1536	1792	2048	2304	36	45	54	63	6	7	8	9
cudd-mtbdd	63	92	125	170	109	65	69	86	11	58	218	709
cudd-bdd	40	54	75	95	**65**	**43**	**42**	**45**	**7**	**25**	**86**	**301**
buddy	**4**	**4**	**6**	**7**	78	46	51	82	**7**	48	165	662
cacbdd	21	28	40	53	87	71	72	85	8	28	95	410
jdd	**4**	**4**	7	**7**	88	49	54	77	8	47	170	637
beedeedee	7	8	12	16	91	55	61	61	11	42	183	853
sylvan-1	5	5	8	8	74	48	50	54	**7**	27	111	615
sylvan-7	5	5	8	8	**29**	**26**	**27**	**28**	**4**	**9**	**28**	**139**
	google / M				phil-nofair / N				dining-crypt / N			
	500	1000	1500	2000	7	8	9	10	25	30	35	40
cudd-mtbdd	8	32	85	144	25	98	339	–MO–	13	44	68	206
cudd-bdd	6	22	56	91	19	74	268	–MO–	9	17	31	51
buddy	**4**	**9**	**23**	**30**	24	122	465	–TO–	18	41	91	169
cacbdd	5	15	42	68	**13**	**51**	**194**	–MO–	5	**8**	**13**	**21**
jdd	**4**	10	25	34	37	203	706	–TO–	19	39	92	172
beedeedee	6	22	56	97	32	136	514	–TO–	20	48	101	166
sylvan-1	5	12	32	46	20	120	500	–TO–	6	11	18	56
sylvan-7	6	12	30	35	**5**	**25**	**102**	–MO–	6	**8**	16	47

and "google" BuDDy and JDD perform better than the other packages, while for the remaining MDP models the best are CUDD as BDD ("firewire-impl" and "leader") and CacBDD ("phil-nofair" and "dining-crypt"). We remark that Sylvan-1 is usually very close to the best-performing BDD packages for "cluster" and "dining-crypt". The CUDD package remains the default choice of most of the symbolic (probabilistic) model checkers, but an order of magnitude in the runtime could be saved sometimes—see the "cluster" and "dining-crypt" examples.

The overall runtime of the packages on all experiments is summarised by the next table, where we sum all entries in Table 3 excluding the failures.

cudd-mtbdd	cudd-bdd	buddy	cacbdd	jdd	beedeedee	sylvan-1	sylvan-7
2837	1522	2156	1433	2493	2598	1838	608

It is worthwhile to note that CUDD (as MTBDD) is always one of the slowest packages and the slowest on the overall set of experiments. This suggests that using only BDD operations sometimes improves the runtime of the model checker for probabilistic systems quite considerably.

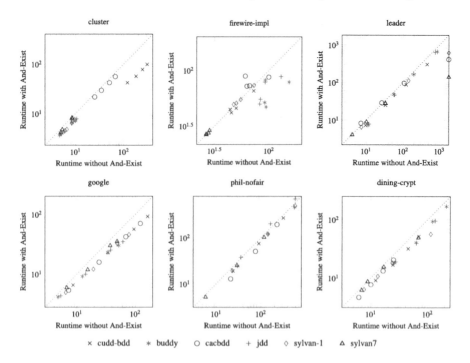

Fig. 2. And-Exist Setting comparison (time).

And-Exist Optimisation. Figure 2 shows the effect of the use of the And-Exist optimisation in the model checking algorithm. We have performed the experiments by using the BDD packages providing native support to the And-Exist optimisation in the same setting as for Table 3; thus, we omitted CUDD (as MTBDD) and BeeDeeDee since they do not provide such an optimisation.

Each mark in the plot corresponds to the execution of the BDD package with and without the And-Exist optimisation for one instance of the models. The points below (above) the dotted line represent the cases where the usage of And-Exist has reduced (increased) the runtime. As we can see, it is in general convenient to use such an optimisation, but there are cases, like for CacBDD on "firewire-impl" and JDD on "phil-nofair" where it is preferable to not use And-Exist.

Figure 3 is similar to Figure 2, except for the fact that we consider the used memory instead of the runtime. We can note that usually the use of And-Exist helps in reducing the memory footprint but there are cases where CUDD (as BDD) and JDD require more memory when And-Exist is used.

Remark 2. Due to space limitations we omit a detailed report of the memory usage of the BDD packages. We have observed, unless a memory-out is reached, irregular behaviour of memory usage. We think that it is due to the fact that different BDD packages have their own way of memory managing strategies, for

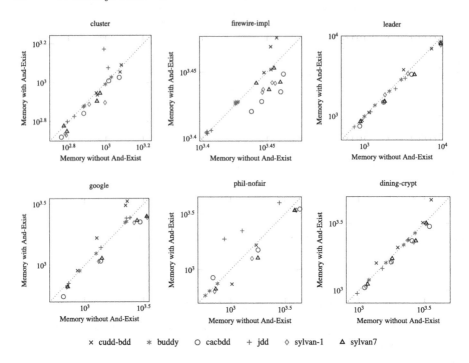

Fig. 3. And-Exist Setting comparison (memory, in MB).

instance by preferring to allocate new memory instead of performing a garbage collection.

Impact of the Initial Cache Size. In Figure 4 we plot the outcomes of several experiments on the "firewire-impl" model with BuDDy by varying only the initial cache size. Note that here the reference value $D = 262\,144 = 2^{18}$ is one tenth of the value we used for Table 3. As one can expect, increasing this value usually improves the running time. However, we can first note a big decrease in the running time going from 0.25D to 1D; then, by enlarging the cache size to 4D, the runtime increases for then decreasing again as expected. Note that by making the

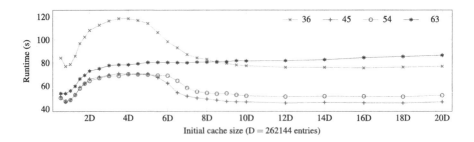

Fig. 4. BuDDy performance on "firewire-impl" with different initial cache sizes.

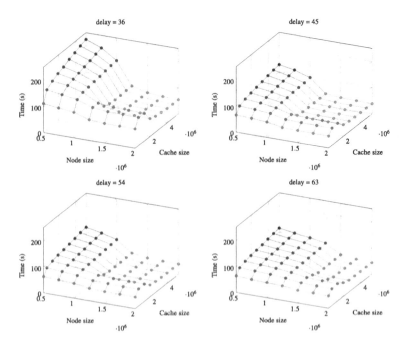

Fig. 5. BuDDy performance on "firewire-impl" with different initial cache and node sizes.

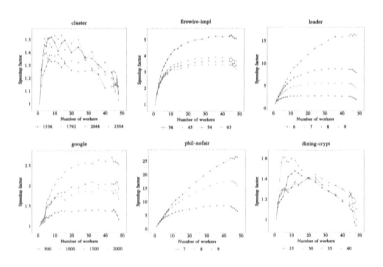

Fig. 6. IsCASMC speedup with Sylvan BDD package with different workers.

cache much larger (from 18D) slightly increases the runtime again. The hashing of the elements in the cache and the locality of the cached data may be the causes of the observed behaviour.

In Figure 5 we plot the result of varying the initial cache size and node size. For the cache size, we range from $D = 262\,144 = 2^{18}$ to 20D; for the node size, we range from $0.5 \cdot 10^6$ to $2 \cdot 10^6$. By looking at the plots, we can note that increasing the cache size is counter-productive if the node size is too small, while it is always worth to increase the node size. Note however that increasing both parameters too much may cause a failure by memory-out.

Effect of the Number of Workers on Sylvan. Figure 6 shows the speedup gained by IscasMC by using Sylvan with a different number of workers. For this case, we used a different machine equipped with 48 cores (4 AMD Opteron 6168 processors) and 128GB of RAM, but with the same time and memory limits as before.

In general, we observe that the gained speedup is correlated to the runtime size of the models. The "leader" and "phil-nofair" models result in a higher speedup. The highest speedup we obtain is with the "phil-nofair" model: here we obtain a speedup of 26.5 with 47 workers. For the "cluster", "google", "dining-crypt" examples, the speedup is at most 3. For the smallest models, the speedup increases first with the number of workers, but with too many workers the gained speedups are lost again. This behavior could be explained as follows. When reachability consists of only small BDD operations, then there is little opportunity for parallelisation. Meanwhile, all workers are competing to execute the same suboperations, which aggravates the overhead from parallelisation. For the "dining-crypt" example with $N = 25$, with more than 46 workers we even observe a slowdown compared to running with 1 worker.

In all experiments we observe reductions of the speedup when nearly all cores are used. This is likely to be due to the fact that all the 48 workers have to share the cores with the system processes and the Java virtual machine, thus there is an increased scheduling activity affecting the workers. Instead, with at most 47 workers, at least one core remains always available for the system processes and the Java virtual machine, so the scheduling activity is not expected to affect the workers. We can derive that in general it is better to use a number of workers at most equal to the number of cores minus 1; this is why in Table 3 and Figure 2 we use 7 workers instead of 8, as confirmed by similar experiments we performed but omitted for lack of space.

Finally, the result of a speedup of 26.5 with 47 workers is similar to results obtained with LTSmin (a C-only model checker) in [36] and suggests that Java and JNA do not have a significant impact on scalability, at least until 44 workers. The performance drop with 45–48 workers, however, is not seen in [36].

4   Conclusion

This paper demonstrates the performances of different BDD packages in the context of probabilistic model checking. From the experiments, we have seen that no BDD package is remarkably faster than the others; CUDD (as BDD) and CacBDD performed rather well on MDP models while BuDDy and JDD were more suitable for continuous time MCs. The parallel BDD package Sylvan can outperform the other packages in cases where the overall running time is sufficiently high and multiple cores are used, and is competitive with the other packages when used sequentially, despite the overhead added by parallelisation. This shows that parallelisation of BDD operations is very good for performance and that other BDD packages might also profit from this approach. The experiments confirmed that BDDs are sufficient for probabilistic model checking and much faster than MTBDDs. We have also shown that the And-Exist optimisation speeds up the whole verification process in some case studies, while for others it does not lead to a considerable speedup or even leads to a decreased performance.

Acknowledgments. This work has been supported by the EU FP7 project SENSATION (318490), the STW-ProRail ExploRail project ArRangeer (12238), the NWO projects MaDriD (612.001.101) and BEAT (612.001.303), the National Natural Science Foundation of China (Grants 61472406, 61472473, 61450110461), the Chinese Academy of Sciences Fellowship for International Young Scientists (Grants 2013Y1GB0006, 2015VTC029), the CAS/SAFEA International Partnership Program for Creative Research Teams, and the Sino-German CDZ project CAP (GZ 1023).

References

1. Akers, S.B.: Binary decision diagrams. IEEE Trans. on Computers **27**, 509–516 (1978)
2. Andersen, H.R.: An introduction to binary decision diagrams. Course Notes on the WWW (1997)
3. Babar, J., Miner, A.: Meddly: Multi-terminal and edge-valued decision diagram library. In: QEST, pp. 195–196. IEEE Comp. Soc., Los Alamitos (2010)
4. Bahar, R.I., Frohm, E.A., Gaona, C.M., Hachtel, G.D., Macii, E., Pardo, A., Somenzi, F.: Algebraic decision diagrams and their applications. In: ICCAD, pp. 188–191. IEEE Comp. Soc., Los Alamitos (1993)
5. Baier, C., Clarke, E.M., Hartonas-Garmhausen, V., Kwiatkowska, M., Ryan, M.: Symbolic model checking for probabilistic processes. In: Degano, P., Gorrieri, R., Marchetti-Spaccamela, A. (eds.) ICALP 1997. LNCS, vol. 1256, pp. 430–440. Springer, Heidelberg (1997)
6. Baier, C., Hahn, E.M., Haverkort, B.R., Hermanns, H., Katoen, J.-P.: Model checking for performability. MSCS **23**(4), 751–795 (2013)
7. Baier, C., Katoen, J.-P.: Principles of Model Checking. MIT Press, Cambridge (2008)
8. Biere, A.: ABCD. http://fmv.jku.at/abcd/
9. Bryant, R.E.: Graph-based algorithms for boolean function manipulation. IEEE Trans. on Computers **100**(8), 677–691 (1986)

10. Burch, J., Clarke, E., McMillan, K., Dill, D., Hwang, L.: Symbolic model checking: 10^{20} states and beyond. I&C **98**(2), 142–170 (1992)
11. Chaum, D.: The dining cryptographers problem: Unconditional sender and recipient untraceability. J. of Cryptology **1**(1), 65–75 (1988)
12. Clarke, E.M., Fujita, M., McGeer, P.C., McMillan, K., Yang, J. C.-Y., Zhao, X.: Multi-terminal binary decision diagrams: An efficient data structure for matrix representation. In: IWLS (1993). http://repository.cmu.edu/compsci/453
13. Cohen, H., Whaley, J., Wildt, J., Gorogiannis, N.: BuDDy. http://sourceforge.net/p/buddy/
14. de Alfaro, L., Kwiatkowska, M., Norman, G., Parker, D., Segala, R.: Symbolic model checking of probabilistic processes using MTBDDs and the Kronecker representation. In: Graf, S. (ed.) TACAS 2000. LNCS, vol. 1785, pp. 395–410. Springer, Heidelberg (2000)
15. Duflot, M., Fribourg, L., Picaronny, C.: Randomized dining philosophers without fairness assumption. Distributed Computing **17**(1), 65–76 (2004)
16. Fujita, M., McGeer, P.C., Yang, J.C.-Y.: Multi-terminal binary decision diagrams: An efficient data structure for matrix representation. FMSD **10**(2–3), 149–169 (1997)
17. Hahn, E.M., Li, Y., Schewe, S., Turrini, A., Zhang, L.: IscasMC: a web-based probabilistic model checker. In: Jones, C., Pihlajasaari, P., Sun, J. (eds.) FM 2014. LNCS, vol. 8442, pp. 312–317. Springer, Heidelberg (2014)
18. Haverkort, B.R., Hermanns, H., Katoen, J.-P.: On the use of model checking techniques for dependability evaluation. In: SRDS, pp. 228–237 (2000)
19. Hermanns, H., Kwiatkowska, M., Norman, G., Parker, D., Siegle, M.: On the use of MTBDDs for performability analysis and verification of stochastic systems. J. of Logic and Algebraic Programming **56**(1–2), 23–67 (2003)
20. IEEE 802.3-2002. Carrier Sense Multiple Access with Collision Detection (CSMA/CD) Standard (2002)
21. Itai, A., Rodeh, M.: Symmetry breaking in distributed networks. I&C **88**(1), 60–87 (1990)
22. Janssen, G.: The Eindhoven BDD package. ftp://ftp.ics.ele.tue.nl/pub/users/geert/bdd.tar.gz
23. Kwiatkowska, M., Norman, G., Parker, D.: PRISM 4.0: verification of probabilistic real-time systems. In: Gopalakrishnan, G., Qadeer, S. (eds.) CAV 2011. LNCS, vol. 6806, pp. 585–591. Springer, Heidelberg (2011)
24. Lee, C.Y.: Representation of switching circuits by binary-decision programs. Bell System Technical Journal **38**(4), 985–999 (1959)
25. Lovato, A., Macedonio, D., Spoto, F.: A thread-safe library for binary decision diagrams. In: Giannakopoulou, D., Salaün, G. (eds.) SEFM 2014. LNCS, vol. 8702, pp. 35–49. Springer, Heidelberg (2014)
26. Lv, G., Su, K., Xu, Y.: CacBDD: A BDD package with dynamic cache management. In: Sharygina, N., Veith, H. (eds.) CAV 2013. LNCS, vol. 8044, pp. 229–234. Springer, Heidelberg (2013)
27. McMillan, K.L.: Symbolic model checking. Springer (1993)
28. Meolic, R.: Biddy a multi-platform academic bdd package. J. of Software, 7(6) (2012)
29. Milvang-Jensen, K., Hu, A.J.: BDDNOW: a parallel BDD package. In: Gopalakrishnan, G.C., Windley, P. (eds.) FMCAD 1998. LNCS, vol. 1522, pp. 501–507. Springer, Heidelberg (1998)
30. Model Checking Group at Carnegie Mellon University: BDD. http://www.cs.cmu.edu/modelcheck/bdd.html

31. PRISM web site. http://www.prismmodelchecker.org
32. Ranjan, R.K., Sanghavi, J..: CAL BDD. http://embedded.eecs.berkeley.edu/Research/cal_bdd/
33. Somenzi, F.: CUDD: CU decision diagram package release 2.5.0. http://vlsi.colorado.edu/fabio/CUDD/
34. Stoelinga, M., Vaandrager, F.W.: Root contention in IEEE 1394. In: Katoen, J.-P. (ed.) AMAST-ARTS 1999, ARTS 1999, and AMAST-WS 1999. LNCS, vol. 1601, pp. 53–74. Springer, Heidelberg (1999)
35. Vahidi, A.: JDD, a pure Java BDD and Z-BDD library. http://javaddlib.sourceforge.net/jdd/
36. van Dijk, T., van de Pol, J.: Sylvan: multi-core decision diagrams. In: Baier, C., Tinelli, C. (eds.) TACAS 2015. LNCS, vol. 9035, pp. 677–691. Springer, Heidelberg (2015)
37. Yang, B., Chen, Y., Bryant, R.E., O'Hallaron, D.R.: Space- and time-efficient BDD construction via working set control. In: ASP-DAC, pp. 423–432, IEEE, Piscataway (1998)

Hybrid and Cyber-Physical Systems

Refinement and Proof Based Development of Systems Characterized by Continuous Functions

Guillaume Babin[1][(✉)], Yamine Aït-Ameur[1], Shin Nakajima[2], and Marc Pantel[1]

[1] Université de Toulouse; IRIT / INPT-ENSEEIHT,
2 Rue Charles Camichel, Toulouse, France
guillaume.babin@irit.fr, {yamine,marc.pantel}@enseeiht.fr
[2] National Institute of Informatics, 2-1-2 Hitotsubashi, Chiyoda-ku, Tokyo, Japan
nkjm@nii.ac.jp

Abstract. The specification of cyber-physical systems usually relies on continuous functions over dense real numbers whereas their implementation is discrete. Proving the correctness of the discrete implementation with respect to the continuous specification remains a challenge in the presence of dense real numbers. In this paper, we propose a refinement-based formal method, relying on Event-B, for such developments. We illustrate our proposal with the development of a simple stability controller for a generic plant model. The continuous function that models the system behavior is refined as a discrete model of the same kind preserving stability expressed as a safety invariants of the continuous model. The obtained discrete model uses discrete time (instants modeled on $\mathbb{N}$), whereas the continuous model is based on dense time (on $\mathbb{R}$). The Rodin Platform, together with the Theory plug-in handling the `Real` datatype and its properties supported the whole developments and proofs.

Keywords: Continuous and discrete behaviors · Dense real numbers · Correct-by-construction · Formal methods · Proved refinements · Event-B

1 Introduction

According to Lee [20], cyber-physical systems (CPS) are defined as *integrations of computation, networking, and physical processes. Embedded computers and networks monitor and control the physical processes, with feedback loops where physical processes affect computations and vice versa.* Most of the time, a software part (the controller) drives the physical part (the plant) through a loop involving sensors and actuators. The CPS plant behavior is given by dense time continuous functions solution of differential equations. The CPS controller behavior is specified by continuous functions over dense time. The CPS software implements a discretization of these functions in order to control the CPS plant. This discretization proof is a key challenge in the CPS correctness proof.

© Springer International Publishing Switzerland 2015
X. Li et al. (Eds.): SETTA 2015, LNCS 9409, pp. 55–70, 2015.
DOI: 10.1007/978-3-319-25942-0_4

In the past years, several approaches relying on formal methods, like Hybrid automata [17] and model checking [5], have been set up to describe the behavior of the software controllers. Our proposal focuses on the verification of correct controllers obtained after discretization.

This paper show how proof and refinement based approaches handle the development of a correct-by-construction discrete controller starting from a dense time continuous function specification of the continuous controller. A complete incremental development relying on a theory of reals is conducted to synthesize a correct discretization of a continuous function. The approach exploits an axiomatization of mathematical reals. It maintains a safety invariant characterizing the physical plant of the studied system. Such invariant defines a safety envelope (which we called *safety corridor*) modeling a *stability property* in which the system must evolve i.e. for a continuous function f, we write $\forall t \in \mathbb{R}^+, f(t) \in [m, M]$ where t is a dense time parameter and the reals m and M define minimum and maximum values in $\mathbb{R}^+$ ensuring a correct behavior of the physical plant. In general, these values come from the physics of the studied system. The Event-B method is used to handle such formal developments. We illustrate our proposal with the development of a simple stability controller for a generic plant model.

This paper is structured as follows. Section 2 overviews the addressed problem of discretization. Section 3 summarizes the Event-B method. Sections 4 and 5 are the core of our proposal: the refinement strategy for any continuous function together with the corresponding requirements are given in section 4 while the complete Event-B development handling these requirements is provided in section 5. Related works and possible applications are sketched in section 6. The conclusion and some perspectives are given in the end.

2   Discretization of Continuous Functions

The behavior of many systems can be characterized by three states: the initial boot, the nominal behavior, and the final halt. Several CPS involving physical plants and software controllers follow this pattern such as energy production systems, smart systems, medical systems, etc. These systems are usually modeled by differential equations specifying dense time continuous functions. In order to control their behavior, one has first to discretize these continuous functions. The main safety property concerns stability where the function values shall be maintained inside a safety envelope i.e. an interval of correct values (called *corridor*).

The correct implementation of such continuous functions is a key point in ensuring the CPS safety. These ones shall be discretized in a correct manner that guarantees that the discrete behavior simulates the continuous one. In other words, the continuous states existing between two observed consecutive states of the discretization are also in the safety corridor. To achieve this goal, we follow a correct-by-construction approach based on a formal development of *any* continuous function discretization, making our development reusable and scalable. The approach relies on refinement and on the preservation of invariants. Discretization information are incrementally added while moving from the continuous level to the discrete one. Event-B [1] and the Rodin Platform [2] have been set up to handle the developments.

3   The Event-B Method

An Event-B model [1] (see Table 1) is defined in a *MACHINE*. It encodes a state transition system which consists of: variables declared in the *VARIABLES* clause to represent the state; and events declared in the *EVENTS* clause to represent the transitions (defined by a Before-After predicate BA) from one state to another.

Table 1. Structure of Event-B machines

CONTEXT	MACHINE
$ctxt\_id\_2$	$machine\_id\_2$
EXTENDS	**REFINES**
$ctxt\_id\_1$	$machine\_id\_1$
SETS	**SEES**
s	$ctxt\_id\_2$
CONSTANTS	**VARIABLES**
c	v
AXIOMS	**INVARIANTS**
$A(s,c)$	$I(s,cv)$
THEOREMS	**THEOREMS**
$T_c(s,c)$	$T_m(s,c,v)$
END	**VARIANT**
	$V(s,c,v)$
	EVENTS
	Event $evt \triangleq$
	any x
	where $G(s,c,v,x)$
	then
	$v : \vert BA(s,c,v,x,v')$
	end
	END

Table 2. Generated proof obligations for an Event-B model

Theorems	$A(s,c) \Rightarrow T_c(s,c)$
	$A(s,c) \wedge I(s,c,v)$
	$\Rightarrow T_m(s,c,v)$
Invariant preservation	$A(s,c) \wedge I(s,c,v)$
	$\wedge G(s,c,v,x)$
	$\wedge BA(s,c,v,x,v')$
	$\Rightarrow I(s,c,v')$
Event feasibility	$A(s,c) \wedge I(s,c,v)$
	$\wedge G(s,c,v,x)$
	$\Rightarrow \exists v'.BA(s,c,v,x,v')$
Variant progress	$A(s,c) \wedge I(s,c,v)$
	$\wedge G(s,c,v,x)$
	$\wedge BA(s,c,v,x,v')$
	$\Rightarrow V(s,c,v') < V(s,c,v)$

A model also holds *INVARIANTS* and *THEOREMS* to represent its relevant properties. A decreasing *VARIANT* may introduce convergence properties when needed. An Event-B machine is related, through the *SEES* clause to a *CONTEXT* which contains the relevant sets, constants axioms, and theorems. The refinement capability [4], introduced by the *REFINES* clause, decomposes a model (thus a transition system) into another transition system containing more design decisions thus moving from an abstract level to a less abstract one. New variables and new events may be introduced at the refinement level. In a refinement, the invariant shall link the variables of the refined machine with the ones of the refining machine. A gluing invariant is introduced for this purpose. It preserves the proved properties and supports the definition of new ones.

Once an Event-B machine is defined, a set of proof obligations is generated. They are submitted to the prover embedded in the RODIN platform. Proof obligations associated to an Event-B model are listed in Table 2, here the prime notation is used to denote the value of a variable after an event is triggered. More details on proof obligations can be found in [1].

Use of Reals in Event-B. A recent evolution of the Event-B method allows to extend it with theories [13] similar to algebraic specifications. In the Rodin Platform, this evolution is provided by the *Theory plugin for Rodin* [3]. We need to model and reason on dense *reals*. We rely on the theory for *reals* and continuous functions, written by Abrial and Butler[1]. It provides a dense mathematical REAL datatype with arithmetic operators, axioms and proof rules.

Remark. From a tool point of view, the use of reals with the *Theory plugin for Rodin* introduces constants like zero and operators defined on the REAL datatype like smr for <, gtr for > or leq for ≤. Casting operators need to be defined in order to work with other data types. These ones are used when discretizing continuous representations by refinement (see section 5.3).

4   Refinement Strategy

The mathematical model and the specification of the system behavior are sketched below. Following the approach defined in [23], the adopted refinement strategy consists in three steps: first, as shown in figure 1, we use three states to define a simple abstract controller that models the system; then, in a first refinement, we introduce a continuous controller characterizing its behaviors with a continuous function; finally, a second refinement builds a discrete controller.

4.1   The Illustrating System

The considered system goes through three phases. Figure 1 depicts its general behavior. First, it is booted (transition *boot* from state 1 to 2). After a while, once in state 2, it becomes operational in a nominal mode (*run* transition). Then, it stays a given amount of time in the nominal or running mode. When in nominal mode, it may be halted (*stop* transition from state 2 to state 3) for example in case a failure occurs or for maintenance purposes. This behavior is the one of a simple *abstract* system controller. When booting, the system cannot be stopped until it reaches the nominal mode. Other complex behavior scenarios can be defined with more complex transition systems.

In order to guarantee a correct behavior of the system, the previously defined controller shall fulfill the requirements from table 3. These ones ensure that the system is correctly controlled. For example, an energy production system requires that the power produced by a given system belongs to a specific interval or a pacemaker must be pacing when a sensed signal belongs to another specific interval.

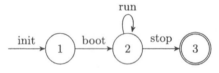

Fig. 1. Controller Automaton

---

[1] http://wiki.event-b.org/index.php/Theory_Plug-in#Standard_Library

Table 3. Requirements at the top level

At any time, the output value of the controlled system shall be less or equal to M in any mode.	Req.1
At any time, the output value of the controlled system shall belong to an interval $[m, M]$ in running mode.	Req.2
At any time, if any future output value of the controlled system does not belong to an interval $[m, M]$, then the system is stopped.	Req. 3

4.2   Continuous Controller

After modeling the system at an abstract level using three states, we introduce the continuous controller through the definition of a continuous function of the dense time $f : \mathbb{R}^+ \to \mathbb{R}^+$ corresponding to the behavior of the system.

The requirements identified in the previous section, are rewritten (refined) to handle the introduced continuous function behavior (see table 4).

Table 4. Requirements at the first refinement

$m < M$	Req.0
$\forall t \in \mathbb{R}^+, f(t) \leq M$	Req.1
$\forall t \in \mathbb{R}^+, state(t) = 2 \Rightarrow f(t) \in [m, M]$	Req.2.1
$\forall t_1, t_2 \in \mathbb{R}^+, t_1 < t_2, state(t_1) = 2 \land f(t_2) \in [m, M] \implies state(t_2) = 2$	Req.2.2
$\forall t_1, t_2 \in \mathbb{R}^+, t_1 < t_2, state(t_1) = 2 \land f(t_2) \notin [m, M] \implies state(t_2) = 3$	Req. 3

The control action over this system is a simple one. It consists in shutting down the system if the value of f goes out of range. The obtained continuous controller corresponds to a refinement of the abstract one from the previous section, it is described by a hybrid automaton [17]. We are aware that the control actions of the defined system are very simple. Our objective is to show how a controller (characterized by a simple state transition system) and a physical plant (characterized by a continuous function) can be formally integrated into a single Event-B formal development encoding incrementally a hybrid automaton.

The previously described behavior is depicted by the graph in figure 2(a). The system is initialized (at point A corresponding to the transition init to enter state 1). It reaches the running mode state at point B (corresponding to the event boot and entering state 2). The system stays in the safety corridor (between m and M in state 2). When point C is reached, the controller switches its state from state 2 to state 3 by the transition stop in order to prevent f from going over the threshold M. The system is then halted to reach point D (corresponding to state 3).

4.3   Discrete Controller

In order to implement the previous controller, we need to discretize the observation of the system behavior. In practice, when using computers to implement such controllers, time is observed according to specific clocks and frequencies. In other words, observations are discrete and depend on the available clocks.

Therefore, it is mandatory to define a correct discretization of time that preserves the continuous behavior introduced previously. This preservation entails the introduction of other requirements on the defined continuous function. Note that, in practice, these requirements correspond to requirements issued from the physical plant.

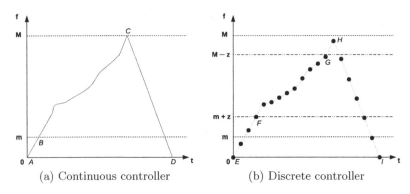

(a) Continuous controller   (b) Discrete controller

Fig. 2. Examples of the evolution of the function f

It is mandatory to introduce a margin allowing the controller to anticipate the next observable behavior before incorrect behavior occurs. Let z be this margin. z is defined such that the derivation of the function f between two observed consecutive instants t_i and t_{i+1} shall not be greater than z. Formally, this is written as $z \geq \max_{i \in \mathbb{N}} |f(t_i) - f(t_{i+1})|$. We assume that a value for z exists (even if it is not the optimal one), it is obtained from the physical properties of the system. This means, that we need to identify the duration δt defining the amount of time between two consecutive states observed by the discrete controller. As a consequence, we write $z \geq \max_{t \in \mathbb{R}^+} |f(t) - f(t + \delta t)|$. In order for the problem to be well-defined, δt must be small enough so that the property $m + z < M - z$ holds. The set $\mathbb{D}$ of observation instants can be defined as $\mathbb{D} = \{t_i \mid t_i \in \mathbb{R} \wedge i \in \mathbb{N} \wedge t_0 = 0 \wedge t_{i+1} = t_i + \delta t\}$ and rewritten as $\mathbb{D} = \{t_i \mid t_i \in \mathbb{R} \wedge i \in \mathbb{N} \wedge t_0 = 0 \wedge t_i = i \times \delta t\}$.

As a consequence of this definition, the safety corridor becomes the interval $[m + z, M - z]$. Moreover, it becomes possible to observe, in the *running mode*,

Table 5. Requirements at the second refinement

$z > 0 \wedge m + z < M - z$	Req.0
$\forall t_i \in \mathbb{D}, f(t_i) \leq M$	Req.1
$\forall t_i \in \mathbb{D}, state(t_i) = 2 \Rightarrow f(t_i) \in [m + z, M - z]$	Req.2.1
$\forall t_i \in \mathbb{D}, state(t_i) = 2 \wedge f(t_i + \delta t) \in [m, M] \Longrightarrow state(t_i + \delta t) = 2$ $\Leftrightarrow \forall t_i \in \mathbb{D}, state(t_i) = 2 \wedge f(t_{i+1}) \in [m, M] \Longrightarrow state(t_{i+1}) = 2$ $\Leftrightarrow \forall n \in \mathbb{N}, state(n\,\delta t) = 2 \wedge f((n+1)\,\delta t) \in [m, M] \Longrightarrow state((n+1)\,\delta t) = 2$	Req.2.2
$\forall t_i \in \mathbb{D}, state(t_i) = 2 \wedge f(t_i + \delta t) \notin [m + z, M - z] \Longrightarrow state(t_i + \delta t) = 3$ $\Leftrightarrow \forall t_i \in \mathbb{D}, state(t_i) = 2 \wedge f(t_{i+1}) \notin [m + z, M - z] \Longrightarrow state(t_{i+1}) = 3$ $\Leftrightarrow \forall n \in \mathbb{N}, state(n\,\delta t) = 2 \wedge f((n+1)\,\delta t) \notin [m + z, M - z]$ $\Longrightarrow state((n+1)\,\delta t) = 3$	Req. 3

two consecutive instants t_i and t_{i+1} such that $f(t_i) \in [m+z, M-z]$ and $f(t_{i+1}) \notin [m+z, M-z] \wedge f(t_{i+1}) \in [m, M]$. This condition characterizes an exit from the safety corridor and thus the condition to stop the system and move to a stopping mode. Again, the previous requirements are refined to consider the discretization of time, using the two new parameters z and δt, and $\mathbb{D}$ (Table 5).

The safety margin z is defined such that if $f(n\,\delta t)$ is in $[m+z, M-z]$ then the value of f observed by the controller, $f((n+1)\,\delta t)$, is in $[m, M]$. The definition of this discretization guarantees that *Req. 2.1* is fulfilled until the next value due to $\forall n \in \mathbb{N}, \quad \forall t \in [n \cdot \delta t, (n+1) \cdot \delta t], \quad |f(t) - f(n\,\delta t)| \leq z$. If the monitor observes a value in $[m, m+z[$ or in $]M-z, M]$, it shuts the system down because in the next step, the value might be out of range (*Req. 3*).

4.4   Top-Down Refinement

According to the previous definitions, the refinement starts from a generic definition of the system with the three identified events. The first refinement introduces the continuous function and the corresponding requirements of table 4. We start with a continuous model M_c of the system, describing the complete relevant physical behavior of the system. Then a second refinement defines the discrete model M_d of the behavior correctly glued with the continuous one. Here, the refined requirements of table 5 are taken into account. Gluing invariants, formalizing the refined requirements, are introduced in order to preserve the proofs and the behavior of the abstraction. When proving the refinement, we demonstrate that our discrete model is a correct implementation of the desired continuous behavior (the specification).

To summarize, in M_c, the continuous function $f_c : \mathbb{R} \longrightarrow \mathbb{R}$ is considered. In M_d, we introduce a discrete function $f_d : \mathbb{N} \longrightarrow \mathbb{R}$, where $i \in \mathbb{N}$ is an instant and δt is the time discretization interval duration. The functions f_d and f_c are glued by the following property: $\forall n \in 0..i, \; f_c(n \times \delta t) = f_d(n)$.

4.5   About Modeling of Time

In order to reduce the complexity of the proof of the discretization refinement corresponding to the introduction of f_d, we have split the behavior of f_c during an ith discrete *macro step* $[t_i, (t_i + \delta t)]$ into three kinds of smaller discrete *micro steps* (see figure 3). For example, at the running state (or nominal phase), we define the following micro steps.

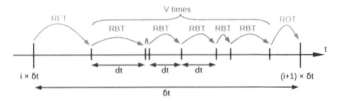

Fig. 3. Collapsing continuous time micro steps into a discrete time macro step

1. RFT: run from tick is the first micro step inside a macro step starting at a *tick* (a discrete time $t_i = i \times \delta t$). Its duration is strictly smaller than δt.
2. RBT: run between ticks is a micro step strictly in the macro step (not the first nor the last micro step in a macro step). Its duration is denoted $dt > 0$. A macro step contains V occurrences of such micro steps.
3. ROT: run on ticks is the last micro step in the macro step.

The Zeno problem is avoided by guaranteeing that the number of micro steps of type RBT is finite, and that $dt > 0$. From a modeling point of view, it will be formalized as a decreasing variant (natural number V in $\mathbb{N}$). The trace of micro steps between t_i and $t_{i+1} = t_i + \delta t$ is defined as RFT (RBT)^V ROT.

Our Event-B models introduce events aligned with these macro and micro steps either in the continuous case of in the discrete one.

5   A Formal Development of a Discrete Controller with Event-B

Our developments expressed within Event-B follow exactly the refinement strategy defined in section 4. According to [23], three development steps have been used. Contexts and machines are defined according to figure 4.

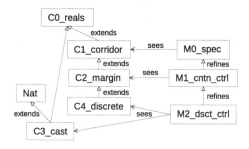

Fig. 4. Project structure

5.1   Abstract Machine: The Top-Level Specification

The top-level specification introduces the abstract controller with three events according to figure 1.

Needed Theories. To be able to handle real numbers and the corresponding theory, we have defined the context C0_reals which uses the theory defining reals. Listing 1.1 gives an extract of this context with axioms and theorems.

Several other axioms and theorems have been defined and proved. We show an extract of this theory. As mentioned in section 3 specific operators for manipulating reals are used.

```
CONTEXT C0_reals
CONSTANTS REAL_POS, REAL_STR_POS
AXIOMS
def01:REAL_POS={x | x ∈ REAL∧ leq(zero,x)}
def02:REAL_STR_POS={x| x∈ REAL
                          ∧ smr(zero,x)}
...
THEOREMS
  thm01: ∀a,b · ( a ∈ REAL ∧b ∈ REAL )
              ⇒( smr(zero,b) ⇒smr(a sub b , a) )
  thm02: ∀a,b · smr(a,b) ⇔¬leq(b,a)
...
END
```

```
CONTEXT C1_corridor
EXTENDS C0_reals
CONSTANTS m, M
AXIOMS
  axm01: m ∈ REAL_STR_POS
  axm02: M ∈ REAL_STR_POS
  axm03: smr(m,M)
END
```

Listing 1.2. Part of context C1_corridor

Listing 1.1. Part of context C0_reals

A second context defines the safety corridor with the values of m and M. Listing 1.2 defines this context C1_corridor extending the context C0_reals.

The Top-Level Event-B Machine. It defines the global continuous values issued from the controlled system. The machine introduces the invariant inv03, guaranteeing *Req*.1 and *Req*.2.1 stating that in running mode (identified by active=true), the continuous value (defining the values of a continuous function introduced in the first refinement) fv shall be correct. This machine also models the abstract controller with three events boot, run and stop corresponding to the transition system of figure 1. These events manipulate fv the real positive value corresponding to the current continuous value.

Listing 1.3 gives an extract of the top specification machine M0_spec. To keep this paper in a reasonable length, only details for the event run are given[2]. Therefore, the *Req*. 3 will not explicitly be handled in this paper, it mainly concerns the stop event.

```
MACHINE M0_spec SEES C1_corridor
VARIABLES fv, active
INVARIANTS
  inv01: fv ∈ REAL_POS
  inv02: active ∈ BOOL
  inv03: active = TRUE ⇒leq(m,fv) ∧leq(fv,M)
  inv04: active = FALSE ⇒fv = zero
EVENTS

INITIALISATION ≜
  THEN
    act01: active := FALSE
    act02: fv := zero
  END
```

```
boot ≜ ...

run ≜
ANY new_fv WHERE
  grd01: active = TRUE
  grd02: new_fv ∈ REAL_POS
  grd03: leq(m,new_fv) ∧leq(new_fv,M)
          // new_fv ∈ [m,M]
THEN
  act01: fv := new_fv
END
stop ≜ ...
END
```

Listing 1.3. Extract of machine M0_spec

---

[2] The complete Event-B developments can be downloaded from http://babin.perso.enseeiht.fr/r/SETTA2015EventBModels.pdf

5.2 The First Refinement: Introducing Continuous Functions

Needed Theories. As shown on figure 4, the context `C2_margin` introducing the margin `z` is defined. Note that `axm02` corresponds to the requirement *Req*.0.

```
CONTEXT C2_margin EXTENDS C1_corridor
CONSTANTS z
AXIOMS
  axm01: z ∈ REAL_POS // z ∈ R+
  axm02: gtr(M sub m , (one plus one) mult z) // M−m > 2∗z
END
```

Listing 1.4. Extract of context C2_margin

The Event-B First Refinement with Continuous Functions. The first refinement `M1_cntn_ctrl` of the controller explicitly introduces

- the continuous function `fc` producing the values `fv` of the abstract machine and the corresponding invariant `prop01`
- dense time with the current instant noted `now`
- an important invariant `glue01` gluing the continuous values of the abstraction with the continuous function defined on dense time `fv = fc(now)`
- the variable `active_t` recoding the dense time where the system enters a running mode and the corresponding invariants `glue02`, `glue03` and `glue04` gluing the behavior of `active_t` with the `active` boolean variable.

The events of the `M1_cntn_ctrl` machine refine the ones of the top level specification. The `boot` event fixes the value of `active_t` and the `run` event builds the continuous function `fc` with steps of duration `dt`. `fc` becomes the function `nfc`, acting until `now+dt` instant.

```
MACHINE M1_cntn_ctrl REFINES M0_spec SEES C2_margin
VARIABLES
  fv, active, fc, now, active_t
INVARIANTS
  type01: now ∈ REAL_POS
  type02: fc ∈ REAL_POS →REAL_POS
  type03: active_t ∈ REAL_POS
  prop01: cnt_int(fc, zero, now) // fc is continous on [0,now]
  glue01: fv = fc(now)
  glue02: active = TRUE ⇒( ∀t ·t ∈ REAL ∧leq(active_t,t) ∧leq(t,now) ⇒
                         ( leq(m plus z , fc(t)) ∧ leq(fc(t) , M sub z) ))
  glue03: ∀t · t ∈ REAL ∧leq(zero,t) ∧leq(t,now) ⇒leq(fc(t),M)
  glue04: active = TRUE ⇒leq(active_t,now)
EVENTS
  boot ≜ REFINES boot ...
    THEN
      ...
      act04: now := now plus dt
      act05: active_t := now plus dt

  run ≜ REFINES run
    ANY dt, nfc, new_fv WHERE
      ...
      grd04: dt ∈ REAL_STR_POS // dt > 0
      grd05: nfc ∈ REAL_POS ↦REAL_POS
      grd06: dom(nfc) = {t | t ∈ REAL ∧leq(now,t) ∧leq(t , now plus dt)} // dom(nf) = [now,now+dt]
      grd07: nfc(now) = fc(now)
```

```
  grd08: nfc(now plus dt) = new_fv
  grd09: leq(fv,new_fv) ⇒(∀ t1,t2 · t1 ∈ dom(nfc) ∧t2 ∈ dom(nfc) ∧leq(t1,t2) ⇒
                              leq(nfc(t1) , nfc(t2)))
  grd10: cnt_int(nfc , now , now plus dt) //  nfc is continuous on [now,now+dt]
  grd11: leq(new_fv,fv) ⇒(∀ t1,t2 · t1 ∈ dom(nfc) ∧t2 ∈ dom(nfc) ∧leq(t1,t2) ⇒
                              leq(nfc(t2) , nfc(t1)))
  grd12: ∀t · t ∈ dom(nfc) ⇒leq(m plus z , nfc(t) ∧ leq(nfc(t) , M sub z)
  THEN
    ...
  act02: now := now plus dt
  act03: fc := fc ⩤nfc
  END
 stop ≜ REFINES stop...
END
```

Listing 1.5. Extract of machine M1_cntn_ctrl

The current instant **now** is incremented by the step duration **dt** as well. The guards of the event **run** introduce the relevant conditions to trigger this event.

Note that during the time interval of the step, the function **fc** shall be continuous and monotonic so as its value is never outside the safety corridor (grd09 to grd11). This condition is fundamental when the function is discretized. Thus, grd09 through grd12 guarantee the requirement Req2.2 and are of particular importance when discretizing.

5.3   The Second Refinement: Introducing Discrete Representation

This refinement introduces the discretization function **fd** corresponding to the continuous function **fc** on each discrete observed instants. This fundamental property corresponds to requirement Req2.2 of table 5. It is expressed by the gluing invariants between the continuous controller and the discrete controller. It links the continuous f_c and and discrete f_d functions by the property $\forall n \in 0 .. i, f_c(n \times \delta t) = f_d(n)$ and is represented by invariant **glue01**.

```
CONTEXT C3_cast EXTENDS C0_reals, Nat
CONSTANTS cast
AXIOMS
  axm01: cast ∈ N→REAL_POS      //  type
  axm02: cast(0) = zero     //  initial case
  axm03: ∀a · a ∈ N ⇒       // induction case
          (cast(a+1) = cast(a) plus one)
THEOREMS
  ...
  thm11: ∀a,b · (a ∈ N ∧ b ∈ N) // equiv over '<'
          ⇒(a < b ⇔smr(cast(a),cast(b)))
  thm12: ∀a,b · (a ∈ N ∧ b ∈ N) // equiv over '='
          ⇒(a = b ⇔cast(a) = cast(b))
  thm13: cast ∈ N ↣ cast[N] // cast is a bijection

END
```

```
CONTEXT C4_discrete EXTENDS C2_margin
SETS VT
CONSTANTS
  tstep    //  discrete time step duration (δt)
  max_df   //  maximum delta for f during tstep
  RBT, RV
AXIOMS
  axm01: tstep ∈ REAL_STR_POS
  axm02: max_df ∈ REAL_POS
                 // max diff of f during tstep
  axm03: leq(max_df,z)
  axm04: partition(VT, {RBT}, {RV})
END
```

Listing 1.6. Definition and properties of the cast function

Listing   1.7.   Extract   of   context C4_discrete

```
MACHINE M2_dsct_ctrl REFINES M1_cntn_ctrl SEES C3_cast, C4_discrete
VARIABLES
  fv, active, fc, now, active_t,
  fd // discrete power function
  i // the current instant number
  et // time elapsed from previous discrete value sampling time
  rs // remaining continuous micro steps inside the discrete macro step
  nv // next variant—related event type
INVARIANTS
  type01: fd ∈ 0..i →REAL_POS
  type02: i ∈ ℕ
  type03: et ∈ REAL_POS
  type04: rs ∈ ℕ
  type05: nv ∈ VT
  glue01: ∀ n · n ∈ 0..i ⇒fc(cast(n) mult tstep) = fd(n) // n ∈ 0..i ⇒fc(n∗tstep) = fd(n)
  glue02: now = (cast(i) mult tstep) plus et // now = i∗tstep + et
  inv01: ∀ n · n ∈ 0..i−1 ⇒(
                  ∀ t · (leq(cast(n) mult tstep , t) ∧ leq(t , cast(n+1) mult tstep)) ⇒(
                         leq(fd(n) sub max_df , fc(t)) ∧ leq(fc(t) , fd(n) plus max_df)))
  inv02: ∀ t · (leq(cast(i) mult tstep , t) ∧ leq(t , now)) ⇒(
                  leq(fd(i) sub max_df , fc(t)) ∧ leq(fc(t) , fd(i) plus max_df))
  inv03: smr(et,tstep)
VARIANT
  rs
EVENTS
  run_from_tick ≜ REFINES run            run_variant ≜
  WHERE                                   WHERE
    ...                                     grd01: nv = RV
    grd13: et = zero                        grd02: rs > 0
    grd14: smr(dt , tstep)                THEN
    grd15: ∀t · t ∈ dom(nfc) ⇒             act01: rs :| rs' ∈ ℕ∧ rs' < rs
           leq(fd(i) sub max_df , nfc(t))  act02: nv := RBT
           ∧ leq(nfc(t) , fd(i) plus max_df) END
           // physical assumption
  THEN                                    run_on_tick ≜ REFINES run
    ...                                   WHERE
    act04: et := et plus dt                 ...
    act05: rs :∈ ℕ                          grd13: et plus dt = tstep
    act06: nv := RBT                        grd14: smr(zero,et)
  END                                       grd15: ∀t · t ∈ dom(nfc) ⇒
                                                    leq(fd(i) sub max_df , nfc(t))
                                                    ∧ leq(nfc(t) , fd(i) plus max_df)
  run_between_ticks ≜ REFINES run          grd16: rs = 0
  WHERE                                   THEOREMS
    ...                                     thm03: cast(i+1) mult tstep = now plus dt
    grd13: smr(zero, et)                  THEN
    grd14: smr(et plus dt , tstep)          ...
    grd15: ∀t · t ∈ dom(nfc) ⇒             act04: i := i + 1
           leq(fd(i) sub max_df , nfc(t))  act05: fd(i+1) := new_f
           ∧ leq(nfc(t) , fd(i) plus max_df) act06: et := zero
    grd16: nv = RBT                       END
    grd17: rs > 0
  THEN                                    END
    ...
    act04: et := et plus dt
    act05: nv := RV
  END
```

Listing 1.8. Extract of machine M2_dsct_ctrl

Needed Theories. Two contexts are introduced. As mentioned in section 3 the first context C3_cast is a technical context related to casting reals and integers. For example, the invariant $\forall n \in 0..i, f_c(n \times \delta t) = f_d(n)$ corresponding to glue01 is written as $\forall n \cdot n \in 0..i \Rightarrow$ fc(cast(n) mult tstep) = fd(n).

Note that the context C3_cast extends the Nat context[3] by Thai Son Hoang needed for handling inductive proofs on sets [4]. The last context C4_discrete introduces the discrete time macro steps duration tstep corresponding to δt on figure 3 and the values RBT and RV to identify the different events corresponding to the run event. It also defines the max_df constant corresponding to the maximum evolution of the function in a macro step is never more that the margin z. This assumption usually comes from the conditions on the physical plant.

The Event-B Refinement with Discretization. The defined machine M2_dsct_ctrl produces the discrete behavior of the continuous function fc with the discrete function fd glued by the invariant glue01. The other invariants inv01 and inv02 preserve Req2.2 and inv03 states that the elapsed time et is less that the discrete time tstep. According to figure 3, three events for ROT, RBT and RFT are defined refine the run event. The run_from_tick (RFT) event starts the computation between two consecutive discrete values of function fd and fixes an arbitrary value of the variant rs.

The most interesting part in this machine relates to the run_between_tick (RBT) event which shall avoid the Zeno problem. For this purpose, each time this event is active, it triggers the event run_variant which decreases the variant. Once, this variant reaches the value 0, the run_on_tick (ROT) event is triggered to compute the final value corresponding to next discrete value of the function fd. Note that the guard grd15 is fundamental to guarantee that the values do not exit the safety corridor. This assumption relates to the physical plant.

5.4   Proofs Statistics

All these models have been encoded within the Rodin Platform [2]. As shown on table 6, the main machine and the refinement led to 265 proof obligations.

Table 6. Rodin proofs statistics

Event-B model	Automatic proofs	Interactive proofs	Total
C0_reals	1	29	30
C1_corridor	0	6	6
C2_margin	0	10	10
C3_cast	11	26	37
C4_discrete	0	1	1
M0_spec (top-level)	11	6	17
M1_cntn_ctrl (1st ref.)	22	51	73
M2_dsct_ctrl (2nd ref.)	22	67	89
Total	67	198	265

---

[3] http://sourceforge.net/p/rodin-b-sharp/mailman/message/30378566/
[4] induction: $\forall S \cdot S \subseteq N \wedge 0 \in S \wedge (\forall x \cdot x \in S \Rightarrow x + 1 \in S) \Rightarrow N \subseteq S$

67 were proved automatically and 198 needed numerous interactive proof steps. The interactive proofs mainly relate to the use of the Theory plugin for handling the reals. The lack of dedicated heuristics due to the representation of reals as an abstract data type, and not as a native type led to more interactive proofs.

6   Related Works and Applications

Two kinds of approaches for modeling hybrid systems can be distinguished. The first one relies on hybrid automata. They are mainly analyzed and verified by model checking [5]. Tools like HyTech [18] have succeeded in analyzing complex hybrid systems. While this approach enables automatic verification, it requires elaborate optimization techniques in order to handle the state space explosion as well as symbolic parameters and non-linear equations. To address these problems, logical analysis of hybrid automata brought interesting results [19]. They address classes of automata. The second kind of approaches relates to analysis of hybrid programs. One of the most successful tool is KeYmaera by Platzer et al. [22]. This tool is dedicated to hybrid system modeling and verification. It is equipped with an interactive theorem prover. Compared to Event-B, it does not provide a built-in refinement development operator. In the meantime, other approaches use Event-B to model hybrid systems. The work initiated in [23], and pursued in [12] proposes to model first the discrete events of a hybrid systems and then refine each event by introducing the continuous elements. It includes the use of a "now" variable, a "click" event that jumps in time to the next instant where an event can be triggered and simulated real numbers. In our proposal, we use this notion of "now" variable on dense time. Time jumps are encoded by the events. We use mathematical reals thanks to the latest developments of the Rodin Platform. Moreover, compared to [23], we have another refinement that introduces discretization of continuous elements. However, [23] incorporate analytical results from the study of differential equations into the Event-B models through the complementary use of Matlab/Simulink. The second proposed approach based on Event-B, initiated by Banach, is Hybrid Event-B [8]. This is an extension of Event-B which includes pliant events [7] as a way to model continuous behavior, allowing the direct use of differential equations in the modeling. However, there is no tool currently supporting this extension whereas our approach enabled us to develop and prove the models using available tools. Banach also worked on similar topics with ASM [9,10]. In our development we use reals defined by a minimal set of axioms. We do not use floating-point numbers, they may be introduced in a further refinement which is out of the scope of this paper. So, we are not exploiting the results from automated verification tools on floating-point numbers [21]. Static analysis [16] or abstract interpretation [14] (with tools such as Astrée [15]) have proved very powerful to analyze such programs. Our approach is at a modeling level. Moreover, the set of axioms for reals in the Theory plug-in we have used does not define reals in a constructive manner. So, we were not able to use the results obtained by the Coq [11] advanced proof tactics on reals. Indeed, our proofs have been discharged using the interactive prover of Rodin, leading to a large proof effort.

7   Conclusion

The development of cyber-physical systems needs to handle the behavior of the physical plant (environment). This behavior is usually described by continuous functions producing feedback information to the controller, which in turns produces orders to the actuators. In this paper, we have shown that it is possible to compose the development of both a controller and the corresponding behavior of the physical plant. The controller corresponds to a hybrid automaton. A simple one has been considered in this paper. It consists in booting, running and then stopping a physical plant (see figure 1). The main contribution of this paper concerns the synthesis of a discrete controller. We have shown that the synthesis of a correct-by-construction discretization of a continuous function associated to the behavior of a physical plant can be obtained by refinement. The proof of the preservation of the invariants gluing the continuous and discrete levels guarantees this correctness. We have introduced at the discrete level a variant guaranteeing that the model is Zeno-free. The Theory plug-in for the Rodin Platform and a theory of real numbers have been used to model continuous functions. To the best of our knowledge, this is the first attempt to model continuous controller discretization with the Event-B method and mathematical reals.

As future work, we plan to address more complex hybrid automata by generalizing the approach presented in this paper. A particular case we expect to study relates to the system substitution in case of failure for example, already addressed in the discrete case in [6]. Another research path concerns the refinement by floating point numbers as another discretization step. This refinement will use the intermediate value theorem as gluing invariant between the obtained discretization level and the floating point level. Finally, an effort should be devoted to handle more efficiently the complex proof process set up in this paper.

References

1. Abrial, J.-R.: Modeling in Event-B: System and Software Engineering, 1st edn. Cambridge University Press, New York, NY, USA (2010)
2. Abrial, J.-R., Butler, M., Hallerstede, S., Hoang, T.S., Mehta, F., Voisin, L.: Rodin: an open toolset for modelling and reasoning in Event-B. Int. J. Softw. Tools Technol. Transfer **12**(6), 447–466 (2010)
3. Abrial, J.-R., Butler, M., Hallerstede, S., Leuschel, M., Schmalz, M., Voisin, L.: Proposals for mathematical extensions for Event-B. Technical report (2009)
4. Abrial, J.-R., Hallerstede, S.: Refinement, decomposition, and instantiation of discrete models: Application to Event-B. Fundamenta Informat. **77**(1), 1–28 (2007)
5. Alur, R.: Formal verification of hybrid systems. In: Chakraborty, S., Jerraya, A., Baruah, S. K., Fischmeister, S. (eds.) Proceedings of the 11th International Conference on Embedded Software, EMSOFT - ESWeek, Taipei, Taiwan, October 9–14, 2011, pp. 273–278. ACM (2011)
6. Babin, G., Ait-Ameur, Y., Pantel, M.: Formal verification of runtime compensation of web service compositions: A refinement and proof based proposal with Event-B. In: International Conference on SCC 2015 IEEE, pp. 98–105, June

7. Banach, R.: Pliant modalities in Hybrid Event-B. In: Liu, Z., Woodcock, J., Zhu, H. (eds.) Theories of Programming and Formal Methods. LNCS, vol. 8051, pp. 37–53. Springer, Heidelberg (2013)

8. Banach, R., Butler, M., Qin, S., Verma, N., Zhu, H.: Core Hybrid Event-B I: Single Hybrid Event-B machines. Science of Computer Programming (2015)

9. Banach, R., Zhu, H., Su, W., Huang, R.: Formalising the continuous/discrete modeling step. In: Derrick, J., Boiten, E.A., Reeves, S. (eds.) Proceedings 15th International Refinement Workshop, Refine 2011, Limerick, Ireland, 20th June 2011, volume 55 of EPTCS, pp. 121–138 (2011)

10. Banach, R., Zhu, H., Su, W., Wu, X.: ASM and controller synthesis. In: Derrick, J., Fitzgerald, J., Gnesi, S., Khurshid, S., Leuschel, M., Reeves, S., Riccobene, E. (eds.) ABZ 2012. LNCS, vol. 7316, pp. 51–64. Springer, Heidelberg (2012)

11. Boldo, S., Lelay, C., Melquiond, G.: Coquelicot: A user-friendly library of real analysis for Coq. Math. Comput. Sci. $9(1)$, 41–62 (2015)

12. Butler, M., Abrial, J.-R., Banach, R.: From Action Systems to Distributed Systems: The Refinement Approach, chapter Modelling and Refining Hybrid Systems in Event-B and Rodin, p. 300. Taylor & Francis, February 2016

13. Butler, M., Maamria, I.: Practical theory extension in Event-B. In: Liu, Z., Woodcock, J., Zhu, H. (eds.) Theories of Programming and Formal Methods. LNCS, vol. 8051, pp. 67–81. Springer, Heidelberg (2013)

14. Cousot, P., Cousot, R.: Abstract interpretation: A unified lattice model for static analysis of programs by construction or approximation of fixpoints. In: Proceedings of the 4th ACM POPL 1977, pp. 238–252, New York, NY, USA. ACM (1977)

15. Cousot, P., Cousot, R., Feret, J., Mauborgne, L., Miné, A., Monniaux, D., Rival, X.: The ASTRÉE analyzer. In: Sagiv, M. (ed.) ESOP 2005. LNCS, vol. 3444, pp. 21–30. Springer, Heidelberg (2005)

16. Goubault, É.: Static analyses of the precision of floating-point operations. In: Cousot, P. (ed.) SAS 2001. LNCS, vol. 2126, p. 234. Springer, Heidelberg (2001)

17. Henzinger. T. A.: The theory of hybrid automata. In: Inan, M.K., Kurshan, R.P. (eds.) Verification of Digital and Hybrid Systems, volume 170 of NATO ASI Series, pp. 265–292. Springer-Verlag (2000)

18. Henzinger, T.A., Ho, P.-H., Wong-Toi, H.: Hytech: A model checker for hybrid systems. International Journal on STTT $1(1–2)$, 110–122 (1997)

19. Ishii, D., Melquiond, G., Nakajima, S.: Inductive verification of hybrid automata with strongest postcondition calculus. In: Johnsen, E.B., Petre, L. (eds.) IFM 2013. LNCS, vol. 7940, pp. 139–153. Springer, Heidelberg (2013)

20. Lee, E.A., Seshia, S.A.: Introduction to Embedded Systems - A Cyber-Physical Systems Approach. LeeSeshia.org, edition 1.5 edition (2014)

21. Muller, J.-M., Brisebarre, N., de Dinechin, F., Jeannerod, C.-P., Lefévre, V., Melquiond, G., Revol, N., Stehlé, D., Torres, S.: Handbook of Floating-Point Arithmetic. Birkhäuser (2010)

22. Platzer, A.: Logical Analysis of Hybrid Systems: Proving Theorems for Complex Dynamics. Springer-Verlag, Heidelberg (2010)

23. Su, W., Abrial, J.-R., Zhu, H.: Formalizing hybrid systems with Event-B and the Rodin platform. Science of Computer Programming, 94, Part 2:164–202 (2014)

Synthesizing Controllers for Multi-lane Traffic Maneuvers

Gregor v. Bochmann[1], Martin Hilscher[2]([✉]), Sven Linker[2],
and Ernst-Rüdiger Olderog[2]

[1] School of Electrical Engineering and Computer Science,
University of Ottawa, Ottawa, ON, Canada
bochmann@uottawa.ca

[2] Department of Computing Science, University of Oldenburg, Oldenburg, Germany
{hilscher,linker,olderog}@informatik.uni-oldenburg.de

Abstract. The dynamic behavior of a car can be modeled as a hybrid system involving continuous state changes and discrete state transitions. However, we show that the control of safe (collision free) lane change maneuvers in multi-lane traffic on highways can be described by finite state machines extended with continuous variables coming from the environment. We use standard theory for controller synthesis to derive the dynamic behavior of a lane-change controller. Thereby, we contrast the setting of interleaving semantics and synchronous concurrent semantics. We also consider the possibility of exchanging knowledge between neighboring cars in order to come up with the right decisions.

Keywords: Multi-lane highway traffic · Lane-change maneuver · Safety · Collision freedeom · Hybrid systems · Controller synthesis · Interleaving and synchronous concurrency

1 Introduction

We consider the safety (collision freedom) of traffic on multi-lane highways. A means to avoid collisions in car maneuvers are advanced driver assistance systems (ADAS) onboard the cars. These systems require that each car is equipped with suitable controllers that interact with other cars by sensors and communication. The development of such a controller is difficult because the interaction of cars on a highway constitutes a distributed hybrid system, combining continuous car dynamics with discrete decisions of the controllers. Therefore every part or pattern of the system that can be automated is of great help.

Well-known is the California PATH (Partners for Advanced Transit and Highways) project that developed automated highway systems for cars driving in

This research was partially supported by the German Research Council (DFG) in the Transregional Collaborative Research Center SFB/TR 14 AVACS, and the Natural Science and Engineering Research Council of Canada.

X. Li et al. (Eds.): SETTA 2015, LNCS 9409, pp. 71–86, 2015.
DOI: 10.1007/978-3-319-25942-0_5

groups called platoons [1]. The maneuvers include joining and leaving the platoon, and lane change. Lygeros et al. [2] sketch a safety proof for car platoons taking car dynamics into account, but admitting collisions at a low speed.

This paper is motivated by previous work in [3], where an abstract model of highway traffic was introduced, consisting of so-called traffic snapshots. The main idea of [3] was that safety is a spatial property. Using a dedicated spatial logic called Multi-Lane Spatial Logic (MLSL) to describe spatial properties concisely, we presented two controllers for the lane-change maneuver on highways and proved that under certain assumptions the controllers guarantee safety. However, the controllers themselves were introduced in an ad-hoc manner.

In this paper, we employ methods from discrete-event systems to synthesize the controllers, thus offering a systematic approach to construct such controllers. The achievement is that we connect methods from discrete-event systems with the application area of traffic maneuvers of multiple cars on highways. We also use methods from protocol derivation to obtain the specification of message exchanges in the case that certain cars need to communicate for their control decisions.

We describe the setting of multi-lane traffic as in [3] (however, without using MLSL), the control architecture, and the control components inside a single car with their interactions. As a formal representation of hybrid systems we consider a variant of Hybrid Input-Output Automata (HIOA), where assumptions on inputs are allowed [4]. However, we focus on the discrete actions needed for lane control, thereby assuming that the car maneuvers of speed control and steering are dealt with separately.

Our main contributions are as follows:

- We show that from a description of the set of all possible discrete behaviors during a lane change we can *synthesize constraints* that yield a safe lane change controller. This is achieved by applying a standard method for controller synthesis in discrete event systems [5].
- We investigate the impact of different semantic models of parallel composition: *interleaving* vs. *synchronous parallelism*. In the latter model more intricate safety risks of a lane change are revealed. We show that the method for controller synthesis can cope with both models.
- We investigate different sensor models that represent different knowledge a car may have about its neighboring cars during a lane change. In [3], the case that a car can sense only the lengths of other cars but not their braking distances was solved by stipulating a helper car and suitable communications with it. Here we show that these *communications can be synthesized* by applying methods for protocol synthesis [6].

This paper is structured as follows. In Section 2 we present the details of our car traffic modelling. In Section 3 we develop stepwise our approach to controller synthesis for multi-lane highway traffic. Conclusions are presented in Section 4.

2   Car Traffic Modeling

2.1   The Multi-lane Highway

The development of a controller is based on models of the system to be controlled. In the case of car traffic, the system consists of the traffic infrastructure, such as roads, traffic lights, etc., and cars that drive within this infrastructure. The traffic infrastructure and the cars can be modelled as consisting of multiple components.

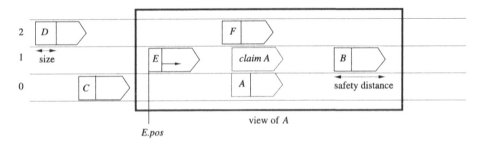

Fig. 1. A multi-lane highway with several cars. The large rectangle shows the view of car A, i.e., the part of the environment visible to A.

In this paper, we consider the infrastructure of multi-lane highways as shown in Fig. 1. In this case, the infrastructure consists of a fixed number of lanes, numbered 0 through L. This infrastructure is passive. It only serves as a coordinate system in which the cars evolve. Each car has a position along the road (from left to right in the figure) and the current lanes used, normally a single lane, but during a lane change a car uses two adjacent lanes.

Each car posssesses a set of sensors, which defines the part of the highway it may perceive, called its *view*. In Fig. 2, a possible view of the car A is indicated by the rectangle surrounding A. The main motivation behind the concept of views is that safety of each car only depends on its local environment. The physical constraints on such a finite set of space ensure that only finitely many cars can be responsible for unsafe situations during each maneuver. Finally, since we assume that all cars behave alike, it is sufficient to analyse the interaction of two cars: if an accident happens, at least two cars are colliding. In this paper, we deal with the conflicting situation where two cars, say cars A and F in Fig. 1, claim space on the same lane. For conflicts between a claiming car and a car already on the claimed lane, say cars A and E in Fig. 1, we refer to our extended version [7].

2.2   A Hybrid Model of a Car

A car can also be modelled as consisting of several components. In this paper, we consider the components shown in Fig. 2: velocity control, steering, and lane control. These components are not passive, but have dynamic behavior. In order to describe such behavior, one first has to define their communication with their

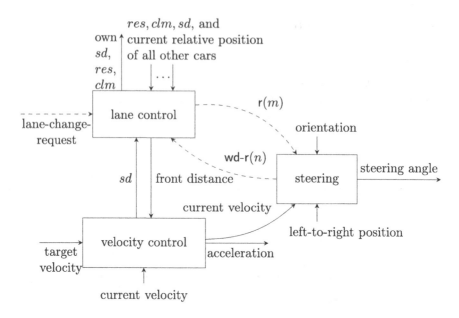

Fig. 2. Control components of a single car.

environment. The interfaces over which the components communicate are indicated in Fig. 2 by arrows. We distinguish between two types of interfaces: (a) shared (real-valued) *interface variables*, and (b) so-called *interaction interfaces* (dashed arrows). The static interconnection structure between components and interface variables is such that each interface variable has exactly one component (possibly the environment) that determines the value of the variable – it represents the output of that component – while several components may read the value of the variable – it is the input for those components. The actions occurring over interaction interfaces are related to discrete transitions (see below). An action is initiated by the component for which the interface is output. Examples of interface variables in Fig. 2 are target-speed and acceleration; examples of actions are r(m) and wd-c(m).

Each component can be modelled as a Hybrid Input-Output Automaton. Its dynamic behavior is determined by (a) continuous state changes (called *trajectories* in [8]) which determine the values of output variables as a function of input variables and the evolving time, and (b) *discrete transitions*, associated with internal actions or interactions, which change the internal state (called mode) which determines the trajectories that are active in this mode and usually associated with an invariant that holds in this mode (see for example [9])

The roles of the components shown in Fig. 2 are as follows. The *velocity control* component receives as input the target velocity set by the driver, the measured current velocity of the car, and the front distance to be maintained, as determined by the lane control component. The defined trajectories determine the value of the acceleration (output variable) as a function of the input variables and time. As dependent output variables, the component also produces the value of the *safety distance*, *sd*, which depends on the speed of the car. This distance is calculated such that the car could stop before that distance in case that a fixed obstacle suddenly occurs at that distance in front of the car. In the normal operation mode, the speed control component will select a trajectory for the acceleration (or deceleration) such that the target speed will be attained under the condition that the front distance is larger than the safety distance. A possible way to construct such a component is described in [9,10].

The *steering* component controls the direction output variable, which acts via the steering angle on the front wheels of the car. It uses as input the orientation (angle of the car to the forward direction of the lane), the current velocity of the car, and the measured left-to-right position of the car over the different lanes. It has an internal variable which contains the target lane of the car. The value of this variable is set by the input action r(m) which sets the target lane to the value m. When the current lane has been changed, the component will perform a discrete transition with the output action wd-r(n) when the reservation of the old lane n is not needed any more. A possible way to construct such a component is described in [10].

The *lane control* component is responsible for determining when a lane change maneuver can be performed. Such a lane change maneuver is requested by the driver through a discrete transition with the input action "lane-change-request" which tells the steering component to which lane it should move. Before performing such a maneuver, the component has to make sure that there is the necessary space on the new lane and that there is no conflict with other cars that may want to change their lane, as described in the following sections. For this purpose, there are a number of input and output variables through which the lane control component interacts with other cars in its environment (see Fig. 2).

2.3   Highway Traffic with Lane Change

In this paper we concentrate on lane change on multi-lane highway which is handled by the lane control component. Its behavior does not involve any trajectories and can be described by a finit-state input-output automaton (IOA) where transitions may have guards that depend on variables.

The following lane change procedure was proposed in [3]: a car that wants to change lane, for instance the car A in Fig. 1, first "claims" the lane to which it wants to move (this corresponds to setting the turn signal ("blinker") in the manual car driving mode), and then "reserves" the new lane before it moves over on to the new lane.

Each car has the following attributes, in addition to those mentioned above:

- *res*: the set of lanes reserved. It has at most two elements, namely the current lane n, and possibly an adjacent lane m to which the car wants to move.
- *clm*: the set of lanes claimed. It has at most one element. The claimed element must be a lane adjacent to the current lane n.

The reserved lanes of the cars define the safety condition for the system. The meaning of a lane reservation by car c is that the lane is reserved for car c over the distance range from the current position of the car, $c.pos$, up to the point of its safety distance, $c.pos + c.sd$. We call this range the *safety envelope* of c.

The dangerous situation of a collision is formalized by the following condition:

$$col = \exists c_1, c_2 : ((c_1.res \cap c_2.res \neq \emptyset) \wedge safetyOverlap(c_1, c_2)), \qquad (1)$$

where $safetyOverlap(c_1, c_2)$ is true if there is an overlap of the ranges from the current position up to the point of the safety distance for the two cars c_1 and c_2:

$$safetyOverlap(c_1, c_2) = (c_1.pos \leq c_2.pos \leq c_1.pos + c_1.sd) \vee$$
$$(c_2.pos \leq c_1.pos \leq c_2.pos + c_2.sd).$$

We say that the system is *safe* if there is no overlap of the safety envelopes of any two cars on any given lane, that is, if the collision condition *col* is false.

To describe the dynamic behavior of the lane change control component during lane change, the following interactions are introduced::

- c(m): introduce a claim for lane m,
- wd-c(m): withdraw the claim for lane m,
- r(m): change a claim for lane m into a reservation for lane m,
- wd-r(m): withdraw the reservation for lane m.

3   Controller Synthesis for Multi-lane Traffic Maneuvers

3.1   Overview of Controller Synthesis

The design of controllers for hybrid systems has to deal with two aspects: the control of the continuous flows, and the control of the discrete actions. In this paper we limit ourselves to the discrete aspects, since we concentrate the discussion on the lane control component, which has a behavior essentially characterized by discrete transitions, such as shown in Fig. 3. The synthesis of controllers for discrete event systems was first described in [11]. Distributed control of systems consisting of several communicating components is described in [5]. It turns out that the method of submodule construction, as introduced in [6], can also be used for this purpose. In [12] this approach is formalized and described for different types of interactions between the controlled system, the environment and the controller. The approach of [12] is used in the following.

The typical system architecture for controlling a single component comprises the plant (to be controlled, called world model in [13]), the environment, and the controller. The behavior of the plant is defined in terms of its interactions with the environment. These interactions are classified into controllable and uncontrollable interactions. The controller can observe a subset of these interactions, called the visible interactions, and it may prevent the occurrence of a visible

controllable interaction, but it has no impact on uncontrollable or invisible interactions. In our modeling framework, we distinguish between input and output
interactions. Plant inputs from the environment are in general uncontrollable,
while input from the controller is controllable. The outputs of the plant to the
controller are either controllable (can be prevented) or uncontrollable.

The environment provides input interactions to the plant, called disturbances
in [13]. These inputs may depend on the outputs received from the plant previously. The order in which these inputs may arrive is sometimes called the
environment assumption. The behavior of the environment may be described
by a state machine model. In this case, the model explicitly describes in which
state which input may be provided, thus defining the environment assumption.
The environment model is also used to define *control objectives*: Safeness objectives, namely that in certain states the plant should not provide certain specific
outputs, can be modeled by including in the behavior of the environment a transition for such outputs into a **Fail** state – and the objective is that such a **Fail**
state should never be reached.

We assume in the following that the set of possible sequences of interactions
of the plant can be described by a finite automaton P where all its states s_P are
accepting, and the set of interaction sequences of the environment are described
by a finite automaton E where its states s_E are accepting, except the **Fail** states.
In the case of full visibility, the most general controller behavior C that avoids the
Fail states of the environment is obtained from the finite automaton $C_1 = P \times E$
(product of P with E where a state (s_P, s_E) of the product is accepting iff s_E
is accepting in E). From this automaton, certain states must be pruned, that is,
eliminated, in order to obtain the controller C.

Pruning is a recursive procedure. In each iteration, the following states are
pruned: (a) any non-accepting states, (b) any states that have a transition with
an uncontrollable interaction to a state that was pruned in an earlier iteration, and (c) any state that is a deadlock (that has no outgoing transition – we
assume here that the plant and the environment, separately, do not have a final
(deadlocking) state). A state is pruned by eliminating all outgoing transitions,
all incoming transitions with controllable (and visible) interactions that lead
into the state, and the state itself. The procedure stops when during the next
iteration no further state is pruned.

If all states are eliminated by the pruning procedure, then there exists no
suitable controller. However, it is important to note that, if a suitable controller
is found, this controller may constrain the plant so much that the remaining
behavior is not useful for the application at hand – in other words, the behavior
satisfies the safety properties defined by the control objectives, but does not
satisfy the liveness properties of the application. Controller synthesis including
liveness objectives is discussed for instance in [14].

In the case of partial visibility, the product automaton C_1 must first be projected onto the visible interactions. The resulting projected automaton, which is
in general non-deterministic, must be determinized before the pruning operations
can be performed. Hence, partial visibility introduces an exponential blow-up of

the set of states. However, in the examples discussed in this paper all interactions are visible, i.e., no blow-up occurs.

For the application of multi-lane traffic control, as described in Section 2, we have a plant that consists of a large number of cars. We would like to obtain a controller per car that is able to control the controllable interactions of that car, and may possibly see some of the interactions of other cars, without being able to control them. In fact, in this paper we are mainly interested in deriving a controller for the lane control component of cars. For such a controller, all output interactions of its lane control component are controllable, but all other inter-actions – including output interactions of other cars – are uncontrollable. This situation is studied in [5] and called distributed control. We note, however, that in general the problem of synthesizing distributed control is undecidable [15].

3.2   A Simple Algorithm for Lane Change

Let us first assume that the lane control component has the simple behavior shown in Fig. 3 (a). In this case no claims are made. The notation $A.qRC$ means that car A is in control state q, it has reserved the lanes in the set R, and it claims the lanes in the set C. The car A in lane n starts with an action $r(m)$ which is an output action that interacts with the steering component which will steer the car on to the new lane m. When this is done, that component will withdraw from the previous lane by producing the wd-r(n) interactions which is received by the lane control component, and the car goes back to the normal driving condition.

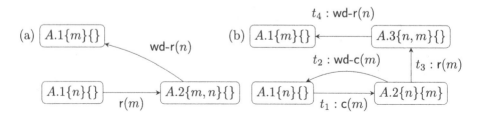

Fig. 3. Behavior of a car A changing from its current lane n to a neighboring target lane $m \in \{n-1, n+1\}$: (a) simple algorithm, (b) protocol with a claim transition c(m) as in [3].

Let us consider a given car *ego* with its lane change controller. Its environment consists of all the other cars in the system and the requirement that the system should be safe in all instants. A safety condition can be proven by showing that it holds in the initial state and remains invariant under all transitions that the system may make. In this example, the safety objective to be satisfied is the condition ¬ *col* (no collision). This can be modeled by an environment E with two states, one where ¬ *col* holds, and one where it is false. The latter is a **Fail** state. The plant P consists of all cars operating concurrently. Consider now two arbitrarily chosen cars A and F. We are interested in understanding what happens if two cars want to reserve the same lane at the same time, as in Fig. 1. In order to understand the situation in more detail, Fig. 4 shows the states of the plant, that is, the global reachability analysis involving the two cars A and F. Building the product $C_1 = P \times E$, we see that the state 4 in the figure is a **Fail** state if the two cars have a safety overlap, that is, if $safetyOverlap(A, F)$ is true (which implies col).

Therefore this **Fail** state must be pruned, if such an overlap exists. To this end, the transitions leading into this state should be pruned (see dashed arrows in the figure). The transition $A.r(n + 1)$ shown in the figure is performed by car A. It should be pruned if $safetyOverlap(A, F)$ is true, because car F has already reserved lane $(n + 1)$ which makes the condition col true for the cars A and F. Generalizing from this example, we conclude that the transition $r(m)$ in Fig. 3(a) should be pruned if the following condition cc, called *collision check* in [3], is false:

$$A.cc(m) = \neg \exists c : ((m \in c.res) \wedge safetyOverlap(A, c)).$$

This means that the predicate $A.cc(m)$ is an enabling condition for the transition $r(m)$ of car A. The same condition for car F restricts the transition $F.r(n+1)$ in Fig. 4 in such a way that the system remains safe.

It is important to note that the global system model uses the interleaving semantics [16], that is, there are never two transitions that occur at the same time. If, on the contrary, transitions may occur concurrently, it would be possible that the cars A and F in Fig. 1 would simultaneously perform a transition $r(1)$, i.e., the dotted transition in the figure, resulting in a collision on lane 1. Interleaving semantics is widely used for modeling concurrent state machines. We note that interleaving semantics was also assumed in the safety proof of [3].

We note that the output action $r(m)$ also induces a mode change in the lane control component which determines the front distance used by the velocity controller for keeping safe distance with the cars in front. The function determining the front distance will have to change because the car must now keep safe distance to the preceding cars on both lanes. Similarly, a mode change occurs with the subsequent wd-r(m) action.

3.3   Interleaving Semantics or Synchronous Models?

It can be argued that interleaving semantics is not a realistic assumption for distributed systems where transitions are controlled independently by different components. Suppose that cars A and F decide at the same time that they want to reserve lane number 1. They will check whether the lane is free and then perform the r(1) transition. If car A does this just before car F, the question arises whether it is realistic to assume that car F will notice this change of reservation made by car A before it performs its own reservation?

A better modeling paradigm appears to be synchronous systems with stuttering. In synchronous systems, all system components perform a transition in parallel during a transition period. Stuttering means that, in each transition period, a component may decide to do no transition, that is, remain in the same state. For the IOA modeling paradigm that we use for the discrete transitions of the lane control component, this means that an output transition of one component will proceed in parallel with the corresponding input transitions of those components receiving the output as input. Other components, during the same transition period, may remain in the same state or perform an internal discrete transition. For the example of lane changing cars considered in this paper, this means that a transition of the lane controller of one car may occur in parallel with a lane controller transition of another car (which is not possible in the context of interleaving semantics).

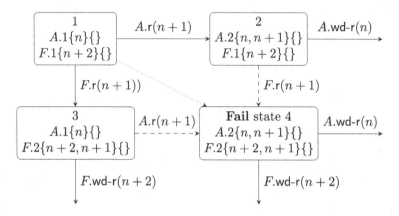

Fig. 4. Reachability analysis for two cars, A and F, behaving as in Fig. 3 (a). Solid and dashed arrows represent transitions in interleaving semantics. The dotted arrow represents an additional transition in the synchronous model.

When this modeling paradigm is used for the simple lane change algorithm discussed above, there are problems as shown in Fig. 4 and discussed above. The dashed transitions are pruned by the cc enabling condition for the $r(m)$ transition, but this condition does not prevent the possibility of simultaneous transitions of both cars from state $(A.1, F.1)$ to state $(A.2, F.2)$, as indicated by the dotted transition in the figure. Because of the independence of the distributed controllers in cars A and F, this dotted transition can only be pruned by also pruning the transitions from $(A.1, F.1)$ to $(A.2, F.1)$ and from $(A.1, F.1)$ to $(A.1, F.2)$, which means that no reservations can be made at all. Therefore, there *does not exist* a suitable controller for the simple algorithm for lane change when simultaneous transitions of different cars are allowed.

3.4   Lane Change Algorithm Allowing for Parallel Transitions

The problem of avoiding car collisions is an instance of the mutual exclusion problem. The space on the lane is the shared resource that must be managed in mutual exclusion by the different cars. One of the earliest mutual exclusion algorithms proposed by Dekker [17] achieves this goal by introducing for each user a variable 'claimed' which can be read by the other user. Before using the resource, a user first has to set its own claimed variable to true, and then he can only use the resource if the claimed variable of the other user is false.

The lane reservation protocol proposed in [3] is based on this principle and represented in Fig. 3 (b). In case of a conflict between the two cars, both cars abandon their reservation and withdraw their claim. In order to avoid infinite looping, it must be assumed that there is some random waiting before each user repeats his claim, similar to the behavior of agents in the ALOHA system [18].

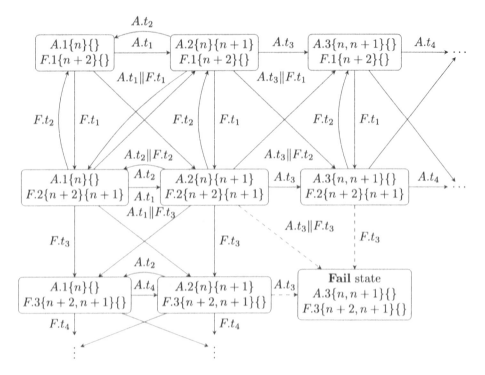

Fig. 5. Reachability analysis for two cars, A and F, behaving according to Figure 3 (b), with concurrent transitions, trying to reserve overlapping space on the same target lane $n + 1$.

The proposed protocol proceeds as follows. First, car A claims a space on the target lane m adjacent to its current lane n by the action c(m). Subsequently, it checks whether this claim intersects with the reservation or claim of any other car. In that case, A withdraws its claim by the action wd-c(m). Otherwise, without any intersection, A turns its claim into a reservation by the action r(m) so that it now reserves space on the two neighboring lanes m and n. During this double reservation A performs the lane change. Once this is completed, A withdraws its reservation on the original lane n by the action wd-r(n) and continues to drive on the target lane m.

In order to derive the necessary control constraints, we proceed along the lines discussed in Section 3.2. Again, we consider the the plant P consisting of two cars that want to reserve the same space on a given lane, for example the cars A and F in Fig. 1. The global plant behavior is shown by the state diagram of Fig. 5 which is the product of two state machines defined by Fig. 3 (b). The figure represents the uncontrolled behavior of two cars on lanes n and $n+2$ that both want to move to lane $m = n + 1$. If we build the product of the plant behavior with the environment objective, $C_1 = P \times E$, we see that the lower right state becomes a **Fail** state where both cars collide.

As in Section 3.2, we can introduce constraints (pruning) in the state machine of Fig. 3 (b) in order to eliminate the transitions into the **Fail** state. This means that we introduce a constraint on the r transition t_3 in Fig. 3 (b), such that this transition is not possible when the global system is in a state where the other car is in state 2 or 3, as shown in Fig. 5 by the dashed transitions. These states are characterized by the fact that the other car either has claimed or reserved an overlapping space on the same lane. Therefore the constraint for the transition of a car ego is the following condition pcc, called *potential collision check*:

$$ego.pcc(m) = \neg \exists c : ((m \in c.res \lor m \in c.clm) \land safetyOverlap(ego, c)).$$

If this constraint is implemented in both cars, then the joint transition from state $(A.2, F.2)$ in Fig. 5 directly into the **Fail** state will also be eliminated and the system is safe.

We note that the lane change algorithm obtained by our derivation approach is very similar to the algorithm proposed in [3], which was verified for interleaving semantics. In fact, they are identical if the states q_1 and q_2 of Fig. 2 in [3] are combined by ignoring the time constraint for state q_2. However, this constraint does not concern safety, but was only included to obtain a upper time-bound for a lane-change maneuver. Therefore this paper shows that the algorithm of [3] is not only correct for interleaving semantics, but also in a synchronous model.

3.5   Using a Helper Car

The preceding discussion assumes that a driving car has local knowledge about the reserved and claimed lanes of other cars in its environment and of the position and safety distance of these other cars. Among this information, the safety distance is probably the most difficult to obtain since it depends on the position and velocity of the other car. Therefore it is considered in [3] that this information may be obtained through message exchanges with another car in the environment, which is called a *helper car*. Such a car c should be on the target lane, but behind the lane changing car ego. It should provide information for the evaluation of the $safetyOverlap(ego, c)$ predicate. This predicate must be evaluated in state 2 of Fig. 3 (b), before the transition $r(m)$ can be performed. In Fig. 1, car E is a helper car for A in its lane change.

We would like to derive the behavior of the lane changing and helper cars from the behavior discussed in Section 3.4 for the case that the safety distance

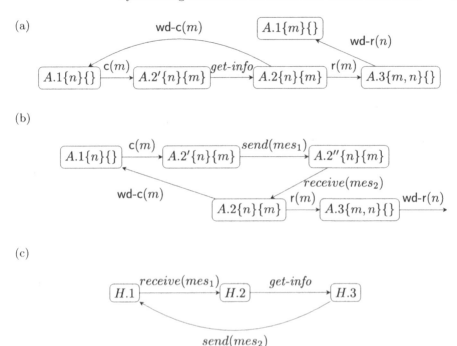

Fig. 6. (a) Global transition diagram involving a helper car that reads its own safety distance. Derived behavior for (b) lane changing car and (c) helper car.

information is available locally in each car. For this purpose, we can use the derivation algorithm described in [19] or use the approach described in [20]. In both cases, one starts out with a global specification of the different actions and their order of execution without being preoccupied by the question which components is responsible for executing each action, such as shown in Fig. 3 (b). After the different actions are allocated to the components that are responsible for their execution, a so-called protocol derivation algorithm constructs the local behavior specification for each component which include, in addition to the actions for which the component is responsible, the exchanges of coordination messages that are required for assuring the orderly execution of all these actions.

The principle of the protocol derivation algorithm [19] is to copy the control flow graph of the global specification for execution by each component, but to ignore all actions performed by other components and include instead the sending and reception of certain coordination messages. These coordination messages depend on the control flow operators in the global specification. For concurrency and weak sequencing (enforcing sequencing only locally inside components [21]), no coordination messages are required. However, they are essential for strict (i.e., global) sequencing, alternatives and loops. If a local action a_1, performed by component c_1, is followed (strictly) by an action a_2 performed by another component c_2, a coordination message will be send by c_1 to c_2, and the message will be received by by c_2 before the local action a_2 is performed.

In the case of the system of a lane changing car with its helper car, we take as global behavior specification a modified version of Fig. 3 (b), where an additional *get-info* action is introduced before entering state 2, as shown in Fig. 6 (a). This action is executed by the helper car, while all other actions are executed by the lane changing car. If we apply the protocol derivation algorithm, we obtain the behaviors for the lane changing car and the helper car shown in Figures 6 (b) and (c). Sending and receiving the synthesized coordination messages mes_1 and mes_2 guarantee the right sequencing of the *get-info* action and the actions of the lane changing car.

The behavior of Fig. 6 (c) should be performed in each car by the lane control component concurrently with its normal behavior described by Fig. 6 (b). The message mes_1 is effectively a request to send the safety distance information, and the message mes_2 sent by the helper car contains the information.

The algorithm obtained here is quite different than the algorithm proposed in [3]. The reason is that in [3], the helper car makes the decision whether a lane change can be done and answers yes or no. In our approach, the helper car simply returns the value of a local variable; the decision whether the lane change can be done remains with the lane changing car. The algorithm proposed in this paper is simpler.

4   Conclusion

This paper revisits the traffic maneuvers on multi-lane highways as discussed in [3]. The main conclusions of the discussions in this paper, which apply to the control of hybrid systems in general, are as follows:

(1) For verifying the safety of systems consisting of several loosely coupled components, where the behavior of a component may depend on the state of other components and where there may be some (even small) delay of communication, a modeling paradigm using interleaving semantics is not suitable. The possibility that different discrete transitions of several components occur in parallel must be considered, which can be modeled by synchronous modeling paradigms. (For a detailed discussion, see Section 3.3).

(2) Well-known algorithms for synthesizing controllers for discrete event systems (e.g. [5]) can be used for synthesizing controllers for the discrete transitions of hybrid systems. Corresponding algorithms exist for interleaving semantics, synchronous systems, and IOA [12]. (For a detailed discussion, see Section 3.1).

(3) When the global behavior involving several system components is known, for instance the actions that should be performed by different controllers of different components, then the behavior of each controller, including the exchange of coordination messages, can be synthesized using an algorithm described in [19]. (For a detailed discussion, see Section 3.5).

We note that an additional difficulty may occur during the lane change maneuver if a fast driving car approaches the claimed space just when the claim is being made. It could happen that the *safetyOverlap* condition with this car becomes false at the same time as the claim is set. It is shown in an extended version of this paper [7] that a collision can be avoided by requiring that the front distance, which is used for the calculation of the safety distance by the approaching car, should take into account the distance to the lane changing car as soon as the claim is made.

References

1. Varaija, P.: Smart cars on smart roads: problems of control. IEEE Trans. on Automatic Control **AC–38**, 195–207 (1993)
2. Lygeros, J., Godbole, D.N., Sastry, S.S.: Verified hybrid controllers for automated vehicles. IEEE Trans. on Automatic Control **43**, 522–539 (1998)
3. Hilscher, M., Linker, S., Olderog, E.-R., Ravn, A.P.: An abstract model for proving safety of multi-lane traffic manoeuvres. In: Qin, S., Qiu, Z. (eds.) ICFEM 2011. LNCS, vol. 6991, pp. 404–419. Springer, Heidelberg (2011)
4. Lynch, N.A., Segala, R., Vaandrager, F.W., Weinberg, H.: Hybrid i/o automata. Technical Report Report CSI-R9907, April 1999, Computing Science Institute, University of Nijmegen (1999)
5. Cai, K., Wonham, W.: Supervisor localization: A top-down approach to distributed control of discrete-event systems. IEEE Trans. Autom. Control **55**, 605–618 (2010)
6. Merlin, P., v. Bochmann, G.: On the construction of submodule specifications and communication protocols. ACM Trans. Program. Lang. Syst. **5**, 1–25 (1983)
7. v. Bochmann, G., Hilscher, M., Linker, S., Olderog, E.R.: Synthesizing and verifying controllers for multi-lane traffic maneuvers. Technical Report 109, AVACS (2015). see www.avacs.org under 'Papers'
8. Lynch, N.A., Segala, R., Vaandrager, F.W.: Hybrid i/o automata. Inf. Comput. **185**, 105–157 (2003)
9. Damm, W., Hungar, H., Olderog, E.R.: Verification of cooperating traffic agents. Intern. Journal of Control **79**, 395–421 (2006)
10. Damm, W., Möhlmann, E., Rakow, A.: Component based design of hybrid systems: A case study on concurrency and coupling. In: Proc. 17th Intern. Conf. on Hybrid Systems: Computation and Control, HSCC 2014, pp.145–150, ACM (2014)
11. Ramadge, P., Wonham, W.: Supervisory control of a class of discrete event processes. SIAM J. Control Optim. **25**, 206–230 (1987)
12. v. Bochmann, G.: Using logic to solve the submodule construction problem. Discrete Event Dynamic Systems **23**, 27–59 (2013)
13. Damm, W., Finkbeiner, B.: Does it pay to extend the perimeter of a world model? In: Butler, M., Schulte, W. (eds.) FM 2011. LNCS, vol. 6664, pp. 12–26. Springer, Heidelberg (2011)
14. Ziller, R., Schneider, K.: Combining supervisor synthesis and model checking. ACM Trans. Embed. Comput. Syst. **4**, 331–362 (2005)
15. Thistle, J.G.: Undecidability in decentralized supervision. Systems & Control Letters **54**, 503–509 (2005)
16. Milner, R.: Communication and Concurrency. Prentice-Hall (1989)
17. Dijkstra, E.W.: Cooperating sequential processes. In: Genuys, F. (ed.) Programming Languages: NATO Advanced Study Institute, pp. 43–112. Academic Press (1968)
18. Abramson, N.: The ALOHA system: Another alternative for computer communications. In: Proc. Fall Joint Computer Conf. AFIPS 1970, pp. 281–285. ACM (1970)

19. Gotzhein, R., v. Bochmann, G.: Deriving protocol specifications from service specifications including parameters. ACM Trans. Comput. Syst. **8**, 255–283 (1990)
20. Castejón, H.N., v. Bochmann, G., Bræk, R.: On the realizability of collaborative services. Software and System Modeling **12**, 597–617 (2013)
21. Mauw, S., Reniers, M.A.: High-level message sequence charts. In: SDL 1997: Time for Testing - SDL, MSC and Trends, pp. 291–306. Elsevier Science B.V. (1997)

Extending Hybrid CSP with Probability and Stochasticity

Yu Peng, Shuling Wang$^{(\boxtimes)}$, Naijun Zhan, and Lijun Zhang

State Key Laboratory of Computer Science, Institute of Software,
Chinese Academy of Sciences, Beijing, China
wangsl@ios.ac.cn

Abstract. Probabilistic and stochastic behavior are omnipresent in computer controlled systems, in particular, so-called safety-critical hybrid systems, because of fundamental properties of nature, uncertain environments, or simplifications to overcome complexity. Tightly intertwining discrete, continuous and stochastic dynamics complicates modelling, analysis and verification of stochastic hybrid systems (SHSs). In the literature, this issue has been extensively investigated, but unfortunately it still remains challenging as no promising general solutions are available yet. In this paper, we give our effort by proposing a general compositional approach for modelling and verification of SHSs. First, we extend Hybrid CSP (HCSP), a very expressive and process algebra-like formal modeling language for hybrid systems, by introducing probability and stochasticity to model SHSs, which is called stochastic HCSP (SHCSP). To this end, ordinary differential equations (ODEs) are generalized by stochastic differential equations (SDEs) and non-deterministic choice is replaced by probabilistic choice. Then, we extend Hybrid Hoare Logic (HHL) to specify and reason about SHCSP processes. We demonstrate our approach by an example from real-world.

1 Introduction

Probabilistic and stochastic behavior are omnipresent in computer controlled systems, such as safety-critical hybrid systems, because of uncertain environments, or simplifications to overcome complexity. For example, the movement of aircrafts could be influenced by wind; in networked control systems, message loss and other random effects (e.g., node placement, node failure, battery drain, measurement imprecision) may happen.

Stochastic hybrid systems (SHSs) are systems in which discrete, continuous and stochastic dynamics tightly intertwine. As many of SHSs are safety-critical, a thorough validation and verification activity is necessary to enhance the quality of SHSs and, in particular, to fulfill the quality criteria mandated by the relevant standards. But modeling, analysis and verification of SHSs is difficult and challenging. An obvious research line is to extend hybrid automata [10], which is the most popular model for traditional hybrid systems, by adding probability and

© Springer International Publishing Switzerland 2015
X. Li et al. (Eds.): SETTA 2015, LNCS 9409, pp. 87–102, 2015.
DOI: 10.1007/978-3-319-25942-0_6

stochasticity. Then, verification of SHSs can be done naturally through reachability analysis, either by probabilistic model-checking [1–3,6,8,20,21], or by simulation i.e., statistical model-checking [15,23]. Along this line, several different notions of *stochastic hybrid automata* have been proposed [1–3,6,8,20,21], with the difference on where to introduce randomness. One option is to replace deterministic jumps by probability distribution over deterministic jumps. Another option is to generalize differential equations inside a mode by stochastic differential equations. Stochastic hybrid systems comprising stochastic differential equations have been investigated in [1,5,13]. More general models can be obtained by mixing the above two choices, and by combining them with memoryless timed probabilistic jumps [4], with a random reset function for each discrete jump [6]. An overview of this line can be found in [4].

To model complex systems, some compositional modelling formalisms have been proposed, e.g., HMODEST [7] and stochastic hybrid programs [18]. HCSP due to He, Zhou, et al [9,22] is an extension of CSP [12] by introducing differential equations to model continuous evolution and three types of interruptions (i.e., communication interruption, timeout and boundary condition) to model interactions between continuous evolutions and discrete jumps in HSs. The extension of CSP to probabilistic setting has been investigated by Morgan et al. [16]. In this paper, we propose a compositional approach for modelling and verification of stochastic hybrid systems. First, we extend Hybrid CSP (HCSP), a very expressive and process algebra-like modeling language for hybrid systems by introducing probability and stochasticity, called stochastic HCSP (SHCSP), to model SHSs. In SHCSP, ordinary differential equations (ODEs) are generalized to stochastic differential equations (SDEs), and non-deterministic choice is replaced by probabilistic choice. Different from Platzer's work [18], SHCSP provides more expressive constructs for describing hybrid systems, including communication, parallelism, interruption, and so on.

Probabilistic model-checking of SHSs does not scale, in particular, taking SDEs into account. For example, it is not clear how to approximate the reachable sets of a simple linear SDEs with more than two variables. Therefore, existing verification techniques based on reachability analysis for SHSs are inadequate, and new approaches are expected. As an alternative, in [18], Platzer for the first time investigated how to extend deductive verification to SHSs. Inspired by Platzer's work, for specifying and reasoning about SHCSP process, we extend Hybrid Hoare Logic [14], which is an extension of Hoare logic [11] to HSs, to SHSs. Comparing with Platzer's work, more computation features of SHSs, and more expressive constructs such as concurrency, communication and interruption, can be well handled in our setting. We demonstrate our approach by modeling and verification of the example of aircraft planning problem from the real-world.

2   Background and Notations

Assume that $\mathcal{F}$ is a σ-algebra on set Ω and P is a probability measure on $(\Omega, \mathcal{F})$, then $(\Omega, \mathcal{F}, P)$ is called a *probability space*. We here assume that every subset of a null set (i.e., $P(A) = 0$) with probability 0 is measurable. A property which holds with probability 1 is said to hold *almost surely* (a.s.). A *filtration* is a sequence of σ-algebras $\{\mathcal{F}_t\}_{t\geq 0}$ with $\mathcal{F}_{t_1} \subseteq \mathcal{F}_{t_2}$ for all $t_1 < t_2$. We always assume that a filtration $\{\mathcal{F}_t\}_{t\geq 0}$ has been completed to include all null sets and is right-continuous.

Let $\mathcal{B}$ represent the Borel σ-algebra on $\mathbb{R}^n$, i.e. the σ-algebra generated by all open subsets. A mapping $X : \Omega \to \mathbb{R}^n$ is called $\mathbb{R}^n$-valued *random variable* if for each $B \in \mathcal{B}$, we have $X^{-1}(B) \in \mathcal{F}$, i.e. X is $\mathcal{F}$-*measurable*. A *stochastic process* X is a function $X : T \times \Omega \to \mathbb{R}^n$ such that for each $t \in T$, $X(t, \cdot) : \Omega \to \mathbb{R}^n$ is a random variable, and for each $\omega \in \Omega$, $X(\cdot, \omega) : T \to \mathbb{R}^n$ corresponds to a *sample path*. A stochastic process X is *adapted* to a filtration $\{\mathcal{F}_t\}_{t\geq 0}$ if X_t is $\mathcal{F}_t$-measurable. Intuitively, a filtration represents all available historical information of a stochastic process, but nothing related to its future. A *càdlàg* function defined on $\mathbb{R}$ is *right continuous* and has *left limit*. A stochastic process X is *càdlàg* iff all of its paths $t \to X_t(\omega)$ (for each $\omega \in \Omega$) are *càdlàg*. A d-dimensional *Brownian motion* W is a stochastic process with $W_0 = 0$ that is continuous almost surely everywhere and has independent increments with time, i.e. $W_t - W_s \sim N(0, t - s)$ (for $0 \leq s < t$), where $N(0, t - s)$ denotes the normal distribution with mean 0 and variance $t - s$. Brownian motion is mathematically extremely complex. Its path is almost surely continuous everywhere but differentiable nowhere. Intuitively, W can be understood as the limit of a random walk. A *Markov time* with respect to a stochastic process X is a random variable τ such that for any $t \geq 0$, the event $\{\tau \leq t\}$ is determined by (at most) the information up to time t, i.e. $\{\tau \leq t\} \in \mathcal{F}_t$.

We use *stochastic differential equation* (SDE) to model stochastic continuous evolution, which is of the form $dX_t = b(X_t)dt + \sigma(X_t)dW_t$, where W_t is a Brownian motion. In which, the drift coefficient $b(X_t)$ determines how the deterministic part of X_t changes with respect to time and the diffusion coefficient $\sigma(X_t)$ determines the stochastic influence to X_t with respect to the Brownian motion W_t. Obviously, any solution to an SDE is a stochastic process.

3   Stochastic HCSP

A system in Stochastic HCSP (SHCSP) consists of a finite set of sequential processes in parallel which communicate via channels synchronously. Each sequential process is represented as a collection of stochastic processes, each of which arises from the interaction of discrete computation and stochastic continuous dynamics modeled by stochastic differential equations.

Let *Proc* represent the set of SHCSP processes, Σ the set of channel names. The syntax of SHCSP is given as follows:

$$P ::= \textbf{skip} \mid x := e \mid ch?x \mid ch!e \mid P; Q \mid B \to P \mid P^*$$
$$\mid P \sqcup_p Q \mid \langle ds = bdt + \sigma dW \& B \rangle$$
$$\mid \langle ds = bdt + \sigma dW \& B \rangle \rhd []_{i \in I} (\omega_i \cdot ch_i * \to Q_i)$$

$$S ::= P \mid S \| S$$

Here $ch, ch_i \in \Sigma$, ch_i* stands for a communication event, e.g. $ch?x$ or $ch!e$, x is a variable, B and e are Boolean and arithmetic expressions, $P, Q, Q_i \in Proc$ are sequential processes, $p \in [0, 1]$ stands for the probability of the choice between P and Q, s for a vector of continuous variables, b and σ for functions of s, W for the Brownian motion process. At the end, S stands for a system, i.e., a SHCSP process.

As defined in the syntax of P, the processes in the first line are original from HCSP, while the last two lines are new for SHCSP. The individual constructs can be understood intuitively as follows:

- **skip**, the assignment $x := e$, the sequential composition $P; Q$, and the alternative statement $B \rightarrow P$ are defined as usual.
- $ch?x$ receives a value along channel ch and assigns it to x.
- $ch!e$ sends the value of e along channel ch. A communication takes place when both the sending and the receiving parties are ready, and may cause one side to wait.
- The repetition P^* executes P for some finite number of times.
- $P \sqcup_p Q$ denotes probabilistic choice. It behaves as P with probability p and as Q with probability $1 - p$.
- $\langle ds = bdt + \sigma dW \& B \rangle$ specifies that the system evolves according to the stochastic process defined by the stochastic differential equation $ds = bdt + \sigma dW$. As long as the boolean expression B, which defines the *domain of s*, turns false, it terminates. We will later use $d(s)$ to return the dimension of s.
- $\langle ds = bdt + \sigma dW \& B \rangle \trianglerighteq []_{i \in I}(\omega_i \cdot ch_i* \rightarrow Q_i)$ behaves like $\langle ds = bdt + \sigma dW \& B \rangle$, except that the stochastic evolution is preempted as soon as one of the communications ch_i* takes place, after that the respective Q_i is executed. I is supposed to be finite and for each $i \in I$, $\omega_i \in \mathbb{Q}^+$ represents the *weight* of ch_i*. If one or more communications are ready at the same time, say they are $\{ch_j*\}_{j \in J}$ with $J \subseteq I$ and $|J| \geq 1$, then ch_j is chosen with the probability $\frac{\omega_j}{\Sigma_{j \in J}\omega_j}$, for each $j \in J$. If the stochastic dynamics terminates before a communication among $\{ch_i*\}_I$ occurring, then the process terminates without communicating.
- $S_1 \| S_2$ behaves as if S_1 and S_2 run independently except that all communications along the common channels connecting S_1 and S_2 are to be synchronized. The processes S_1 and S_2 in parallel can neither share variables, nor input nor output channels.

3.1   A Running Example

We use SHCSP to model the aircraft position during the flight, which is inspired from [19]. Consider an aircraft that is following a flight path consisting of a sequence of line segments at a fixed altitude. Ideally, the aircraft should fly at a constant velocity v along the nominal path, but due to the wind or cloud disturbance, the deviation of the aircraft from the path may occur. For safety, the aircraft should follow a correction heading to get back to the nominal path as quickly as possible. On one hand, the correction heading should be orthogonal to the nominal path for the shortest way back, but on the other hand, it should also go ahead to meet the destination. Considering these two objectives, we assume the correction heading always an acute angle with the nominal path.

Here we model the behavior of the aircraft along one line segment. Without loss of generality, we assume the segment is along x-axis, with $(x_s, 0)$ as the starting point and $(x_e, 0)$ as the ending point. When the aircraft deviates from the segment with a vertical distance greater than λ, we consider it enters a dangerous state. Let (x_s, y_0) be the initial position of the aircraft in this segment, then the future position of the aircraft $(x(t), y(t))$ is governed by the following SDE:

$$\begin{pmatrix} dx(t) \\ dy(t) \end{pmatrix} = v \begin{pmatrix} cos(\theta(t)) \\ sin(\theta(t)) \end{pmatrix} dt + dW(t)$$

where $\theta(t)$ is the correction heading and is defined with a constant degree $\frac{\pi}{4}$ when the aircraft deviates from the nominal path:

$$\theta(t) = \begin{cases} -\frac{\pi}{4} & \text{if } y(t) > 0 \\ 0 & \text{if } y(t) = 0 \\ \frac{\pi}{4} & \text{if } y(t) < 0 \end{cases}$$

Let B be $x_s \leq x \leq x_e$, the movement of the aircraft described above can be modelled by the following SHCSP process P_{Air}:

$$x = x_s; y = y_0; \langle [dx, dy]^T = v[cos(\theta(t)), sin(\theta(t))]^T dt + dW(t) \& B \rangle$$

4   Operational Semantics

Before giving operational semantics, we introduce some notations first.

System Variables. In order to interpret SHCSP processes, we use non-negative reals $\mathbb{R}^+$ to model time, and introduce a global clock *now* as a system variable to record the time in the execution of a process. A *timed communication* is of the form $\langle ch.c, b \rangle$, where $ch \in \Sigma$, $c \in \mathbb{R}$ and $b \in \mathbb{R}^+$, representing that a communication along channel ch occurs at time b with value c transmitted. The set $\Sigma \times \mathbb{R} \times \mathbb{R}^+$ of all timed communications is denoted by $T\Sigma$. The set of all timed traces is

$$T\Sigma_{\leq}^* = \{\gamma \in T\Sigma^* \mid \text{ if } \langle ch_1.c_1, b_1 \rangle \text{ precedes } \langle ch_2.c_2, b_2 \rangle \text{ in } \gamma, \text{ then } b_1 \leq b_2 \}.$$

If $C \subseteq \Sigma$, $\gamma \lceil_C$ is the projection of γ onto C such that only the timed communications along channels of C in γ are preserved. Given two timed traces γ_1, γ_2, and $X \subseteq \Sigma$, the *alphabetized parallel* of γ_1 and γ_2 over X, denoted by $\gamma_1 \gamma_2$, results in the following set of timed traces

$$\{\gamma \mid \gamma \lceil_{\Sigma - (\Sigma(\gamma_1) \cup \Sigma(\gamma_2))} = \epsilon, \gamma \lceil_{\Sigma(\gamma_1)} = \gamma_1, \gamma \lceil_{\Sigma(\gamma_2)} = \gamma_2 \text{ and } \gamma \lceil_X = \gamma_1 \lceil_X = \gamma_2 \lceil_X \},$$

where $\Sigma(\gamma)$ stands for the set of channels that occur in γ.

To model synchronization of communication events, we need to describe their readiness. Because a communication itself takes no time when both parties get ready, thus, at a time point, multiple communications may occur. In order to record the execution order of communications occurring at the same time point, we prefix each communication readiness a timed trace that happened before the ready communication event. Formally, each *communication readiness* has the form of $\gamma.ch?$ or $\gamma.ch!$, where $\gamma \in T\Sigma_{\leq}^*$. We denote by RDY the set of communication readiness in the sequel.

Finally, we introduce two system variables, rdy and tr, to represent the ready set of communication events and the timed trace accumulated at the considered time, respectively. In what follows, we use $Var(P)$ to represent the set of process variables of P, plus the system variables $\{rdy, tr, now\}$ introduced above, which take values respectively from $\mathbb{R} \cup RDY \cup T\Sigma_{\leq}^* \cup \mathbb{R}^+$, denoted by Val.

States and Functions. To interpret a process $P \in Proc$, we define a state ds as a mapping from $Var(P)$ to Val, and denote by $\mathcal{D}$ the set of such states. Because of stochasticity, we introduce a random variable $\rho : \Omega \to \mathcal{D}$ to describe a distribution of all possible states. In addition, we introduce a stochastic process $H : Intv \times \Omega \to \mathcal{D}$ to represent the continuous flow of process P over the time interval $Intv$, i.e., state distributions on the interval. In what follows, we will abuse state distribution as state if not stated otherwise.

Given two states ρ_1 and ρ_2, we say ρ_1 and ρ_2 are parallelable iff for each $\omega \in \Omega$, $Dom(\rho_1(\omega)) \cap Dom(\rho_2(\omega)) = \{rdy, tr, now\}$ and $\rho_1(\omega)(now) = \rho_2(\omega)(now)$. Given two parallelable states ρ_1 and ρ_2, paralleling them over $X \subseteq \Sigma$ results in a set of new states, denoted by $\rho_1 \uplus \rho_2$, any of which ρ is given by

$$\rho(\omega)(v) \stackrel{\text{def}}{=} \begin{cases} \rho_1(\omega)(v) & \text{if } v \in Dom(\rho_1(\omega)) \setminus Dom(\rho_2(\omega)), \\ \rho_2(\omega)(v) & \text{if } v \in Dom(\rho_2(\omega)) \setminus Dom(\rho_1(\omega)), \\ \rho_1(\omega)(now) & \text{if } v = now, \\ \gamma, \text{ where } \gamma \in \rho_1(\omega)(tr)\rho_2(\omega)(tr) & \text{if } v = tr, \\ \rho_1(\omega)(rdy) \cup \rho_2(\omega)(rdy) & \text{if } v = rdy. \end{cases}$$

It makes no sense to distinguish any two states in $\rho_1 \uplus \rho_2$, so hereafter we abuse $\rho_1 \uplus \rho_2$ to represent any of its elements. $\rho_1 \uplus \rho_2$ will be used to represent states of parallel processes.

Given a random variable ρ, the update $\rho[v \to e]$ represents a new random variable such that for any $\omega \in \Omega$ and $x \in Var$, $\rho[v \to e](\omega)(x)$ is defined as the value of e if x is v, and $\rho(\omega)(x)$ otherwise. Given a stochastic process $X : [0, d) \times \Omega \to R^{d(s)}$, for any t in the domain, $\rho[s \to X_t]$ is a new random variable such that for any $\omega \in \Omega$ and $x \in Var$, $\rho[s \to X_t](\omega)(x)$ is defined as $X(t, w)$ if x is s, and $\rho(\omega)(x)$ otherwise.

At last, we define H_d^ρ as the stochastic process over interval $[\rho(now), \rho(now) + d]$ such that for any $t \in [\rho(now), \rho(now) + d]$ and any w, $H_d^\rho(t, \omega) = \rho[now \mapsto t](\omega)$, and moreover, $H_d^{\rho,s,X}$ as the stochastic process over interval $[\rho(now), \rho(now) + d]$ such that for any $t \in [\rho(now), \rho(now) + d]$ and any w, $H_d^{\rho,s,X}(t, \omega) = \rho[now \mapsto t, rdy \mapsto \emptyset, s \mapsto X_t](\omega)$.

4.1 Operational Semantics

Each transition relation has the form of $(P, \rho) \xrightarrow{\alpha} (P', \rho', H)$, where P and P' are processes, α is an event, ρ, ρ' are states, H is a stochastic process. It expresses that starting from initial state ρ, P evolves into P' by performing event α, and ends in state ρ' and the execution history of α is recorded by continuous flow H. When the transition is discrete and thus produces a flow on a point interval (i.e. current time now), we will write $(P, \rho) \xrightarrow{\alpha} (P', \rho')$ instead of $(P, \rho) \xrightarrow{\alpha} (P', \rho', \{\rho(now) \mapsto \rho'\})$. The label α represents events, which can be an internal event like skip, assignment, or a termination of a continuous etc, uniformly denoted by τ, or an external communication event $ch!c$ or $ch?c$, or an internal communication $ch.c$, or a time delay d that is a positive real number. We call the events but the time delay $discrete\ events$, and will use β to range over them. We define the dual of $ch?c$ (denoted by $\overline{ch?c}$) as $ch!c$, and vice versa, and define $comm(ch!c, ch?c)$ or $comm(ch?c, ch!c)$ as the communication $ch.c$. In the operational semantics, besides the timed communications, we will also record the internal events that have occurred till now in tr.

For page limit, we present the semantics for the new constructs of SHCSP in the paper in Table 1. The semantics for the rest is same to HCSP, which can be found at [17]. The semantics for probabilistic choice is given by rules (PCho-1) and (PCho-2): it is defined with respect to a random variable U which distributes uniformly in $[0, 1]$, such that for any sample ω, if $U(\omega) \leq p$, then P is taken, otherwise, Q is taken. In either case, it is assumed that an internal action happened. A stochastic dynamics can continuously evolve for d time units if B always holds during this period, see (Cont-1). In (Cont-1), the variable X solves the stochastic process and the ready set keeps unchanged, reflected by the flow $H_d^{\rho,s,X}$. The stochastic dynamics terminates at a point whenever B turns out false at a neighborhood of the point (Cont-2). Communication interrupt evolves for d time units if none of the communications ch_{i^*} is ready (IntP-1), or is interrupted to execute $ch_{i_j}*$ whenever $ch_{i_j}*$ occurs first (IntP-2), or terminates immediately in case the continuous terminates before any communication happening (IntP-3).

The following theorem indicates that the semantics of SHCSP is well defined.

Theorem 1. *For each transition* $(P, \rho) \xrightarrow{\alpha} (P', \rho', H)$, H *is an almost surely càdlàg process and adapted to the completed filtration* $(\mathcal{F}_t)_{t \geq 0}$ *(generated by* ρ, *the Brownian motion* $(B_s)_{s \leq t}$, *the weights* $\{\omega_i\}_{i \in I}$ *and uniform* U *process) and the evolving time from* P *to* P', *denoted by* $\Delta(P, P')$, *is a Markov time.*

Proof. The proof of this theorem can be found at [17].

5 Assertions and Specifications

In this section, we define a specification logic for reasoning about SHCSP programs. We will first present the assertions including syntax and semantics, and then the specifications based on Hoare triples. The proof system will be given in next section.

5.1 Assertion Language

The assertion language is essentially defined by a first-order logic with emphasis on the notion of explicit time and the addition of several specific predicates on occurrence of communication traces and events. Before giving the syntax of assertions, we introduce three kinds of expressions first.

$$h ::= \varepsilon \mid \langle ch.E, T \rangle \mid h \cdot h \mid h^*$$
$$E ::= c \mid x \mid f^k(E_1, ..., E_k)$$
$$T ::= o \mid now \mid u^l(T_1, ..., T_l)$$

h defines trace expressions, among which $\langle ch.E, T \rangle$ represents that there is a value E transmitted along channel ch at time T. E defines value expressions,

Table 1. The semantics of new constructs of SHCSP

$$\frac{U \text{ is a random variable distributed uniformly in } [0,1], U(\omega) \le p}{(P \sqcup_p Q, \rho) \xrightarrow{\tau} (P, \rho[tr \mapsto tr \cdot \langle \tau, now \rangle])} \quad \text{(PCho-1)}$$

$$\frac{U \text{ is a random variable distributed uniformly in } [0,1], U(\omega) > p}{(P \sqcup_p Q, \rho) \xrightarrow{\tau} (Q, \rho[tr \mapsto tr \cdot \langle \tau, now \rangle])} \quad \text{(PCho-2)}$$

$$\frac{\begin{array}{l} X : [0,d) \times \Omega \to \mathbb{R}^{d(s)} \text{ is the solution of} \\ ds = bdt + \sigma dW \wedge \forall t \in [0,d), \forall \omega. \rho[now \mapsto now + t, s \mapsto X_t](\omega)(B) = \mathbf{T} \end{array}}{(\langle ds = bdt + \sigma dW \& B \rangle, \rho) \xrightarrow{d} \left(\begin{array}{l} \langle ds = bdt + \sigma dW \& B \rangle, \\ \rho[now \mapsto now + d, s \mapsto X_d], H_d^{\rho,s,X} \end{array} \right)} \quad \text{(Cont-1)}$$

$$\frac{\begin{array}{l} \exists \omega. (\rho(\omega)(B) = \mathbf{F}) \text{ or } (X : [0,d) \times \Omega \to \mathbb{R}^{d(s)} \text{ is the solution of } ds = bdt + \sigma dW, \\ \exists \varepsilon > 0 \forall t \in (0, \varepsilon) \exists \omega. \rho[now \mapsto now + t, s \mapsto X_t](\omega)(B) = \mathbf{F}) \end{array}}{(\langle ds = bdt + \sigma dW \& B \rangle, \rho) \xrightarrow{\tau} (\epsilon, \rho[tr \mapsto tr \cdot \langle \tau, now \rangle])} \quad \text{(Cont-2)}$$

$$\frac{\begin{array}{l} (chi*; Q_i, \rho) \xrightarrow{d} (chi*; Q_i, \rho_i', H_i), \quad \forall i \in I \\ (\langle ds = bdt + \sigma dW \& B \rangle, \rho) \xrightarrow{d} (\langle ds = bdt + \sigma dW \& B \rangle, \rho', H) \end{array}}{\begin{array}{l} (\langle ds = bdt + \sigma dW \& B \rangle \trianglerighteq []_{i \in I}(\omega_i \cdot chi* \to Q_i), \rho) \xrightarrow{d} \\ \left(\begin{array}{l} \langle ds = bdt + \sigma dW \& B \rangle \trianglerighteq []_{i \in I}(\omega_i \cdot chi* \to Q_i), \\ \rho'[rdy \mapsto \cup_{i \in I}\rho_i'(rdy)], H[rdy \mapsto \cup_{i \in I}\rho_i'(rdy)] \end{array} \right) \end{array}} \quad \text{(IntP-1)}$$

$$\frac{\begin{array}{l} \{\overline{chi_k *}\}_{1 \le k \le n} \text{ get ready simultaneously while others not} \\ U \text{ is a random variable distributed uniformly in } [0,1], \text{ and for } 1 \le j \le n \\ \frac{\sum_{k=1}^{j-1} \omega_{i_k}}{\sum_{k=1}^{n} \omega_{i_k}} \le U(\omega) < \frac{\sum_{k=1}^{j} \omega_{i_k}}{\sum_{k=1}^{n} \omega_{i_k}} \text{ and } (chi_j*; Q_{i_j}, \rho) \xrightarrow{chi_j*} (Q_{i_j}, \rho') \end{array}}{(\langle ds = bdt + \sigma dW \& B \rangle \trianglerighteq []_{i \in I}(\omega_i \cdot chi* \to Q_i), \rho) \xrightarrow{chi_j*} (Q_{i_j}, \rho')} \quad \text{(IntP-2)}$$

$$\frac{(\langle ds = bdt + \sigma dW \& B \rangle, \rho) \xrightarrow{\tau} (\epsilon, \rho')}{(\langle ds = bdt + \sigma dW \& B \rangle \trianglerighteq []_{i \in I}(\omega_i \cdot chi* \to Q_i), \rho) \xrightarrow{\tau} (\epsilon, \rho')} \quad \text{(IntP-3)}$$

including a value constant c, a variable x, or arithmetic value expressions. T defines time expressions, including a time constant o, system variable now, or arithmetic time expressions.

The categories of the assertion language include terms, denoted by θ, θ_1 etc., state formulas, denoted by S, S_1 etc., formulas, denoted by φ, φ_1 etc., and probability formulas, denoted by $\mathcal{P}$ etc., which are given by the following BNFs:

$$\theta ::= E \mid T \mid h \mid tr$$
$$S ::= \perp \mid R^n(\theta_1, ..., \theta_n) \mid h.ch? \mid h.ch! \mid \neg S \mid S_1 \vee S_2$$
$$\varphi ::= \perp \mid S \text{ at } T \mid \neg \varphi \mid \varphi_1 \vee \varphi_2 \mid \forall v.\varphi \mid \forall t.\varphi$$
$$\mathcal{P} ::= P(\varphi) \bowtie p \mid \neg \mathcal{P} \mid \mathcal{P} \vee \mathcal{P}$$

The terms θ include value, time and trace expressions, plus trace variable tr. The state expressions S include false (denoted by $\perp$), truth-valued relation R^n on terms, readiness, and logical combinations of state formulas. In particular, the readiness $h.ch?$ or $h.ch!$ represents that the communication event $ch?$ or $ch!$ is enabled, and prior to it, the sequence of communications recorded in h has occurred. The formulas φ include false, a primitive S at T representing that S holds at time T; and logical combinations of formulas (v, t represent logical variables for values and time resp.). For time primitive, we have an axiom that $(S_1 \text{ at } T \wedge S_2 \text{ at } T) \Leftrightarrow (S_1 \wedge S_2) \text{ at } T$. We omit all the other axiom and inference rules for the formulas, that are same to first-order logic. The probability formula $\mathcal{P}$ has the form $P(\varphi) \bowtie p$, where $\bowtie \in \{<, \leq, >, \geq\}$, $p \in \mathbb{Q} \cap [0, 1]$, or the logical composition of probability formulas free of quantifiers. In particular, $P(\varphi) \bowtie p$ means that φ is true with probability $\bowtie p$. For the special case $P(\varphi) = 1$, we write φ for short.

In the sequel, we use the standard logical abbreviations, as well as

$$\varphi \text{ dr } [T_1, T_2] \overset{\text{def}}{=} \forall t.(T_1 \leq t \leq T_2) \Rightarrow \varphi \text{ at } t$$
$$\varphi \text{ in } [T_1, T_2] \overset{\text{def}}{=} \exists t.(T_1 \leq t \leq T_2) \wedge \varphi \text{ at } t$$

Interpretation. In the following, we will use a random variable $Z : \Omega \to (Var \to Val)$ to describe the current state and a stochastic process $\mathcal{H} : [0, +\infty) \times \Omega \to (Var \to Val)$ to represent the whole evolution. The semantics of a term θ is a function $\llbracket \theta \rrbracket : (\Omega \to (Var \to Val)) \to (\Omega \to Val)$ that maps any random variable Z to a random variable $\llbracket \theta \rrbracket^Z$, defined as follows:

$$\llbracket c \rrbracket^Z = c$$
$$\llbracket x \rrbracket^Z = Y \text{ where } Y(\omega) = Z(\omega)(x) \text{ for } \omega \in \Omega$$
$$\llbracket f^k(E_1, ..., E_k) \rrbracket^Z = f^k(\llbracket E_1 \rrbracket^Z, ..., \llbracket E_k \rrbracket^Z)$$
$$\llbracket o \rrbracket^Z = o$$
$$\llbracket now \rrbracket^Z = Y \text{ where } Y(\omega) = Z(\omega)(now) \text{ for } \omega \in \Omega$$
$$\llbracket u^l(T_1, ..., T_l) \rrbracket^Z = u^l(\llbracket T_1 \rrbracket^Z, ..., \llbracket T_l \rrbracket^Z)$$
$$\llbracket \varepsilon \rrbracket^Z = \varepsilon$$
$$\llbracket \langle ch.E, T \rangle \rrbracket^Z = \langle ch.\llbracket E \rrbracket^Z, \llbracket T \rrbracket^Z \rangle$$
$$\llbracket h_1 \cdot h_2 \rrbracket^Z = \llbracket h_1 \rrbracket^Z \cdot \llbracket h_2 \rrbracket^Z$$
$$\llbracket h^* \rrbracket^Z = (\llbracket h \rrbracket^Z)^*$$

The semantics of state formula S is a function $[\![S]\!] : (\Omega \to (Var \to Val)) \to (\Omega \to \{0,1\})$ that maps any random variable Z describing the current state to a boolean random variable $[\![S]\!]^Z$, defined as follows:

$$[\![\bot]\!]^Z = 0$$
$$[\![R^n(\theta_1,\ldots,\theta_n)]\!]^Z = R^n([\![\theta_1]\!]^Z,\ldots,[\![\theta_n]\!]^Z)$$
$$\text{where } R^n([\![\theta_1]\!]^Z,\ldots,[\![\theta_n]\!]^Z)(\omega) = R^n([\![\theta_1]\!]^Z(\omega),\ldots,[\![\theta_n]\!]^Z(\omega))$$
$$[\![h.ch?]\!]^Z = \mathcal{I}_{\{\omega\in\Omega|[\![h]\!]^Z(\omega).ch?\in Z(\omega)(rdy)\}}$$
$$[\![h.ch!]\!]^Z = \mathcal{I}_{\{\omega\in\Omega|[\![h]\!]^Z(\omega).ch!\in Z(\omega)(rdy)\}}$$
$$[\![\neg S]\!]^Z = 1 - [\![S]\!]^Z$$
$$[\![S_1 \vee S_2]\!]^Z = [\![S_1]\!]^Z + [\![S_2]\!]^Z - [\![S_1]\!]^Z * [\![S_2]\!]^Z$$

where given a set S, the characteristic function $\mathcal{I}_S$ is defined such that $\mathcal{I}_S(w) = 1$ if $w \in S$ and $\mathcal{I}_S(w) = 0$ otherwise. The semantics of formula φ is interpreted over a stochastic process and an initial random variable. More precisely, it's a function $[\![\varphi]\!] : ([0,+\infty) \times \Omega \to (Var \to Val)) \to (\Omega \to (Var \to Val)) \to (\Omega \to \{0,1\})$ that maps a stochastic process $\mathcal{H}$ with initial state Z to a boolean random variable $[\![\varphi]\!]^{\mathcal{H},Z}$. The definition is given below:

$$[\![\bot]\!]^{\mathcal{H},Z} = 0$$
$$[\![S \text{ at } T]\!]^{\mathcal{H},Z} = [\![S]\!]^{\mathcal{H}([\![T]\!]^Z)}$$
$$[\![\neg\varphi]\!]^{\mathcal{H},Z} = 1 - [\![\varphi]\!]^{\mathcal{H},Z}$$
$$[\![\varphi_1 \vee \varphi_2]\!]^{\mathcal{H},Z} = [\![\varphi_1]\!]^{\mathcal{H},Z} + [\![\varphi_2]\!]^{\mathcal{H},Z} - [\![\varphi_1]\!]^{\mathcal{H},Z} * [\![\varphi_2]\!]^{\mathcal{H},Z}$$
$$[\![\forall v.\varphi]\!]^{\mathcal{H},Z} = \inf\{[\![\varphi[b/v]]\!]^{\mathcal{H},Z} : b \in \mathbb{R}\}$$
$$[\![\forall t.\varphi]\!]^{\mathcal{H},Z} = \inf\{[\![\varphi[b/t]]\!]^{\mathcal{H},Z} : b \in \mathbb{R}^+\}$$

The semantics of probability formula $\mathcal{P}$ is defined by function $[\![\mathcal{P}]\!] : ([0,+\infty) \times \Omega \to (Var \to Val)) \to (\Omega \to (Var \to Val)) \to \{0,1\}$ that maps a stochastic process $\mathcal{H}$ with initial state Z to a boolean variable $[\![\mathcal{P}]\!]^{\mathcal{H},Z}$. Formally,

$$[\![P(\varphi) \bowtie p]\!]^{\mathcal{H},Z} = (P([\![\varphi]\!]^{\mathcal{H},Z} = 1) = P(\{\omega \in \Omega : [\![\varphi]\!]^{\mathcal{H},Z}(\omega) = 1\}) \bowtie p)$$

The semantics for $\neg$ and $\vee$ can be defined as usual.

We have proved that the terms and formulas of the assertion language are measurable, stated by the following theorem:

Theorem 2 (Measurability). *For any random variable Z and any stochastic process $\mathcal{H}$, the semantics of $[\![\theta]\!]^Z$, $[\![S]\!]^Z$ and $[\![\varphi]\!]^{\mathcal{H},Z}$ are random variables (i.e. measurable).*

Proof. The proof of this theorem can be found at [17].

5.2   Specifications

Based on the assertion language, the specification for a SHCSP process P is defined as a Hoare triple of the form $\{A; E\} P \{R; C\}$, where A, E, R, C are probability formulas. A and R are *precondition* and *postcondition*, which specify the initial state and the terminating state of P respectively. For both of them, the formulas φ occurring in them have the special form S at now, and we will write S for short. E is called an *assumption* of P, which expresses the timed occurrence of the dual of communication events provided by the environment. C is called a *commitment* of P, which expresses the timed occurrence of communication events, and the real-time properties of P.

Definition 1 (Validity). *We say a Hoare triple $\{A; E\} P \{R; C\}$ is valid, denoted by $\models \{A; E\} P \{R; C\}$, iff for any process Q, any initial states ρ_1 and ρ_2, if P terminates, i.e.$(P\|Q, \rho_1 \uplus \rho_2) \xrightarrow{\alpha^*} (\epsilon\|Q', \rho_1' \uplus \rho_2', \mathcal{H})$ then $[\![A]\!]^{\rho_1}$ and $[\![E]\!]^{\mathcal{H}, \rho_2}$ imply $[\![R]\!]^{\rho_1'}$ and $[\![C]\!]^{\mathcal{H}, \rho_1'}$, where $\mathcal{H}$ is the stochastic process of the evolution.*

6   Proof System

We present a proof system for reasoning about all valid Hoare triples for SHCSP processes. First we axiomatize SHCSP language by defining the axioms and inference rules for all the primitive and compound constructs, and then the general rules and axioms that are applicable to all processes.

Skip. The rule for skip is very simple. Indicated by $\top$, the skip process requires nothing from the environment for it to execute, and guarantees nothing during its execution.

$$\{A; \top\} \, \mathbf{skip} \, \{A; \top\}$$

Assignment. The assignment $x := e$ changes nothing but assigns x to e in the final state, taking no time to complete.

$$\{A[e/x]; \top\} \, x := e \, \{A; \top\}$$

Input. For input $ch?x$, we use logical variables o to denote the starting time, h the initial trace, and v the initial value of x respectively, in the precondition. The assumption indicates that the compatible output event is not ready during $[o, o_1)$, and at time o_1, it becomes ready. As a consequence of the assumption, during the whole interval $[o, o_1]$, the input event keeps waiting and ready, as indicated by the commitment. At time o_1, the communication occurs and terminates immediately. As indicated by the postcondition, x is assigned by some value v' received, the trace is augmented by the new pair $\langle ch.v', o_1 \rangle$, and now is increased to o_1. Assume A does not contain tr and o_1 is finite (and this assumption will be adopted for the rest of the paper). Let h' be $h[v/x, o/now] \cdot \langle ch.v', o_1 \rangle$, the rule is presented as follows:

$$\{A \wedge now = o \wedge tr = h \wedge x = v; \neg h.ch! \, \mathsf{dr} \, [o, o_1) \wedge h.ch! \, \mathsf{at} \, o_1\}ch?x$$
$$\{A[o/now] \wedge now = o_1 \wedge \exists v'.(x = v' \wedge tr = h'); h.ch? \, \mathsf{dr} \, [o, o_1]\}$$

A communication event is equivalent to a sequential composition of a wait statement and an assignment, both of which are deterministic. Thus, as shown above, the formulas related to traces and readiness hold with probability 1.

If such finite o_1 does not exist, i.e., the compatible output event will never become available. As a consequence, the input event will keep waiting forever, as shown by the following rule:

$$\{A \wedge now = o \wedge tr = h; \neg h.ch! \text{ dr } [o, \infty)\}ch?x$$
$$\{A[o/now] \wedge now = \infty; h.ch? \text{ dr } [o, \infty)\}$$

Output. Similarly, for output $ch!e$, we have one rule for the case when the compatible input event becomes ready in finite time. Thus the communication occurs successfully.

$$\{A \wedge now = o \wedge tr = h; \neg h.ch? \text{ dr } [o, o_1) \wedge h.ch? \text{ at } o_1\}ch!e$$
$$\{A[o/now] \wedge now = o_1 \wedge tr = h[o/now] \cdot \langle ch.e, o_1 \rangle, h.ch! \text{ dr } [o, o_1]\}$$

We also have another rule for the case when the compatible input event will never get ready.

$$\{A \wedge now = o \wedge tr = h; (\neg h.ch?) \text{ dr } [o, \infty)\} ch!e$$
$$\{A[o/now] \wedge now = \infty; h.ch! \text{ dr } [o, \infty)\}$$

Stochastic Differential Equation. Let f be a function, and $\lambda > 0, p \geq 0$ are real values. We have the following rule for $\langle ds = bdt + \sigma dW \& B \rangle$.

$$\frac{f(s) \in C^2(\mathbb{R}^n, \mathbb{R}) \text{ has compact support on } B, \lambda, p > 0 \text{ and}}{A \to B \to (f \leq \lambda p) \quad B \to (f \geq 0) \wedge (Lf \leq 0)}$$

$$\{A \wedge s = s_0 \wedge now = o; \top\}\langle ds = bdt + \sigma dW \& B\rangle\{P(f(s) \geq \lambda) \leq p \wedge A[s_0/s, o/now]$$
$$\wedge now = o + d \wedge cl(B); B \wedge P(f(s) \geq \lambda \text{ dr } [o, o + d]) \leq p\}$$

where o, s_0 are logical variables denoting the starting time and the initial value of s resp., d is the execution time of the SDE, and $cl(B)$ returns the closure of B, e.g. $cl(x < 2) = x \leq 2$; and the Lie derivative $Lf(s)$ is defined as $\sum_i b_i(s) \frac{\partial f}{\partial s_i}(s) +$

$\frac{1}{2}\sum_{i,j}(\sigma(s)\sigma(s)^T)_{i,j} \frac{\partial^2 f}{\partial s_i \partial s_j}(s)$. The rule states that, if the initial state of the SDE satisfies $f \leq \lambda p$, and in the domain B, f is always non-negative and Lf is non-positive, then during the whole evolution of the SDE, the probability of $f(s) \geq \lambda$ is less than or equal to p; on the other hand, during the evolution, the domain B holds almost surely, while at the end, the closure of B holds almost surely.

Sequential Composition. For $P; Q$, we use o to denote the starting time, and o_1 the termination time of P, if P terminates, which is also the starting time of Q. The first rule is for the case when P terminates.

$$\frac{\{A \wedge now = o; E\} P \{R_1 \wedge now = o_1; C_1\} \quad \{R_1 \wedge now = o_1; C_1\} Q \{R; C\}}{\{A; E\} P; Q \{R; C\}}$$

On the other hand, if P does not terminate, the effect of executing $P; Q$ is same to that of executing P itself.

$$\frac{\{A \wedge now = o; E\} P \{R \wedge now = \infty; C\}}{\{A \wedge now = o; E\} P; Q \{R \wedge now = \infty; C\}}$$

Conditional. There are two rules depending on whether B holds or not initially.

$$\frac{A \Rightarrow B \quad \{A; E\}\, P\, \{R; C\}}{\{A; E\}\, B \to P\, \{R; C\}} \quad \text{and} \quad \frac{A \Rightarrow \neg B}{\{A; \top\}\, B \to P\, \{A; \top\}}$$

Probabilistic Choice. The rule for $P \sqcup_p Q$ is defined as follows:

$$\frac{\{A \wedge now = o; E\}\, P\, \{P(S) \Join_1 p_1; P(\varphi) \Join_2 p_2\}}{\{A \wedge now = o; E\}\, Q\, \{P(S) \Join_1 q_1; P(\varphi) \Join_2 q_2\}}{\{A \wedge now = o; E\}\, P \sqcup_p Q\, \{P(S) \Join_1 pp_1 + (1-p)q_1; P(\varphi) \Join_2 pp_2 + (1-p)q_2\}}$$

where $\Join_1, \Join_2$ are two relational operators. The final postcondition indicates that, if after P executes S holds with probability $\Join_1 p_1$, and after Q executes S holds with probability $\Join_1 q_1$, then after $P \sqcup_p Q$ executes, S holds with probability $\Join_1 pp_1 + (1-p)q_1$; The history formula can be understood similarly.

Communication Interrupt. We define the rule for the special case $\langle ds = bdt + \sigma dW \& B \rangle \rhd (ch?x \to Q)$ for simplicity, which can be generalized to general case without any difficulty. We use o_F to denote the execution time of the SDE. The premise of the first rule indicates that the compatible event (i.e. $h.ch!$) is not ready after the continuous terminates. For this case, the effect of executing the whole process is thus equivalent to that of executing the SDE.

$$\frac{\{A \wedge now = o; E\}\langle ds = bdt + \sigma dW \& B \rangle\{R \wedge now = o + o_F; C\}}{A \wedge now = o \wedge E \Rightarrow (tr = h \wedge \neg h.ch!\ \mathrm{dr}\ [o, o + o_F])}{\{A \wedge now = o; E\}\ \langle ds = bdt + \sigma dW \& B \rangle \rhd (ch?x \to Q)\ \{R \wedge now = o + o_F; C\}}$$

In contrary, when the compatible event gets ready before the continuous terminates, the continuous will be interrupted by the communication, which is then followed by Q. Thus, as shown in the following rule, the effect of executing the whole process is equivalent to that of executing $ch?x; Q$, plus that of executing the SDE before the communication occurs, i.e. in the first o_1 time units.

$$\frac{\{A \wedge now = o; E\}\langle ds = bdt + \sigma dW \& B \rangle\{R \wedge now = o + o_F; C\}}{(A \wedge now = o \wedge E) \Rightarrow (tr = h \wedge h.ch!\ \mathrm{at}\ (o + o_1) \wedge o_1 \leq o_F)}{\{A \wedge B \wedge now = o; E\}\, ch?x; Q\, \{R_1; C_1\}}{\{A \wedge now = o; E\}\ \langle ds = bdt + \sigma dW \& B \rangle \rhd (ch?x \to Q)}{\{R_1; R\|_{[o,o+o_1)} \wedge C_1\}}$$

where $R\|_{[o,o+o_1]}$ extracts from R the formulas before $o + o_1$, e.g., $(P(S\ \mathrm{at}\ T) \Join p)\|_{[o,o+o_1]}$ is equal to $P(S\ \mathrm{at}\ T) \Join p$ if T is less or equal to $o + o_1$, and true otherwise.

Parallel Composition

For $P\|Q$, let X be $X_1 \cap X_2$ where $X_1 = \Sigma(P)$ and $X_2 = \Sigma(Q)$, then

$$\frac{A \Rightarrow A_1 \wedge A_2, \quad \{A_1 \wedge now = o; E_1\}\, P\, \{R_1 \wedge tr = \gamma_1 \wedge now = o_1; C_1\}}{\{A_2 \wedge now = o; E_2\}\, Q\, \{R_2 \wedge tr = \gamma_2 \wedge now = o_2; C_2\}}{\forall ch \in X.(C_1[o_1/now] \upharpoonright_{ch} \Rightarrow E_2 \upharpoonright_{ch}) \wedge (C_2[o_2/now] \upharpoonright_{ch} \Rightarrow E_1 \upharpoonright_{ch})}{\forall dh \in X_1 \setminus X.E \upharpoonright_{dh} \Rightarrow E_1 \upharpoonright_{dh} \quad \forall dh' \in X_2 \setminus X.E \upharpoonright_{dh'} \Rightarrow E_2 \upharpoonright_{dh'}}{\{A \wedge now = o; E\}\, P\|Q\, \{R; C_1' \wedge C_2'\}}$$

where A_1 is a property of P (i.e., it only contains variables of P), A_2 a property of Q, and o_1 and o_2, γ_1 and γ_2 logical variables representing the time and trace at termination of P and Q respectively. Let o_m be $\max\{o_1, o_2\}$, R, C_1' and C_2' are defined as follows:

$$R \overset{\text{def}}{=} R_1[\gamma_1/tr, o_1/now] \wedge R_2[\gamma_2/tr, o_2/now] \wedge now = o_m \wedge \gamma_1 \lceil x = \gamma_2 \lceil x \wedge tr = \gamma_1 \gamma_2$$
$$C_i' \overset{\text{def}}{=} C_i[o_i/now] \wedge R_i'[o_i/now] \text{ dr } [o_i, o_m) \text{ for } i = 1, 2$$

where for $i = 1, 2$, $R_i \Rightarrow R_i'$ but $tr \notin R_i'$. At termination of $P\|Q$, the time will be the maximum of o_1 and o_2, and the trace will be the alphabetized parallel of the traces of P and Q, i.e. γ_1, γ_2. In C_1' and C_2', we specify that none of variables of P and Q except for now and tr will change after their termination.

Repetition. For P^*, let k be an arbitrary non-negative integer, then $(tr \notin A)$

$$\frac{\{A \wedge now = o + k * t \wedge tr = (h \cdot \alpha^k); E[o/now]\} \; P}{\{A \wedge now = o + (k+1) * t \wedge tr = (h \cdot \alpha^{k+1}); C\}}$$
$$\frac{}{\{A \wedge now = o \wedge tr = h; E\} \; P^* \; \{A \wedge now = o' \wedge tr = (h \cdot \alpha^*) + \tau; C \vee (o = o' \text{ at } now)\}}$$

t and α are logical variables representing the time elapsed and trace accumulated respectively by each execution of P, and o and o' denote the starting and termination time of the loop (o' could be infinite).

The general rules that are applicable to all processes, such as Monotonicity, Case Analysis, and so on, are similar to the traditional Hoare Logic. We will not list them here for page limit.

Theorem 3 (Soundness). *If* $\vdash \{A; E\} P \{R; C\}$*, then* $\models \{A; E\} P \{R; C\}$*, i.e. every theorem of the proof system is valid.*

Proof. The proof of this theorem can be found at [17].

Example 1. For the aircraft example, define $f(x, y)$ as $|y|$, assume $f(x_s, y_0) = |y_0| \leq \lambda p$, where $p \in [0, 1]$. Obviously, $B \rightarrow (f \geq 0) \wedge (Lf \leq 0)$ holds. By applying the inference rule of SDE, we have the following result:

$$\{now = o; True\} P_{Air} \left\{ \begin{matrix} \exists d.now = o + d \wedge B \wedge P(f \geq \lambda) \leq p; \\ B \wedge P(f \geq \lambda \text{ dr } [o, o+d]) \leq p \end{matrix} \right\}$$

which shows that, the probability of the aircraft entering the dangerous state is always less than or equal to p during the flight. Thus, to guarantee the safety of the aircraft, p should be as little as possible. For instance, if the safety factor of the aircraft is required to be 99.98%, then p should be less than or equal to 0.0002, and in correspondence, $|y_0| \leq \frac{\lambda}{5000}$ should be satisfied.

7   Conclusion

This paper presents stochastic HCSP (SHCSP) for modelling hybrid systems with probability and stochasticity. SHCSP is expressive but complicated with interacting discrete, continuous and stochastic dynamics. We have defined the semantics of stochastic HCSP and proved that it is well-defined with respect to stochasticity. We propose an assertion language for specifying time-related and probability-related properties of SHCSP, and have proved the measurability of it. Based on the assertion language, we define a compositional Hoare Logic for specifying and verifying SHCSP processes. The logic is an extension of traditional Hoare Logic, and can be used to reason about how the probability of a property changes with respect to the execution of a process. To illustrate our approach, we model and verify a case study on a flight planing problem at the end.

References

1. Abate, A., Prandini, M., Lygeros, J., Sastry, S.: Probabilistic reachability and safety for controlled discrete time stochastic hybrid systems. Automatica **44**(11), 2724–2734 (2008)
2. Altman, E., Gaitsgory, V.: Asymptotic optimization of a nonlinear hybrid system governed by a Markov decision process. SIAM Journal of Control and Optimization **35**(6), 2070–2085 (1997)
3. Bujorianu, M.L.: Extended stochastic hybrid systems and their reachability problem. In: Alur, R., Pappas, G.J. (eds.) HSCC 2004. LNCS, vol. 2993, pp. 234–249. Springer, Heidelberg (2004)
4. Bujorianu, M.L., Lygeros, J.: Toward a general theory of stochastic hybrid systems. In: Blom, H.A.P., Lygeros, J. (eds.) Stochastic Hybrid Systems. LNCIS, vol. 337, pp. 3–30. Springer, Heidelberg (2006)
5. Bujorianu, M.L., Lygeros, J., Bujorianu, M.C.: Bisimulation for general stochastic hybrid systems. In: Morari, M., Thiele, L. (eds.) HSCC 2005. LNCS, vol. 3414, pp. 198–214. Springer, Heidelberg (2005)
6. Fränzle, M., Hahn, E.M., Hermanns, H., Wolovick, N., Zhang, L.: Measurability and safety verification for stochastic hybrid systems. In: HSCC 2011, pp. 43–52. ACM (2011)
7. Hahn, E.M., Hartmanns, A., Hermanns, H., Katoen, J.: A compositional modelling and analysis framework for stochastic hybrid systems. Formal Methods in System Design **43**(2), 191–232 (2013)
8. Hahn, E.M., Hermanns, H., Wachter, B., Zhang, L.: PASS: abstraction refinement for infinite probabilistic models. In: Esparza, J., Majumdar, R. (eds.) TACAS 2010. LNCS, vol. 6015, pp. 353–357. Springer, Heidelberg (2010)
9. He, J.: From CSP to hybrid systems. In: A Classical Mind, Essays in Honour of C.A.R. Hoare, pp. 171–189. Prentice Hall International (UK) Ltd. (1994)
10. Henzinger, T.A.: The theory of hybrid automata. In: LICS 1996, pp. 278–292, July 1996
11. Hoare, C.A.R.: An axiomatic basis for computer programming. Commun. ACM **12**(10), 576–580 (1969)
12. Hoare, C.A.R.: Communicating Sequential Processes. Prentice-Hall (1985)
13. Hu, J., Lygeros, J., Sastry, S.S.: Towards a theory of stochastic hybrid systems. In: Lynch, N.A., Krogh, B.H. (eds.) HSCC 2000. LNCS, vol. 1790, p. 160. Springer, Heidelberg (2000)
14. Liu, J., Lv, J., Quan, Z., Zhan, N., Zhao, H., Zhou, C., Zou, L.: A calculus for hybrid CSP. In: Ueda, K. (ed.) APLAS 2010. LNCS, vol. 6461, pp. 1–15. Springer, Heidelberg (2010)
15. Meseguer, J., Sharykin, R.: Specification and analysis of distributed object-based stochastic hybrid systems. In: Hespanha, J.P., Tiwari, A. (eds.) HSCC 2006. LNCS, vol. 3927, pp. 460–475. Springer, Heidelberg (2006)

16. Morgan, C., McIver, A., Seidel, K., Sanders, J.W.: Refinement-oriented probability for CSP. Formal Asp. Comput. **8**(6), 617–647 (1996)
17. Peng, Y., Wang, S., Zhan, N., Zhang, L.: Extending hybrid CSP with probability and stochasticity. Technical report, Institute of Software, Chinese Academy of Sciences (2015). http://arxiv.org/abs/1509.01660
18. Platzer, A.: Stochastic differential dynamic logic for stochastic hybrid programs. In: Bjørner, N., Sofronie-Stokkermans, V. (eds.) CADE 2011. LNCS, vol. 6803, pp. 446–460. Springer, Heidelberg (2011)
19. Prandini, M., Hu, J.: Application of reachability analysis for stochastic hybrid systems to aircraft conflict prediction. In: 47th IEEE Conference on Decision and Control (CDC), pp. 4036–4041. IEEE (2008)
20. Sproston, J.: Decidable model checking of probabilistic hybrid automata. In: Joseph, M. (ed.) FTRTFT 2000. LNCS, vol. 1926, p. 31. Springer, Heidelberg (2000)
21. Zhang, L., She, Z., Ratschan, S., Hermanns, H., Hahn, E.M.: Safety verification for probabilistic hybrid systems. In: Touili, T., Cook, B., Jackson, P. (eds.) CAV 2010. LNCS, vol. 6174, pp. 196–211. Springer, Heidelberg (2010)
22. Zhou, C., Wang, J., Ravn, A.P.: A formal description of hybrid systems. In: Alur, R., Sontag, E.D., Henzinger, T.A. (eds.) HS 1995. LNCS, vol. 1066. Springer, Heidelberg (1996)
23. Zuliani, P., Platzer, A., Clarke, E.M.: Bayesian statistical model checking with application to stateflow/simulink verification. Formal Methods in System Design **43**(2), 338–367 (2013)

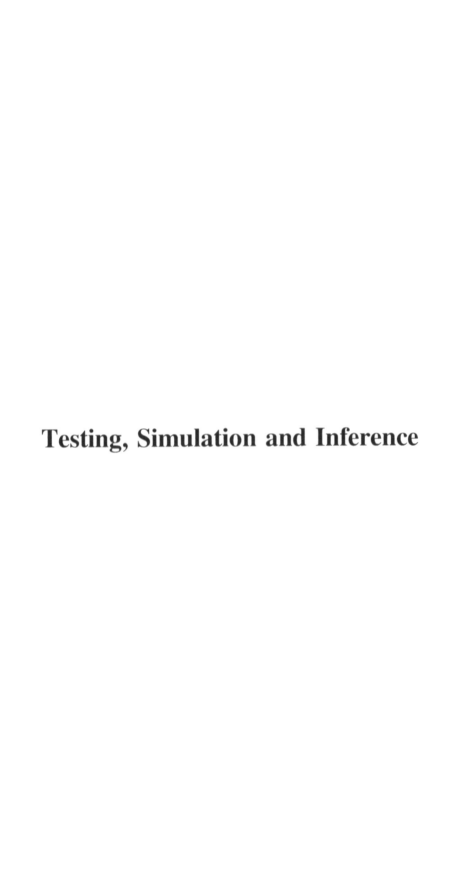

Testing, Simulation and Inference

Towards Verified Faithful Simulation

Vania Joloboff[1,2,3]($\boxtimes$), Jean-François Monin[4], and Xiaomu Shi[5]

[1] East China Normal University, Shanghai, China
vania.Joloboff@inria.fr
[2] INRIA, Sophia Antipolis, France
[3] LIAMA, Beijing, China
[4] Université de Grenoble - Verimag, Grenoble, France
[5] Tsinghua University, Beijing, China

Abstract. This paper presents an approach to construct a verified virtual protoyping framework of embedded software. The machine code executed on a simulated target architecture can be proven to provide the same results as the real hardware, and the proof is verified with a theorem prover. The method consists in proving each instruction of the instruction set independently, by proving that the execution of the C code simulating an instruction yields an identical result to that obtained by a formal executable model of the processor architecture. This formal model itself is obtained through an automated translation process from the architecture specifications. Each independent proof draws a number of lemmas from a generic lemma library and also uses the automation of inversion tactics in the theorem prover. The paper presents the proof of the ARM architecture version 6 Instruction Set Simulator of the SimSoC open source simulator, with all of the proofs being verified by the Coq proof assistant, using automated tactics to reduce manual proof development.

1 Introduction

In many embedded systems applications nowadays, virtual prototyping is used to design, develop and test new applications. Most of these virtual prototypes include an Instruction Set Simulator (ISS) to simulate the target processor. The ISS runs the target executable binary code in emulating the hardware and generate the outputs that the executable should produce when run on the target platform. An ISS can be used for example to optimize algorithms such as cryptographic software, or to debug new compiler developments, or in the design of many embedded systems applications. Instead of using real hardware prototypes, simulated platforms are more convenient and less expensive. Then, it is important to be sure that the simulator used is faithful to the hardware that it emulates. A *faithful ISS* must produce exactly the same results as the executable would if run on hardware implementation of the instruction set specification, and this guarantee must be proven.

The purpose of our work is to formally verify that the execution of a program on our Instruction Set Simulator for the target ARM architecture indeed

X. Li et al. (Eds.): SETTA 2015, LNCS 9409, pp. 105–119, 2015.
DOI: 10.1007/978-3-319-25942-0_7

produces the expected results, to be certain that the data output from the simulator, the final processor and memory states are indeed identical to the result obtained with the real hardware. This requires sequential steps, to prove first that the translation from the C code of the simulator to the simulation machine is correct, and second that the simulation of the target machine code is also correct, that is, it preserves the semantics of the computer architecture, together with the fact that all of these proofs are verified using a theorem prover, or proof checker, not subject to human error in the proof elaboration or verification.

The next sections of the paper are organized as follows. Section 2 reviews related work. Section 3 describes the tools that we have used, in particular the Compcert C compiler, a certified compiler for the C language, the Coq proof assistant, and the SimSoC simulator in which our work is integrated. Section 4 presents our contribution to prove the correctness of an ARM Instruction Set Simulator, integrated within SimSoC. In summary, the method consists in proving each instruction of the instruction set independently, by proving that the execution of the C code simulating an instruction yields identical result to that obtained by a formal executable model of the architecture. Each independent proof requires using a number of lemmas from a generic lemmas library and usage of a new inversion tactics in the theorem prover. Finally, our conclusion mentions lessons learned and directions for future work.

2 Related Work

Program certification has to be based on a formal model of the program under study. Such a formal model is itself derived from a formal semantics of the programming language. Axiomatic semantics and Hoare logic have been widely used for proving the correctness of programs. For imperative programming languages such as C, a possible approach is to consider tools based on axiomatic semantics, like Frama-C [5], a framework for a set of interoperable program analyzers for C. Most of the modules integrated inside rely on ACSL (ANSI/ISO C Specification Language), a specification language based on an axiomatic semantics for C.

Frama-C software leverages off from Why technology [3,7], a platform for deductive program verification, which is an implementation of Dijkstra's calculus of weakest preconditions. Why compiles annotated C code into an intermediate language. The result is given as input to the VC (Verification Conditions) generator, which produces formulas to be sent to both automatic provers or interactive provers like Coq.

In our case of verifying an instruction set implementation, we have to deal with a very large specification including complex features of the C language. A framework is required that is rich enough to make the specification manageable, using abstraction mechanisms for instance, and in which an accurate definition of C features is available. As we need to verify specific properties referring to a formal version of the ARM architecture, operational semantics offer a more concrete approach to program semantics as it is based on states. The behavior of a piece of program corresponds to a transition between abstract states.

This transition relation makes it possible to define the execution of programs by a mathematical computation *relation*. This approach is quite convenient for proving the correctness of compilers, using operational semantics for the source and target languages (and, possibly intermediate languages). Operational semantics are used in CompCert (described below) to define the execution of C programs, or more precisely programs in the subset of C considered by the CompCert project. The work presented in this paper is based on this approach. Interesting examples are given by Brian Campbell in the CerCo project [4], in order to show that the evaluation order constraints in C are lax and not uniform.

A very significant verification work has been done to prove the SEL4 operating system[11]. It is comparable to our work in that they have considered a C implementation. The main difference is that they have not considered operational semantics of C, but deduced the proof obligations from the C code, considering the compiler and the architecture as correct. In our work, we believe that the subset of C accepted by CompCert is even larger than the subset accepted in SEL4.

Regarding formalization and proofs related to an instruction set, a Java byte code verifier has been proved by Cornelia Pusch[15], the Power architecture semantics has been formally specified in [1], and closer to our work, the computer science laboratory in Cambridge University has used HOL4 to formalize the instruction set architecture of ARM [8]. The objective of their work was to verify an implementation of the ARM architecture with *logical gates*, whereas we consider a ARM architecture simulator coded in C. Reusing the work done at Cambridge in [8] was considered. But, because we need a certified C compiler and our approach is based on CompCert C, which is itself coded in Coq, it would have required us to translate all of the C operational semantics as well, which would have been error prone, not to mention the very large effort. It was more convenient to develop our formal model and our proofs in Coq.

Our work is based on the SimSoC simulation framework [10], available as open source software at http://gforge.inria.fr/projects/simsoc, described in the next section.

3   Background

3.1   Coq

Coq [2] is an interactive theorem prover, implemented in OCaml. It allows the expression of mathematical assertions, mechanically checks proofs of these assertions, helps to discover formal proofs, and may extract a certified program from the constructive proof of its formal specification. Coq can also be presented as a dependently typed λ-calculus (or functional language). For a detailed presentation, the reader can consult [6] or [2]. Coq proofs are typed functions and checking the correctness of a proof boils down to type-checking.

The logic supported by Coq includes arithmetic, therefore it is too rich to be decidable. As full automation is not possible for generating proofs, human interaction is essential. The latter is realized by *proof scripts*, which are sequences of commands for building a proof step by step. Coq also provides built-in *tactics* implementing various decision procedures for suitable fragments of the calculus of inductive constructions and a language which can be used for automating the search of proofs and shortening scripts.

When a proof has been interactively developed, Coq automatically verifies the proof, or possibly signals where errors are located. Our work has consisted in developing proofs demonstrating that the C functions simulating the behavior of the ARM processor indeed implement the ARM architecture semantics.

3.2   Compert-C

CompCert is a formally verified compiler for the C programming language provided by INRIA [12,13], which currently targets Power, ARM and 32-bit x86 architectures. The compiler is specified, programmed, and proved in Coq. It aims to be used for programming embedded systems requiring high reliability. The generated assembly code is proved to behave exactly the same as the input C program, according to a formally defined operational semantics of the language.

A key point is that we are considering here C programs compliant with the definition of ISO-C 99 standard of *correct C programs*. Indeed the ISO-C standard identifies many constructions that are syntactically correct, but have undefined semantics such as a[i++] = i;. The document identifies about one hundred such constructions, and says that a C compiler in that case basically may choose its own interpretation of the abstract syntax, resulting in *unspecified behavior*. This is very important in our work. All of the C code implementing the ISS is correct with respect to the ISO C standard, meaning that it does not contain any construction with unspecified behavior. Compcert-C does not accept such ill-defined expressions and only well formed programs can be translated according to the formal, unambiguous, semantics. All of the C code considered here has unique and well defined semantics. We need to prove that it implements the ARM semantics, but we do not need to worry about multiple interpretations.

Three parts of CompCert C are used in this work. The first is that we use the correct machine code generated by the C compiler. The second is the C language operational semantics in Coq from which we get a formal model of the program. Third, we use the CompCert Coq library for words, half-words, bytes etc., and bitwise operations to describe the instruction set model. These low level functions have been proven already in CompCert, so we can safely re-use them.

It must be noted that the C code of an ISS does not use functions from the C library that invoke the operating system, such as gettimeofday(), It uses a very limited number of functions from the C library such as memset() or memcpy(). CompCert provides the formalized properties of such built-in external functions, so we can reason formally on their potential side effects in our proofs.

3.3   SimSoC

There is abundant literature covering Instruction Set Simulation. Using *interpretive simulation*, such as used in Insulin [16], each instruction of the target program is fetched from memory, decoded, and executed. With *static transla-tion*, the target application program is decoded at compile time and translated into a new program for the simulation host. The simulation speed is vastly improved [18] , but it is not suitable for application programs that generate, or dynamically load code at run-time. Most ISS'es today use some kind of *dynamic binary translation*, initiated with systems such as Embra [17].

As mentioned above, the target ISS for the verification is integrated within SimSoC [10], a full system simulator of System-on-Chips, available as open source software. SimSoC takes as input real binary code and executes simulation models of the complete embedded system: processor, memory units, interconnect, and peripherals. The chip simulator also includes a network controller simulator, so that the simulator can communicate with the real world. Our proof assumes the existence of a correct decoder to dynamically generate the translation of the input binary into C structures, e.g. the program that takes the binary input sequence and translates it into a sequence of qualified instructions. It is out of scope of the proof.

SimSoC uses the SystemC kernel to simulate hardware parallellism and trans-action level modeling (TLM) to model communications between the modules. It includes ISS'es to execute embedded applications on various processors. We are considering here the ARM Version 6 ISS. SimSoC supports two modes of dynamic translation. In the first mode, our verification target, the binary decoder trans-lates each instruction into a C structure that has a *semantics function* [9]. It is these C semantic functions that we are verifying here.

4   Verified Simulation

The general objective is to obtain a verified simulator is illustrated in Figure 1. Considering the ARM architecture, we need to have the following:

- a formal model of the ARM instruction set.
- an instruction set simulator of the ARM arcchitecture coded in the (CompCert) C programming language.

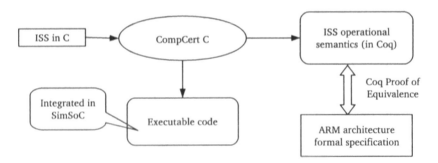

Fig. 1. Overall goal

- a formal operational semantics of the ISS. As shown in Figure 1, from the ISS source code in C, we can obtain through `CompCert` C on one hand the Coq formal semantics of the compiled C program constructed by `CompCert`, since the intermediate representation of the C compiler is a Coq representation and, on the other hand, the verified machine code, which conforms to this operational semantics as guaranteed by CompCert. We use both, the compiled machine code to run simulations, and the formal semantics for the proof.
- prove, using the Coq proof assistant, that the resulting ISS semantics indeed implement the formal model of the ARM processor, which boils down to verifying that the semantics of the simulator accurately modifies the processor (and memory) state representation at each step and ends up in results that comply with the formal model of the ARM architecture.

These steps are described in the following paragraphs.

4.1 Constructing the Formal Model

Ideally the formal specification of the ARM architecture should be provided by the vendor. But it is not the case, an issue already raised in the work with HOL4 mentioned above [8]. We decided to derive the formal model of ARM architecture in Coq from the architecture reference manual as output of a semi-automated process. The main relevant chapters of the manual are:

- `Programmer's Model` introduces the main features in ARMv6 architecture, the data types, registers, exceptions, etc;
- `The ARM Instruction Set` explains the instruction encoding in general and puts the instructions in categories;
- `ARM Instructions` lists all the ARM instructions in ARMv6 architecture in alphabetical order and the `ARM Addressing modes` section explains the five kinds of addressing modes.

There are 147 ARM instructions in the ARM V6 architecture. For each instruction, the manual provides its encoding table, its syntax, a piece of pseudo-code explaining its own operation, its exceptions, usage, and notes. Three kinds of information are extracted for each ARM operation: its binary encoding format, the corresponding assembly syntax, and the instruction semantics, which is an algorithm operating on the processor state. This algorithm may call basic functions defined elsewhere in the manual, for which we provide a Coq library defining their semantics. Other than these extracted data files, there is still useful information left in the document which cannot be automatically extracted, such as validity constraints information required by the decoder generator. However, the most tedious (then, arguably, error prone) part is described using fairly simple, precise and regular pseudo-code, allowing us to extract the Coq formal model in three automated steps: (i) extracting information from the .pdf file; (ii) parsing the data into abstract syntax trees (iii) automated translation from the abstract syntax into Coq formal model.

During this process, a dozen documentation problems were found but none that were relevant to instruction semantics. These documentation mistakes have been acknowledged by ARM Ltd. Moreover, a single mistake in our automated extractor would impact the formal model of many or even all instructions and then become rather easy to detect. The model has then tested on real programs to verify that we obtain the same results, which gives reasonable confidence in the model.

4.2   Proof Structure

The proof starts from an ISS coded in C, where each instruction is coded as a C function that modifies the processor state and possibly the memory state (but everything is represented in memory on the simulation host machine). Each C function may also call basic functions from a library. As mentioned above, this C code does not include any construction with "unspecified behavior" of the C language specification. To prove that the simulator is correct, we need to prove that, given the initial state of the system, the execution of an instruction as implemented by a C function results in the same state as the formal specification. To establish the proof, a formal model of that C implementation is provided by CompCert, which defines operational semantics of C formalized in Coq.

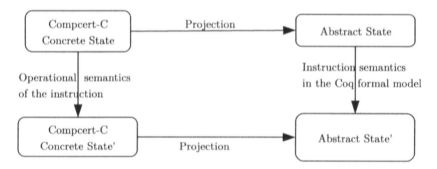

Fig. 2. Theorem statement for a given ARM instruction

The proof shall demonstrate that the operational semantics of the C code corresponds to the ARM formal specification. The complete proof is too lengthy for this article, and we only provide here an outline of the method. The state of the ARM V6 processor defined in the formal model is called the *abstract state*. Alternatively, the same state is represented by the data structures corresponding to C semantics that we shall call the *concrete state*. In order to establish correctness theorems we need to relate these two models. Executing the same instruction on the two sides produces a pair of new processor states which should be related as equivalent. Informally, executing the same instruction on a pair of equivalent states should produce a new pair of equivalent states, as schematized by Figure 2. Equivalent states are defined according to a suitable projection from the C concrete state to the abstract model, as represented in Figure 3.

This projection constructs a formal structure from the concrete one. The formal structure obtained should be identical to that obtained through the formal model, otherwise the C code is incorrect.

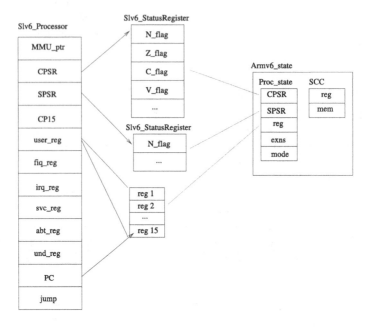

Fig. 3. Projection

4.3   Projection

In order to achieve a high speed simulation, the C ISS includes optimizations. In particular, processor state representation in the C implementation is complex, not only due to the inherent complexity of the C language memory model, but also because of optimization and design decisions targeting efficiency. Despite the complexity of the C memory model, the `CompCert` C semantics makes it possible to define and prove the projection. Fortunately, all of the instructions operate on the processor state and there is a single representation of that state in the simulator. It is necessary and sufficient to prove the projection for each variant case of the representation structure. For example, the projection of a register performs a case analysis on possible values, whereas the projection of saved data upon exceptions depends on the type of exception modes. Although there are a number of specific cases to handle, the proof of the projection is relatively straightforward. In more detail:

– The C implementation uses large embedded *struct*s to express the ARM processor state. Consequently the model of the state is a complex Coq record type, including not only data fields but also proofs to verify access permission, next block pointer, etc.

– Transitions are defined with a relational style (as opposed to a functional style where reasoning steps can be replaced by computations). Relational style is more flexible, especially when dealing with constraints; and fits well with operational semantics.
– The global state is based on a memory model with load and store functions that are used for read/write operations.

The proofs for instructions start from the abstract state described by the formal specification. To verify the projection of the original state, we need the following data: the initial memory state, the local environment, and the formal initial processor state. The projection is meaningful only after the C memory state is prepared for evaluating the current function body representing a ARM instruction. In the abstract Coq model, we directly use the processor state st. But on the C side, the memory state is described by the contents of several parameters, including the memory representation of the processor state. We also need to observe the modifications of certain memory blocks corresponding to local variables.

The semantics of CompCert C considers two environments. The global environment *genv* maps global function identifiers, global variables identifiers to their blocks in memory, and function pointers to a function definition body. The local environment *env* maps local variables of a function to their memory blocks reference. It maps each variable identifier to its location and its type, and its value is stored in the associated memory block. The value associated to a C variable or a parameter of a C function is obtained by applying load to the suitable reference block in memory. These two operations are performed when a function is called, building a local environment and an initialized memory state. When the program starts its execution, *genv* is built. The local environment *env* is built when the associated function starts to allocate its variables. Therefore, on the concrete side, a memory state and a local environment is prepared initially using two steps. First, from an empty local environment, all function parameters and local variables are allocated, resulting into some memory state and the local environment. Second, function parameters are set up using a dedicated function bind_parameters and the initial state is thus created.

4.4   Lemmas Library

Next, we need to consider the execution of the instruction. In the C ISS, there is a standalone C function for each ARM V6 instruction. Each function (instruction) has its own correctness proof. Each function is composed of its return type, arguments variables, local variables, and the function body. The function body is a sequence of statements including assignments and expressions. Let us consider as an example the ARM instruction BL (Branch and Link). The C code is:

```
void B(struct SLv6_Processor *proc,
       const bool L,
       const SLv6_Condition cond,
       const uint32_t signed_immed_24){
```

```
if (ConditionPassed(&proc->cpsr, cond)){
  if ((L == 1))
    set_reg(proc,14,address_of_next_instruction(proc));
    set_pc_raw(proc,reg(proc,15)+(SignExtend_30(signed_immed_24)<<2));
 }
}
```

CompCert has designed semantics for CompCert C in big-step inductive types for evaluating expressions, which we reuse for the proof. The semantics is defined as a relation between an initial expression and an output expression after evaluation. Then, the body of the function is executed. On the concrete side, the execution yields a new state **mfin**. On the abstract side, the new state is obtained by running the formal model. We have to verify that the projection from the concrete state **mfin** is related to this abstract state. The proof is performed in a top-down manner. It follows the definition of the instruction, analyzing the expression step by step. The function body is split into statements and then into expressions. When evaluating an expression, one has to search for two kinds of information. The first one is how the memory state changes on the concrete side; the other is whether the results on the abstract and the concrete model are related by the projection. To this end, a library of lemmas had to be developed, identifying five categories summarized below.

1. Evaluating a CompCert expression with no modification on the memory state
Such lemmas are concerned with the expression evaluation on CompCert C side and in particular the C memory state change issue. Asserting that a memory state is not modified has two aspects: one is that the memory contents are not modified; the other is that the memory access permission is not changed. For example, evaluating the boolean expression *Sbit* $==$ 1 returns an unchanged memory state.

$$\text{if } G, E \vdash \text{eval\_binop}_c \ (Sbit \ == \ 1), M \xrightarrow{\varepsilon} v, M'$$
$$\text{then } M = M'.$$

In Coq syntax, the relation in premise is expressed with eval_binop. In this lemma and the following, E is the local environment, G is the global environment, M is the memory state, ε is the empty event (we may have here a series of events, e.g. system call, volatile load/store) and v is the result. The evaluation is performed under environments G and E. Before evaluation, we are in memory state M. With no event occurring, we get the next memory state M'. According to the definition of eval_binop, an internal memory state will be introduced.

$$\frac{G, E \vdash a_1, M \Rightarrow M' \quad G, E \vdash a_2, M' \Rightarrow M''}{G, E \vdash (a_1 \ binop \ a_2), M \Rightarrow M''}$$

In the example, expression a_1 is the value of *Sbit* and a_2 is the constant value 1. By inverting the hypothesis of type eval_binop, we obtain several new hypotheses, including on the evaluation of the two subexpressions and the introduction of an intermediate memory state M''. Evaluating them has no change on the C memory state, hence we have $M = M'' = M'$. In more detail, from the `CompCert` C semantics definition, we know that the evaluation of an expression will change the memory state if the evaluation contains uses of `store_value_of_type`. In `CompCert`, the basic store function on memory is represented by an inductive type `assign_loc` instead of `store_value_of_type`. As a note, since `CompCert` version supports volatile memory access, we also have to determine whether the object type is volatile before storage.

2. Result of the evaluation of an expression with no modification on the memory
Continuing the example above, we now discuss the result of evaluating the binary operation *Sbit* $==$ 1 both in the abstract and the concrete model. At the end of evaluation, a boolean value *true* or *false* is returned in both the concrete and the abstract models.

> if Sbit_related M Sbit,
> and $G, E \vdash$ eval_rvalue_binop$_c$ (*Sbit* $==$ 1), $M \Rightarrow v, M'$
> then $v = (Sbit == 1)_{coq}$

Intuitively, the projection corresponding to the parameter `sbit` in the concrete model must yield the same value as in the abstract model. Here, the expression is a so-called "simple expression" that always terminates in a deterministic way, and preserves the memory state. To evaluate the value of simple expressions, `CompCert` provides two big-step relations `eval_simple_rvalue` and `eval_simple_lvalue` for evaluating respectively their left and right values. The rules have the following shape:

$$\frac{G, E \vdash a_1, M \Rightarrow v_1 \quad G, E \vdash a_2, M \Rightarrow v_2 \quad \text{sem\_binary\_operation}(op, v_1, v_2, M) = v}{G, E \vdash (a_1 \; op \; a_2), M \Rightarrow v}$$

In order to evaluate the binary expression $a_1 \; op \; a_2$, the sub-expressions a_1 and a_2 are first evaluated, and their respective results v_1 and v_2 are used to compute the final result v.

3. Memory state changed by storage operation or side effects
As mentioned before, evaluating some expressions such as `eval_assign` may modify the memory state. Lemmas are required to state that corresponding variables in the abstract and in the concrete model must evolve consistently. For example, considering an assignment on register Rn, the projection relation `register_related` is used. Expressions with side effects of modifying memory are very similar.

> if rn_related M rn
> and $G, E \vdash$ eval_assign$_c$ ($rn := rx$), $M \Rightarrow M', v$
> then rn_related M' rn

4. Internal function call.

The simulation code is sometimes using functions from libraries. We distinguish `internal` functions and `external` functions. An internal function is a function that belongs to a library, the code of which is part of the simulator, that we have coded ourselves, or the C code is provided by compcert C. An external function is a function for which we do not have access to the operational semantics. After an internal function is called, a new stack of blocks is typically allocated in memory. After the evaluation of the function, these blocks will be freed. Unfortunately, this may not bring the memory back to the previous state: the memory contents may stay the same, but pointers and memory organization may have changed.

$$\text{if } \texttt{proc\_state\_related } M \text{ } st$$
$$\text{and } \text{ } G, E \text{ } \vdash \texttt{eval\_funcall}_c(copy\_StatusRegister)_c, M \Rightarrow v, \text{ } M'$$
$$\text{and } \text{ } st' = (copy\_StatusRegister)_{coq} \text{ } st$$
$$\text{then } \texttt{proc\_state\_related } M' \text{ } st'.$$

Lemmas must be developed regarding the evaluation of internal functions, so that one can observe the returned results, compare it with the corresponding evaluation in the formal specification, and verify some conditions. For example, the lemma above is about the processor state after evaluating an internal function call `copy_StatusRegister`, which reads the value of the CPSR (Current Processor Status Register) and copies it into the SPSR (Saved Processor Status Register) when an exception occurs. The evaluation of `copy_StatusRegister` must be protected by a check on the current processor mode. If it is in authorized mode, the function `copy_StatusRegister` can be called. Otherwise, the result is "unpredictable", which is defined by ARM architecture

It is necessary to reason on the newly returned states, which should still be related by the projection. This step is usually easy to prove, by calculation on the two representations of the processor state to verify that they match.

5. External function call

The `CompCert` C AST of an external function call contains the types of input arguments and of the returned value, and an empty body. For each external function (e.g. `memcpy()`), we have its asserted properties. mostly provided by `CompCert` C. The general expected properties of an external call are that (i) the call returns a result, which has to be related to the abstract state, (ii) the arguments must comply with the signature. (iii) after the call, no memory blocks are invalidated, (iv) the call does not increase the access permission of any valid block, and finally that the memory state can be modified only when the access permission of the call is granted. For each external call, such required properties are verified.

4.5   Inversion

Equipped with these lemmas we can build the proof scripts for ARM instructions. For that, we are decomposing the ARM instruction execution step by step to perform the execution of the C programs. `CompCert` C operational semantics define large and complex inductive relations. Each constructor describes the memory state transformation of an expression, statement, or function. As soon as we want to discover the relation between memory states before and after evaluating the C code, we have to *invert* the hypotheses of operational semantics to follow the clue given by its definition, to verify the hypotheses relating concrete memory states according to the operational semantics.

An *inversion* is a kind of forward reasoning step that allows for users to extract all useful information contained in a hypothesis. It is an analysis over the given hypothesis according to its specific arguments, that removes absurd cases, introduces relevant premises in the environment and performs suitable substitutions in the whole goal. Most proof assistants provide an inversion mechanism. In the case of Coq, it is a general tactic called inversion [6].

Every instruction contains complex expressions, but each use of inversion will go one step only. If we want to find the relation between the memory states affected by these expressions, we have to invert many times. For illustration, let us consider the simple example from the ARM reference manual CPSR = SPSR, that assigns to register CPSR the value of SPSR (defined above). As the status register is not implemented by a single value, but a set of individual fields, the corresponding C code is a call to the function copy_StatusRegister, which sets the CPSR field by field with the values from SPSR. Lemma same_cp_SR below states that the C memory state of the simulator and the corresponding formal representation of ARM processor state evolve consistently during this assignment.

```
Lemma same_copy_SR :
  ∀ e m l b s t m' v em,
  proc_state_related m e (Ok tt (mk_semstate l b s)) →
    eval_expression (Genv.globalenv prog_adc) e m expr_cp_SR t m' v  →
    ∀ l b, proc_state_related m' e
                        (Ok tt (mk_semstate l b (Arm6_State.set_cpsr s
                                                 (Arm6_State.spsr s em))))
```

In its proof, 18 consecutive inversions are needed in order to exhaust all constructors occuring in the assumptions. Unfortunately, inversion generates uncontrolable names which pollute proof scripts. Here, an intensive use of inversion makes proofs scripts unmanageable, and not robust to version changes of Coq or CompCert. In order to reduce the script size and get better maintainability, we studied a general solution to the inversion problem, and developed a new mechanism described in [14]. On top of it, we could program a Coq tactic able to automatically find the hypothesis to invert by matching the targeted memory states, properly manage other hypotheses, perform our inversion, clean up the goal, and repeat the above steps until all transitions between the two targeted memory states are discovered.

As a result, proofs script have become much shorter and more manageable. Considering the former example of same_copy_SR, the 18 calls to standard inversion reduce into one single step: inv_eval_expr m m'.

4.6   Instruction Proofs

Proofs of instructions rely heavily on the library of lemmas and the controlable inversion mechanism described above. Scripts size vary with the instructions complexity from less than 200 lines (e.g 170 for LDRB) to over 1000 (1204 for ADC). As a result, for each ARM instruction, we have established a theorem proving that the C code simulating an ARM instruction is equivalent to the formal specification of the ARM processor.

5   Conclusion

Using the approach presented in this paper, we have constructed a tool chain that makes it possible to certify that the simulation of a binary executable program on some simulation platform is compliant with the formal model of the target hardware architecture. Using Compcert-C, that has defined formal C semantics, we have formally proved, using the Coq theorem prover, the ARM v6 Instruction Set Simulator of SimSoc.

We certainly acknowledge the limits of our approach: the quality of our "verified simulation" relies on the faithfulness of our formal model of the ARM processor to the real hardware. Because the vendor companies do not provide a formal description of their hardware, one has to build them[1]. This issue is partly solved in this work by automatically deriving the most tedious parts of the Coq formal model from pseudo-code extracted from the vendor reference manual. If the vendors would make public formal specifications of their architectures, then our toolchain would become fully verified.

We believe this work has further impact on proofs of programs. First, we have proved here a significantly large C program. Second, because the proved program is a hardware simulator, it can be used as a tool to prove execution of target programs. For example considering a cryptographic algorithm implemented for the ARM archiecture and compiled with Compcert-C, it could then be proved that the execution of that program provides the exact encryption required, and nothing else. Therefore, the tool presented is an enabler for the proofs of other programs, which offers a direction for future research.

Another consequence of this work is that, supposing one could compile the C instructions to silicon using a silicon compiler, and that compiler would also be certified, ala `CompCert`, it would then make it possible to prove real hardware...

References

1. Alglave, J., Fox, A., Ishtiaq, S., Myreen, M.O., Sarkar, S., Sewell, P., Nardelli, F.Z.: The semantics of power and ARM multiprocessor machine code. In: DAMP 2009, pp. 13–24. ACM, New York (2008)
2. Bertot, Y., Castéran, P.: Interactive Theorem Proving and Program Development. Coq'Art: The Calculus of Inductive Constructions. Springer (2004)

---

[1] Note that this problem is the same as for the work done by Cambridge University.

3. Bobot, F., Filliâtre, J., Marché, C., Paskevich, A.: Why3: Shepherd your herd of provers. Boogie **53–64**, 2011 (2011)
4. Campbell, B.: An executable semantics for CompCert C. In: Hawblitzel, C., Miller, D. (eds.) CPP 2012. LNCS, vol. 7679, pp. 60–75. Springer, Heidelberg (2012)
5. Canet, G., Cuoq, P., Monate, B.: A value analysis for C programs. In: SCAM 2009, pp. 123–124. IEEE (2009)
6. Coq Development Team. The Coq Reference Manual, Version 8.2. INRIA Rocquencourt, France (2008). http://coq.inria.fr/
7. Filliâtre, J.-C., Marché, C.: The why/krakatoa/caduceus platform for deductive program verification. In: Damm, W., Hermanns, H. (eds.) CAV 2007. LNCS, vol. 4590, pp. 173–177. Springer, Heidelberg (2007)
8. Fox, A., Myreen, M.O.: A trustworthy monadic formalization of the ARMv7 instruction set architecture. In: Kaufmann, M., Paulson, L.C. (eds.) ITP 2010. LNCS, vol. 6172, pp. 243–258. Springer, Heidelberg (2010)
9. Hao, H., Song, J., Helmstetter, C., Joloboff, V.: Generation of executable representation for processor simulation with dynamic translation. In: Proceedings of the International Conference on Computer Science and Software Engineering, Wuhan, China. IEEE (2008)
10. Helmstetter, C., Joloboff, V., Xiao, H.: SimSoC: a full system simulation software for embedded systems. In: IEEE (ed.) 2009 IEEE International Workshop on Opensource Software for Scientific Computation (OSSC), pp. 49–55, Sept 2009
11. Klein, G., Elphinstone, K., Heiser, G., Andronick, J., Cock, D., Derrin, P., Elkaduwe, D., Engelhardt, K., Kolanski, R., Norrish, M., Sewell, T., Tuch, H., Winwood, S.: sel4: Formal verification of an os kernel. In: Proceedings of the ACM SIGOPS 22Nd Symposium on Operating Systems Principles, SOSP 2009, pp. 207–220. ACM, New York (2009)
12. Leroy, X.: Formal verification of a realistic compiler. Communications of the ACM **52**(7), 107–115 (2009)
13. Leroy, X.: The CompCert C verified compiler. Documentation and user's manual. INRIA Paris-Rocquencourt, March 2012
14. Monin, J.-F., Shi, X.: Handcrafted inversions made operational on operational semantics. In: Blazy, S., Paulin-Mohring, C., Pichardie, D. (eds.) ITP 2013. LNCS, vol. 7998, pp. 338–353. Springer, Heidelberg (2013)
15. Pusch, C.: Proving the soundness of a java bytecode verifier specification in isabelle/HOL. In: Cleaveland, W.R. (ed.) TACAS 1999. LNCS, vol. 1579, p. 89. Springer, Heidelberg (1999)
16. Sutarwala, S., Paulin, P.G., Kumar, Y.: Insulin: An instruction set simulation environment. In: CHDL 1993: 11th IFIP WG10.2 International Conference, pp. 369–376. North-Holland, Amsterdam (1993)
17. Witchel, E., Rosenblum, M.: Embra: fast and flexible machine simulation. In: SIGMETRICS 1996, pp. 68–79. ACM, New York (1996)
18. Zhu, J., Gajski, D.D.: An ultra-fast instruction set simulator. IEEE Trans. Very Large Scale Integr. Syst. **10**(3), 363–373 (2002)

Cardinality of UDP Transmission Outcomes

Franz Weitl[1]([✉]), Nazim Sebih[3], Cyrille Artho[2], Masami Hagiya[3],
Yoshinori Tanabe[4], Yoriyuki Yamagata[2], and Mitsuharu Yamamoto[1]

[1] Chiba University, Chiba, Japan
`franz@chiba-u.jp, mituharu@math.s.chiba-u.ac.jp`
[2] AIST/RISEC, Amagasaki/tsukuba, Japan
`{yoriyuki.yamagata,c.artho}@aist.go.jp`
[3] The University of Tokyo, Tokyo, Japan
`n.sebih@gmail.com, hagiya@is.s.u-tokyo.ac.jp`
[4] Tsurumi University, Yokohama, Japan
`tanabe-y@tsurumi-u.ac.jp`

Abstract. This paper examines the cost of testing network applications
using the User Datagram Protocol (UDP). Such applications must deal
with packet loss, duplication, and reordering. Ideally, a UDP application should be tested against all possible outcomes of unreliable UDP
transmissions. Their number, however, grows at least exponentially in
the number of transmitted packets.

To estimate the cost of the exhaustive testing of UDP applications,
we determine the number of UDP transmission outcomes analytically.
Based on this combinatorial analysis, we derive a sound, complete, and
optimal algorithm for generating outcomes of unreliable UDP transmissions. The algorithm is implemented in the net-iocache extension of the
software model checker Java Pathfinder (JPF).

Experimental results confirm the consistency of the implementation
with the analytical results. In addition, we found that JPF's state matching reduces the explored state space significantly and ensures the practicability of the approach despite of its exponential complexity.

Keywords: User datagram protocol · Software model checking · Java
Pathfinder · Combinatorial analysis

1 Introduction

Modern software often involves both multi-threading and network communication. Testing such systems is complex due to non-determinism in thread scheduling and network behavior. When applying the User Datagram Protocol (UDP),
the application must be tested against non-deterministic outcomes of network
input/output (I/O) including packet loss, duplication, and reordering.

Despite of its unreliability, UDP is favorable over the Transmission Control
Protocol (TCP) for applications that require low latency and high throughput. These include real-time and multimedia applications such as gaming and

© Springer International Publishing Switzerland 2015
X. Li et al. (Eds.): SETTA 2015, LNCS 9409, pp. 120–134, 2015.
DOI: 10.1007/978-3-319-25942-0_8

media streaming [11,22], but also high performance computing [13], widely used application-level protocols such as DNS [17], DHCP [5], and the new protocol QUIC [21] for web applications. Studies [32] report on a significant and increasing portion of UDP traffic on the Internet.

Testing a distributed application against all possible outcomes of UDP I/O is challenging because of the explosion of cases when combining packet loss, duplication, and reordering. Network emulators [7,15,19,26] that use stochastic methods for the injection of such *packet perturbation*, avoid a combinatorial explosion but cannot guarantee the coverage of all combinations. Recent work [23,31] proposes the application of software model checking with Java Pathfinder (JPF) [29] for testing UDP applications *exhaustively* against possible outcomes of UDP I/O but it is unclear which problem sizes these exhaustive methods scale up to.

In this paper, we analyze the practical feasibility of model checking UDP applications. We describe unreliable UDP I/O in a formal model and analyze the number of possible outcomes for a sequence of n transmitted packets. The formal model and its analysis yield a sound, complete, and optimal algorithm of generating outcome sets which is a formal and generally applicable version of the algorithms presented in previous work [23]. In experiments, we determine its cost in terms of runtime and memory consumption and compare the number of generated cases with the analytically derived cardinality results. A major finding is that the runtime grows less than the analytical results suggest because JPF recognizes visited states and prunes the exploration of the state space.

These results encourage the application of software model checking for UDP applications despite of its exponential complexity. The availability of efficient formal methods promotes the use of UDP for a broader range of applications, including dependable systems. The contributions of this paper are:

Formal Analysis: We formalize the set of UDP transmission outcomes for n packets and analyze its cardinality. This is an indicator of the computational cost of exhaustively testing UDP applications.

General Algorithm: We derive a new generally applicable algorithm for generating outcome sets which is sound, complete, and optimal. In contrast to previous algorithms [23], it can be implemented independently from JPF.

Evaluation: In experiments, we compare the analytical results with the number of cases generated by the JPF extension net-iocache, and evaluate the impact JPF's state matching on the runtime.

This paper is structured as follows. We introduce relevant concepts of JPF and its extension net-iocache for networked systems in Section 2. Section 3 defines outcome sets of unreliable UDP transmissions and proves their cardinality while Section 4 presents algorithms for generating them. We report on experimental results in Section 5 and discuss related work in Section 6 before concluding the paper in Section 7.

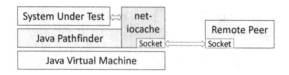

Fig. 1. Java Pathfinder and its extension net-iocache for network communication.

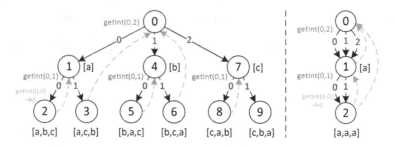

Fig. 2. State space exploration for input sequence a,b,c (left) and a,a,a (right) with JPF v8.0 rev 25; Dotted arrows: backtracking.

Table 1. Explored state space for different input sequences.

input	cases	branches	states	transitions
a,b,c	6	6	10	9
a,a,a	6	4	3	5

2   Background

Java Pathfinder (JPF) [10,29] is a custom Java Virtual Machine (JVM) written in Java. It runs on top of a host JVM (Fig. 1). The application verified by JPF is called the system under test (SUT). Net-iocache [3,14] extends JPF towards major parts of the java.net application programmig interface (API): It intercepts method calls of the SUT to classes such as java.net.DatagramSocket and forwards network I/O to the remote peers (Fig. 1 center). This way, instances of packet loss, duplication, or reordering can be injected transparently.

For non-deterministic operations such as thread scheduling or random number generation, JPF creates a *choice generator* and explores the rest of the SUT for each of the possible choices on a separate execution branch. JPF offers an application programming interface (API) for creating custom choice generators. Net-iocache uses this API for the exhaustive exploration of non-deterministic outcomes of UDP I/O [23]. E. g., permutations can be generated as follows:

```
1 List<Character> l=new ArrayList<Character>(Arrays.asList('a','b','c'));
  for(int i=0; i<perm.length; i++) {
    int max=l.size()-1;
    perm[i]=l.remove(Verify.getInt(0, max));
5 }
  System.out.print(Arrays.toString(perm)+" ");
```

The program stores the character sequence 'a','b','c' in a list l (line 1) and moves it to an array perm (lines 2–5). Verify.getInt(0,max) in line 4 creates a data choice generator with choices 0,1,...,max. When executing on a standard JVM, Verify.getInt returns a randomly chosen value in [0,max] and the program outputs a single permutation of a,b,c, for instance [c,a,b]. In contrast, when executing the same program on JPF, it outputs all permutations [a,b,c] [a,c,b] [b,a,c] [b,c,a] [c,a,b] [c,b,a]. This is because JPF executes the SUT for all possible return values of each call to Verify.getInt in a depth-first-search manner (Fig. 2 lhs). For the input sequence a,b,c, each alternative choice results in a new program state, numbered in the order of their first visit (0: initial state, 9: last visited state). When reaching one of the 6 terminal states {2, 3, 5, 6, 8, 9}, JPF backtracks the SUT to a previous state with open choices. Note that the result of Verify.getInt(0,0) is deterministic. JPF merges it into the same transition as the preceding invocation Verify.getInt(0,1) (Fig. 2 lhs bottom).

When the arguments of method Arrays.asList in line 1 are changed to "'a','a','a'", different return values of Verify.getInt lead to the same program state (Fig. 2 rhs). By default, JPF recognizes previously visited states by *state matching* and prunes the search as follows (dotted arrows indicate backtracking): $0 \rightarrow 1 \rightarrow 2 \dashrightarrow 1 \rightarrow 2$ (visited) $\dashrightarrow 0 \rightarrow 1$ (visited) $\dashrightarrow 0 \rightarrow 1$ (visited). Note that only 4 execution branches and 5 forward transitions are executed instead of 6 branches and 9 transitions in the scenario of Fig. 2 lhs. Table 1 summarizes the size and structure of the explored state space for each of the two input sequences a,b,c and a,a,a. Column 'cases' refers to the number of permutations of length 3, while 'branches' refers to the number of combined choices generated by calls of Verify.getInt. If state matching detects visited states, the number of explored 'branches' can be smaller than the number of 'cases'. State matching can be disabled in the JPF settings via property vm.storage.class to save memory. If enabled, it leads to a significant speed up in our experiments (Section 5).

3   Formal Analysis of Unreliable UDP Behavior

When a message consisting of a sequence of n packets is sent by UDP, *which messages* possibly arrive at the destination? *How many possibilities* are there, taking arbitrary combinations of packet loss, duplication and reordering into account?

Consider a message being fragmented into the three packets (p_1, p_2, p_3) put onto the network subsequently. Since each packet may get lost, duplicated, and/or reordered, the packet sequences, which possibly arrive at the destination, include

ϵ	empty sequence, all packets lost
(p_1, p_2, p_3)	normal delivery, no loss/duplication/reordering
(p_1, p_3, p_3)	p_2 lost, p_3 duplicated, no reordering
$(p_2, p_3, p_2, p_1, p_3)$	p_2, p_3 duplicated, reordered
...	

How many such messages are there? Let us assume first that packets are duplicated at most once and do not get reordered. Then there are three possibilities
for each individual packet: 1) loss, 2) delivery once, 3) delivery twice, resulting
in 3^n combinations for n packets, i.e., 27 in the given case of $n = 3$. This means
that even in scenarios without reordering, the number of transmission outcomes
grows already exponentially in the number of transmitted packets.

We will show that the number of transmission outcomes increases up to 271
for messages of 3 packets (Table 2), if cases of reordering are considered in
addition. Their number depends on the network capacity which is the maximum
number of packets the network can hold at a certain time. For instance, the
number of transmission outcomes for messages of 3 packets drops to 135 on a
network with a capacity of 2 packets and to 27 on a network with capacity 1
which does not permit any reordering (Table 2).

Why is it important to know the number of transmission outcomes precisely?
Obviously it is an indicator of the cost of testing a UDP application exhaustively.
More importantly, the cardinality analysis reveals the structure of outcome sets
and yields an algorithm for generating them which is sound, complete, and optimal by construction.

3.1   Unreliable UDP Transmissions

We denote the set of *natural numbers including 0* as $\mathbb{N}$. $\mathbb{N}_1 =_{\mathrm{def}} \mathbb{N} \setminus \{0\}$ denotes
the set of *positive* natural numbers; $[n, m] =_{\mathrm{def}} \{i \in \mathbb{N} : n \leq i \leq m\}$ denotes a
closed interval in $\mathbb{N}$; $\mathcal{P}(A) =_{\mathrm{def}} \{S : S \subseteq A\}$ denotes the *powerset* of set A; $A \uplus B$
denotes the *union of disjoint sets* A, B, i.e., $A \uplus B = A \cup B$ and $A \cap B = \emptyset$.

Definition 1 (Packet, Packet Sequence)

P denotes an infinite set of packets.

*P^n with $n \in \mathbb{N}$ denotes the set of packet sequences of length n. Elements of
P^n are denoted as $(p_1, ..., p_n)$. ϵ denotes the empty sequence for $n = 0$.*

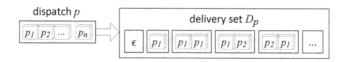

Fig. 3. Set of possible deliveries for a sequence of n dispatched packets $(p_1, ..., p_n)$.

In our model we fix a sequence of n unique packets $p \in P^n$, forwarded to the
network (*dispatch*), and define the possible UDP transmission outcomes of p as
delivery set (Fig. 3):

Definition 2 (Dispatch, Delivery, Dispatch Order)

Let $p \in P^n$ be a packet sequence of length $n \in \mathbb{N}$. Then

- *p is a* dispatch *iff $p_i = p_j$ implies $i = j$ for all $i, j \in [1, n]$.*

- $D_p =_{def} \bigcup_{m \in \mathbb{N}} \{p_i : i \in [1, n]\}^m$ denotes the set of deliveries *of dispatch p*.
- *The* dispatch order *is:* $p_i < p_j \Leftrightarrow_{def} i < j$ *for all* $i, j \in [1, n]$.

Each element of D_p is a sequence of packets of p with arbitrary order and number of instances: $(p_1, p_2, p_1) \in D_{(p_1, p_2)}$ and $\epsilon \in D_{(p_1, p_2)}$ but $(p_1, p_2, p_3) \notin D_{(p_1, p_2)}$ with $p_1, p_2, p_3 \in P$ being distinct packets.

The network has a limited capacity; it can hold at most c packets at a time. After a packet p_i is delivered, at most $c - 1$ *late* packets can be delivered that have been sent before p_i. This limits the delivery set for p as follows:

Definition 3 (Capacity-Bounded Deliveries)
Let D_p be the set of deliveries of a dispatch $p \in P^n$. Let $c \in \mathbb{N}_1$ be the maximum number of packets the network can hold at a given time.
For a delivery $q \in D_p$ with length m and $i \in [1, m - 1]$, let $L_{q,i} =_{def} \{q_j : j > i \land q_j < q_i\}$ denote the set of packets which are late in q w. r. t. q_i. Then

$$D_{p,c} =_{def} \{(q_1, ..., q_m) \in D_p : \forall i \in [1, m - 1]. |L_{(q_1,...,q_m),i}| < c\}$$

is the set of capacity-c-bounded deliveries *of p.*

As an example, consider the delivery $q = (p_2, p_3, p_1, p_3, p_2)$ of dispatch $p = (p_1, p_2, p_3)$. Then $L_{q,1} = \{p_1\}$, $L_{q,2} = \{p_1, p_2\}$, $L_{q,3} = \emptyset$, and $L_{q,4} = \{p_2\}$. Thus $q \in D_{p,c}$ if and only if $c > |L_{q,2}| = 2$. Note that $D_{p,c} = D_p$ if $c \geq n$. Furthermore, a network with capacity 1 does not permit reordering. For instance, $(p_1, p_1, p_2) \in D_{(p_1, p_2),1}$ but $(p_1, p_2, p_1) \notin D_{(p_1, p_2),1}$.

In the example above one may argue that a network capacity of 3 is still not sufficient for delivering $(p_2, p_3, p_1, p_3, p_2)$ because after the first delivery of p_3 there are three more packets delivered which must have been on the network at the time p_3 is delivered. Definition 3 is based on the assumption that a packet is not necessarily duplicated at dispatch time but at any time while it is on the network. The latest possible time is just the time of delivery. This most general assumption regarding duplication maximizes the cases of reordering permitted by a given network capacity in our model. For instance, a network with capacity 3 can generate the delivery $(p_2, p_3, p_1, p_3, p_2)$ as follows:

Event	Packets on the network	Delivered packets
p_1, p_2, p_3 dispatched	$\{p_1, p_2, p_3\}$	$()$
duplicate of p_2 delivered	$\{p_1, p_2, p_3\}$	(p_2)
duplicate of p_3 delivered	$\{p_1, p_2, p_3\}$	(p_2, p_3)
p_1 delivered	$\{p_2, p_3\}$	(p_2, p_3, p_1)
p_3 delivered	$\{p_2\}$	(p_2, p_3, p_1, p_3)
p_2 delivered	$\emptyset$	$(p_2, p_3, p_1, p_3, p_2)$

Delivery sets of non-empty dispatches are infinite because deliveries may contain arbitrarily many instances of dispatched packets. We identify finite subsets by constraining the number of times each dispatched packet may appear in a delivery, using a set of *multiplicity choices*:

Definition 4 (Multiplicity-Bounded Deliveries)

Let $M \subset \mathbb{N}$ be a non-empty, finite set of natural numbers, called multiplicity choices. Let D_p be the delivery set of dispatch $p \in P^n$. Then

$$D_{p,M} =_{\text{def}} \{(q_1, ..., q_m) \in D_p : \forall i \in [1, n]. \ |\{j \in [1, m] : q_j = p_i\}| \in M\}$$

is the set of multiplicity-M-bounded deliveries of p.

For instance, $\{1, 2\}$ is the set of multiplicity choices that permits each packet to be delivered once or twice. Hence $(p_1, p_2, p_1) \in D_{(p_1,p_2),\{1,2\}}$ but $(p_1, p_2, p_1, p_1) \notin D_{(p_1,p_2),\{1,2\}}$ and $(p_1, p_1) \notin D_{(p_1,p_2),\{1,2\}}$. In general, we consider the deliveries that are both multiplicity- and capacity-bounded:

Definition 5 (Multiplicity-and-Capacity-Bounded Deliveries)

Let $p \in P^n$ be a dispatch, $M \subset \mathbb{N}$ a non-empty, finite set of multiplicity choices, and $c \in \mathbb{N}_1$ a network capacity. Then

$$D_{p,M,c} =_{\text{def}} D_{p,M} \cap D_{p,c}$$

is the set of multiplicity-M-and-capacity-c-bounded deliveries of p.

3.2   Cardinality of Unreliable UDP Transmissions

We analyze the cardinality of the delivery set $D_{p,M,c}$ by splitting it into partitions whose cardinality can be determined easier. This partitioning also provides the formal ground for a sound, complete, and optimal algorithm for generating delivery sets (Section 4).

Delivery sets are partitioned along the two independent dimensions of variation: 1) the number of delivered instances of each dispatched packet, called *multiplicity vector* and 2) reordering as permitted by the network's capacity.

For instance, $(p_2, p_4, p_2, p_1, p_4)$ is a delivery of (p_1, p_2, p_3, p_4) with multiplicity vector $(1, 2, 0, 2)$, meaning that p_1 is delivered exactly once, p_2 and p_4 are delivered exactly twice, and p_3 is not delivered. Other instances with this multiplicity vector are obtained by reordering, e.g., $(p_1, p_2, p_2, p_4, p_4)$, $(p_1, p_2, p_4, p_2, p_4)$, ... For determining the number of such permutations with repetition, we can apply known results of combinatorics.

Formally, we divide $D_{p,M,c}$ into partitions using *multiplicity vectors* as follows:

Definition 6 (Multiplicity-Vector-Bounded Delivery Sets)

Let $p \in P^n$ be a dispatch. Then $\mu \in \mathbb{N}^n$ is a multiplicity vector for p and

$$D_{p,\mu} =_{\text{def}} \{(q_1, ..., q_m) \in D_p : \forall i \in [1, n]. \ |\{j \in [1, m] : q_j = p_i\}| = \mu_i\}$$

is the set of multiplicity-vector-μ-bounded deliveries of p.

For $c \in \mathbb{N}_1$, $D_{p,\mu,c} =_{\text{def}} D_{p,\mu} \cap D_{p,c}$ is the set of multiplicity-vector-μ-and-capacity-c-bounded deliveries of p.

A multiplicity vector μ defines for each individual packet p_i of a dispatch $p \in P^n$, how often it appears in a delivery of $D_{p,\mu}$. For instance, the multiplicity vector $(2,1)$ permits such deliveries of dispatch (p_1, p_2) where p_1 appears twice and p_2 once. Thus $(p_1, p_2, p_1) \in D_{(p_1,p_2),(2,1)}$ but $(p_2, p_1, p_2) \notin D_{(p_1,p_2),(2,1)}$.

Multiplicity vectors partition the set of multiplicity-M-and-capacity-c-bounded deliveries $D_{p,M,c}$ into pairwise disjoint sets. By Definitions 4 and 6, it holds for $\mu \in M^n$ and $\mu' \in M^n \setminus \{\mu\}$: $D_{p,\mu,c} \cap D_{p,\mu',c} = \emptyset$ and $\bigcup_{\mu \in M^n} D_{p,\mu,c} = D_{p,M,c}$. This gives the following Lemma:

Lemma 1 (Partitioning of Delivery Set)
For a dispatch $p \in P^n$, a non-empty, finite set of multiplicity choices $M \subset \mathbb{N}$, and a network capacity $c \in \mathbb{N}_1$ it holds:

$$D_{p,M,c} = \biguplus_{\mu \in M^n} D_{p,\mu,c} \tag{1}$$

$$|D_{p,M,c}| = \sum_{\mu \in M^n} |D_{p,\mu,c}| \tag{2}$$

Next we derive the cardinality of $D_{p,\mu,c}$, using the following operations:

Definition 7 (Vector Operations)
Let $p \in P^n$ be a dispatch, $c \in \mathbb{N}_1$ a network capacity, and $\mu \in \mathbb{N}^n$ a multiplicity vector. Then

- $|\mu| =_{def} |\{i \in [1,n] : \mu_i \neq 0\}|$ *denotes the number of packets that appear at least once in any delivery $q \in D_{p,\mu,c}$.*
- $\mathbf{u}_i$ *denotes the i-th unit vector in $\mathbb{N}^n$ for $i \in [1,n]$. I. e., with $x = \mathbf{u}_i$ it holds: $x_i = 1$ and $x_j = 0$ for all $j \in [1,n] \setminus \{i\}$.*
- $\mu - \mathbf{u}_i$ *denotes the vector subtraction of $\mathbf{u}_i$ from μ. I. e., with $x = \mu - \mathbf{u}_i$ it holds: $x_i = \mu_i - 1$ and $x_j = \mu_j$ for all $j \in [1,n] \setminus \{i\}$.*
- $F_{\mu,c} =_{def} \{i \in [1,n] : \mu_i > 0 \wedge |\{j \in [1,i] : \mu_j > 0\}| \leq c\}$ *denotes the first c indices where μ has a value greater than zero. These are the indices of the first c packets of a dispatch p which appear at least once in any delivery $q \in D_{p,\mu,c}$.*

Lemma 2 (Partitioning of Multiplicity-Vector-Bounded Deliveries)
For a dispatch $p \in P^n$, capacity $c \in \mathbb{N}_1$, and multiplicity vector $\mu \in \mathbb{N}^n$ it holds:

$$D_{p,\mu,c} = \begin{cases} \{\epsilon\} & \text{if } |\mu| = 0 \\ \biguplus_{i \in F_{\mu,c}} \{p_i\} \times D_{p,\mu - \mathbf{u}_i,c} & \text{if } |\mu| > 0 \end{cases} \tag{3}$$

Proof (Sketch)
$D_{p,\mu,c} = \{\epsilon\}$ for $|\mu| = 0$ follows directly from Definitions 2 and 6.

Assume $|\mu| > 0$. On a network with capacity c, the first packet q_1 of a delivery $q \in D_{p,\mu,c}$ of length $m \in \mathbb{N}$ is one of the first c packets of dispatch p which appear at least once in q, i. e., $q_1 = p_i$ for some $i \in F_{\mu,c}$. Packet p_i appears $\mu_i - 1$ times in the remaining delivery sequence $(q_2, ..., q_m)$ Thus the multiplicity vector of $(q_2, ..., q_m)$ is $\mu - \mathbf{u}_i$ and we get Equation (3) for $|\mu| > 0$. $\square$

Proposition 1 (Cardinality of Multiplicity-Vector-Bounded Deliveries)

For a dispatch $p \in P^n$, capacity $c \in \mathbb{N}_1$, and multiplicity vector $\mu \in \mathbb{N}^n$ with $|\mu| > 0$ it holds:

$$|D_{p,\mu,c}| = \sum_{i \in F_{\mu,c}} |D_{p,\mu-\mathbf{u}_i,c}| \qquad (4)$$

For $|\mu| \leq c$ it holds:

$$|D_{p,\mu,c}| = |D_{p,\mu}| = \frac{(\sum_{i=1}^{n} \mu_i)!}{\prod_{i=1}^{n} \mu_i!} \qquad (5)$$

Proof

Equation (4) is direct consequence of Lemma 2.

Equation (5) is shown as follows. For $|\mu| \leq c$ we get: $D_{p,\mu,c} = D_{p,\mu}$ since reordering is not limited by c if less than c packets are delivered.

$D_{p,\mu}$ is the set of permutations of n packets where each packet p_i with $i \in [1,n]$ appears μ_i times (multiset permutation [4]). Its cardinality is given by the multinomial coefficient $\binom{m}{\mu_1,\dots,\mu_n}$ with $m = \sum_{i=1}^{n} \mu_i$ [4,9]. We get:

$$|D_{p,\mu,c}| = |D_{p,\mu}| = \binom{\sum_{i=1}^{n} \mu_i}{\mu_1,\dots,\mu_n} = \frac{(\sum_{i=1}^{n} \mu_i)!}{\prod_{i=1}^{n} \mu_i!} \quad \square$$

Lemma 1 and Proposition 1 enable the calculation of $|D_{p,M,c}|$ with $p \in P^n$, by unfolding the recursive Equation (4) until $|\mu| \leq c$ and then applying Equation 5. Table 2 displays the numbers for $M = \{0,1,2\}$ (packet loss/normal delivery/duplication), $n \in [1,5]$, and $c \in [1,6]$.

Table 2. Cardinality of delivery sets $D_{p,\{0,1,2\},c}$ with $p \in P^n$, $n \in [1,5]$ and $c \in [1,6]$; Numbers in blue are referred in the beginning of Section 3 and in Section 5.

$n \backslash c$	1	2	3	4	5	6
1	3	3	3	3	3	3
2	9	19	19	19	19	19
3	27	135	271	271	271	271
4	81	955	3825	7365	7365	7365
5	243	6711	51331	176011	326011	326011

4 Generating UDP Transmission Outcomes

According to Lemmata 1 and 2, the delivery set $D_{p,M,c}$ for a given dispatch $p \in P^n$, a non-empty, finite set of multiplicity choices $M \subset \mathbb{N}$, and a network capacity $c \in \mathbb{N}_1$ is partitioned as

$$D_{p,M,c} = \biguplus_{\mu \in M^n} D_{p,\mu,c}$$

$$D_{p,\mu,c} = \begin{cases} \{\epsilon\} & \text{if } |\mu| = 0 \\ \biguplus_{i \in F_{\mu,c}} \{p_i\} \times D_{p,\mu-\mathbf{u}_i,c} & \text{if } |\mu| > 0 \end{cases}$$

Algorithm 1 is a direct operational reformulation of these equations. This ensures its soundness, completeness, and optimality in the sense that each element in $D_{p,M,c}$ is calculated exactly once.

Function delivery of Algorithm 2 returns an arbitrary element of the delivery set $D_{p,M,c}$. Function **chooseOneOf**, similar to JPF's `Verify.getInt` (see Section 2), performs a non-deterministic choice, returning an arbitrary element of a non-empty set. The combination of all non-deterministic choices in Algorithm 2 yields the delivery set $D_{p,M,c}$. Parameters M and c of function delivery are configuration settings chosen by the user according to the test goals for a given SUT [23, 24].

Function deliveries(p, M, c)
  $n \leftarrow$ arity(p);
  $D \leftarrow \emptyset$;
  for $\mu \in M^n$ **do**
   $D \leftarrow D \uplus$ delivsRec(p, μ, c);
  return D;

Function delivsRec(p, μ, c)
  if $|\mu| = 0$ **then**
   return $\{\epsilon\}$;
  $F \leftarrow$ getFirst(μ, c);
  $D \leftarrow \emptyset$;
  for $i \in F$ **do**
   $\mu' \leftarrow \mu$;
   $\mu'_i \leftarrow \mu'_i - 1$;
   $D' \leftarrow$ delivsRec(p, μ', c);
   $D \leftarrow D \uplus (\{p_i\} \times D')$;
  return D;

Function getFirst(μ, c)
  $F \leftarrow \emptyset$;
  $i \leftarrow 1$;
  while $i \leq$ arity(μ) $\wedge |F| < c$ **do**
   if $\mu_i > 0$ **then**
    $|F| \leftarrow |F| \uplus \{i\}$;
   $i \leftarrow i + 1$;
  return F;

Algorithm 1. Delivery set generation.

Function delivery(p, M, c)
  $n \leftarrow$ arity(p);
  for $i \in [1, n]$ **do**
   $\mu_i \leftarrow$ **chooseOneOf**(M);
  return delivRec(p, μ, c);

Function delivRec(p, μ, c)
  if $|\mu| = 0$ **then**
   return ϵ;
  $F \leftarrow$ getFirst(μ, c);
  $i \leftarrow$ **chooseOneOf**(F);
  $\mu' \leftarrow \mu$;
  $\mu'_i \leftarrow \mu'_i - 1$;
  $(q_1, ..., q_m) \leftarrow$ delivRec(p, μ', c);
  return $(p_i, q_1, ..., q_m)$;

Algorithm 2. Non-deterministic generation of a single delivery.

5 Experimental Results

We implemented an adapted version of Algorithm 2 in net-iocache [23]: It generates packet perturbation for *individually* sent and received packets rather than for packet *sequences*.

In a scenario inspired by the UDP-based file transfer protocols TFTP [27] and MFTP [20], we determine the number of cases generated by net-iocache and compare them with the analytical results on the cardinality of delivery sets (Proposition 1). In addition, we evaluate the impact of JPF's state matching (Section 2) on the performance. The source repository of net-iocache v2 [30] comprises this and other experiments.

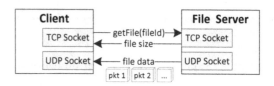

Fig. 4. Components of the file transfer application.

Fig. 4 shows the setting: A *client* connects to a TCP port of a *file server* for exchanging control information and listens on a UDP port for receiving files. The server adds a sequence number to each UDP packet, allowing the client to detect missing or duplicated packets, and to restore their original order. The server does not read files from the disk but synthesizes them on demand in such a way that each packet of each file is distinct. This maximizes the number of program states of the client (cf. scenario in Fig. 2). The client checks the validity of the received file content but does not store it to the file system. This avoids effects of file I/O on the runtime behavior. Dropped packets are not retransmitted to keep the number of packets sent by the server independent from the generated packet perturbation.

We analyze the runtime behavior of JPF when checking the client, receiving files with increasing number of packets (packet size: 512 bytes), for UDP transmissions with possible packet loss, duplication and reordering, according to multiplicity choices $M = \{0, 1, 2\}$ and capacity $c = 2$.

JPF does not detect any errors and thus explores the entire state space of the SUT. Both the client and file server were executed on the same 8 core Mac Pro workstation with 24 GB of memory running Ubuntu 14.04.2 LTS (64 Bit), Java RTE 1.8.0_45-b14, JPF v8.0 (rev 25), and net-iocache v2 (rev 76) [30].

Table 3 shows the runtime results when transferring one file with an increasing number of packets. Column 'cases' refers to the cardinality of the delivery set $D_{p,\{0,1,2\},2}$ (second data column of Table 2) while 'branches' refers to number of combined choices actually explored by JPF (cf. Section 2, especially Table 1). When state matching is disabled, the number of cases is identical with the number of branches JPF explores. This confirms the consistency of the implementation with the analytical results for the cardinality of delivery sets in Section 3.2. Enabled state matching, however, reduces the number of explored execution branches significantly and enables the exhaustive exploration of much larger problems than the analytical results suggest.

Table 3. File transfer client explored by JPF for **one** file with $n \in [1, 12]$ packets and delivery set $D_{p,\{0,1,2\},2}$, permitting packet loss, duplication, and reordering.

packets	cases	no state matching			state matching			speed-up factor
		branches	time[s]	mem[MB]	branches	time[s]	mem[MB]	
1	3	3	0.3	362	3	0.3	362	1.00
2	19	19	0.5	362	19	0.4	362	1.25
4	955	955	3.4	457	303	0.8	362	4.25
8	2,305,819	2,305,819	5437.3	1,782	17,383	11.4	1,021	476.96
16	$13.9 \cdot 10^{12}$	–	–	–	$12.2 \cdot 10^{6}$	6693.7	1,782	–

Equivalent states detected by JPF's state matching arise from the reaction of the SUT on packet duplication and reordering. Duplicated packets are discarded immediately [23] and do not lead to a new program state. Similarly, the compensation of packet reordering eventually leads to the same program state for all generated packet permutations. A similar speed up by state matching can be expected for applications such as multimedia streaming that cope with duplicated and reordered packets in this way.

6   Related Work

In previous work [23,24], we created a new version of net-iocache [30] for the exhaustive exploration of UDP transmission outcomes with JPF and conducted first experiments to confirm the feasibility and usefulness of the approach. This paper describes UDP transmissions and their enumeration formally and analyzes its cardinality. The proposed algorithm for generating the set of possible outcomes of unreliable UDP transmissions extends existing algorithms for enumerating permutations [12] towards a limited reorder window according to the assumed network capacity. The non-deterministic version of the algorithm can be considered as a variant of the Fisher-Yates shuffle algorithm [6,8] for generating random permutations, extended in two aspects: 1) Instead of choosing each element *exactly once*, each element (packet) is chosen a *number of times* according to the configured number of duplications; 2) Instead of choosing an *arbitrary* element from the set of not yet chosen elements, only one of the remaining *first c* elements (packets) is chosen in each iteration to account for the network capacity c.

Rathje and Richards [31] use JPF for exploring non-deterministic outcomes of UDP I/O. They apply a *centralization-* and stub-based approach: All communicating peers are transformed into a single multi-threaded program and network I/O is replaced by inter-thread communication using message queues. Packet loss and reordering is generated but packet duplication is not covered. The adopted approach is not entirely automatic: A small implementation effort is required for each individual SUT. Stoller and Liu [28] coined the term *centralization* for merging multiple processes into one. In their work, Java RMI method invocations are replaced by local method calls. This has been extended to TCP sockets [2,16]. A similar approach analyzes the complete state space of all processes by extending JPF itself [25] rather than pre-processing the SUT.

In contrast to centralization, net-iocache adopts a modular approach [3,14]: A single peer is selected as SUT and explored by JPF while the other peers run as remote processes outside of JPF. Net-iocache stores and replays network I/O in a cache to synchronize the backtracked SUT with the remote peers. The modular approach leads to smaller number of concurrent threads in the SUT, reducing the state space and increasing scalability. In general, however, only a part of the state space of the distributed system is covered. For an in-depth discussion of the differences between centralization and net-iocache, we refer the reader to previous work [14].

Instead of software model checking, stochastic methods have been applied for the testing of UDP applications: Farchi et al. [7] propose to instrument Java bytecode related to the UDP API to introduce a layer for creating "automatic noise" which subsumes delay, packet loss, duplication, and reordering. In their approach, each packet is randomly selected to be subject to noise with an equal probability. The network emulator netem [15] and its extensions [19,26] are Linux modules that inject stochastically packet delays, loss, duplication, reordering, and IP packet corruption to simulate non-deterministic unreliable UDP I/O. Stochastic methods are more scalable but cannot guarantee complete coverage.

The reordering of network packets has been described formally and the impact of re-sequencing on the *performance* of streaming applications has been evaluated [18]. Two metrics are considered: *reordering density*, defining the distribution of the displacement of packets from their original position, and *reordering buffer occupancy density* which is the degree of occupancy of a buffer used for re-sequencing out-of-order packets. To the best of our knowledge, the number of outcomes of unreliable UDP I/O has not been addressed in previous work.

Work on verifying programs with unreliable channels [1] shows that the *reachability problem* as well as *safety* and *eventuality* properties become decidable for communicating *infinite* state systems when lossy instead of lossless channels are used. In our work, we address the verification of *finite* state systems by exhaustively enumerating the outcomes of non-deterministic UDP I/O. The implementation of the proposed algorithm in the software model checker JPF enables the direct checking of Java programs without modeling effort, but it cannot be applied to models of infinite state systems.

7   Conclusion

Based on a formal model of UDP's unreliable transmission behavior, we analyzed the number of transmission outcomes and derived a sound, complete, and optimal algorithm for generating them. The algorithm is implemented in the JPF extension net-iocache. In experiments, the behavior of net-iocache is consistent with the analytical results: It generates the same number of cases as predicted by the formal analysis. We observed in addition, that JPF's state matching reduces the state space significantly which enables the exhaustive exploration of scenarios with trillions of cases.

Future work addresses the following issues: 1) By mapping multiplicity-and-capacity-bounded delivery sets onto known problems in combinatorics, it may be possible to derive a *non*-recursive precise formula and/or tight approximations of their cardinality. 2) Additional experiments would help to evaluate the effectiveness and scalability of the approach for a broader range of applications. 3) Since techniques such as state matching cannot solve the inherent combinational complexity of exhaustive techniques, the combination of software model checking with other, more scalable methods such as runtime verification, is an important issue of our future work.

Acknowledgments. This work was supported by JSPS KAKENHI Grants Number 23240003, 23300004, and 26280019. The authors thank Lei Ma for his helpful comments.

References

1. Abdulla, P.A., Jonsson, B.: Verifying programs with unreliable channels. Information and Computation **127**(2), 91–101 (1996)
2. Artho, C., Garoche, P.: Accurate centralization for applying model checking on networked applications. In: Proceedings of the 21st International Conference on Automated Software Engineering (ASE 2006). pp. 177–188. Tokyo, Japan (2006)
3. Artho, C., Leungwattanakit, W., Hagiya, M., Tanabe, Y.: Efficient model checking of networked applications. In: Paige, R.F., Meyer, B. (eds.) TOOLS EUROPE 2008. LNBIP, vol. 19, pp. 22–40. Springer, Heidelberg (2008)
4. Bona, M.: Combinatorics of Permutations. CRC Press, second edition edn. (2012)
5. Droms, R.: Dynamic host configuration protocol. IETF RFC 2131 (1997). http://www.ietf.org/rfc/rfc2131 Accessed: 13th Feb 2015
6. Durstenfeld, R.: Algorithm 235: Random permutation. Communications of the ACM 7(7), 420 (1964)
7. Farchi, E., Krasny, Y., Nir, Y.: Automatic simulation of network problems in UDP-based Java programs. In: Proceedings of the 18th International Parallel and Distributed Processing Symposium. IEEE (2004)
8. Fisher, R.A., Yates, F.: Statistical tables for biological, agricultural and medical research. Oliver & Boyd, London, 3rd edn, pp. 26–27 (1948)
9. Hall, M.: Combinatorial theory. Wiley (1986)
10. Havelund, K., Pressburger, T.: Model checking Java programs using Java PathFinder. International Journal on Software Tools for Technology Transfer **2**(4), 366–381 (2000)
11. Huitema, C.: Real time control protocol (RTCP) attribute in session description protocol (SDP). IETF RFC 3605 (2003). http://tools.ietf.org/html/rfc3605 Accessed: 13th Feb 2015
12. Ives, F.M.: Permutation enumeration: four new permutation algorithms. Communications of the ACM **19**(2), 68–72 (1976)
13. Junqueira, F., Reed, B.: ZooKeeper: Distributed Process Coordination. O'Reilly (2013)
14. Leungwattanakit, W., Artho, C., Hagiya, M., Tanabe, Y., Yamamoto, M., Takahashi, K.: Modular software model checking for distributed systems. IEEE Transactions on Software Engineering **40**(5), 483–501 (2014)
15. Linux Foundation: Network emulation with netem. www.linuxfoundation.org/collaborate/workgroups/networking/netem (accessed on October 7, 2014

16. Ma, L., Artho, C., Sato, H.: Analyzing distributed Java applications by automatic centralization. In: Proceedings of the 2nd IEEE Workshop on Tools in Process. IEEE, Kyoto, Japan (2013)
17. Mockapetris, P.: Domain names – implementation and specification. IETF RFC 1035 (1987). http://www.ietf.org/rfc/rfc1035 Accessed: 13th Feb 2015
18. Narasiodeyar R., J.A.: Improvement in packet-reordering with limited re-sequencing buffers: An analysis. In: 2013 IEEE 38th Conference on Local Computer Networks (LCN), pp. 453–457. IEEE (2013)
19. Reinecke, P., Drager, M., Wolter, K.: Netemcg – IP packet-loss injection using a continuous-time Gilbert model. Tech. Rep. TR-B-11-05, Freie Universitt Berlin, Germany (2011)
20. Robertson, K., Miller, K., White, M., Tweedly, A.: Starburst multicast file transfer protocol (MFTP) specification. IETF-DRAFT (1998). http://tools.ietf.org/html/draft-miller-mftp-spec-03 Accessed: 12th Feb 2015
21. Roskind, J.: QUIC: Multiplexed stream transport over UDP. Google working design document (2013)
22. Schulzrinne, H.: RTP: A transport protocol for real-time applications. IETF RFC 3550 (2003). http://tools.ietf.org/html/rfc3550 Accessed: 13th Feb 2015
23. Sebih, N., Weitl, F., Artho, C., Hagiya, M., Yamamoto, M., Tanabe, Y.: Software model checking of UDP-based distributed applications. In: Proceedings of the Second International Symposium on Computing and Networking (CANDAR 2014). pp. 96–105. IEEE, Shizuoka, Japan (2014)
24. Sebih, N., Weitl, F., Artho, C., Hagiya, M., Yamamoto, M., Tanabe, Y.: Software model checking of UDP-based distributed applications. International Journal of Networking and Computing (IJNC) 5(2), 373–402 (2015)
25. Shafiei, N., Mehlitz, P.C.: Extending JPF to verify distributed systems. ACM SIG-SOFT Software Engineering Notes 39(1), 1–5 (2014)
26. Sliwinski, J., Beben, A., Krawiec, P.: EmPath: tool to emulate packet transfer characteristics in IP network. In: Ricciato, F., Mellia, M., Biersack, E. (eds.) Proceedings of the Second International Workshop on Traffic Monitoring and Analysis (TMA 2010). LNCS, vol. 6003, pp. 46–58. Springer, Heidelberg (2010)
27. Sollins, K.: The TFTP protocol (revision 2). IETF RFC 1350 (1992). http://tools.ietf.org/html/rfc1350 Accessed: 1th May 2015
28. Stoller, S.D., Liu, Y.A.: Transformations for model checking distributed java programs. In: Dwyer, M.B. (ed.) Proceedings of the 8th International SPIN Workshop (SPIN 2001). LNCS, vol. 2057, p. 192. Springer, Heidelberg (2001)
29. Visser, W., Havelund, K., Brat, G., Park, S., Lerda, F.: Model checking programs. Automated Software Engineering Journal 10(2), 203–232 (2003)
30. Weitl, F., Sebih, N., Artho, C.: jpf-net-iocache v2 – source code repository. https://bitbucket.org/weitl/jpf-net-iocache Accessed: 15th Apr 2015
31. Rathje, W., Richards, B.: A framework for model checking UDP network programs with Java Pathfinder. In: HILT 2014 Proceedings of the 2014 ACM SIGAda Annual Conference on High Integrity Language Technology (2014)
32. Zhang, M., Dusi, M., John, W., Chen, C.: Analysis of UDP traffic usage on Internet backbone links. In: Ninth Annual International Symposium on Applications and the Internet (SAINT 2009), pp. 280–281. IEEE (2009)

Inferring Software Behavioral Models
with MapReduce

Chen Luo[1,2,3], Fei He[1,2,3]([✉]), and Carlo Ghezzi[4]

[1] Tsinghua National Laboratory for Information Science and Technology (TNList),
Beijing, China
luoc13@mails.tsinghua.edu.cn, hefei@tsinghua.edu.cn
[2] Key Laboratory for Information System Security, Ministry of Education,
Beijing, China
[3] School of Software, Tsinghua University, Beijing 100084, China
[4] Politecnico di Milano, Milano, Italy
carlo.ghezzi@polimi.it

Abstract. Software systems are often built without developing any explicit model and therefore research has been focusing on automatic inference of models by applying machine learning to execution logs. However, the logs generated by a real software system may be very large and the inference algorithm can exceed the capacity of a single computer.

This paper focuses on inference of *behavioral models* and explores to use of MapReduce to deal with large logs. The approach consists of two distributed algorithms that perform *trace slicing* and *model synthesis*. For each job, a distributed algorithm using MapReduce is developed. With the parallel data processing capacity of MapReduce, the problem of inferring behavioral models from large logs can be efficiently solved. The technique is implemented on top of Hadoop. Experiments on Amazon clusters show efficiency and scalability of our approach.

Keywords: Model inference · Parametric trace · Log analysis · MapReduce

1 Introduction

Software behavioral models play an important role in the whole life cycle of software systems. Through models, software engineers may gain a deep understanding of how a system behaves without dealing with the intricacies of the implementation. Although good software engineering practices suggest that models should be developed first and then used to derive an implementation, reality shows that often models do not exist, or they are inconsistent with the implementation. In fact, building a proper model is hard and requires both mathematical skills and ingenuity. Moreover, even if they are developed, they are often not kept in sync with changes to the implementation.

One promising approach to tackle this problem is to use machine learning to infer the software behavioral models automatically from execution logs [7,14].

© Springer International Publishing Switzerland 2015
X. Li et al. (Eds.): SETTA 2015, LNCS 9409, pp. 135–149, 2015.
DOI: 10.1007/978-3-319-25942-0_9

Many model inference algorithms [4,10,13] have been proposed by recent research. To infer accurate models, the logs should contain as much detail information as possible. However, a log with more information also increases the difficulty of model inference task. The logs generated by real systems are usually very large. For example, the production systems in Google generate billions of log events each day [18], which far exceeds the capacity of a single computer.

It is thus desirable to parallelize the processing of massive logs. In prior work [11], Lee et al. proposed an algorithm for slicing traces by parametric events. This algorithm is useful for log processing and model inference. However, one cannot parallelize this algorithm by simply dividing the trace into N segments and running N copies of the algorithm on these segments in parallel. Note that the events in different segments may be correlated and should be sliced together (Section 3). Processing the segments independently can lead to incorrect results.

To this end, we propose to use MapReduce [9] to deal with large logs in model inference tasks. Using the MapReduce model, we can effectively distribute the processing of massive logs to numerous computing nodes, meanwhile ensuring the related events are always processed together. With the powerful data processing capacity of MapReduce, the problem of inferring behavioral models from large logs can be efficiently solved.

In a nutshell, our approach consists of two stages: *trace slicing* and *model synthesis*. The first stage parses and slices the log into different trace slices, and constructs a prefix tree acceptor as the intermediate result. The second stage reads the prefix tree acceptor, and synthesizes the behavioral model. Both stages are realized under the MapReduce framework. We develop a distributed algorithm for the trace slicing and model synthesis, respectively. With these two algorithms, we propose a novel MapReduce framework for inferring software behavioral models.

The main contributions are summarized as follows:

- We propose a distributed trace slicing algorithm using MapReduce;
- We propose a distributed model synthesis algorithm using MapReduce;
- With these algorithms, we developed an inference method that, to the best of our knowledge, represents a novel attempt to use the MapReduce framework for inferring software behavioral models;
- We implemented a prototype of our technique. The experimental results show the promising performance of our approach.

The rest of the paper is organized as follows: Section 2 provides an overview of our approach. Section 3 introduces some formal definitions of this work. Section 4 and Section 5 introduce our distributed algorithms for trace slicing and model synthesis, respectively. Section 6 reports the experimental results. Section 7 discusses the related work and Section 8 concludes this paper.

2 Approach Overview

2.1 MapReduce

MapReduce [9] is a large-scale parallel data processing framework based on distributed architectures. It hides the details of data distribution, load balancing, and failure recovery while providing simple yet powerful interfaces to users. Hadoop [1] is an open-source implementation of MapReduce.

In MapReduce, the data is stored in a distributed file system (DFS) and the computation is based on key-value pairs. A MapReduce job consists of three phases, i.e., *map*, *shuffle* and *reduce*. In the *map* phase, the input data are partitioned and distributed to a number of mappers. At each mapper, a user-defined MAP function is invoked to handle the input data and produce intermediate results (in the form of key-value pairs). These intermediate results are then partitioned and sorted in the *shuffle* phase. Each partition corresponds to a reducer in the *reduce* phase. At each reducer, a user-defined REDUCE function is invoked to handle that partition. Note that the MapReduce framework ensures the values for the same key are passed to a single reduce call. The output of a reducer is written to the DFS.

When solving a problem on top of MapReduce, one major concern is to design the distributed algorithm with MAP and REDUCE functions. Once the algorithm is well encoded, one can leverage clusters and parallel computing to speed up the computation. The interested reader may refer to [12] for more information.

2.2 Behavioral Model Inference

The workflow of a typical behavioral model inference mainly consists of three steps: *log parsing*, *trace slicing*, and *model synthesis*. First, we rely on a parser to extract relevant events from the log files as defined in the *event specification*. The events are usually associated with some parameters, called *parametric events*. A parameter corresponds to an entity in the system. We say an *interaction* happens when two or more events with the same parameter are detected in the log file. After parsing, we get a sequence of parametric events, called a *parametric trace*. The parametric trace may contain many independent interactions, and thus cannot be directly used for model synthesis. A trace slicer then slices the parametric trace into many slices, each of which corresponds to an interaction scenario. Finally, a synthesis algorithm is called to infer the behavioral model from the set of trace slices.

Consider the online shopping system shown in Figure 1 as a running example. The relevant events and their corresponding parameters are as follows:

- the user *userid* *logins* in the system,
- the user *userid* *creates* an order with the ID of *orderid*,
- the item *itemid* is *added* to the order *orderid*,
- the item *itemid* is *removed* from the order *orderid*,

---

[1] http://hadoop.apache.org/

- the user *userid* *pays* the order *orderid*, and
- the user *userid* *cancels* the order *orderid*.

An example parametric trace excerpt for the system is shown in Figure 1a, and the behavioral model is depicted in Figure 1b.

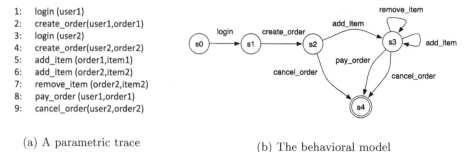

```
1:  login (user1)
2:  create_order(user1,order1)
3:  login (user2)
4:  create_order(user2,order2)
5:  add_item (order1,item1)
6:  add_item (order2,item2)
7:  remove_item (order2,item2)
8:  pay_order (user1,order1)
9:  cancel_order(user2,order2)
```

(a) A parametric trace   (b) The behavioral model

Fig. 1. An online shopping system example

2.3   Our Approach

To deal with the large logs generate by the software system, we propose to apply MapReduce to parallelize the model inference process. As shown in Figure 2, our approach consists of two stages, i.e., the distributed trace slicing stage and the distributed model synthesis stage, both of which are realized using MapReduce. The first stage takes as input a log file, performs the log parsing and trace slicing, and outputs a prefix tree acceptor (PTA) [13]. The log parsing task is performed by mappers, while the trace slicing task is executed by reducers. The second stage takes as input the PTA generated in the former stage, and infers the behavioral model by a distributed model synthesis algorithm. With the large-scale data processing capacity of MapReduce framework, the problem of inferring behavioral models from large log files can be efficiently solved.

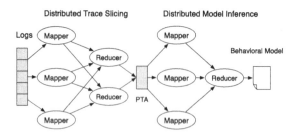

Fig. 2. Model inference with MapReduce

Although the basic algorithms for trace slicing [11] and model synthesis [7] exist, our contribution is to realize a novel MapReduce version of both algorithms and integrate them seamlessly.

3   Formal Definitions

This section introduces the formal definitions needed in our framework. Some of these definitions originate from [11].

Definition 1. *An* event specification *is a pair* $\langle \mathcal{E}, X \rangle$, *where* $\mathcal{E}$ *is a set of* base events, *and* X *is a set of* parameters.

An event specification specifies the events of interest and the parameters. The event specification for the running example is $\mathcal{E}=\{login, create\_order, add\_item, remove\_item, pay\_order, cancel\_order\}$, $X = \{userid, orderid, itemid\}$.

Let $[A \rightarrow B]$ (or $[A \rightharpoonup B]$) be the sets of total (or partial) functions from A to B. For any partial function $\theta \in [A \rightharpoonup B]$, $Dom(\theta) = \{x \in A \mid \theta(x) \text{ is defined}\}$. Let $\perp$ be the partial function for which $Dom(\perp) = \emptyset$.

Definition 2. *A* parameter instance θ *is a partial function from* X *to* V_X, *i.e.,* $\theta \in [X \rightharpoonup V_X]$, *where* V_X *is a set of parameter values for the parameter set* X. *A parameter instance* θ *is called* complete *if* $Dom(\theta) = X$. *Let* $Y \subseteq Dom(\theta)$, *a* restriction $\theta\restriction_Y$ *of* θ *to* Y *is a parameter instance such that* $Dom(\theta\restriction_Y) = Y$ *and for any* $y \in Y$, $\theta\restriction_Y (y) = \theta(y)$.

To simplify the notation, we often ignore the parameter names X and use the parameter values V_X to represent the parameter instance, if the mapping from X to V_X is clear from the context. For example, the parameter instance $\langle userid \mapsto user1, orderid \mapsto order1 \rangle$ can be simplified as $\langle user1, order1 \rangle$.

Definition 3. *The* parametric event definition $\mathcal{D}_e$ *is a function from* $\mathcal{E}$ *to* 2^X, *i.e.,* $\mathcal{D}_e \in [\mathcal{E} \rightarrow 2^X]$. *A* parametric event *is* $e\langle\theta\rangle$, *where* e *is a base event,* θ *is a parameter instance such that* $Dom(\theta) = \mathcal{D}_e(e)$.

A parametric event definition provides parameter information for each base event $e \in \mathcal{E}$, and we assume parameters for each base event to be fixed as in [11].

Definition 4. *A* trace *is a finite sequence of base events. A* parametric trace *is a finite sequence of parametric events. Denote* $e \in \tau$ *(or* $e\langle\theta\rangle \in \tau$*) if base event* e *(or parametric event* $e\langle\theta\rangle$*) appears in trace (or parametric trace)* τ.

Definition 5. *A parameter instance* θ' *is called* less informative *than another parameter instance* θ *(written* $\theta' \sqsubseteq \theta$*), if for any* $x \in X$, $\theta'(x)$ *is defined implies* $\theta(x)$ *is also defined and* $\theta'(x) = \theta(x)$.

For example, $\langle user1 \rangle$ is less informative than $\langle user1, order1 \rangle$.

Definition 6. *Let* τ *be a parametric trace and* θ *be a parameter instance, the* θ-trace slice $\tau\restriction_\theta$ *of* τ *is a (non-parametric) trace defined as:*

- $\epsilon\restriction_\theta = \epsilon$, *where* ϵ *is the empty trace, and*
- $(\tau e\langle\theta'\rangle)\restriction_\theta = \begin{cases} (\tau\restriction_\theta)e, & \text{if } \theta' \sqsubseteq \theta \\ \tau\restriction_\theta, & \text{otherwise} \end{cases}$

Intuitively, the θ-trace slice $\tau \upharpoonright_\theta$ first filters out the irrelevant parametric events to θ, then leaves out the parameter instances and only keeps the base events. For example, let τ_1 be the parametric trace in Figure 1a. For $\theta_1 = \langle user1, order1 \rangle$, $\tau_1 \upharpoonright_{\theta_1}$ is the sequence of: $login, create\_order, pay\_order$.

A trace slice corresponds to a parameter instance. However, all parameter instances appearing in τ_1 are incomplete. With the following operator, incomplete parameter instances can be combined to form a complete one.

Definition 7. *Two parameter instances θ and θ' are* compatible *if for any $x \in Dom(\theta) \cap Dom(\theta')$, $\theta(x) = \theta'(x)$. If θ and θ' are compatible, we define their* combination *(written $\theta \sqcup \theta'$) as:*

$$(\theta \sqcup \theta')(x) = \begin{cases} \theta(x) & \text{if } \theta(x) \text{ is defined} \\ \theta'(x) & \text{if } \theta'(x) \text{ is defined} \\ undefined & otherwise \end{cases}$$

For example, the parameter instances $\langle user1, order1 \rangle$ and $\langle order1, item1 \rangle$ are compatible, and their combination gives $\langle user1, order1, item1 \rangle$. However, the parameter instances $\langle user1 \rangle$ and $\langle user2, order2 \rangle$ are incompatible.

The combination of parameter instances may lead to meaningless results. For example, the parameter instance $\langle user1 \rangle$ and $\langle order2, item2 \rangle$ are compatible, but their combination $\langle user1, order2, item2 \rangle$ is meaningless since $user1$ and $order2$ do not interact in any event. To avoid such meaningless combinations, we require only *connected* parameter instances to be combined.

Definition 8. *Two parameter instances θ_1 and θ_2 are* strong compatible *(written $\theta_1 \bowtie \theta_2$), if θ_1 and θ_2 are compatible, and $Dom(\theta_1) \cap Dom(\theta_2) \neq \emptyset$.*

Definition 9. *Given a parametric trace τ and a parameter instance θ, we say θ is τ-connected (or connected if τ is clear from the context), if*

- $e\langle\theta\rangle \in \tau$, or
- *there exist θ_1, θ_2 such that both θ_1 and θ_2 are τ-connected, $\theta_1 \bowtie \theta_2$, and $\theta = \theta_1 \sqcup \theta_2$.*

Considering the running example. The parameter instances $\langle user1, order1 \rangle$ and $\langle order1, item1 \rangle$ satisfy the first condition in above definition, and $\langle user1, order1 \rangle \sqcup \langle order1, item1 \rangle = \langle user1, order1, item1 \rangle$, thus the parameter instance $\langle user1, order1, item1 \rangle$ is connected. In the remainder of this paper, we only consider trace slices for complete and connected parameter instances to avoid meaningless results as in [11].

4   Distributed Trace Slicing with MapReduce

This section presents our distributed trace slicing algorithm with MapReduce. The basic idea is to group all related parameter events and send then to the same reducer to generate correct trace slices. In the following, we first propose a data encoding mechanism, and then introduce the mapper and reducer functions.

4.1   Data Encoding

In MapReduce, the transmitted data between mappers and reducers are organized as key-value pairs. The transmitted data for our problem are basically
parametric events. We thus need a mechanism to set a *key* for each parametric
event to distribute them to reducers.

The basic idea is to watch a subset of X, and for each parametric event $e\langle\theta\rangle$,
we report the watched value on θ as its key, which is used by MapReduce to
determine to which reducer the parameter event should be passed.

Definition 10. *A* parameter window $\mathcal{X}$ *is a subset of* X, *such that for all* $e \in \mathcal{E}$,
either $\mathcal{X} \subseteq \mathcal{D}_e(e)$ *or* $\mathcal{X} \cap \mathcal{D}_e(e) = \emptyset$. *A parameter window* $\mathcal{X}$ *is nontrivial if*
$\mathcal{X} \neq \emptyset$.

Note that any singleton parameter set is always a well-formed and nontrivial parameter window. Consider the running example, a nontrivial parameter
window can be $\mathcal{X} = \{orderid\}$.

Definition 11. *The* key *of a parametric event* $e\langle\theta\rangle$ *(written* $key(e\langle\theta\rangle)$*) with
respect to the parameter window* $\mathcal{X}$ *is*

- *the restriction of* θ *to* $\mathcal{X}$, *i.e.*, $\theta\lceil_\mathcal{X}$, *if* $\mathcal{X} \subseteq \mathcal{D}_e(e)$, *or*
- $\perp$, *if* $\mathcal{X} \cap \mathcal{D}_e(e) = \emptyset$.

For example, with the parameter window $\mathcal{X} = \{orderid\}$, the key of the first
parametric event $login\langle user1\rangle$ in Figure 1a is $\perp$. And the keys of the remaining
parametric events in Figure 1a are: $\langle order1\rangle$, $\perp$, $\langle order2\rangle$, $\langle order1\rangle$, $\langle order2\rangle$,
$\langle order2\rangle$, $\langle order1\rangle$ and $\langle order2\rangle$, respectively.

With a parameter window $\mathcal{X}$, we divide all parametric events into two disjoint
sets: $T_1 = \{e\langle\theta\rangle | \mathcal{X} \subseteq \mathcal{D}_e(e)\}$ and $T_2 = \{e\langle\theta\rangle | \mathcal{X} \cap \mathcal{D}_e(e) = \emptyset\}$. Continue the
previous example, the parametric events labeled 2, 4, 5, 6, 7, 8 and 9 belong to
T_1, and the parametric events labeled 1 and 3 belong to T_2.

Lemma 1. *Let* $e_1\langle\theta_1\rangle$ *and* $e_2\langle\theta_2\rangle$ *be two parametric events in* T_1, *if*
$key(e_1\langle\theta_1\rangle) \neq key(e_2\langle\theta_2\rangle)$, *then* $e_1\langle\theta_1\rangle$ *and* $e_2\langle\theta_2\rangle$ *must be incompatible.* [2]

Let $hash()$ be a hash function that takes a key as input and returns the
ID of a reducer. For a parametric event $e_1\langle\theta_1\rangle \in T_1$, let $k_1 = key(e_1\langle\theta_1\rangle)$,
we pass the key-value pair $(k_1, e_1\langle\theta_1\rangle)$ to the reducer with the ID of $hash(k_1)$.
However, parametric events in T_2 may be combined with any parametric events
in T_1. Thus, for any parametric event $e_2\langle\theta_2\rangle \in T_2$, we pass the key-value pair
$(\perp, e_2\langle\theta_2\rangle)$ to all reducers.

We now discuss how to choose $\mathcal{X}$ automatically. Since the parametric events
in T_2 need to be passed to all reducers, $\mathcal{X}$ should be chosen such that T_2 is as
small as possible. However, the optimal $\mathcal{X}$ cannot be determined unless we have
processed the entire log. To handle this, we define non-parametric version of T_2
as $\hat{T}_2 = \{e | \mathcal{X} \cap \mathcal{D}_e(e) = \emptyset\}$, and relax the criteria as follows.

---

[2] Due to space limitation, all proofs can be found in the extended version [15].

Heuristic 1. *The set $\mathcal{X}$ should be chosen such that $\hat{T}_2$ is as small as possible.*

This heuristic is an approximation, since minimizing $\hat{T}_2$ does not necessarily mean that T_2 is minimized. However, one advantage is that $\hat{T}_2$ can be computed with the event definition, which is known a priori. Thus, the parameter window $\mathcal{X}$ can be decided before MapReduce computations.

Moreover, for parametric events in T_1, we want them to be distributed evenly to reducers, i.e., we want keys in T_1 to be as many as possible. Notice that the number of different keys is influenced by $|\mathcal{X}|$, we thus have another heuristic.

Heuristic 2. *The set $\mathcal{X}$ should be as large as possible.*

With above heuristics, the parameter window $\mathcal{X}$ can be decided with a brute-force search as follows. We first find all non-trivial parameter windows according to Definition 10, then apply the first heuristic to maximize $\hat{T}_2$. If there is more than one candidate $\mathcal{X}$, we then apply the second heuristic to select the one with the largest size.

4.2   Mapper

The log is split (implicitly by the MapReduce) into blocks, each of which is passed to a mapper. We call each line in the log a *log entry*. A log entry records a parametric event, and the time when it happens. In the remainder of the paper, we assume each event to be associated with a *timestamp*. However, for simplicity, we will consider them only when we need to sort the parametric events.

Figure 3 shows the pseudocode of the MAP function, which takes as input a log entry and outputs a key-value pair. Note that the parameter window $\mathcal{X}$ is provided a priori to all mappers. For each log entry, the PARSE function is called (line 2) to get the parametric event $e\langle\theta\rangle$. If the event is not in $\mathcal{E}$, the PARSE function returns NULL and this log entry is simply skipped (line 4). Otherwise, the mapper outputs a key-value pair (lines 5-8) based on Definition 11.

Consider the example trace in Figure 1a. Suppose there are two mappers and two reducers respectively. We assume each key-value pair output by the mappers is with the same label as the parametric event. Let $hash(\langle order1\rangle) = 1$ and $hash(\langle order2\rangle) = 2$. Then the key-value pairs labeled 1, 2, 3, 5, 8 are passed to $Reducer_1$; the key-value pairs labeled 1, 3, 4, 6, 7, 9 are passed to $Reducer_2$.

4.3   Reducer

Recall that during the shuffle phase, MapReduce merges and sorts key-value pairs to ensure that values corresponding to the same key are passed to a single reduce call. Denote $values[]$ the list of parametric events with the key of key. The REDUCE function is called for each pair of key and $values[]$.

The REDUCE function is shown in Figure 3. Note that all parametric events in $values[]$ are with the same key, but their parameter instances may be different. The RESTORE function first reorganizes $values[]$ into several lists (lines 3-6), each list $\Delta_{tmp}(\theta)$ corresponds to a parameter instance θ, and consists of base events

```
1: function MAP(line)
2:    e⟨θ⟩ ← PARSE(line);
3:    if e⟨θ⟩ = NULL then
4:        return ;
5:    if X ⊆ D_e(e) then
6:        OUTPUT(θ↾_X, e⟨θ⟩);
7:    else
8:        OUTPUT(⊥, e⟨θ⟩);
```

```
1: function REDUCE(key, values[])
2:    if key = ⊥ then
3:        Δ_⊥ ←RESTORE(values[]);
4:        return ;
5:    Δ ←RESTORE(values[]);
6:    while ∃θ_1 ∈ Dom(Δ_⊥), θ_2 ∈ Dom(Δ)
7: s.t. θ_1 ∉ Dom(Δ) ∧ θ_1 ⋈ θ_2 do
8:        Δ(θ_1) ← Δ_⊥(θ_1);
9:    CONSTRUCT(Δ);
```

```
1: function RESTORE(values[])
2:    Δ_tmp ← ∅;
3:    for e⟨θ⟩ ∈ values[] do
4:        if θ ∉ Dom(Δ_tmp) then
5:            Initialize Δ_tmp(θ);
6:        Insert e into Δ_tmp(θ);
7:    return Δ_tmp;
```

```
1: function CONSTRUCT(Δ)
2:    Ω ← Dom(Δ);
3:    while ∃θ_1, θ_2 ∈ Ω
4: s.t. θ_1 ⋈ θ_2, (θ_1 ⊔ θ_2 ∉ Ω)  do
5:        Ω ← Ω ∪ {θ_1 ⊔ θ_2};
6:    for complete θ ∈ Ω do
7:        Γ ← {Δ(θ')|θ' ⊑ θ, θ' ∈ Dom(Δ)};
8:        τ↾_θ← merging event lists in Γ;
9:        Update PTA using τ↾_θ;
```

Fig. 3. Distributed trace slicing

only. Here we abuse the notion of $Dom(Δ)$, which denotes the set of parameter instances $θ$ where the list $Δ(θ)$ is defined, i.e., $Dom(Δ) = \{θ|Δ(θ)$ is defined$\}$. Recall that each event is associated with a *timestamp*. At line 6, the base event e is inserted to a proper position in $Δ_{tmp}(θ)$ such that $Δ_{tmp}(θ)$ is in ascending order of *timestamp*.

Note that $Δ_⊥$ is global and shared by multiple calls of the REDUCE function. And the MapReduce framework is configured such that key-value pairs in T_2 always come before pairs in T_1. As a result, when the REDUCE function proceeds to line 5, $Δ_⊥$ must have already been initialized.

The while loop at line 6 tries to retrieve some lists $Δ_⊥(θ_1)$ into $Δ$ such that $θ_1$ can be combined with some $θ_2 ∈ Dom(Δ)$. According to Definition 9, if $θ_1$ and $θ_2$ are connected, and $θ_1 ⋈ θ_2$, then $θ_1 ⊔ θ_2$ is also *connected*, thus the list $Δ_⊥(θ_1)$ can be added to $Δ$ (line 7). Note that $θ_1$ may again be strong compatible to other parameter instances in T_2; this process is thus iterative.

The CONSTRUCT function is called at line 9 to compute trace slices and then update the intermediate structure PTA. $Ω$ is the set of parameter instances in $Δ$. The function tries to combine (lines 3-5) all strong compatible parameter instances in $Ω$. This process is iterative, since the newly generated parameter instance may be combined to the existing ones. Then the trace slice for each complete and connected parameter instance $θ$ is constructed by merging the event sequences of $θ$'s less informative parameter instances (lines 7-9).

Consider $Reducer_1$ of our running example. After line 5 of the REDUCE function, $Δ_⊥$ and $Δ$ are defined as follows. For $Δ_⊥$, $Δ_⊥(⟨user1⟩) = login$ and $Δ_⊥(⟨user2⟩) = login$. For $Δ$, $Δ(⟨user1, order1⟩) = create\_order, pay\_order$ and $Δ(⟨order1, item1⟩) = add\_item$. Then at line 6, since $⟨user1⟩$ is strong compatible with $\langle user1, order1 \rangle$, the list $\Delta_\perp(\langle user1 \rangle)$ is added to Δ. After the while loop at line 3 of the CONSTRUCT function, $\Omega = \{\langle user1 \rangle, \langle user1, order1 \rangle, \langle order1, item1 \rangle, \langle user1, order1, item1 \rangle\}$. Let $\theta = \langle user1, order1, item1 \rangle$, then $\tau \lceil_\theta = login, create\_order, add\_item, pay\_order$.

We take the prefix tree acceptor (PTA) as the intermediate structure. Each reducer keeps a partial PTA, which only maintains trace slices generated at the reducer. However, since the model inference algorithm (see Section Section 5) takes as input a complete PTA, we then merge the PTAs in each reducer to form a complete one after the reduce process terminates. The complete PTA accepts all trace slices generated, and an example is shown in Figure 4.

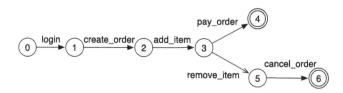

Fig. 4. PTA for the running example

5   Distributed Model Synthesis with MapReduce

Once the complete PTA has been generated, as previously shown, many off-the-shelf model synthesis algorithms [7,16] can be applied to infer the system model. However, since these are centralized algorithms and the PTA can be a very large data structure, we further propose a distributed model synthesis algorithm based on k-tail [7] with MapReduce to improve efficiency.

The most expensive operation of k-tail is to decide which states can be merged. Our idea is to distribute the most expensive operations to a number of mappers. With the intermediate results computed by the mappers, the model construction is comparatively simple, and is performed by a single reducer.

5.1   Data Encoding

To implement the distributed model synthesis algorithm with MapReduce, the intermediate results must be in the form of key-value pairs. The "value" here is a state, we thus need a mechanism to set a key for each state. Moreover, as states with the same key are grouped together by MapReduce, the key should convey information about the merged state of these states.

We first introduce some notation relevant to the description of the behavioral model. A behavioral model M is defined as a finite-state automaton $M = (\Sigma, S, s_0, \sigma, F)$, where Σ is the set of base events, S is a finite, non-empty set of states, $s_0 \in S$ is an initial state, σ is the state-transition function, and $F \subseteq S$ is the set of non-final states. Let $\sigma^* : S \times \Sigma^* \to S$ be the extended transition function, i.e., $\sigma^*(s, \epsilon) = s$ and $\sigma^*(s, e\omega) = \bigcup_{s' \in \sigma(s,e)} \sigma^*(s', \omega)$. Denote the input PTA model as M_{PTA}, and the target finite-state model as M_{FSM}.

Let k be a predefined integer. Let $\omega \in \Sigma^*$ be a word, i.e. a trace of base events. Let $\Sigma^{\leq k} = \Sigma^0 \cup \Sigma^1 \cdots \cup \Sigma^k$, then $\omega \in \Sigma^{\leq k}$ is a word of maximum length k. Given an automaton M, let f be a function from $S \times \Sigma^*$ to Boolean, such that for any state $s \in S$ and any word $\omega \in \Sigma^*$, $f(s, \omega) = 1$ iff starting from s, the word ω is *accepted* by σ^* [3].

Definition 12. *Let s_1, s_2 be two states in M, we say s_1 and s_2 are k-equivalent, if for any word $\omega \in \Sigma^{\leq k}$, $f(s_1, \omega) = 1$ iff $f(s_2, \omega) = 1$.*

The k-equivalence class that contains s is

$$[s] = \{t \in S \,|\, s \text{ and } t \text{ are } k\text{-equivalent}\}.$$

All states in a k-equivalent class can be merged. A k-equivalent class in M_{PTA} corresponds to a state in M_{FSM}. The function f can be lifted to a equivalent class: $\forall \omega \in \Sigma^{\leq k}$, $f([s], \omega) = f(s', \omega)$, where s' can be any state in $[s]$.

Lemma 2. *For any two k-equivalent classes $[s]$ and $[t]$, there must exist a word $\omega \in \Sigma^{\leq k}$, such that $f([s], \omega) \neq f([t], \omega)$.*

We can use the valuations of $f([s], \omega)$ for all $\omega \in \Sigma^{\leq k}$ to characterize $[s]$. Assume words in $\Sigma^{\leq k}$ to be indexed from 1 to $|\Sigma^{\leq k}|$. We use following definition to compute the signature of a state.

Definition 13. *Let s be a state in S, the signature sig of s is a Boolean vector of length $|\Sigma^{\leq k}|$, such that $sig[i] = 1$ iff with the i-th word ω in $\Sigma^{\leq k}$, $f(s, \omega) = 1$ for $1 \leq i \leq |\Sigma^{\leq k}|$.*

By Lemma 2, the signatures of s and t are identical, if and only if they are in the same k-equivalent class. We thus choose the key of a given state s as the signature of s.

5.2   Mapper and Reducer

The pseudocode of distributed model synthesis is shown in Figure 5. Let S_i be the set of states distributed to $Mapper_i$. For each state $s \in S_i$, $Mapper_i$ computes the signature sig for s, and outputs the signature-state pair.

When all states signatures have been computed, the synthesis of M_{FSM} is simple, and can be performed by a single reducer. MapReduce sorts all signature-state pairs and puts the states with the same signature into one list. Let $states[]$ be the list of states with the same signature sig. The REDUCE function is called for each pair of sig and $states[]$, and simply creates a new state in M_{FSM} in correspondence to the given signature.

After all signatures have been processed, the POSTREDUCE function is invoked, which adds transitions to M_{FSM}. For each transition in M_{PTA} from s to t due to event e, a transition from $[s]$ to $[t]$ labeled e is added to M_{FSM}. The POSTREDUCE function is called once and returns the synthesized model M_{FSM}.

---

[3] We do not require that a word ends in a final state, as in [8].

1: **function** MAP(*state*)
2:      compute signature *sig* of *state* by Definition 13;
3:      OUTPUT(*sig, state*);

4: **function** REDUCE(*sig, states*[])
5:      Create a new state in M_{FSM} w.r.t. *sig*;

6: **function** POSTREDUCE
7:      **for** each transition (s_1, e, s_2) in M_{PTA} **do**
8:          Add a transition $([s_1], e, [s_2])$ in M_{FSM};

Fig. 5. Distributed model synthesis

6 Experimental Evaluation

We implemented our approach on top of Hadoop 1.2.1, and conducted experiments on Amazon Elastic MapReduce clusters [4]. Each computing node has a dual-core CPU and 7.5 GB memories. We let each node serve as two mappers and one reducer simultaneously. The running time spent on both MapReduce jobs (trace slicing and model synthesis) is measured separately. Each experiment is performed 3 times, and the average value is reported.

The datasets used in our experiments are synthetically generated as follows. (1) An automaton is randomly generated as the target model, which contains 50 states and maximally 5 transitions per state. (2) The automaton is randomly simulated to generate parametric traces. Each parametric trace is with 10 to 100 parametric events. (3) All generated parametric traces are randomly mixed up. (4) The same number of irrelevant entries are randomly added to the log as noises. Other parameters are set as: $|\mathcal{E}| = 15$, $|X| = 4$ and $k = 1$. The event definition $\mathcal{D}_e$ is randomly determined, and the parameter value is randomly chosen from integer domain. The size of the largest log file exceeds 10 GB.

We designed several sets of experiments to evaluate our approach, ranging from basic performance, speed up to scalability. The experimental results are reported and discussed below.

Basic Performance. The first set of experiments tests the running time of our approach for logs with increasing size. Sizes of these logs range from 20 to 100 million events. The cluster size is fixed to 10 nodes. The results are plotted in Figure 6a. Each column in the graph contains two parts, representing the running time of trace slicing and model synthesis, respectively. Most of the running time is spent on trace slicing. The total processing time for the largest log (the file size exceeds 10GB) is less than 7 minutes.

Speed-Up. In the second set of experiments, we test the speed-up of our approach with increasing number of computing nodes. The log size is fixed to 40 million events, while the cluster size varies from 1 node to 10 nodes. The experimental results are plotted in Figure 6b. We observed that the total running time

---

[4] http://aws.amazon.com/elasticmapreduce/

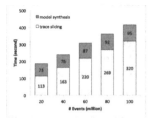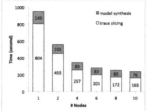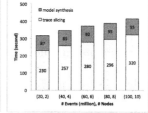

(a) Running time with inreasing log size

(b) Running time with increasing nodes

(c) Running time with increasing nodes and log size

Fig. 6. Experimental results

of our approach decreases considerably when given more computing nodes. This is well understandable. Moreover, along with the increase of computing nodes, the speed-up ratio goes down slowly. This is also reasonable, since the communication cost increases and there are some operations (for example, the REDUCE and POSTREDUCE functions in model synthesis) that cannot be parallelized or completely parallelized.

Scalability. The third set of experiments tests the scalability of our approach. We increase the log size (from 20 million to 100 million events) and the cluster size (from 2 to 10 nodes) by the same factor, and then observe the running time of our approach. Note that the ratio between log size and cluster size remains unchanged. The experimental results are shown in Figure 6c. When both log size and cluster size increase, the total running time increases a little. This phenomenon is very encouraging, which means our approach scales well.

Threat to Validity. The main threat to validity is the synthetic logs used in the evaluation. To mitigate this, the log generator is designed as practical as possible by imitating the practical parameter settings and the noises. Another possible threat to validity is certain characteristics of logs, e.g., the event definition, because of the heuristics we used for determining the parameter windows. To eliminate the bias involved in designing the data sets, we also choose synthetic logs and randomly generated event definitions in our evaluation.

7   Related Works

The related works fall into two categories: behavioral model inference and trace checking with MapReduce.

Behavioral Model Inference. A lot of work exists on inferring software behavioral models from execution traces. Ammons et al. [1] first proposed the technique of *specification mining* to mine program specifications from program execution traces. GK-Tail [14] extends the k-tail algorithm and infers extended finite state machines. Walkinshaw and Bogdanov [17] considered LTL constraints as additional input, and used model checking technique to guide the state merging process. Lo et al. [13] mined temporal invariants from execution traces and used the invariants to guide the model inference. Synoptic [5] adopted similar idea and incorporated refinement and coarsening to generate accurate but concise models. Lee et al. [11] proposed the trace slicing technique to mine parametric specifications. Ghezzi et al. [10] inferred users' behavior models from web application logs. However, to the best of our knowledge, there is no previously published work on applying MapReduce to model inference.

Trace Checking with MapReduce. Recently, there have been several works on checking trace compliance against temporal logics using MapReduce. Barre et al. [2] presented an iterative algorithm for checking Linear Temporal Logic (LTL) formula over event traces with MapReduce. Bianculli et al. [6] further improved the work [2] by supporting metric temporal logic with aggregating modalities. Basin et al. [3] presented a formal log slicing framework for checking policies expressed with metric first-order temporal logic. These works share some similarities with ours, i.e., log processing with MapReduce. But the major difference is that our work focus on behavioral model inference from large logs, rather than checking compliance against temporal logics.

8   Conclusion

In this paper, we presented an approach to infer software behavioral models from large logs using MapReduce. In our approach, the logs are first parsed and sliced, then the model is inferred by the distributed k-tail algorithm. Our approach can also be used as a log preprocessor and combined with existing model inference algorithms. Experiments on Amazon clusters and large datasets show the efficiency and scalability of our approach.

We plan to perform case studies on logs generated by real software systems to further evaluate the performance and applicability of our approach. We also plan to investigate the parallelization of more precise and robust model inference algorithms [16] or incorporating temporal invariants [13] during inference phase.

Acknowledgment. This work was supported in part by the Chinese National 973 Plan (2010CB328003), the NSF of China (61272001, 91218302), the Chinese National Key Technology R&D Program (SQ2012BAJY4052), the Importation and Development of High-Caliber Talents Project of Beijing Municipal Institutions (YETP0167), and the Tsinghua University Initiative Scientific Research Program.

References

1. Ammons, G., Bodík, R., Larus, J.R.: Mining specifications. In: Proceedings of the 29th ACM SIGPLAN-SIGACT Symposium on Principles of Programming Languages, POPL 2002, pp. 4–16. ACM, New York (2002)

2. Barre, B., Klein, M., Soucy-Boivin, M., Ollivier, P.-A., Hallé, S.: MapReduce for parallel trace validation of LTL properties. In: Qadeer, S., Tasiran, S. (eds.) RV 2012. LNCS, vol. 7687, pp. 184–198. Springer, Heidelberg (2013)
3. Basin, D., Caronni, G., Ereth, S., Harvan, M., Klaedtke, F., Mantel, H.: Scalable offline monitoring. In: Bonakdarpour, B., Smolka, S.A. (eds.) RV 2014. LNCS, vol. 8734, pp. 31–47. Springer, Heidelberg (2014)
4. Beschastnikh, I., Brun, Y., Ernst, M.D., Krishnamurthy, A.: Inferring models of concurrent systems from logs of their behavior with CSight. In: Proceedings of the 36th International Conference on Software Engineering, pp. 468–479. ACM (2014)
5. Beschastnikh, I., Brun, Y., Schneider, S., Sloan, M., Ernst, M.D.: Leveraging existing instrumentation to automatically infer invariant-constrained models. In: Proceedings of the 19th ACM SIGSOFT symposium and the 13th European Conference on Foundations of Software Engineering, pp. 267–277. ACM (2011)
6. Bianculli, D., Ghezzi, C., Krstić, S.: Trace checking of metric temporal logic with aggregating modalities using MapReduce. In: Giannakopoulou, D., Salaün, G. (eds.) SEFM 2014. LNCS, vol. 8702, pp. 144–158. Springer, Heidelberg (2014)
7. Biermann, A., Feldman, J.: On the synthesis of finite-state machines from samples of their behavior. Computers, IEEE Transactions on C $21(6)$, 592–597 (1972)
8. Cook, J.E., Wolf, A.L.: Discovering models of software processes from event-based data. ACM Trans. Softw. Eng. Methodol. $7(3)$, 215–249 (1998)
9. Dean, J., Ghemawat, S.: Mapreduce: Simplified data processing on large clusters. Commun. ACM $51(1)$, 107–113 (2008)
10. Ghezzi, C., Pezzè, M., Sama, M., Tamburrelli, G.: Mining behavior models from user-intensive web applications. In: Proceedings of the 36th International Conference on Software Engineering, pp. 277–287. ACM (2014)
11. Lee, C., Chen, F., Roşu, G.: Mining parametric specifications. In: Proceedings of the 33rd International Conference on Software Engineering, pp. 591–600. ICSE 2011. ACM, New York (2011)
12. Lee, K.H., Lee, Y.J., Choi, H., Chung, Y.D., Moon, B.: Parallel data processing with mapreduce: A survey. SIGMOD Rec. $40(4)$, 11–20 (2012)
13. Lo, D., Mariani, L., Pezzè, M.: Automatic steering of behavioral model inference. In: Proceedings of the 7th Joint Meeting Of The European Software Engineering Conference and the ACM SIGSOFT symposium on The foundations of software engineering, pp. 345–354. ACM (2009)
14. Lorenzoli, D., Mariani, L., Pezzè, M.: Automatic generation of software behavioral models. In: Proceedings of the 30th international conference on Software engineering, pp. 501–510. ACM (2008)
15. Luo, C., He, F., Ghezzi, C.: Inferring software behavioral models with mapreduce (extended version). http://sts.thss.tsinghua.edu.cn/beagle/paper/model-2015.pdf
16. Thollard, F., Dupont, P., Higuera, C.d.l.: Probabilistic dfa inference using kullback-leibler divergence and minimality. In: Proceedings of the Seventeenth International Conference on Machine Learning, ICML 2000, pp. 975–982. Morgan Kaufmann Publishers Inc., San Francisco, CA, USA (2000)
17. Walkinshaw, N., Bogdanov, K.: Inferring finite-state models with temporal constraints. In: Proceedings of the 2008 23rd IEEE/ACM International Conference on Automated Software Engineering, pp. 248–257. IEEE Computer Society (2008)
18. Xu, W., Huang, L., Fox, A., Patterson, D., Jordan, M.: Experience mining google's production console logs. In: Proceedings of the 2010 Workshop on Managing Systems via Log Analysis and Machine Learning Techniques, SLAML 2010, pp. 5–5. USENIX Association, Berkeley, CA, USA (2010)

Bisimulation and Correctness

An Application of Temporal Projection
to Interleaving Concurrency

Ben Moszkowski[1]($\boxtimes$) and Dimitar P. Guelev[2]

[1] School of Computing Science, Newcastle University, Newcastle upon Tyne, UK
benmos63@gmail.com
[2] Department of Algebra and Logic,
Institute of Mathematics and Informatics, Sofia, Bulgaria
gelevdp@math.bas.bg

Abstract. We revisit the earliest temporal projection operator Π in discrete-time Propositional Interval Temporal Logic (PITL) and use it to formalise interleaving concurrency. The logical properties of Π as a normal modality and a way to eliminate it in both PITL and conventional point-based Linear-Time Temporal Logic (LTL), which can be viewed as a PITL subset, are examined. We also formalise concurrency without Π, and relate the two approaches. Furthermore, Π and another standard PITL projection operator are interdefinable and both suitable for reasoning about different time granularities. We mention other (mostly interval-based) temporal logics with similar forms of projection, as well as some related applications and international standards.

Keywords: Interleaving concurrency · Interval temporal logic · Temporal projection · Time granularities

1 Introduction

Temporal intervals, which are finite and infinite state sequences, offer a compellingly natural and flexible way to model computational processes involving hardware or software. *Interval Temporal Logic* (ITL) [35],[19],[36] is an established formalism for reasoning about such phenomena. In ITL, satisfaction of formulas is defined at intervals rather than time points which are used in other temporal logics. ITL operators for sequentially combining formulas $A; B$ (*"A chop B"*) and A^* (*"A chop-star"*) are related to the concatenation and Kleene star operators for regular expressions.

In the early 1980s, we proposed in [35],[19] a simple binary temporal operator Π for time granularities and projection to enhance ITL's usefulness for formalising digital circuits. Here we revisit Π's logical properties and use it to formalise interleaving concurrency. We also discuss a related operator for modelling time granularities and related work on temporal projection in general.

Structure of the Paper: Section 2 overviews propositional ITL. Section 3 looks at the projection operator Π. Section 4 uses Π to formalise concurrent programs and also shows how to do this without Π. Section 5 discusses related work.

© Springer International Publishing Switzerland 2015
X. Li et al. (Eds.): SETTA 2015, LNCS 9409, pp. 153–167, 2015.
DOI: 10.1007/978-3-319-25942-0_10

2   Propositional Interval Temporal Logic

For an in-depth presentation of PITL we refer the reader to [39]; see also [36],[31] and the ITL web pages [27]. The version of PITL used here has the syntax

$$A ::= \; true \mid p \mid \neg A \mid A \vee A \mid \bigcirc A \mid A \,\mathcal{U}\, A \mid A; A \mid A^* , \qquad (1)$$

where p denotes a propositional variable. Owing to our purposes here, the Until operator $\mathcal{U}$ is included. We define $false$, $\wedge$, $\supset$ and $\equiv$ as usual.

PITL models time using discrete (linear) state sequences. The *set of states* Σ is the powerset 2^V of the set V of propositional variables, so each state in Σ sets every propositional variable $p, q, \ldots$ to $true$ or $false$. *Local* PITL is the (standard) version of PITL with such state-based variables (instead of interval-based ones). An *interval* $\sigma = \sigma^0 \sigma^1 \ldots$ is any element of $\Sigma^+ \cup \Sigma^\omega$. If σ is finite, its *interval length* $|\sigma|$ is the number of σ's states minus 1, otherwise ω. Given $i \leq j \leq |\sigma|$, $j < \omega$, $\sigma^{i..j}$ denotes $\sigma^i \ldots \sigma^j$, and $\sigma^{i\uparrow}$ is the suffix subinterval $\sigma^i \sigma^{i+1} \ldots$ of σ. We write $\sigma \models A$ for *interval σ satisfies A*. Formula A is *valid* if all intervals satisfy A. The definition of $\sigma \models A$ by induction on the construction of A is as follows, where i, j, k, k_i and n are natural numbers:

$\sigma \models true$ for any σ $\qquad \sigma \models p$ iff $p \in \sigma^0$ $\qquad \sigma \models \neg A$ iff $\sigma \not\models A$

$\sigma \models A \vee B$ iff $\sigma \models A$ or $\sigma \models B$ $\qquad \sigma \models \bigcirc A$ iff $|\sigma| \geq 1$ and $\sigma^{1\uparrow} \models A$

$\sigma \models A \,\mathcal{U}\, B$ iff, for some $k \leq |\sigma|, \sigma^{k\uparrow} \models B$ and for all $j < k, \sigma^{j\uparrow} \models A$

$\sigma \models A; B$ iff for some $k \leq |\sigma|$, $\sigma^{0..k} \models A$ and $\sigma^{k\uparrow} \models B$, or $|\sigma| = \omega$ and $\sigma \models A$

$\sigma \models A^*$ iff either (1) $|\sigma| = 0$,

or (2) there exists a finite sequence $k_0 = 0 < k_1 < \ldots < k_n \leq |\sigma|$ such that for all $i < n$, $\sigma^{k_i..k_{i+1}} \models A$, and $\sigma^{k_n\uparrow} \models A$,

or (3) $|\sigma| = \omega$ and there exists an infinite sequence $k_0 = 0 < k_1 < \ldots$ such that $\sigma^{k_i..k_{i+1}} \models A$ for all $i < \omega$.

In the first case for chop, intervals $\sigma^{0..k}$ and $\sigma^{k\uparrow}$ have overlapping state σ^k. Cases (1)-(3) for chop-star concern zero, nonzero but finite, and infinite ("*chop-omega*") iterations, respectively. Chop here is *weak*, like the weak version $\mathcal{W}$ of $\mathcal{U}$, for potentially nonterminating programs which ignore B. *Strong* chop, which forces the left subinterval to be finite, is derivable.

Consider a sample 5-state interval σ with the following alternating values for the variable p: $p \; \neg p \; p \; \neg p \; p$. Here are four formulas σ satisfies:

$$p \quad (\bigcirc \neg \bigcirc true); \neg p \quad p \wedge (true; \neg p) \quad (p \wedge \bigcirc \bigcirc (p \wedge \neg \bigcirc true))^* .$$

For example, $(\bigcirc \neg \bigcirc true); \neg p$ is true since σ's prefix subinterval $\sigma^0 \sigma^1$ satisfies $\bigcirc \neg \bigcirc true$ (which is true exactly on 2-state intervals) and the adjacent suffix subinterval $\sigma^1 \ldots \sigma^4$ satisfies $\neg p$ because $p \notin \sigma^1$. The formula $(p \wedge \bigcirc \bigcirc \neg \bigcirc true)^*$ is true since σ's subintervals $\sigma^0 \sigma^1 \sigma^2$ and $\sigma^2 \sigma^3 \sigma^4$ both satisfy $p \wedge \bigcirc \bigcirc \neg \bigcirc true$, but σ does not satisfy formulas $\neg p$, $(\bigcirc \neg \bigcirc true); p$ and $true; (\neg p \wedge \neg (true; p))$.

Table 1. Some Useful Derived LTL Operators

$ⓦ A \mathrel{\hat{=}} \neg\bigcirc\neg A$	Weak Next	$more \mathrel{\hat{=}} \bigcirc true$	≥ 2 states
$empty \mathrel{\hat{=}} \neg more$	One state	$skip \mathrel{\hat{=}} \bigcirc empty$	$= 2$ states
$\Diamond A \mathrel{\hat{=}} true\,\mathcal{U}\,A$	Eventually	$\Box A \mathrel{\hat{=}} \neg\Diamond\neg A$	Always
$inf \mathrel{\hat{=}} \Box more$	Infinite interval	$finite \mathrel{\hat{=}} \neg inf$	Finite interval
$fin\,A \mathrel{\hat{=}} \Box(empty \supset A)$	Final state (weak)	$halt\,w \mathrel{\hat{=}} \Box(w \equiv empty)$	Halt upon test

Let w, w_1 and w_2 denote *state formulas*, which have no temporal operators. Conventional LTL can be viewed as the subset of PITL with just the temporal operators $\bigcirc$ and $\mathcal{U}$. The infinite state sequences that are common with LTL are just infinite intervals. Table 1 shows useful derived LTL operators.

Here are some sample valid PITL formulas:

$$A \supset (A;true)\quad skip^*\quad inf \equiv true; false\quad (w \wedge A);B \equiv w \wedge (A;B)\quad A \equiv (empty;A)\ .$$

We note that PITL without chop-star has the same expressiveness as LTL. With chop-star, PITL has the same expressiveness as LTL with the addition of propositional quantification (explicitly defined later in Sect. 4). That is, having propositional quantification instead of chop-star gives the same *regular* expressiveness for finite intervals and ω-*regular expressive power* (i.e., MSO(ω,<)) for infinite intervals. The LTL operator $\mathcal{U}$ is also expressible using chop, $\bigcirc$ and quantification. More details about PITL's expressiveness are found in [35],[38],[39].

3 Temporal Projection

The binary temporal operator Π for *state projection* [35],[19] provides a way to examine dynamic behaviour at certain points in time and ignore all intermediate states. Given an interval σ and a state formula w, let $\sigma|_w$ denote the sequence of σ's states satisfying w. If σ is infinite, $\sigma|_w$ can be finite or infinite. The definition of Π, whose first argument is supposed to be a state formula, is

$$\sigma \models w\,\Pi\,A \quad \text{iff} \quad \sigma^i \models w,\ \text{for some } i \leq |\sigma|,\ \text{and}\ \sigma|_w \models A\ .$$

For example, $\sigma \models p\,\Pi\,\Box q$ if p is true at some state of σ, and q is true whenever p is, i.e., if $\sigma \models \Diamond p \wedge \Box(p \supset q)$. We can generalise Π to permit arbitrary formulas for selecting projected states by using $\sigma|_B = \langle \sigma^i : i \leq |\sigma|,\ \sigma^{i\uparrow} \models B \rangle$ to define $\sigma \models B\,\Pi\,A$. This does not alter Π's meaning when B is a state formula.

For a fixed w, $w\,\Pi\,A$ is a normal unary modality on A. Its accessibility relation $\sigma \mapsto \sigma|_w$ is deterministic. This entails the validity of the standard modal axioms **K** and **D$_c$**, and the *necessitation rule* N [6,23]. These are normally written in terms of the "universal" *dual* $\neg(w\,\Pi\,\neg A)$ of $w\,\Pi\,A$, denoted $w\,\Pi^u\,A$:

$$\textbf{(K)}\ w\,\Pi^u\,(A \supset B) \supset (w\,\Pi^u\,A \supset w\,\Pi^u\,B),\quad \textbf{(D}_c\textbf{)}\ w\,\Pi\,A \supset w\,\Pi^u\,A,\quad \textbf{(N)}\ \frac{A}{w\,\Pi^u\,A}.$$

$\mathbf{K}$, $\mathbf{D_c}$ and N are sufficient to infer equivalences such as

$$w \, \Pi \, (A \wedge B) \quad \equiv \quad w \, \Pi \, A \, \wedge \, w \, \Pi \, B$$
$$w \, \Pi^{\mathrm{u}} \, A \, \wedge \, w \, \Pi \, B \quad \supset \quad w \, \Pi \, (A \wedge B)$$
$$w \, \Pi^{\mathrm{u}} \, (A \supset B) \, \wedge \, w \, \Pi \, A \quad \supset \quad w \, \Pi \, B \ .$$

The following valid formulas are specific to Π:

$$\Box(w_1 \equiv w_2) \quad \supset \quad (w_1 \, \Pi \, A) \equiv (w_2 \, \Pi \, A)$$

$$w_1 \, \Pi \, (w_2 \, \Pi \, A) \quad \equiv \quad (w_1 \wedge w_2) \, \Pi \, A \tag{2}$$

$$w \, \Pi^{\mathrm{u}} \, A \equiv \Box \neg w \vee w \, \Pi \, A, \qquad w \, \Pi \, A \equiv \Diamond w \, \wedge \, w \, \Pi^{\mathrm{u}} \, A \tag{3}$$

$$w_1 \, \Pi \, \Diamond w_2 \supset \Diamond w_2, \qquad \Box w_2 \supset w_1 \, \Pi^{\mathrm{u}} \, \Box w_2 \tag{4}$$

The equivalences (3) give a simple way to define Π and Π^{u} in terms of each other because $\Diamond w$ is available to indicate whether the reference interval has a nonempty projection. The implications (4) facilitate importing and exporting properties into and from the scope of Π.

The valid equivalences below form a complete axiomatisation of Π relative to basic PITL and show that every PITL formula with Π has a Π-free equivalent.

$$w \, \Pi \, \mathit{true} \equiv \Diamond w \qquad\qquad w \, \Pi \, (A \vee B) \equiv w \, \Pi \, A \vee w \, \Pi \, B$$
$$w \, \Pi \, p \quad \equiv (\neg w) \, \mathcal{U} \, (w \wedge p) \qquad w \, \Pi \, (A \, \mathcal{U} B) \equiv (w \, \Pi \, A) \, \mathcal{U} \, (w \, \Pi \, B)$$
$$w \, \Pi \, \neg A \equiv \Diamond w \, \wedge \, \neg (w \, \Pi \, A) \qquad w \, \Pi \, \bigcirc A \quad \equiv (\neg w) \, \mathcal{U} \, (w \wedge \bigcirc (w \, \Pi \, A))$$
$$w \, \Pi \, (A;B) \equiv (w \, \Pi \, A); (w \, \wedge \, w \, \Pi \, B)$$
$$w \, \Pi \, (A^*) \equiv \neg w \, \mathcal{U} \, \big(w \wedge ((w \, \Pi \, A) \wedge \mathit{fin} \, w)^*; \circledcirc \Box \neg w \big)$$

The equivalences about the LTL operators show that LTL formulas with Π have Π-free LTL equivalents too.

By (2), $A \equiv w \, \Pi \, B$ entails $w \, \Pi \, A \equiv w \, \Pi \, B$, so A has an equivalent of the form $w \, \Pi \, B$ iff $\models A \equiv w \, \Pi \, A$. This may be useful for *synthesising* a controller to be run in parallel with other code from a global requirement R. The synthesis is possible only if $\models R \equiv (w \, \Pi \, R)$, where w marks the controller's time slices. The latter reduces to a basic ITL validity after eliminating Π from $w \, \Pi \, R$.

We originally defined Π so that $\sigma \models w \, \Pi \, A$ *vacuously* holds when $\sigma|_w$ has no states [19],[35]. This holds for Π^{u} in this paper. Projection is *false* when no projection interval exists for the real-time projection operators from [15–17], and likewise for the projection operator from [36],[37] discussed in Sect. 4.2.

4   Formalisation of Imperative Concurrent Programs

We now look at a way to formalise in ITL imperative concurrent programs in which processes are interleaved. The availability of sequential composition operators such as chop has long made ITL well suited for expressing sequential and concurrent programs and executing them in ITL-based interpreters, as we previously investigated in [36]. Such an interpreter for an ITL programming language subset called *Tempura* is available from [27]. ITL has also been productively used for *symbolic execution* for theorem proving [2,3]. Some later research by others on expressing concurrent programs in variants of ITL is discussed in Sect. 5.

The approach described here is specifically meant to correspond to the popular notion of *state transition systems* (based on Keller's work [30] and extensively surveyed by Baier and Katoen [1]; see also [7],[31]), where at any time only one of the program's processes is allowed in *global* time to make a transition from the current state to its immediate successor state and possibly make assignments involving just these two adjacent states. This is a quite widely employed standard assumption for interleaving found in frameworks including Manna-Pnueli *Reactive Systems* [33] (see also [4],[31]), Lamport's TLA+ [32] (including the TLC model checker), Jones' *Rely-Guarantee Conditions* [28] (see also [43]), the SPIN model checker [22] and *Partial Order Reduction* [7],[1] used by some model checkers such as SPIN. Our intention is to develop a framework that *a priori* seeks to maximise the use of ITL together with the operator Π for the interleaving model. Projection constructs are not strictly required (since they can be eliminated, as discussed later in Sect. 4.1), but we consider them here because they bring succinctness and clarity.

Interleaved parallel composition. We now define

$$A \mathbin{|||}_p B \; \mathrel{\widehat{=}} \; p \,\Pi\, A \;\wedge\; (\neg p) \,\Pi\, B$$

to express that two formulas A and B operate concurrently in an interleaved manner with a boolean variable p indicating which is active in any given state. We refer to this *three-operand* interleaving operator as $\mathbin{|||}_\_$. It is commutative and associative, subject to suitable manipulations of the middle operand:

$$\models \quad A \mathbin{|||}_p B \;\equiv\; B \mathbin{|||}_{\neg p} A \tag{5}$$

$$\models \quad (A \mathbin{|||}_p B) \mathbin{|||}_q C \;\equiv\; A \mathbin{|||}_{p\wedge q} (B \mathbin{|||}_q C) \tag{6}$$

$$\models \quad A \mathbin{|||}_p (B \mathbin{|||}_q C) \;\equiv\; (A \mathbin{|||}_p B) \mathbin{|||}_{p\vee q} C \tag{7}$$

Commutativity is easily proved, as is associativity, using the validity of

$$p \,\Pi\, (A \mathbin{|||}_q B) \;\equiv\; (p \wedge q) \,\Pi\, A \;\wedge\; (p \wedge \neg q) \,\Pi\, B \;.$$

When irrelevant, $\mathbin{|||}_\_$'s middle operand can be quantified away:

$$A \mathbin{|||} B \; \mathrel{\widehat{=}} \; \exists p.\,(A \mathbin{|||}_p B) \;.$$

Here, $\sigma \models \exists p.\,C$ holds iff $\sigma' \models C$ holds for some interval σ' identical to σ except possibly for p's behaviour. [1] The definition of $\mathbin{|||}$ here corresponds to

---

[1] As noted in the introduction, such quantification does not increase PITL's expressiveness: quantified formulas have equivalent quantifier-free ones. Here is how to express $\mathcal{U}$: $\models A \,\mathcal{U}\, B \equiv \Diamond B \wedge \exists p.\,(p \wedge \Box(p \supset (B \vee (A \wedge \bigcirc p))))$ (e.g., see [31, p.84]), where the following straightforward valid equivalences are used: $inf \equiv (true; false)$, $finite \equiv \neg inf$, $\Diamond C \equiv (finite; C)$ (with $\Box$ still being $\Diamond$'s dual: $\Box C \equiv \neg \Diamond \neg C$).

Table 2. Some imperative programming constructs expressed in ITL

$$
\begin{aligned}
a := e \quad &\hat{=} \quad skip \;\wedge < nval > [.a] = e \\
&\wedge \; \forall v \in (< dom > (< nval >) \setminus \{.a\}).(< nval > [v] = v\,\hat{\;}) \\[4pt]
a_1,\ldots,a_n := e_1,\ldots,e_n \quad &\hat{=} \quad skip \;\wedge < nval > [.a_1] = e_1 \wedge \cdots \wedge < nval > [.a_n] = e_n \\
&\wedge \; \forall v \in (< dom > (< nval >) \setminus \{.a_1,\ldots,.a_n\}).(< nval > [v] = v\,\hat{\;}) \\[4pt]
< noop > \quad &\hat{=} \quad skip \;\wedge \; \forall v \in < dom > (< nval >).(< nval > [.v] = v\,\hat{\;}) \\[4pt]
l_i : A \quad &\hat{=} \quad < lab >= l_i \;\wedge\; A \\[4pt]
empty \quad &\quad (\text{Already defined in Table 1}) \\[4pt]
A; B \quad &\quad (\text{Already defined as primitive ITL operator in Sect. 2}) \\[4pt]
if\ w\ then\ A\ else\ B \quad &\hat{=} \quad (w \wedge A) \vee (\neg w \wedge B) \\[4pt]
while\ w\ do\ A \quad &\hat{=} \quad (\neg w \wedge A)^*; (empty \wedge w) \\[4pt]
for\ some\ times\ do\ A \quad &\hat{=} \quad A^* \\[4pt]
A \sqcup B \quad &\hat{=} \quad A \vee B \qquad (\text{Nondeterministic choice})
\end{aligned}
$$

Baier and Katoen's notion in [1]. With the middle operand quantified away, $|||$ is commutative and associative in the usual way. Both Π and $|||_-$ are expressible using either $|||$ or $|||_-$, so these operators can be taken as primitive instead of Π:

$$
\begin{aligned}
\models \quad A \,|||_w\, B \quad &\equiv \quad (\Box w \wedge A) \,|||\, (\Box\neg w \wedge B) \\
\models \quad w \,\Pi\, A \quad &\equiv \quad (A \,|||_w\, true) \vee (\Box w \wedge A) .
\end{aligned}
$$

The equivalence for expressing $w \,\Pi\, A$ needs two cases because, unlike $w \,\Pi\, A$, the disjunct $A \,|||_w\, true$ ensures that sometimes w is *false*.

Multiple Processes with Process Identifiers. When dealing with multiple processes, it can be convenient to associate a numerical index with each one. An auxiliary variable ¡pid¿ can be readily used for this. For instance, for a formula $A \,|||_p\, B$ with two processes, we can take ¡pid¿ to range over $\{0,1\}$ and construct it using the formula $\Box(< pid >= if\ p\ then\ 0\ else\ 1)$. For any expression e and formula A, define $e :: A$ to specify that e is the process id for A:

$$
e :: A \quad \hat{=} \quad \Box(< pid >= e) \;\wedge\; A .
$$

The existence of a suitable ¡pid¿ then readily ensures the validity of $A \,|||\, B \equiv \exists < pid >.(0 :: A \,|||\, 1 :: B)$. The proof uses the validity of $A \,|||_{<pid>=0}\, B \equiv (0 :: A \,|||\, 1 :: B)$. The techniques easily generalise to any number of processes (e.g., $0 :: A_1 \,|||\, 1 :: A_2 \,|||\, 2 :: A_3$).

The Rest of the Imperative Constructs. When formalising programs and processes, the framework here takes the liberty of assuming that data variables range over finite domains. Besides various constants such as the bit values 0 and 1, we also employ some finite sets and lists to deal with program variables. For any given finite set of program variables, this all can in principle be propositionally encoded.

Table 2 contains imperative programming constructs which can be viewed as derived operators in ITL. We let $\setminus$ denote *set difference*. Labels are optional, normally only added to each atomic assignment and noop, and do not affect program operation. When specified, ¡lab¿'s value is the active process's current label. Labelling just the atomic statements suffices to *fully* determine ¡lab¿'s value in all states but the final one, if the process terminates. Hence, each process ends with another labelled formula of the form l_i: *empty*.

As we already noted, interleaving-based transition systems only perform assignments involving two states adjacent in *global* time. However, a process within $|||_-$ in *projected* time might not see the <u>next</u> global state even if the <u>current</u> *projected* and <u>current</u> *global* states are identical. For example, suppose the <u>current</u> *global* interval is $s_1 s_2 s_3 s_4 \ldots$. Therefore, assignments from <u>current</u> *global* state s_1 should involve s_1 and the <u>next</u> global state s_2. If a process in $|||_-$ sees the <u>current</u> *projected* interval $s_1 s_4 \ldots$ without states s_2 and s_3, then any := within $|||_-$ that sees the current state s_1 cannot see *global* state s_2 and so cannot access s_2 with $\bigcirc$ to assign variables. Such an instance of $\bigcirc$ instead sees the <u>next</u> projected state s_4 (although an alternative approach *without projection* in Sect. 4.1 can indeed see state s_2 by simply employing $\bigcirc$). *Exactly* the same issue applies to the remaining program variables which := needs to *frame* (i.e., leave unchanged) and likewise for *noop*.

The assignment construct := instead uses *state formulas* and a *state variable* *nval* which is a *record* (i.e., a finite list indexed by field names and like records in Lamport's TLA+ [32]). The purpose of ¡nval¿ is to store in the <u>current</u> *projected* state the values which are to be assigned to variables in the <u>next</u> *global* state (itself normally only accessible from *outside* of the scope of $|||_-$). In effect, ¡nval¿ helps *tunnel* from projected to global time. For each program variable a, ¡nval¿ has an element $< nval > [.a]$, where .a is a *field name constant* (like a quoted atom in Lisp) serving as a subscript (TLA+ uses strings such as "a" to index records). The assignment $a := e$ *does not actually change* a or *frame* the remaining program variables (i.e., it does not explicitly keep them unchanged). Instead, in the <u>current</u> *projected* state (which is also the <u>current</u> *global* state), $a := e$ treats its first operand as a kind of *reference* (i.e., .a) and just sets $< nval > [.a]$ equal to e, and $< nval > [.b]$ equal to b's current value for every other (unaltered) program variable b. The desired setting of a's and b's values in the <u>next</u> *global* state (to equal the *current* values of $< nval > [.a]$ and $< nval > [.b]$, respectively) is handled separately outside of $|||_-$ in *global* time, as discussed later, where the operator $\bigcirc$ can indeed access the next global state.

The field name constant .a can serve as a *reference* to the variable a itself because we let a be accessible via .a using the *dereferencing* construct .a^ (e.g., the equality .a^ = a is valid). We can abbreviate $< nval > [.a]$ as $< nval.a >$ (as in TLA+, where $< nval > ["a"] = < nval.a >$). This shorthand is not applicable if the subscript is a variable whose value is a field name constant. For example, if b equals .a, then $< nval > [b]$ equals both $< nval[.a] >$ and $< nval.a >$ (e.g., $\models b = .a \supset < nval > [b] = < nval > .a$) but not necessarily $< nval.b >$.

As in TLA+, we can regard the record ¡nval¿ as a function from field name constants to values, and let $< dom > (< nval >)$ denote ¡nval¿'s domain which is in fact the set of these field name constants. Hence, $< dom > (< nval >)$ can

		Process Pr'_0:	Process Pr'_1:
Process Pr_0:	Process Pr_1:	$l'_0 : x := 1;$	$\quad$ while $y = 0$ do
$l_0 : x := 1;$	$l_2 : x := 1 - x;$	$l'_1 : y := 1;$	$l'_3 : \quad noop;$
$l_1 : empty$	$l_3 : empty$	$l'_2 : empty$	$l'_4 : x := 1 - x;$
			$l'_5 : empty$

A. Let $dom(nval_{Pr}) = \{.x\}$. Initially $x = 0$. $\qquad$ B. Let $dom(nval_{Pr'}) = \{.x, .y\}$.
Initially both $x = 0$ and $y = 0$.

Fig. 1. Simple concurrent programs ¡Pr¿ and $< Pr >'$

serve as a set of references to the program variables for use in the semantics of atomic statements (given above in Table 2) when *framing* variables (e.g., for an assignment $a := e$, we need to explicitly formalise in the logic that all program variables referenced by $< dom > (< nval >)$ besides a remain unchanged.) For example, one concurrent program $< Pr >'$ considered shortly has just two program variables x and y, so $< dom > (< nval >) = \{.x, .y\}$, where $.x$ and $.y$ are the field name constants associated with x and y, respectively. The set $< dom > (< nval >)$ especially helps to formalise framing for programs with several variables.

The framing construct *iframe* now defined, when used in *global* states, ensures that *intended* assignments of values recorded in ¡nval¿ in each *projected* state actually *take effect* on the program variables themselves in the <u>next</u> global state:

$$iframe \quad \hat{=} \quad \Box\big(more \supset \forall v \in < dom > (< nval >). (< nval > [v] = \bigcirc v\hat{\,})\big) \ .$$

For example, if $< dom > (< nval >) = \{.a\}$, then *iframe* is semantically equivalent to both of the formulas $\Box(more \supset < nval > [.a] = .a\hat{\,})$ and $\Box(more \supset < nval > .a = a)$.

Here are sample valid formulas involving *iframe* (assume $< dom > (< nval >) = \{.a\}$):

$$\models \quad iframe \wedge \Box(more \supset < nval > .a = a) \quad \supset \quad \Box(more \supset (\bigcirc a) = a) \quad (8)$$

$$\models \quad iframe \wedge (\neg p)\,\Pi^u \,\Box(more \supset < nval > .a = a) \supset p\,\Pi^u \, iframe \ . \qquad (9)$$

According to (8), if *iframe* controls a and also $< nval > .a$ always equals a (except maybe at the end), then $\bigcirc a$ also always equals a (except maybe at the end), so, in other words, a is *stable*. Implication (9) describes that if *iframe* controls a and also in time projected by $\neg p$, $< nval > .a$ always equals a (except maybe at the end), then *iframe* as well controls a within time projected by p.

Figure 1 shows two simple concurrent programs ¡Pr¿ and $< Pr >'$. The next formula for ¡Pr¿ includes initialisation and framing (as noted in Fig. 1, $< dom > (< nval >_{<Pr>}) = \{.x\}$):

$$x = 0 \ \wedge \ iframe \ \wedge < Pr >_0 |||_r < Pr >_1 \ .$$

The middle operand r of $|||_-$ here need not be quantified away because we only use $|||_-$ on the left side of $\supset$. The first program can terminate with x equal to 0

Process $< Peterson >_i$, for $i \in \{0,1\}$

for some times do (

$l_0:$ $< noop >;$

$l_1:$ $flag_i := 1;$

$l_2:$ $turn := 1;$

       $while(flag_{1-i} = 1 \wedge turn = 1 - i)$ *do*

$l_3:$ $< noop >;$

$l_4:$ $< noop >;$ /* Enter critical section */

$l_5:$ $< noop >;$ /* Critical section */

$l_6:$ $flag_i := 0;$ /* Leave critical section */

$l_7:$ $< noop >$

     );

$l_8:$ *empty*

Let $< dom > (< nval >_{<Peterson>}) = \{.flag_0, .flag_1, .turn\}$.

Initially both $flag_0 = 0$ and $flag_1 = 0$, but $turn$'s initial value is unimportant.

Fig. 2. Version of Peterson's algorithm with processes $<\ Peterson\ >_0$ and $<\ Peterson >_1$

or 1, but the second program ensures x ends equal to 0, as formalised below (as noted in Fig. 1, $< dom > (< nval >_{<Pr>'}) = \{.x, .y\}$):

$$\models\quad x = 0 \wedge y = 0 \wedge iframe \wedge < Pr >_0'|||_r < Pr >_1' \quad \supset \quad fin(x = 0 \wedge y = 1) .$$

The labels help link conditions on state to control points. Here is an example stating that x will equal 1 when process $< Pr >_1'$ is at label l_4':

$$\models\quad x = 0 \wedge y = 0 \wedge iframe \wedge < Pr >_0'|||_r < Pr >_1' \quad \supset \quad \neg r\ \Pi\ (< lab >= l_4' \supset x = 1) .$$

The next construct is a shorthand to test a process's current label:

$$at_p\, l_i \quad \hat{=} \quad p\, \Pi\, (< lab >= l_i)$$
$$at_p\{l_{i_1}, \ldots, l_{i_k}\} \quad \hat{=} \quad p\, \Pi\, (< lab >\in \{l_{i_1}, \ldots, l_{i_k}\}) .$$

The previously discussed translation of Π to LTL in Sect. 3 ensures that $at_p\, l_i$ can be expressed in LTL as $\neg p\, \mathcal{U}\, (p \wedge < lab >= l_i)$.

Figure 2 shows Peterson's mutual exclusion algorithm [42]. The two processes do not simultaneously access their critical sections (labels l_5 and l_6). Below are some valid properties, where we let ¡init¿ denote $flag_0 = 0 \wedge flag_1 = 0$ (also, as noted in Fig. 2, $< dom > (< nval >_{<Peterson>}) = \{.flag_0, .flag_1, .turn\}$):

$$\models\quad < init > \wedge\ iframe\ \wedge < Peterson >_0|||_r < Peterson >_1 \qquad (10)$$
$$\supset\quad \Box\neg(at_r\{l_5, l_6\} \wedge at_{\neg r}\{l_5, l_6\})$$

$$\models\quad < init > \wedge\ iframe\ \wedge < Peterson >_0|||_r < Peterson >_1$$
$$\supset\quad \Box(at_r\, l_0 \supset \Diamond at_r\, l_5) \wedge \Box(at_{\neg r}\, l_0 \supset \Diamond at_{\neg r}\, l_5)$$

$$\models\quad < init > \wedge\ iframe\ \wedge\ (inf \wedge < Peterson >_0)\ |||_r\ (inf \wedge < Peterson >_1)$$
$$\supset\quad \Box\Diamond\, at_r\, l_0 \wedge \Box\Diamond\, at_r\, l_5 \wedge \Box\Diamond\, at_{\neg r}\, l_0 \wedge \Box\Diamond\, at_{\neg r}\, l_5$$

$$\models\quad < Peterson >_i \quad \supset \quad \Box(more \supset\, < nval > .flag_{1-i} = flag_{1-i})$$
$$\models\quad < Peterson >_i \quad \supset \quad \Box(more \supset\, < nval > .turn = turn\, \vee < nval > .turn = 1 - i) .$$

Implication (10) concerns mutual exclusion. Surprisingly, variants with l_4 or $\{l_4, l_5\}$ instead of $\{l_5, l_6\}$ are *not* valid: Suppose $< Peterson >_0$'s process is active (i.e., r is true) with $< lab >= l_4$ (so $at_r \, l_4$ holds). If $< Peterson >_1$'s currently inactive process is beyond l_2 and l_3 but before l_4, it could *later on* have $< lab >= l_4$ when in its next active state entering its critical section. Then $at_{\neg r} \, l_4$ would be true now! Hence, our approach has an interesting idiom to formalise behaviour.

4.1 Formalising Interleaving without Projection

As already discussed above, modelling of interleaving with Π needs the variable ¡nval¿ and the *iframe* construct to ensure that each assignment to a program variable is suitably performed between two *globally* adjacent states. An alternative framework without Π now presented avoids the need for either ¡nval¿ or *iframe* and so is even closer to the interleaving semantics described by Baier and Katoen [1]. Instead of using a record ¡nval¿, we simply let ¡pvars¿ denote the set of program variables' field name constants to play a role like that of $< dom > (< nval >)$.

The only constructs in Table 2 which need to be changed are the assignment operator :=, ¡noop¿ and *empty*. Below is a definition of the alternative construct $:='$ for assigning to a single variable, where ¡pvars¿ is the set of program variables' field name constants:

$$a :=' e \quad \widehat{=} \quad (\bigcirc a) = e \,\wedge\, \forall v \in < pvars > \setminus \{.a\}. \, ((\bigcirc v\hat{\,}) = v\hat{\,})$$
$$\wedge < active > \wedge \, \bigcirc \big(finite \wedge \square (more \, \supset \, \neg < active >) \big) \ .$$

Here the operator $\bigcirc$ helps assign to a and frame other program variables over the first two (global) states. The variable ¡active¿ is initially *true*, but then *false* in the finite number of subsequent (intermediate) states, except in the last state, to indicate inactivity. Note that $:='$ does not determine ¡active¿'s value in the last state since this is left for a follow-on atomic statement to do. Similar definitions for multiple assignments and the alternative construct $< noop >'$ are omitted here. A variant of *empty* ensures ¡active¿ holds in a process's final state:

$$empty' \quad \widehat{=} \quad empty \wedge < active > \ .$$

Any such process A has the valid implication $A \supset (< active > \wedge \, fin < active >)$. Here are variants of Π and $|||_{-}$ which seem suitable:

$$w \, \pi \, A \quad \widehat{=} \quad \neg w \, \mathcal{U} \, ((w \wedge A^w_{<active>}); (w \wedge \textcircled{w}\square\neg w))$$
$$A \, |||'_w \, B \quad \widehat{=} \quad (< active > \wedge \, w) \, \pi \, A \,\wedge\, (< active > \wedge \, \neg w) \, \pi \, B \ .$$

The construct $w \, \pi \, A$ is similar to $w \, \Pi \, A$, but instead of projection, π uses the variable ¡active¿ to restrict A's active steps to when w holds.   Properties of Π such as (2) can be adapted to π. The role of π in the definition of $|||'_{-}$ is similar to that of Π in the definition of $|||_{-}$. Variants of the properties of commutativity (5) and associativity (6)-(7) for $|||\_$ can also be shown for $|||'\_$. It is possible to formally relate programs with the projected and global constructs. Here is one possibility:

$$\models \quad iframe \wedge \Box < active > \quad \supset \quad < Pgm >_1 \equiv < Pgm >_2 \ ,$$

where $< Pgm >_1$ uses $:=, |||$ and so forth, which are replaced in $< Pgm >_2$ with primed versions such as $:='$ and $|||'$, and we let sets $< dom > (< nval >)$ and ¡pvars¿ be equal.

Incidentally, as a handy shorthand we can let $< pvars > \,\hat{}$ denote the record with indices in $< pvars >$ such that for each $.a \in < pvars >$, the record element $< pvars > \,\hat{}\,[.a]$ equals a's value. For example, the equality $(\bigcirc < pvars > \,\hat{}\,) =< pvars > \,\hat{}$ keeps program variables' values unchanged in the next state. Also, $< nval > [< dom > (< nval >) \backslash \{.a\}]$ can denote the record equalling $< nval >$ but without element $< nval > [.a]$.

4.2   Comparison of State Projection with Time-Step Projection

Somewhat after Π was introduced in [19],[35], another binary ITL operator was proposed in [36] (see also [37],[31]) for what can be referred to as *time-step projection*. It is alternatively written as *proj*, $\triangle$ or $\backslash\backslash$. Unlike for Π, temporal connectives almost always occur in both operands of *proj*. For finite σ,

$$\sigma \models A \ proj \ B \ \text{iff there exists } n \geq 0 \text{ and } i_0 = 0 < i_1 < \ldots < i_n = |\sigma| \text{ such that}$$
$$\sigma_{i_k} \ldots \sigma_{i_{k+1}} \models A, \text{ for each } k < n, \text{ and } \sigma_{i_0} \ldots \sigma_{i_n} \models B \ .$$

Intuitively, A defines time steps and B is interpreted over the interval formed of the endpoints of a sequence of such steps that links the endpoints of the reference interval. The formula A^* is expressible as $A \ proj \ true$, so it expresses the mere possibility to represent the reference interval as a sequence of time steps specified by A. Note that an interval may admit more than one suitable partitioning.

The definition of *proj* generalises to infinite time by allowing an infinite number of adjacent finite subintervals. The validity of the implication

$$inf \quad \supset \quad A \ proj \ true \ \equiv \ (finite \wedge A)^*$$

shows how the operator *proj* can express *chop-omega*.

A primary application of *proj* is to define coarser time granularities, and it is included in the Tempura programming language for such purposes, whereas Π is best fit for interleaving concurrency. A variant of *proj* for projecting from real to discrete time has been studied in [20],[15].

Π and, consequently, parallel composition $|||\_$, can be expressed using *proj*:

$$\models \quad p \ \Pi \ A \quad \equiv \quad \neg p \ \mathcal{U} \ (p \wedge ((\bigcirc halt \ p) \ proj \ A); \circledw\Box\neg p) \ .$$

Conversely, *proj* can be defined using Π and propositional quantification, which, as noted in Sect. 2, does not add expressiveness to PITL:

$$\models \quad A \ proj \ B \quad \equiv \quad \exists p. \, (p \wedge (A \wedge finite \wedge \bigcirc halt \ p)^* \wedge p \ \Pi \ B) \ ,$$

where variable p does not occur in A or B.

5   Related Work

Projection in the Duration Calculus. Dang [8] proposed for the Duration Calculus (DC) [45],[44],[41] a real-time version of the projection operator Π written / to reason about interleaving concurrency in hybrid systems. An operator for parallel composition involving global time is also defined by Dang. The definition does not use projection, although some connections to it are demonstrated. Guelev and Dang [17] further investigated this topic and other aspects of /. A complete axiomatisation of DC with / is given in [18]. In [16], / is used to specify that pairs of corresponding flexible non-logical symbols from isomorphic predicate ITL vocabularies have the same meaning in projected subintervals. It is shown that this entails the existence of *interpolants* for implications between formulas written in the two vocabularies as in Craig's classical interpolation theorem.

Other kinds of Temporal Projection. Several research groups have subsequently proposed and studied other forms of temporal projection [36],[37],[20] for use with ITL, DC and further variants such as Projection Temporal Logic [9–11] and RGITL [2,3]. RGITL, which combines Jones' *Rely-Guarantee Conditions* [28] with ITL, also assumes interleaving and involves temporal projection and local time. It has concurrency operators which are akin to ||| but defined without using an explicit projection operator, and, as the authors acknowledge, are much more complicated to handle. RGITL has been used extensively to reasoning about interleaved concurrent programs in the KIV proof verifier. Maybe Π can help elucidate RGITL's operators.

Our new approach aims to avoid as much as possible the need to introduce new primitive temporal constructs (such as RGITL's addition of branching-time constructs) and assumptions about time. For example, reasoning in RGITL about an individual process involving both its own next step and the system's (environment's) next step uses for each program variable x two additional primed variants x' and x'' associated with these. Of course, our purist approach (both with and without a projection operator) will have some limitations (e.g., it might indeed be incompatible with RGITL's overall goals), but we would like to thoroughly research and assess the situation in future case studies and comparisons involving a range of concurrent applications.

Jones et al. observe in [29] that RGITL could perhaps be quite attractive ("seductive" in their words), although it might be *too expressive*, particularly for an unskilled person. On the other hand, recent experience by Newcombe et al. [40] at Amazon Web Services with successfully specifying and verifying subtle industrial-strength concurrent algorithms using Lamport's TLA+ [32] supports the view that logics which can equally express algorithms *and* their correctness properties are desirable, and can with care be made sufficiently accessible to significantly benefit nonspecialists. More evaluation and comparison will be needed to see whether powerful and general interval-based frameworks are overkill in relation to other approaches specifically developed for the required purposes.

Eisner et al. [13,14] have developed $LTL^@$, which adds a *clock operator* to LTL to deal with time granularities in hardware systems. This is included in the international standards Property Specification Language (PSL, IEEE Standard 1850 [24]) [12] and SystemVerilog Assertions (SVA, in IEEE Standard 1800 [26]) [5]. The clock operator adds succinctness but not expressiveness and is its own dual. It requires modifying the semantics of formulas (e.g., "$\models$" includes both a state sequence and clock). The authors point out that the use of the term "projection" for the clock operator in $LTL^@$ and standards which adapt it is imprecise since states in between the projected ones are still accessible (unlike for Π). A similar construct called the *sampling operator* is found in *temporal 'e'* (part of IEEE Standard 1647 [25] and influenced by ITL [34],[21]).

Conclusions

We have explored new uses of the oldest known projection operator for ITL and also related it with other such constructs. In future work, we would like to apply this approach to larger concurrent applications. This research would include of an evaluation of the merits of the two approaches presented here for formalising concurrency in ITL with and without projection. Our plans also include exploring formal connections with RGITL and Projection Temporal Logic as well as clocked-based logics such as $LTL^@$ (all mentioned in Sect. 5).

Acknowledgments. This research was partially supported by Royal Society International Exchanges grant IE141148 and the EPSRC UNCOVER project (Ref.: EP/K001698/1). We thank Maciej Koutny and the anonymous reviewers for their comments and suggestions.

References

1. Baier, C., Katoen, J.: Principles of Model Checking. MIT Press (2008)
2. Bäumler, S., Balser, M., Nafz, F., Reif, W., Schellhorn, G.: Interactive verification of concurrent systems using symbolic execution. AI Commun. **23**(2–3), 285–307 (2010)
3. Bäumler, S., Schellhorn, G., Tofan, B., Reif, W.: Proving linearizability with temporal logic. Formal Aspects of Computing **23**(1), 91–112 (2011)
4. Ben-Ari, M.: Principles of Concurrent and Distributed Programming. Addison-Wesley, second edn. (2006)
5. Cerny, E., Dudani, S., Havlicek, J., Korchemny, D.: SVA: The Power of Assertions in SystemVerilog, 2nd edn. Springer, Heidelberg (2015)
6. Chellas, B.F.: Modal Logic: An Introduction. Cambridge University Press, Cambridge (1980)
7. Clarke, E.M., Grumberg, O., Peled, D.A.: Model Checking. MIT Press, Cambridge (1999)
8. Hung, D.V.: Projections: A technique for verifying real-time programs in DC. Tech. Rep. 178, UNU/IIST, Macau (1999). In: Proc. Conf. on Information Technology and Education, Ho Chi Minh City, Vietnam, January 2000

9. Duan, Z.: An Extended Interval Temporal Logic and a Framing Technique for Temporal Logic Programming. Ph.D. thesis, Dept. Comp. Sci., tech. rep. 556, Newcastle University, UK (1996). http://hdl.handle.net/10443/2075

10. Duan, Z., Koutny, M., Holt, C.: Projection in temporal logic programming. In: Pfenning, F. (ed.) LPAR 1994. LNCS, vol. 822, pp. 333–344. Springer, Heidelberg (1994)

11. Duan, Z., Yang, X., Koutny, M.: Framed temporal logic programming. Science of Computer Programming 70(1), 31–61 (2008)

12. Eisner, C., Fisman, D.: A Practical Introduction to PSL. Springer, Heidelberg (2006)

13. Eisner, C., Fisman, D.: Temporal logic made practical. In: Clarke, E.M., Henzinger, T.A., Veith, H. (eds.) Handbook of Model Checking. Springer (Expected 2016). http://www.cis.upenn.edu/~fisman/documents/EF_HBMC14.pdf

14. Eisner, C., Fisman, D., Havlicek, J., McIsaac, A., Van Campenhout, D.: The definition of a temporal clock operator. In: Baeten, J.C.M., Lenstra, J.K., Parrow, J., Woeginger, G.J. (eds.) ICALP 2003. LNCS, vol. 2719, pp. 857–870. Springer, Heidelberg (2003)

15. Guelev, D.P.: A complete proof system for first-order interval temporal logic with projection. J. Log. Comput. 14(2), 215–249 (2004)

16. Guelev, D.P.: Logical interpolation and projection onto state in the Duration Calculus. J. Applied Non-Classical Logics 14(1–2), 181–208 (2004)

17. Guelev, D.P., Van Hung, D.: Prefix and projection onto state in duration calculus. Electr. Notes Theor. Comput. Sci. 65(6), 101–119 (2002)

18. Guelev, D.P., Van Hung, D.: A relatively complete axiomatisation of projection onto state in the Duration Calculus. J. Applied Non-Classical Logics 14(1–2), 149–180 (2004)

19. Halpern, J., Manna, Z., Moszkowski, B.: A hardware semantics based on temporal intervals. In: Diaz, J. (ed.) ICALP 1983. LNCS, vol. 154, pp. 278–291. Springer, Heidelberg (1983)

20. Kleinberg, R.D.: A behavioral model for co-design. In: Wing, J.M., Woodcock, J., Davies, J. (eds.) FM 1999. LNCS, vol. 1709, p. 1420. Springer, Heidelberg (1999)

21. Hollander, Y., Morley, M., Noy, A.: The e language: a fresh separation of concerns. In: Proc. TOOLS Europe 2001: 38th Int'l Conf. on Technology of Object-Oriented Languages and Systems, Components for Mobile Computing, pp. 41–50. IEEE Computer Society Press (2001)

22. Holzmann, G.: The SPIN Model Checker: Primer and Reference Manual. Addison-Wesley Professional (2003)

23. Hughes, G.E., Cresswell, M.J.: A New Introduction to Modal Logic. Routledge, London (1996)

24. IEEE: Standard for Property Specification Language (PSL), Standard 1850–2010. ANSI/IEEE, New York (2010)

25. IEEE: Standard for the Functional Verification Language e, Standard 1647–2011. ANSI/IEEE, New York (2011)

26. IEEE: Standard for SystemVerilog-Unified Hardware Design, Specification, and Verification Language, Standard 1800–2012. ANSI/IEEE, New York (2012)

27. ITL web pages. http://www.antonio-cau.co.uk/ITL/

28. Jones, C.B.: Tentative steps toward a development method for interfering programs. ACM Trans. Program. Lang. Syst. 5(4), 596–619 (1983)

29. Jones, C.B., Hayes, I.J., Colvin, R.J.: Balancing expressiveness in formal approaches to concurrency. Formal Asp. Comput. 27(3), 475–497 (2015)

30. Keller, R.M.: Formal verification of parallel programs. Commun. ACM **19**(7), 371–384 (1976)
31. Kröger, F., Merz, S.: Temporal Logic and State Systems. Texts in Theoretical Computer Science (An EATCS Series). Springer, Heidelberg (2008)
32. Lamport, L.: Specifying Systems: The TLA+ Language and Tools for Hardware and Software Engineers. Addison-Wesley Professional (2002)
33. Manna, Z., Pnueli, A.: The Temporal Logic of Reactive and Concurrent Systems: Specifications. Springer, New York (1992)
34. Morley, M.J.: Semantics of temporal e. In: Melham, T.F., Moller, F.G. (eds.) Banff'99 Higher Order Workshop: Formal Methods in Computation, Ullapool, Scotland, 9–11 Sept. 1999. pp. 138–142. Univ. Glasgow, Dept. Comp. Sci., tech. rep. (1999)
35. Moszkowski, B.: Reasoning about Digital Circuits. Ph.D. thesis, Department of Computer Science, Stanford University, tech. rep. STAN-CS-83-970 (June 1983)
36. Moszkowski, B.: Executing Temporal Logic Programs. Cambridge University Press, Cambridge (1986)
37. Moszkowski, B.: Compositional reasoning about projected and infinite time. In: Proc. 1st IEEE Int'l Conf. on Engineering of Complex Computer Systems (ICECCS'95), pp. 238–245. IEEE Computer Society Press (1995)
38. Moszkowski, B.: A hierarchical completeness proof for Propositional Interval Temporal Logic with finite time. J. Applied Non-Classical Logics **14**(1–2), 55–104 (2004)
39. Moszkowski, B.: A complete axiom system for propositional Interval Temporal Logic with infinite time. Log. Meth. Comp. Sci. **8**(3:10), 1–56 (2012)
40. Newcombe, C., Rath, T., Zhang, F., Munteanu, B., Brooker, M., Deardeuff, M.: How Amazon Web Services uses formal methods. Commun. ACM **58**(4), 66–73 (2015)
41. Olderog, E.R., Dierks, H.: Real-Time Systems: Formal Specification and Automatic Verification. Cambridge University Press, Cambridge (2008)
42. Peterson, G.L.: Myths about the mutual exclusion problem. Inf. Process. Lett. **12**(3), 115–116 (1981)
43. de Roever, W.P., de Boer, F., Hanneman, U., Hooman, J., Lakhnech, Y., Poel, M., Zwiers, J.: Concurrency Verification: Introduction to Compositional and Noncompositional Methods. Cambridge University Press (2001)
44. Chaochen, Z., Hansen, M.R.: Duration Calculus: A Formal Approach to Real-Time Systems. Springer, Heidelberg (2004)
45. Chaochen, Z., Hoare, C.A.R., Ravn, A.P.: A calculus of durations. Inf. Process. Lett. **40**(5), 269–276 (1991)

A High-Level Model for an Assembly Language Attacker by Means of Reflection

Adriaan Larmuseau[1]([⊠]), Marco Patrignani[2], and Dave Clarke[1,2]

[1] Uppsala University, Uppsala, Sweden
Adriaan.Larmuseau@it.uu.se
[2] iMinds-Distrinet, K.U. Leuven, Leuven, Belgium
Marco.Patrignani@cs.kuleuven.be

Abstract. Many high-level functional programming languages are compiled to or interoperate with, low-level languages such as C and assembly. Research into the security of these compilation and interoperation mechanisms often makes use of high-level attacker models to simplify formalisations. In practice, however, the validity of such high-level attacker models is frequently called into question. In this paper we formally prove that a light-weight ML equipped with a reflection operator can serve as an accurate model for malicious assembly language programs, when reasoning about the security threats such an attacker model poses to the abstractions of ML programs that reside within a protected memory space. The proof proceeds by relating bisimulations over the assembly language attacker and the high-level attacker.

1 Introduction

High-level functional programming languages such as ML and Haskell offer programmers numerous security features through abstractions such as type systems, module systems and encapsulation primitives. Motivated by speed and memory efficiency, these high-level functional programming languages are often compiled to low-level target languages such as C and assembly [7] or extended with Foreign Function Interfaces (FFIs) that enable interoperation with these low-level target languages [2]. The security features of these low-level languages, however, rarely coincide with those of functional languages. In practice, the high-level programs are often compromised by low-level components and/or libraries that may be written with malicious intent or susceptible to code injection attacks.

Accurately modeling the impact that such malicious low-level code has on high-level programs is rather challenging, as the semantics of low-level code differs greatly from that of high-level functional programming languages. As an alternative, high-level models that capture the capabilities of certain low-level attackers have been introduced. Jagadeesan *et al.* [3], for example, make use of a λ-calculus extended with low-level memory access operators to model a low-level attacker within a memory with randomized address spaces. The validity of such high-level models for low-level attackers is, however, often called into question.

In this paper we present $\mathcal{L}^a$, a high-level attacker model derived directly from a source language $\mathcal{L}$ by removing type safety and adding a reflection operator.

© Springer International Publishing Switzerland 2015
X. Li et al. (Eds.): SETTA 2015, LNCS 9409, pp. 168–182, 2015.
DOI: 10.1007/978-3-319-25942-0_11

Our claim in previous works [5] has been that this attacker model accurately captures the threats posed by an assembly language attacker to the abstractions of a source language $\mathcal{L}$, when the programs of that language reside within a protected memory space. This protected memory space is provided by the Protected Module Architecture (PMA) [19]. PMA is a low-level memory isolation mechanism, that protects a certain memory area by restricting access to that area based on the location of the program counter. PMA will be supported in a future generation of commercial processors [10]. Our high-level model of the threats that the assembly language attacker, residing outside of the protected memory, poses to the abstractions of programs residing within the protected memory, is thus bound to be useful for many different practical applications.

In what follows, we prove that $\mathcal{L}^a$, despite being simple to derive and formalise, is an accurate model of this assembly language attacker. We do so for an example source language MiniML: a light-weight ML featuring references and recursion, from which we derive a $\mathcal{L}^a$ attacker model MiniML^a. The proof technique proceeds as follows: first we develop a notion of bisimulation over the interactions between the high-level attacker MiniML^a and programs in the source language MiniML. Next we develop a notion of bisimulation over the interactions between the assembly language attacker and programs in MiniML by adopting the labels of a previously developed fully abstract trace semantics for the attacker model [11]. Finally, we establish our result by proving that the latter bisimulation is a full abstraction of the former and vice versa.

The remainder of this paper is organised as follows. Firstly the paper introduces the assembly language attacker and its high-level replacement (Section 2). Secondly it details the example source language MiniML, the derived attacker model MiniML^a and the bisimulation over MiniML^a (Section 3). Next, the paper introduces a bisimulation over the assembly language attacker (Section 4) and then presents a proof of full abstraction between both bisimulations (Section 5). Finally the paper presents related work (Section 6) and concludes (Section 7).

2   Security Overview

This section presents the security-relevant notions of this paper. Firstly it details the PMA enhanced low-level machine model and the associated assembly language attacker (Section 2.1). Then it details contextual equivalence: the formalism used to reason about the abstractions of high-level programming languages as well as the threats that attackers pose to them (Section 2.2). Lastly we introduce our high-level attacker model $\mathcal{L}^a$, for which we prove further on in this paper, that it captures all threats that the low-level attacker poses to the contextual equivalence of a source language $\mathcal{L}$ (Section 2.3).

2.1   PMA and the Assembly Language Attacker

Our low-level attacker is a standard untyped assembly language attacker running on a von Neumann machine consisting of a program counter p, a register file r, a flags register f and a memory space m that maps addresses to words and contains all code and data. The supported instructions are the standard assembly instructions for integer arithmetic, value comparison, address jumping, stack pushing and popping, register loading and memory storing. For a full formalisation of these instructions and their operational semantics we refer the interested reader to Patrignani and Clarke's formalisation [11].

To enable the development of secure applications, for this paper the development of secure programs in MiniML, this machine model has been enhanced with the Protected Module Architecture (PMA). PMA is a fine-grained, program counter-based, memory access control mechanism that divides memory into a protected memory module and unprotected memory [13]. The protected module is further split into two sections: a protected code section accessible only through a fixed collection of designated entry points, and a protected data section that can only be accessed by the code section. As such the unprotected memory is limited to executing the code at entry points. The code section can only be executed from the outside through the entry points and the data section can only be accessed by the code section. An overview of the access control mechanism is given below.

From \ To	Protected			Unprotected
	Entry Point	*Code*	*Data*	
Protected	r x	r x	r w	r w x
Unprotected	x			r w x

A variety of PMA implementations exist. While current implementations of PMA are still research prototypes [13], Intel is developing a new instruction set, referred to as SGX, that will enable the usage of PMA in future commercially available processors [10].

The attacker. The attacker considered in this work is an assembly program that has kernel-level code injection privileges that can be used to introduce malware into a software system. Kernel-level code injection is a critical vulnerability that bypasses all existing software-based security mechanisms: disclosing confidential data, disrupting applications and so forth. The attacker can thus inspect and manipulate every bit of code and data in the system except for the programs that reside within the protected memory of the PMA mechanism. As noted above, PMA is a program counter-based mechanism, which the kernel-level code injection capabilities of this attacker model cannot bypass [13].

2.2 Contextual Equivalence

As detailed in Section 1 our interest in the assembly language attacker of Section 2.1, revolves around the security threat this attacker poses to the abstractions of programs that reside within a protected memory space. We formally reason about this threat by means of *contextual equivalence*, as is often the case in this research field [12]. Contextual equivalence (also known as observational equivalence) provides a notion of observation of the behaviour of a program and states when two programs exhibit the same observable behaviour. Only what can be observed by the context is of any relevance, and this changes from language to language, since different languages have different levels of abstractions. Languages that feature many strong abstractions will thus produce a larger set of contextually equivalent programs then those languages that do not.

Informally, a context C is a program with a single hole $[\cdot]$ that can be filled with a program P, generating a new program $C[P]$. For example, if P is a λ-calculus expression $\lambda x.x$, a context is another λ-calculus expression with a hole, such as $((\lambda y.y)[\cdot])$. Two programs P_1 and P_2 are said to be contextually equivalent if and only if there exists no context C, that can distinguish between the two programs. Contextual equivalence is formalised as follows.

Definition 1. Contextual equivalence $(\simeq)$ *is defined as:*

$$P_1 \simeq P_2 \overset{def}{=} \forall C.\ C[P_1]\Uparrow \iff C[P_2]\Uparrow$$

where $\Uparrow$ denotes divergence [12].

From our security based perspective, contexts model malicious attackers that interoperate with a program P and attack it. Consider, for example, the following two higher-order λ-terms:

$$(a)\ (\lambda x.(x\ 2) + (x\ 2)) \qquad (b)\ (\lambda x.(x\ 2) * 2) \qquad \text{(Ex-1)}$$

In a purely functional λ-calculus with no side-effects, these two terms are contextually equivalent as there is no context that can distinguish them. In a λ-calculus that includes references these two terms are, however, not equivalent as the following context/attack can distinguish between them.

$$\text{let } r = (\textbf{ref } 0) \text{ in } ([\cdot]\ (\lambda y.r :=!r + 1; y)); \text{ if } !r = 2 \text{ then } \Omega \text{ else } 1$$

Applying λ-term (a) will result in divergence as the reference r will be increased twice, whereas applying λ-term (b) will not. The above is thus considered a successful attack against the implementation details of the two λ-terms.

Our low-level assembly-language attacker of Section 2.1 poses an incredibly strong threat to the contextual equivalences of any source language $\mathcal{L}$ as it can compare and manipulate any sequence of bits it has access to. When interoperating with the λ-terms of Ex-1 our low-level attacker could thus distinguish them by doing a bit-wise comparison on their memory encodings.

2.3   The High-Level Attacker Model $\mathcal{L}^a$

Our high-level attacker model $\mathcal{L}^a$ aims to accurately model the threats posed by the assembly-language attacker to the contextual equivalences of a source language $\mathcal{L}$, whose programs reside in the protected memory space of PMA. To ensure that this attacker model can be formalised quickly and easily, we specify it as three simple transformations that one must apply to a source language $\mathcal{L}$ to derive the high-level, but accurate, attacker model $\mathcal{L}^a$.

Transformation 1: removal of type safety. Type safety forces programs to preserve types and avoids stuck states. Removing the typing rules of $\mathcal{L}$ ensures that $\mathcal{L}^a$ has no such restrictions.

Transformation 2: introduction of reflection. The assembly language attacker is not constrained by the source level restrictions of any programming language as it can inspect and manipulate any sequence of bits it has access to. To replicate this observational power we apply an insight from Wand [15], who discovered that the inclusion of reflection into a programming language renders all abstractions and associated source level restrictions meaningless.

Transformation 3: limit control flow. The assembly language attacker is in complete control of its execution. The assembly language attacker can thus apply reflection to any execution mechanisms of the original source language $\mathcal{L}$. The high-level attacker model $\mathcal{L}^a$, however, is derived from $\mathcal{L}$ and is thus susceptible to the same execution mechanisms as $\mathcal{L}$. For $\mathcal{L}^a$ to be an accurate model of the assembly language attacker these mechanisms must be relaxed or removed.

In all of our experimentations with applying the $\mathcal{L}^a$ attacker model to different source languages $\mathcal{L}$, we have encountered but one constraint. It is only possible to derive an accurate attacker model $\mathcal{L}^a$ from a source language $\mathcal{L}$ whose function calls are observable, as an assembly-language attacker can accurately observe function calls and their arguments. It is thus not possible to derive an $\mathcal{L}^a$ style attacker from a purely functional λ-calculus, for example, because, as illustrated in Ex-1 of Section 2.2, function calls are not observable there.

3   A Bisimulation over the High-Level Attacker

To prove the accuracy of the $\mathcal{L}^a$ attacker models in a general manner would require a proof technique capable of reasoning over all source languages. This not being possible, we instead introduce an example source language MiniML (Section 3.1), for which we derive an instance of our $\mathcal{L}^a$ attacker model denoted as MiniML^a (Section 3.2). Next, we model the interactions between MiniML and the high-level attacker MiniML^a by applying our previously developed interoperation semantics [5], resulting in a combined calculus MiniML$^+$ (section 3.3). Lastly a bisimulation $\mathcal{B}^a$ that captures the observations and inputs of the high-level MiniML^a attacker is derived over the semantics of this MiniML$^+$ (Section 3.4). Later on, in Section 5, this bisimulation is related to a bisimulation $\mathcal{B}^l$ over the observations and inputs of the assembly-language attacker (Section 4), to prove the accuracy of the high-level MiniML^a attacker.

In what follows, the source language MiniML is typeset in a `black font`, The attacker model MiniML^a is typeset in a **bold red font**.

3.1   The Source Language MiniML

The source language is MiniML: an extension of the typed λ-calculus featuring constants, references and recursion. The syntax is as follows.

$$t \quad ::= v \mid x \mid (t_1 \ t_2) \mid t_1 \ \mathsf{op} \ t_2 \mid \mathsf{if} \ t_1 \ t_2 \ t_3 \mid \mathsf{ref} \ t \mid t_1 := t_2 \mid t_1; t_2$$
$$\mid \ \mathsf{let} \ x = t_1 \ \mathsf{in} \ t_2 \mid \ !t \mid \mathsf{fix} \ t \mid \mathsf{hash} \ t \mid \mathsf{letrec} \ x : \tau = t_1 \ \mathsf{in} \ t_2$$

```
op ::= + | − | * | < | > | ==
v  ::= unit | l_i | n̄ | (λx : τ.t) | true | false
τ  ::= Bool | Int | Unit | τ₁ → τ₂ | Ref τ
E  ::= [·] | E t | v E | op E t | op v E | if E t₂ t₃ | ...
```

Here $\bar{n}$ indicates the syntactic term representing the number n, τ denotes the types and E is a Felleisen-Hieb-style evaluation context with a hole [·] that lifts the basic reduction steps to a standard left-to-right call-by-value semantics [1]. The letrec operator is syntactic sugar for a combination of let and fix. The operators op apply only to booleans and integers. Locations l_i are an artefact of the dynamic semantics that do not appear in the syntax used by programmers and are tracked at run-time in a store $\mu ::= \emptyset \mid \mu, l_i = v$. Allocating new locations is done deterministically $l_1, .., l_n$. The term hash t maps a location to its index: $l_i \mapsto \bar{i}$, similar to how Java's .hashCode method converts references to integers.

The reduction and type rules are standard and are thus omitted. The interested reader can find a full formalisation of the semantics of MiniML in a companion technical report [6].

3.2 The High-Level Attacker Model MiniML^a

We now apply the three transformations specified for $\mathcal{L}^a$ to MiniML, resulting in a new calculus MiniML^a: the high-level attacker.

Transformation 1: removal of type safety. Removing type safety is a straightforward transformation. The types and type checking rules of MiniML are removed from the formalism and a new term wr is introduced that captures non reducible expressions such as the following one:

$$\mu \mid E[\text{if } v\ t_2\ t_3] \longrightarrow \mu \mid E[\text{wr}] \qquad \textit{where } v \neq true \textit{ or } v \neq false$$

where μ is the run-time store of MiniML^a. While capturing the stuck states of the attacker is not required, removing them from the semantics does significantly simplify proofs over the attacker model without reducing its effectiveness.

Transformation 2: introduce reflection. The most important feature of the $\mathcal{L}^a$ attacker model is the inclusion of a reflection operator, as it renders the abstractions and the associated source level restrictions of a language meaningless [15]. Reflection is added to MiniML^a by means of a syntactic equality testing operator modulo α-equivalence $=_\alpha$. It enables a program in MiniML^a to compare the syntax of any two terms as follows.

$$\frac{t_1 \text{ and } t_2 \text{ are } \alpha\text{-}equiv}{\mu \mid E[t_1 =_\alpha t_2] \longrightarrow \mu \mid E[true]} \qquad \frac{t_1 \text{ and } t_2 \text{ are } not\ \alpha\text{-}equiv}{\mu \mid E[t_1 =_\alpha t_2] \longrightarrow \mu \mid E[false]}$$

Transformation 3: limit control flow. MiniML enforces an evaluation order through the evaluation contexts E (Section 3.1). The α-equivalence testing operator $=_\alpha$ works around this enforced control flow, by not reducing its sub-terms to values.

Attacks in MiniML^a. While MiniML^a is clearly not a low-level code formalism, it does capture all relevant threats to contextual equivalence by the assembly language attacker, as the addition of reflection in MiniML^a by means of the α-equivalence operator, reduces contextual equivalence to α-equivalence [15]. Consider, for example, the following two contextually equivalent MiniML terms.

$$(\lambda x : \texttt{Int}.(+\ x\ x)) \qquad (\lambda x : \texttt{Int}.(*\ 2\ x)) \qquad \text{(Ex-2)}$$

There exists no context/attack in MiniML that can distinguish these two terms. The following MiniML^a context, however, is an attack against this equivalence.

$$\mathbf{C} = (\texttt{if} \ ((\lambda \mathbf{y}.(*\ 2\ \mathbf{y})) \equiv_\alpha [\cdot]) \ \Omega \ \texttt{true})$$

The context distinguishes the two equivalent terms due to the $\equiv_\alpha$ operator's ability to inspect the syntax of MiniML terms, where Ω is a diverging MiniML^a term. A similar context $\mathbf{C}$ can thus be built for every pair of contextually equivalent terms in MiniML apart from α-equivalent terms.

3.3   MiniML$^+$: Interoperation Between MiniML^a and MiniML

To accurately capture the inputs and observations of the high-level attacker we must first introduce a formalism for its interactions with programs in MiniML. To do so we apply our previously developed language interoperation semantics [5]. While there exists many different multi-language semantics (Section 6), our interoperation semantics is the only one that supports separated program states and explicit marshalling rules. The former is required to accurately capture the behaviour of the attacker, the latter is used to simplify and streamline the transition to the low-level attacker model in Section 4.

Concretely the MiniML$^+$-calculus combines the attacker model MiniML^a and the source language MiniML by defining separated program states, specifying marshalling rules, encoding cross boundary function calls through call stacks and sharing data structures through reference objects.

Separated program states. The program state $P = \mathbf{A} \parallel \mathbf{S}$ of MiniML$^+$ is split into two sub-states: an attacker state $\mathbf{A}$ and a MiniML program state $\mathbf{S}$. The reduction rules for MiniML$^+$ programs are denoted as follows: $\mathbf{A} \parallel \mathbf{S} \twoheadrightarrow \mathbf{A}' \parallel \mathbf{S}'$.

The MiniML state $\mathbf{S}$ is either (1) executing a term t of type τ, (2) marshalling out values, (3) marshalling in input from the attacker that is expected to be of type τ or (4) waiting on input.

$$(1)\ \mathtt{N}; \mu \Vdash \Sigma \circ t : \tau \quad (2)\ \mathtt{N}; \mu \Vdash \Sigma \rhd m : \tau \quad (3)\ \mathtt{N}; \mu \Vdash \Sigma \lhd m : \tau \quad (4)\ \mathtt{N}; \mu \Vdash \Sigma$$

where $m = \mathtt{v} \mid v$ as the marshalling rules convert MiniML values to MiniML^a values, and vice versa. The attacker state takes two forms: (1) it executes a MiniML^a term t or (2) is suspended waiting on input from the MiniML program.

$$(1)\ \mathbf{A} = \mu \Vdash \overline{\mathbf{C}} \bullet \mathbf{t} \qquad (2)\ \mathbf{A} = \mu \Vdash \overline{\mathbf{C}}$$

The states never compute concurrently. Whenever the MiniML state $\mathbf{S}$ computes, the attacker state $\mathbf{A}$ is suspended and vice-versa.

Marshalling. Marshalling converts the result of MiniML programs to MiniML^a values and inputs from the MiniML^a attacker to MiniML values. Marshalling, booleans for example, is done as follows.

$$\text{A} \parallel \text{N}; \mu \Vdash \Sigma \lhd b : \text{Bool} \twoheadrightarrow \text{A} \parallel \text{N}; \mu \Vdash \Sigma \lhd b : \text{Bool} \qquad \text{(In-B)}$$

$$\text{A} \parallel \text{N}; \mu \Vdash \Sigma \rhd b : \text{Bool} \twoheadrightarrow \text{A} \parallel \text{N}; \mu \Vdash \Sigma \rhd b : \text{Bool} \qquad \text{(Out-B)}$$

Note that when marshalling, the typing information encoded in the MiniML state is used to ensure that the input does not violate MiniML typing rules.

Call stacks. To ensure that the program state is separable, the combined language must explicitly encode the depth of the interactions between MiniML and the attacker MiniML^a. To do so each state is extended with a call stack. The MiniML state S encodes this call stack as a type annotated stack of evaluation contexts $\Sigma ::= \bar{\text{E}} : \overline{\tau \to \tau'} \mid \varepsilon$, where $\bar{\text{E}}$ denotes a sequence of evaluation contexts E that represent the continuation of computation when a call to the attacker returns and are thus only to be filled in by input originating from the attacker. The stack of evaluation contexts is type annotated, these types are incorporated into the dynamic type checks of the marshalling rules to ensure that the input from the attacker does not break type safety.

In contrast the attacker encodes the call stack through a sequence of contexts/attacks $\overline{C}$, enabling it to attack each interaction with the MiniML program. The attacker stack $\overline{C}$ is updated directly (Share), the MiniML stack Σ is plugged by the result of the marshalling rules (Plug), as follows.

$$\mu \Vdash \overline{C}, C \parallel \text{N}; \mu \Vdash \Sigma \rhd v : \tau \twoheadrightarrow \mu \Vdash \overline{C} \bullet C[v] \parallel \text{N}; \mu \Vdash \Sigma \qquad \text{(Share)}$$

$$\mu \Vdash \overline{C} \parallel \text{N}; \mu \Vdash \Sigma, \text{E} : \tau \to \tau' \lhd v : \tau \twoheadrightarrow \mu \Vdash \overline{C} \parallel \text{N}', \mu \Vdash \Sigma \circ \text{E}[v] : \tau' \qquad \text{(Plug)}$$

Reference objects. Security relevant MiniML terms, namely λ-terms and locations, are shared by providing the attacker with reference objects, objects that refer to the original terms of the program in MiniML. These reference objects, have two purposes: firstly they mask the contents of the original term and secondly they enable the MiniML program residing within the protected memory, to keep track of which locations or λ-terms and locations have been shared with the attacker. MiniML$^+$ models reference objects for λ-terms and locations through names n_i^f and n_i^l respectively. Both names are tracked in the MiniML state S through a map N that records the associated term and type, as follows.

$$\text{N} ::= \star \mid \text{N}, \text{n}_i^f \mapsto (t, \tau) \mid \text{N}, \text{n}_i^l \mapsto (t, \tau)$$

A *fresh* name n_i^f is created deterministically every time a λ-term is shared between the MiniML program and the attacker, in contrast the index i of the name n_i^l will correspond to the index of the location it refers to ($\text{n}_i^l \mapsto l_i$).

The MiniML^a attacker shares only its functions with the MiniML programs. These attacker functions are embedded through a term $^\tau \text{F}(\lambda \text{x}.t)$. A MiniML program calls this embedded attacker function, as follows.

$$\mu \Vdash \overline{C}, C \parallel \text{N}; \mu \Vdash \Sigma \circ \text{E}[(^{\tau_1 \to \tau_2}\text{F}(\lambda \text{x}.t)\ v)] : \tau \twoheadrightarrow \qquad \text{(M-Call)}$$

$$\mu \Vdash \overline{C}, C[((\lambda \text{x}.t)\ [\cdot])] \parallel \text{N}; \mu \Vdash \Sigma, \text{E} : \tau_2 \to \tau \rhd v : \tau_1$$

3.4 $\mathcal{B}^a$: A Bisimulation over the MiniML^a Attacker

To capture the inputs and observations of the high-level MiniML^a attacker in a formalism that can be easily related to the inputs and observations of the assembly language attacker, we define a notion of bisimulation $\mathcal{B}^a$. To do so we define an applicative bisimulation in the style of Jeffrey and Rathke's applicative bisimulation for the $vref$-calculus [4]. The applicative bisimulation is defined through a labelled transition system (LTS), that models the inputs and observations of the high-level MiniML^a attacker in its interactions with the MiniML program. The LTS is a triple $(S, \alpha, \xrightarrow{\alpha})$ where the MiniML states S of MiniML$^+$ are the states of the LTS, α the set of labels and $\xrightarrow{\alpha}$ the labelled transitions between states. The attacker state A is thus not represented in these labelled reductions, instead the labels α denote the observations of the high-level MiniML^a attacker as follows.

$$\alpha ::= \gamma \mid \tau \mid \sqrt{}$$
$$\gamma ::= v? \mid v! \mid wr \mid \gg (\lambda x.t) \mid \gg n_i^l \mid \gg n_i^f \mid \gg ref^\tau \mid !n_i^l$$

The labelled reductions of the LTS are of the form: $S \xrightarrow{\gamma} S'$. The most relevant transitions are as follows.

$$\frac{A \parallel N; \mu \Vdash \Sigma \circ t : \tau \twoheadrightarrow A \parallel N; \mu' \Vdash \Sigma \circ t' : \tau}{N; \mu \Vdash \Sigma \circ t : \tau \xrightarrow{\tau} N; \mu' \Vdash \Sigma \circ t' : \tau} \quad \text{(S-Inner)}$$

$$N; \mu \Vdash \Sigma, E : \tau \to \tau' \xrightarrow{v?} N \Vdash \Sigma, E : \tau \to \tau' \lhd v : \tau \quad \text{(A-V)}$$

$$N; \mu \Vdash \Sigma \xrightarrow{!n_i^l} N; \mu \Vdash \Sigma \circ !l_i : \tau \quad \text{where } N(n_i^l) = (l_i, \text{Ref } \tau) \quad \text{(D-N)}$$

$$N; \mu \Vdash \Sigma \xrightarrow{\gg ref^\tau} N; \mu \Vdash \Sigma, (\text{ref } [\cdot]) : \tau \to \text{Ref } \tau \quad \text{(A-R)}$$

$$N; \mu \Vdash \Sigma \xrightarrow{\gg n_i^f} N; \mu \Vdash \Sigma, (t [\cdot]) : \tau \to \tau' \quad \text{where } N(n_i^f) = (t, \tau \to \tau') \quad \text{(C-N)}$$

$$N; \mu \Vdash \Sigma \circ E[(^{\tau_1 \to \tau_2}F(\lambda x.t)\ v)] : \tau \xrightarrow{\gg (\lambda x.t)} N; \mu \Vdash \Sigma, E : \tau_2 \to \tau \rhd v : \tau_1 \quad \text{(C-L)}$$

$$N; \mu \Vdash \Sigma \lhd wr : \tau \xrightarrow{wr} \star; \emptyset \Vdash \varepsilon \quad \text{(Wr-I)}$$

$$N; \mu \Vdash \Sigma \rhd v : \tau \xrightarrow{v!} N; \mu \Vdash \Sigma \quad \text{(M-V)} \qquad N; \mu \Vdash \Sigma \xrightarrow{wr} \star; \emptyset \Vdash \varepsilon \quad \text{(Wr-C)}$$

The internal reduction steps (S-Inner) and the marshalling transitions are *not observable* to the attacker and are thus labelled as silent through the label τ. The values v that the attacker returns or inputs are decorated with ? (A-V). The values returned by the MiniML program to the attacker, returned as marshalled values v, are decorated with ! (M-V). The attacker can dereference a shared location in a one step transition that is labeled as $!n_i$ (D-N). The attacker can also set locations, create shared locations (A-R) and apply shared MiniML λ-terms through two transitions. In the first step, whose label is decorated with $\gg$, the MiniML program is updated with the requested operation and the targeted term. In the second step the attacker injects an argument as captured by the value sharing rule (A-V). Whenever, an MiniML program calls a function of the attacker (C-L) the attacker observes the call as well as the, immediately following, argument to the function (M-V). If the marshalling fails (Wr-I) or the attacker makes an inappropriate call (Wr-C), the transition is labelled as wrong (wr).

We define a weak bisimulation over this LTS. In contrast to a strong bisimulation, such a bisimulation does not use the silent transitions between two states, thus capturing the fact that the attacker cannot directly observe the number of internal reduction steps within a MiniML program. Define the transition relation $S \overset{\gamma}{\Rightarrow} S'$ as $S \overset{\tau}{\longrightarrow}^* \overset{\gamma}{\longrightarrow} S'$ where $\overset{\tau}{\longrightarrow}^*$ is the reflexive transitive closure of the silent transitions $\overset{\tau}{\longrightarrow}$. Our bismulation $\mathcal{B}^a$ over the observations and inputs of the MiniML^a attacker is now defined as follows.

Definition 2. *The relation $\mathcal{B}^a$ is a **bisimulation** iff* $S_1 \mathcal{B}^a S_2$ *implies:*
  (1) Given $S_1 \overset{\gamma}{\Rightarrow} S_1'$ *there is* S_2' *such that:* $S_2 \overset{\gamma}{\Rightarrow} S_2'$ *and* $S_1' \mathcal{B}^a S_2'$
  (2) Given $S_2 \overset{\gamma}{\Rightarrow} S_2'$ *there is* S_1' *such that:* $S_1 \overset{\gamma}{\Rightarrow} S_1'$ *and* $S_1' \mathcal{B}^a S_2'$

We denote bisimilarity, the largest bisimulation, as $\approx^a$.

Congruence. Just defining a bisimulation over the observations and inputs of the MiniML^a attacker is not enough. We must also prove that the bisimulation accurately captures those observations and inputs. We do this by proving that the bisimulation $\mathcal{B}^a$ is a *congruence*: it coincides with contextual equivalence in MiniML$^+$ where the contexts of MiniML$^+$ are all possible attacks definable in MiniML^a. Formally contextual equivalence over MiniML$^+$ is defined as follows.

Definition 3. Contextual equivalence for MiniML$^+$ ($\simeq^a$) *is defined as:*

$$S_1 \simeq^a S_2 \overset{def}{=} \forall A.(A \parallel S_1)\Uparrow \iff (A \parallel S_2)\Uparrow$$

Theorem 1 (Congruence of the Bisimilarity). $S_1 \simeq^a S_2 \iff S_1 \approx^a S_2$.

A proof of this property is an adaptation of existing results [5], as such we leave it to the companion technical report [6].

4   A Bisimulation over the Assembly Language Attacker

In this section we introduce a bisimulation over the assembly language that captures its interactions with an MiniML program residing in the protected memory of the PMA mechanism. To accurately capture the inputs and observations of the assembly language attacker we adopt the labels of a fully abstract trace semantics over the interactions between the attacker and the protected memory space (Section 4.1). Next, we define the applicative bisimulation $\approx^l$ over an LTS whose state is a low level extension of the MiniML state of Section 3.3 (Section 4.2). Later on in Section 5, we relate this bisimulation to the bisimulation over the high-level attacker to prove the accuracy of the high-level attacker.

4.1   A Trace Semantics for the Assembly Language Attacker

To accurately reason about the capabilities and behaviour of the assembly attacker we make use of the *labels* used by the fully abstract trace semantics of Patrignani and Clarke [11] for assembly programs enhanced with PMA. These trace semantics transitions over a state $\Lambda = (p, r, f, m, s)$ where p is the program counter, m is the protected memory of PMA and s is a descriptor that details where the protected memory partition starts as well as the number of entry points. Additionally Λ can be $(\textbf{unkown}, m, s)$ when modeling the attacker. The attacker thus does not feature an explicit state, instead the labels L capture its observations and inputs as follows.

$$L ::= \alpha \mid \tau \qquad \alpha ::= \sqrt{} \mid \gamma! \mid \gamma? \qquad \gamma ::= call\ p(r) \mid ret\ p(r)$$

A label L can be either an observable action α or a non-observable action τ. Decorations ? and ! indicate the direction of the observable action: from the attacker to the protected memory (?) or vice-versa (!). Observable actions include a tick $\sqrt{}$ indicating termination, and actions γ: function calls or returns to a certain address p, combined with the registers r. These registers convey the arguments of the calls and returns.

The traces provide an accurate model of the attacker as they coincide with contextual equivalence for assembly programs enhanced with PMA.

Proposition 1 (Full Abstraction [11]). $P_1 \simeq_l P_2 \iff \mathsf{Tr}(P_1) = \mathsf{Tr}(P_2)$

Where $\simeq_l$ denotes contextual equivalence between low-level programs and where $\mathsf{Tr}(P)$ computes the traces of a program, with an initial state $\Lambda(P)$ as follows.

$$\mathsf{Tr}(P) = \{\overline{\gamma} \mid \exists \Lambda'.\Lambda(P) \overset{\overline{\gamma}}{\Longrightarrow} \Lambda'\}$$

Note that this trace semantics does not include explicit reads or writes from the protected memory to the unprotected memory or reads and writes from the attacker to the protected memory. The latter is not possible as it violates PMA (Section 2.1), the former is not required in our work as the data shared by MiniML programs fits in to the registers r. Incorporating larger data structures that require low-level reads and writes, has been left for future work.

4.2 $\mathcal{B}^l$: A Bisimulation over the Assembly Language Attacker

While the trace semantics of Section 4.1 provides an accurate method for reasoning about the attacker, the states Λ of that semantics include many low-level details of the protected memory that are not relevant to the result of this paper. We thus define a bisimulation $\mathcal{B}^l$ that keeps the labels of the trace semantics, to denote the inputs and observations of the assembly language attacker, but features a more high-level state that denotes only the relevant information.

This state is a triple $\langle \mathsf{S}, e, \overline{p} \rangle$: the MiniML state of MiniML$^+$ extended with static set of entry points e and a stack of return pointers $\overline{p}$. The MiniML state S captures the current state of the MiniML program interacting with the attacker from within protected memory. The set of entry points e contains the addresses p^e of the entry points into the protected memory that the attacker can call. The stack of return pointers $\overline{p}$ enables the MiniML program to return to the address of the attacker were a call to an entry point originated from.

Note that assembly language attacker inputs and outputs words of bytes w instead of the high-level values v. The marshalling rules of MiniML$^+$ over the

MiniML state S are thus adapted to convert to and from words w. Marshalling *in* a `true` value and marshalling *out* a `false` value, for example, is as follows.

$$\mathsf{N}; \mu \Vdash \Sigma \rhd \mathtt{false} : \mathtt{Bool} \twoheadrightarrow \mathsf{N}; \mu \Vdash \Sigma \rhd \mathtt{0x0} : \mathtt{Bool} \qquad \text{(Out-False)}$$

$$\mathsf{N}; \mu \Vdash \Sigma \lhd \mathtt{0x01} : \mathtt{Bool} \twoheadrightarrow \mathsf{N}; \mu \Vdash \Sigma \lhd \mathtt{true} : \mathtt{Bool} \qquad \text{(In-True)}$$

The numbers $\bar{n}$, and names $\mathrm{n}^l_{\ j}$ and $\mathrm{n}^f_{\ i}$ are converted into a word of bytes w, in a similar manner. Functions p_f from the attacker are embedded as $^{\tau_1 \to \tau_2}\mathsf{F}p_f$.

The bisimulation $\mathcal{B}^l$ is now over defined an LTS $(\langle \mathsf{S}, e, \bar{p} \rangle, L, \xrightarrow{L})$, where L are the labels of the fully abstract trace semantics and $\xrightarrow{L}$ denotes the labelled transitions between the states. The most relevant transitions are as follows.

$$\frac{\mathsf{N}; \mu \Vdash \Sigma \circ t : \tau \twoheadrightarrow \mathsf{N}; \mu' \Vdash \Sigma \circ t' : \tau}{\langle (\mathsf{N}; \mu \Vdash \Sigma \circ t : \tau), e, p_r : \bar{p} \rangle \xrightarrow{\tau} \langle (\mathsf{N}; \mu' \Vdash \Sigma \circ t' : \tau), e, p_r : \bar{p} \rangle} \qquad \text{(S-Inner)}$$

$$\langle (\mathsf{N}; \mu \Vdash \Sigma \circ t : \tau), e, \emptyset \rangle \xrightarrow{call\ p^e_{start}(p_r)?} \langle (\mathsf{N}; \mu \Vdash \Sigma \circ t : \tau), e, p_r : \emptyset \rangle \qquad \text{(A-Start)}$$

$$\langle (\mathsf{N}; \mu \Vdash \Sigma \rhd w : \tau), e, p_r : \bar{p} \rangle \xrightarrow{ret\ p_r\ (w)!} \langle (\mathsf{N}; \mu \Vdash \Sigma), e, \bar{p} \rangle \qquad \text{(M-Ret)}$$

$$\langle (\mathsf{N}; \mu \Vdash \Sigma, \mathsf{E} : \tau \to \tau'), e, \bar{p} \rangle \xrightarrow{ret\ p^e_{retb}(w)?} \langle (\mathsf{N}; \mu \Vdash \Sigma, \mathsf{E} : \tau_f \lhd w : \tau), e, \bar{p} \rangle \quad \text{(A-R)}$$

$$\langle (\mathsf{N}; \mu \Vdash \Sigma), e, \bar{p} \rangle \xrightarrow{call\ p^e_{deref}(w_n, p_r)?} \langle (\mathsf{N}; \mu \Vdash \Sigma \circ !l_i : \tau), e, p_r : \bar{p} \rangle \qquad \text{(A-Deref)}$$
$$where\ \mathsf{N}(w_n) = (l_i, \mathsf{Ref}\ \tau)$$

$$\langle (\mathsf{N}; \mu \Vdash \Sigma), e, \bar{p} \rangle \xrightarrow{call\ p^e_{appl}(w_n, w, p_r)?} \langle (\mathsf{N}; \mu \Vdash \Sigma, (t\ [\cdot]) : \tau \to \tau' \lhd w : \tau), e, \bar{p}' \rangle$$
$$where\ \mathsf{N}(w_n) = (t, \tau \to \tau')\ and\ \bar{p}' = p_r : \bar{p} \qquad \text{(A-Apply)}$$

$$\langle (\mathsf{N}; \mu \Vdash \Sigma \lhd wr : \tau), e, p_r : \bar{p} \rangle \xrightarrow{\checkmark} \langle (\star; \emptyset \Vdash \epsilon), e, \emptyset \rangle \qquad \text{(Wr-I)}$$

$$\langle (\mathsf{N}; \mu \Vdash \Sigma, \mathsf{E} : \tau \to \tau'), e, \bar{p} \rangle \xrightarrow{ret\ p(w)?} \langle (\star; \emptyset \Vdash \epsilon), e, \emptyset \rangle\ where\ p \neq p^e_{retb} \quad \text{(Wr-R)}$$

$$\langle (\mathsf{N}; \mu \Vdash \Sigma), e, p_r : \bar{p} \rangle \xrightarrow{call\ p(\bar{w})?} \langle (\star; \emptyset \Vdash \epsilon), e, \emptyset \rangle \quad where\ p \notin e \qquad \text{(Wr-C)}$$

$$\text{(M-Call)}$$
$$\frac{\begin{array}{c} \mathsf{N}; \mu \Vdash \Sigma \circ \mathsf{E}[(^{\tau_1 \to \tau_2}\mathsf{F}p_f\ v)] : \tau \twoheadrightarrow \mathsf{N}; \mu \Vdash \Sigma, \mathsf{E} : \tau_2 \to \tau \rhd v : \tau_1 \\ \mathsf{N}; \mu \Vdash \Sigma, \mathsf{E} : \tau_2 \to \tau \rhd v : \tau_1 \twoheadrightarrow^* \mathsf{N}; \mu \Vdash \Sigma, \mathsf{E} : \tau_2 \to \tau \rhd w : \tau_1 \end{array}}{\langle (\mathsf{N}; \mu \Vdash \Sigma \circ \mathsf{E}[(^{\tau_1 \to \tau_2}\mathsf{F}p_f\ v)] : \tau), e, \bar{p} \rangle \xrightarrow{call\ p_f(w)!} \langle (\mathsf{N}; \mu \Vdash \Sigma, \mathsf{E} : \tau_2 \to \tau), e, \bar{p} \rangle}$$

Transitions within the MiniML program, such as for example S-Inner, are not observable the attacker and are thus again labelled as silent. To start the computation of the MiniML program, the low-level attacker calls the entry point p^e_{start} passing as its only argument p_r the address at which it expects the result returned (A-Start). When the MiniML program returns to that address (M-Ret), it makes use of modified marshalling rules to return a word w to the address at the head of the stack $\bar{p}$ instead of MiniML^a values, as detailed earlier. The assembly language attacker, in contrast, has less freedom for its returns. Because it cannot jump to an address of the protected memory outside of the entry points, it must return its values through a return entry point p^e_{retb} (A-R). Whereas each operation by the high-level attacker on the MiniML terms shared to it through names n_i was denoted with its own label, the assembly language attacker calls a separate entry point for each operation (A-Deref,A-Apply) passing a byte word representation of the names (w_n) as an argument to the call. Whenever the assembly-language attacker makes a mistake by either providing words that cannot be marshalled (Wr-I) or by calling or returning to an inaccessible address (Wr-C,Wr-R) the protected memory is terminated to the empty state $\langle(\star; \emptyset \Vdash \varepsilon), e, \emptyset\rangle$. While the attacker makes many different types of calls to the protected memory, the MiniML program, only calls attacker functions p_f whenever it applies them to an MiniML value (M-Call).

We now define a notion of *weak* bisimulation, that does not take into account the silent transitions τ only the actions α, over the LTS. Define the transition relation $\langle S, e, \overline{p}\rangle \stackrel{\alpha}{\Longrightarrow} \langle S', e, \overline{p}'\rangle$ as $\langle S, e, \overline{p}\rangle \stackrel{\tau}{\longrightarrow}^* \stackrel{\alpha}{\longrightarrow} \langle S', e, \overline{p}'\rangle$ where $\stackrel{\tau}{\longrightarrow}^*$ is the reflexive transitive closure of the silent transitions $\stackrel{\tau}{\longrightarrow}$.

Definition 4. $\mathcal{B}^l$ *is a bisimulation iff* $\langle S_1, e_1, \overline{p_1}\rangle \mathcal{B} \langle S_2, e_2 \overline{p_2}\rangle$ *implies:*

1. *Given* $\langle S_1, e_1, \overline{p_1}\rangle \stackrel{\alpha}{\Longrightarrow} \langle S'_1, e_1, \overline{p_1}'\rangle$, *There is* $\langle S'_2, e_2, \overline{p_2}'\rangle$ *such that* $\langle S_2, e_2, \overline{p_2}\rangle \stackrel{\alpha}{\Longrightarrow} \langle S'_2, e_2, \overline{p_2}'\rangle$ *and* $\langle S'_1, e_1, \overline{p_1}'\rangle \mathcal{B} \langle S'_2, e_2, \overline{p_2}'\rangle$
2. *Given* $\langle S_2, e_2, \overline{p_2}\rangle \stackrel{\alpha}{\Longrightarrow} \langle S'_2, e_2, \overline{p_2}'\rangle$, *There is* $\langle S'_1, e_1, \overline{p_1}'\rangle$ *such that* $\langle S_1, e_1, \overline{p_1}\rangle \stackrel{\alpha}{\Longrightarrow} \langle S'_1, e_1, \overline{p_1}'\rangle$ *and* $\langle S'_1, e_1, \overline{p_1}'\rangle \mathcal{B} \langle S'_2, e_2, \overline{p_2}'\rangle$

We denote bisimilarity, the largest bisimulation as, $\approx^l$.

5   Full Abstraction

We now establish the accuracy of the high-level attacker by proving that the bisimulation over the assembly-language attacker is a full abstraction of the bisimulation over the high-level MiniML^a attacker. We thus prove that there is no assembly language attacker action that affects the abstractions of MiniML programs residing in the protected memory, that cannot be replicated by the high-level attacker MiniML^a.

Theorem 2 (Full Abstraction). $\{t_1\}^\uparrow \approx^a \{t_2\}^\uparrow \iff \{t_1\}^\downarrow \approx^l \{t_2\}^\downarrow$

where $\{t\}^\uparrow$ denotes the start state: $(\star; \emptyset \Vdash \varepsilon \circ t : \tau)$ of an MiniML term t when faced with the MiniML^a attacker and where $\{t\}^\downarrow$ denotes the start state: $\langle(\star; \emptyset \Vdash \varepsilon \circ t : \tau), e, \emptyset\rangle$ of an MiniML term when faced with the assembly language attacker.

The proof splits the thesis into two sublemma: preservation and reflection.

Lemma 1. (Preservation) $\{t_1\}^\uparrow \approx^a \{t_2\}^\uparrow \Rightarrow \{t_1\}^\downarrow \approx^l \{t_2\}^\downarrow$.

Proof Sketch. We must establish that there exists a relation $\mathcal{R}$, so that: (1) $\{t_1\}^\downarrow \mathcal{R} \{t_2\}^\downarrow$ and (2) that $\mathcal{R}$ relates low-level states $\langle S, e, \overline{p}\rangle$ and $\langle S', e', \overline{p}'\rangle$ as would $\mathcal{B}^l$. We define $\mathcal{R}$ as a union of relations $\mathcal{R} = \mathcal{R}_0 \cup \mathcal{R}_1 \cup \mathcal{R}_2 \cup \mathcal{R}_3$: one relation for each possible kind of low-level state. The relation $\mathcal{R}_0$ relates halted states: $\langle(N; \mu \Vdash \Sigma), e, \overline{p}\rangle$ and $\langle(N'; \mu' \Vdash \Sigma'), e', \overline{p}'\rangle$ and enforces that the name maps are equivalent: $Dom(N) = Dom(N') \wedge \forall n_i.N(n_i) \simeq N'(n_i)$, the evaluation stacks are equivalent: $|\Sigma| = |\Sigma'| \wedge \forall E, E', t.E[t] \simeq E'[t]$, the entry point sets are equal

$e = e'$, and that the return address stacks are equal as well $\bar{p} = \bar{p}'$. The relation $\mathcal{R}_1$ relates two states reducing terms contextually equivalent terms t and t' in addition to upholding $\mathcal{R}_0$. The relations $\mathcal{R}_2$ and $\mathcal{R}_3$ relate the marshalling states, they require that $\mathcal{R}_0$ holds and that the marshalled terms are equal if they are assembly language terms. Case (1) now follows from the assumption. Case (2) proceeds by analysis on the label L. The most challenging sub-case is the call from MiniML to the low-level attacker labelled as $L = call\ p_f(w)!$. To prove that both states will perform the same outward calls, we rely on the insight that by including references in MiniML we have that two equivalent MiniML terms will perform the same function calls, as illustrated for (Ex-1) in Section 2.2.

Lemma 2. (Reflection) $\{t_1\}^\downarrow \approx^l \{t_2\}^\downarrow \Rightarrow \{t_1\}^\uparrow \approx^a \{t_2\}^\uparrow$.

Proof Sketch. We prove the contrapositive: $\{t_1\}^\uparrow \not\approx^a \{t_2\}^\uparrow \Rightarrow \{t_1\}^\downarrow \not\approx^l \{t_2\}^\downarrow$. The proof has two cases. In the first case the bisimulation fails immediately as the MiniML terms t_1 and t_2 embedded in S either reduce to difference values or diverge. These differing LTS transitions are replicated directly in the low-level bisimulation, the only difference being the inclusion of a start transition with label: $call\ p^e_{\text{start}}(p_r)$ that starts the reduction of the embedded MiniML terms. In the second case there is a sequence of context actions ($\gg (\lambda x.t)\ |\ \gg n^i_i\ |\ \gg n^f_i\ |\ \gg \text{ref}^\tau\ |\ !n^i_i$) that result in two states where different LTS transitions apply. In this case we establish the thesis by showing that each high-level attacker action can be replicated by an assembly-language attacker action.

Full proofs for both lemmas are provided in a companion report [6].

6   Related Work

Our attacker model is based on the insights of Wand [15] on the nature of programming language reflection. Alternative attacker models are Jagadeesan *et al.*'s attacker language with low-level memory access operators [3] or the erasure function approach of several non-interference works [8]. The former is only suitable for low-memory models with address space randomization, the latter does not lend itself to low-level attackers.

In Section 3.3 we use the interoperation semantics of Larmuseau *et al.* [5] to model the interoperation between the MiniML^a attacker and the source language MiniML. There exist multiple alternatives for language interoperation: Matthews and Findler's multi-language semantics [9] enables two languages to interoperate through direct syntactic embedding and Zdancewic *et al.*'s multi-agent calculus that treats the different modules or calculi that make up a program as different principals, each with a different view of the environment [16]. These alternatives, however, do not provide separated program states or explicated marshalling rules both required to model the assembly language attacker.

Our notions of bisimulation over the interactions of the high-level and low-level attackers are based on the bisimulations for the νref-calculus by Jeffrey and Rathke [4]. An alternative approach could be the environmental bisimulations of Sumii and Pierce [14], which would not require a hash operation in MiniML to make the locations observable within the labels. Their bisimulations, however, do not provide a clear formalism to reason about the observations of an attacker.

7   Conclusions

This paper presented a high-level attacker model $\mathcal{L}^a$ that captures the threat that an assembly-language attacker poses to the abstractions of a program that resides within the memory space protected by PMA, a low-level memory isolation mechanism. The accuracy of this high-level attacker model was proven for an example language MiniML, by relating a bisimulation over the the high-level attacker model to a bisimulation over the assembly language attacker.

References

1. Felleisen, M., Hieb, R.: The revised report on the syntactic theories of sequential control and state. Theoret. Comput. Sci. **103**(2), 235–271 (1992)
2. Furr, M., Foster, J.S.: Checking type safety of foreign function calls. In: PLDI 2005, pp. 62–72. ACM (2005)
3. Jagadeesan, R., Pitcher, C., Rathke, J., Riely, J.: Local memory via layout randomization. In: CSF 2011, pp. 161–174. IEEE (2011)
4. Jeffrey, A., Rathke, J.: Towards a theory of bisimilarity for local names. In: Logic in Computer Science, pp. 56–66. IEEE (2000)
5. Larmuseau, A., Clarke, D.: Formalizing a secure foreign function interface. In: Calinescu, R., Rumpe, B. (eds.) SEFM 2015. LNCS, vol. 9276, pp. 215–230. Springer, Heidelberg (2015)
6. Larmuseau, A., Clarke, D.: Modelling an Assembly Attacker by Reflection. Technical Report 2015–026, Uppsala University (2015)
7. Leroy, X., Doligez, D., Garrigue, J., Rémy, D., Vôuillon, J.: The Objective Caml system, release 4.02. Technical report, INRIA, August 2014
8. Li, P., Zdancewic, S.: Arrows for secure information flow. Theoret. Comput. Sci. **411**(19), 1974–1994 (2010)
9. Matthews, J., Findler, R.B.: Operational semantics for multi-language programs. TOPLAS, 31(3):12:1–12:44 (2009)
10. McKeen, F., Alexandrovich, I., Berenzon, A., Rozas, C.V., Shafi, H., hanbhogue, V., Savagaonkar, U.R.: Innovative instructions and software model for isolated execution. In: HASP 2013, pp. 10:1–10:1. ACM (2013)
11. Patrignani, M., Clarke, D.: Fully Abstract Trace Semantics of Low-level Isolation Mechanisms. In: SAC 2014, pp. 1562–1569. ACM (2014)
12. Plotkin, G.: LCF considered as a programming language. Theor. Comput. Science **5**, 223–255 (1977)
13. Strackx, R., Piessens, F.: Fides: Selectively hardening software application components against kernel-level malware. In: CCS 2012, pp. 2–13. ACM
14. Sumii, E., Pierce, B.C.: A bisimulation for dynamic sealing. In: POPL 2004, pp. 161–172. ACM (2004)
15. Wand, M.: The theory of fexprs is trivial. Lisp and Symbolic Computation **10**(3), 189–199 (1998)
16. Zdancewic, S., Grossman, D., Morrisett, G.: Principals in programming languages:a syntactic proof technique. In: ICFP 1999, pp. 197– 207. ACM

Design and Implementation

Improving Design Decomposition

David Faitelson[1]([✉]) and Shmuel Tyszberowicz[2]

[1] Afeka Tel-Aviv Academic College of Engineering, Tel Aviv, Israel
davidf@afeka.ac.il
[2] The Academic College Tel Aviv-Yaffo, Tel Aviv, Israel
tyshbe@tau.ac.il

Abstract. Decomposing a system into subsystems is essential to the design of large software systems. Traditionally, it is performed intuitively without rigorously analyzing the system model. This makes it difficult to check the decomposition correctness, and risks creating subsystems that are either too tightly coupled or not cohesive enough. An aggravating factor is that traditionally classes are the atomic design units. In many cases, however, the same classes play a role in more than one subsystem, and partitioning them unbroken among the subsystems may increase coupling and reduce cohesion. We present an analytical approach that enables reasoning about early exploration of decomposition alternatives. In addition, we describe a visual notation for diagramming the composition of subsystems, and an automatic technique for suggesting good decompositions. A key to our approach is that individual relations, not classes, are the atomic design units. We illustrate the approach with examples and demonstrate its effectiveness on a commercial system.

Keywords: Decomposition · Coupling · Cohesion · Visualization · Refinement

1 Introduction

Decomposing a system into subsystems is an essential activity in the design of large software systems. Traditionally, subsystem decomposition is performed intuitively, based on the experience of the system designers [12], not on any rigorous analysis of the actual dependencies between the system's functionality and structure. While intuition is indispensable, relying solely on it has caused many systems to fail to meet their requirements due to poor design [19].

There is not a lot of modern work on functional decomposition. Software architecture explores different decomposition styles to address non-functional concerns (e.g. peer-to-peer to address distribution, pipe and filter to address throughput, layers to address security and incremental development, etc. [9]). Similarly, the aspect oriented approach deals with non-functional concerns that crosscut the entire system (tracing, logging, synchronization, etc.). Neither, however, address functional decomposition.

This work has been partially supported by GIF (grant No. 1131-9.6/2011).

X. Li et al. (Eds.): SETTA 2015, LNCS 9409, pp. 185–200, 2015.
DOI: 10.1007/978-3-319-25942-0_12

The object-oriented design (OOD) literature does not say much about subsystem decomposition, as most discussions focus on finding classes. Even when this problem is addressed, it receives little treatment and often the advice is to partition the system into "loosely coupled, strongly cohesive" modules, without saying how to find such a decomposition. An exception is [9], that offers two heuristics: one is to create subsystems from groups of classes that are densely connected and the other is to create a subsystem from the classes that participate in each use case. In practice, however, this advice is very hard to follow. The problem is that traditional OOD assumes that classes are atomic design units and decomposition is defined as partitioning classes between subsystems. In many cases, however, such an approach leads to fundamental difficulties. For example, consider a restaurant management system that keeps track of orders, reservations, and a waiting list of people waiting outside. As ordering food, managing reservations, and managing the wait list are separate areas of functionality, it is reasonable to partition the system into three subsystems. The concept of a table is essential to this domain, thus we define a class to model it. But in which subsystem should we put it? In the subsystem that manages the orders? In the subsystem that keeps track of reservations? Or should we create a special subsystem to hold the class?

In general, many conceptual entities may be shared by the different areas of functionality that a system manages. But if we model each entity as an atomic class we create an artificial problem of where to put the class (i.e., in which subsystem). Creating subsystems to hold the overlapping concepts is bad, because such subsystems have poor cohesion and no coherent behavior. Instead, we argue that it is better to allocate individual relations to the subsystems according to how they are used by the system operations. The class, once broken, is used only to represent the unique identity of its instances, to ensure that the subsystems refer to the same (problem domain) objects.

Regarding our restaurant example, it may be better to split the attributes and associations of the table class into subsets of coherent functionality: the attributes that correspond to taking orders become a part of the orders subsystem, the attributes and associations that keep track of the waiting list become a part of the waiting list subsystem, etc. Instances of the table class can be used as identifiers, to ensure that all the subsystems refer to the same set of tables.

Our contribution consists of: (1) a method for scaling formal system models by breaking them into modular subsystems, (2) criteria for reasoning about the decomposition correctness, (3) a technique for visualizing the impact of decomposition choices on the system's functional structure, and (4) an approach for automatically finding good (low coupling/high cohesion) subsystem candidates.

In the following sections we describe a formal model of software systems that takes relations as atomic units of design. We then explain how we can use it to model software systems and subsystem decompositions, and how we can reason about their correctness. Next, we show how to visualize the dependencies between the system operations and state variables, and how this facilitates the

```
sig Table { occupied : set Diner }
sig Diner { reservations : set Table }
fact { ∀ t  : Table • lone t.occupied }
```

Fig. 1. A simple Alloy model. Note that w are using a LaTeX package that replaces Alloy keywords with their equivalent mathematical symbols.

selection of good decompositions. We explain how to use the approach even when the system is developed without a formal model. Finally, we provide a case study to demonstrate the approach's scalability.

2   A Relational Model of Software Systems

The relational state based model is a familiar approach to the specification of software systems [2,3,15,26]. In essence, a relational model consists of: (i) a finite collection of sets of atomic entities (basic sets in Z, atoms in Alloy), (ii) a finite set of state variables, each being a relation between the basic sets, (iii) an invariant predicate that constrains the sets and relational variables to fit the requirements of the system that we model, and (iv) a finite set of operation-specifications, each a predicate that defines the effect of an operation by describing the relation of the state variables before the operation begins to their value after it ends.

As we are using Alloy in this paper, we explain briefly its essential concepts and the modeling style that we are using. For more details see [15]. In a nutshell, the Alloy language describes constraints over relational variables that range over relations between sets of atoms. The constraints are first order predicates on the variables. To make Alloy more friendly to software engineers, these concepts are presented in a syntax similar to that of popular object oriented languages. For example, the Alloy model in Fig. 1 appears similar to a class model with two classes, `Table` having an `occupied` field and `Diner` having a `reservations` field. But actually, this model defines two sets of atoms (`Table` and `Diner`) and two relational variables (`occupied` is a relation between `Table` and `Diner` and `reservations` is a relation between `Diner` and `Table`). The relational semantics behind the object-oriented skin becomes apparent when we write expressions such as `~occupied` (the inverse relation of `occupied`) or `reservations.occupied` (the relational composition of `reservations` and `occupied`). In addition the model defines a constraint (`fact`) that ensures a table can be occupied by at most one (`lone`) diner[1].

Alloy has no predefined notion of a software system. Therefore, we must adopt a particular style and a set of conventions for writing such models. In the style that we use[2], each system variable that represents a relation of arity n is modeled as a relational variable with an arity of $n+1$, the extra dimension representing the moment in time (aka the system's state, because the system evolves through

---

[1] This can be written more concisely; we write it this way to illustrate facts in general.

[2] This style is explained in detail in chapter 6 of [15].

Table 1. A summary of the operations provided by the restaurant management system.

Operation	Description
reserve	reserve a table for a diner at a future date
unreserve	cancel an existing reservation
leave	remove a diner from the waiting list
wait	add a diner to the waiting list
order	order food for an occupied table
cancel	cancel an order
checkin	assign a diner to a free table
checkout	clear the table of a diner that has left the restaurant
prepare	setup reserved tables and release stale reservations

```
sig State { today : Date }
sig Dish {}
sig Diner {
  waiting : set State,
  head : set State, // last person in waiting list
  next : Diner lone -> State, // next in waiting list
  reservations : Table -> Date -> State }
sig Table {
  free, occupied : set State,
  reserved : Diner -> Date -> State,
  orders : Dish -> State }
pred wait[s,s': State,p: Diner] {
  s.today = s'.today and p ∉ waiting.s and no free.s
  waiting.s' = waiting.s + p
  next.s' = next.s + p -> head.s
  head.s' = p
  reservations.s' = reservations.s
  orders.s' = orders.s
  occupied.s' = occupied.s
  reserved.s' = reserved.s
  free.s' = free.s }
```

Fig. 2. An Alloy fragment of the restaurant system model.

a sequence of discrete time steps) in which the variable held this particular value. For example, to model how the occupied relation changes when the system operates, we replace its definition with occupied: Diner->State. We can now write occupied.s1 and occupied.s2 to refer to the value of occupied at different system states. Note that in this modeling style the State signature has no fields of its own. In general, given a system with n state variables $v_1, \ldots, v_n$ the state of the system at a particular moment s is defined as the value of all the state variables at moment s, that is as $v_1.s, \ldots, v_n.s$.

Finally, to model system operations, we use Alloy pred definitions. For example, the predicate *wait* in Fig. 2 models the operation that adds a diner to

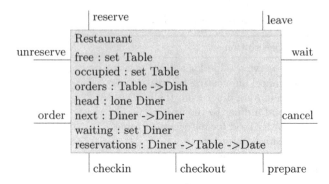

Fig. 3. A subsystem diagram of the entire restaurant system model.

the waiting list when the restaurant is full. The states s and s' represent the system state just before the operation begins (s) and immediately after it ends (s'). The operation is enabled when the restaurant is full and the diner is not already waiting. It adds the diner p to the end of the waiting list, and keep everything else unchanged. All other system operations are similarly described. A complete model is available online [1]. We summarize the system operations in Table 1.

As a system model can be long, we will summarize it in a *subsystem diagram* (see Fig. 3). [3] The subsystem diagram represents the system as a box with its state variables inside, and its operations as short line segments protruding from the edges of the box. There are two important differences between the way the state variables appear in the model and in the diagram. First, in the diagram they appear as relations without using the `sig` keyword (remember that a field `x: T` in signature `A` is a relation `x: A->T`). Second, as each state variable has a final `State` component we omit it from the diagram. E.g., the field `free: set State` of sig `Table` (the relation `free: Table->State`), becomes, after removing `State`, the variable `free: set Table` that represents the set of free tables at a particular state. As we will see in the next section, this diagram is very useful to describe the structure of subsystem models.

3   Subsystem Decomposition

Modeling. Now that we have formalized the notion of a software system model, we can rephrase the problem of decomposition in precise terms: given a system model that consists of a state space, an invariant, and a finite set of operations, how can we partition it into subsystems, each with its own state space, invariant and operations, such that when these subsystems communicate with each other, the result refines [21] the original system?

---

[3] We have borrowed the idea for these diagrams from the informal diagrams that are often used to summarize CSP [25] models.

```
pred WaitingList_wait[s,s': State,p: Diner] {
  s.today = s'.today and p ∉ waiting.s
  waiting.s' = waiting.s + p
  next.s' = next.s + p -> head.s
  head.s' = p }
pred Reception_is_full[s,s': State] {
    no free.s
    occupied.s' = occupied.s
    free.s' = free.s  }
pred wait[s,s': State,p: Diner] {
  WaitingList_wait[s,s',p]
  Reception_is_full[s,s']
  Orders_skip[s,s']
  Reservations_skip[s,s'] }
```

Fig. 4. Assembling the *wait* operation in the restaurant subsystem (modular) model.

Our solution is to model decomposition as a syntactical partition of the state space; i.e., the subsystems partition the set of system state variables. The operations of each subsystem may access only the subsystem's variables. Each subsystem operation is still a predicate on the entire state space, but it refers only to the variables of the subsystem, leaving the other variables unspecified. This facilitates composition of subsystems by conjoining their operations (in Alloy, predicates on separate lines are implicitly conjoined). For example, we have decomposed the restaurant system into 4 subsystems: *Orders* keeps track of the food served to tables, *Reception* is responsible for allocating tables to incoming diners, *WaitingList* manages the queue of waiting customers, and *Reservations* manages reservation requests. The system operation *wait* (Fig. 4) is now achieved by cooperation with the *Reception* and *WaitingList* subsystems, while the other subsystems are not involved. Figure 5 is a subsystem diagram that summarizes the structure of the decomposition. The diagram clearly shows which parts of the state space belong to which subsystems, and how the subsystem operations are used to support the system operations. Note that we do not specify how the subsystems communicate, only what information is passed between them. Essentially, we assume a perfect communication medium. We could, in principle, describe the medium explicitly by adding buffer components between the subsystems, each one will hold variables for the messages in transit. But unless we are interested in designing mechanisms for overcoming communication problems (e.g., messages disappearing or getting out of order) adding such components will only complicate the model without providing any additional value.

We can verify the decomposition by checking that the compositional (modular) form of each system operation refines the original unpartitioned (monolithic) version.[4] We are using data-refinement ([26], Chapter 18) with the special case of

---

[4] We could insist that the two versions be equivalent but refinement gives more freedom for specifying the subsystems.

an identity function for the retrieve relation.[5] E.g., to check that *wait* is correctly implemented, we must show that

$$\forall\, s, s' : State, d : Diner \bullet Modular/wait[s, s', d] \Rightarrow Monolithic/wait[s, s', d]$$
$$\forall\, s, s' : State, d : Diner \bullet$$
$$Monolithic/wait[s, s', d] \Rightarrow \exists\, s'' : State \mid Modular/wait[s, s'', d]$$

The first predicate ensures that every behavior of the modular model is also a behavior of the monolithic model, and the second ensures that the modular version of the operation can be used whenever the monolithic version can be used. A similar check must be made to every operation. As the focus of this paper is not on proof methods, we leave the question of how to check these predicates open. One could use a theorem prover, informal reasoning, or a model finder.[6]

Once we are satisfied with the correctness of the decomposition, we can create a separate model for each subsystem. We can then develop each subsystem independently, e.g. by data refinement [26] or by decomposing the subsystem itself into further subsystems. Every time we refine the model, we increase the number of its state space variables, thus complexity grows. Every time we decompose the system, we decrease the number of state space variables in each subsystem, hence decreasing complexity. Provided that the subsystems are decoupled, the decomposition effect is to offset the increase in complexity that results from making the model more concrete. This combination of data refinement and subsystem decomposition steps, facilitates scalable development of large formal models. To illustrate, if we start with an abstract model that consists of k state variables, and perform 3 data refinement steps in which we double the number of state variables, interleaved with 3 decomposition steps in which we halve the number of state variables, we end with 2^3 subsystems, each consisting of k state variables. Without decomposition we will have a single model that consists of $8k$ state variables. It is much easier to reason about each individual subsystem (and all can be analyzed in parallel) than to reason about the large monolithic model.

So far we have described a relational approach to model software systems, and illustrated how it can be used to create an abstract version of an entire system, how it can be decomposed into a subsystem model, and how the decomposition can be verified. We have also introduced the subsystem diagram, which summarizes the decomposition by listing the state variables and operations of each subsystem and by showing how the subsystem operations collaborate to support the system operations. But how can we find a good decomposition?

Visualizing. A good decomposition partitions a system into loosely coupled, yet cohesive subsystems. Our approach to finding such a decomposition is to visualize the relationships between the system operations and the state variables that they use, in such a way that we can recognize clusters of dense relationships

---

[5] because we do not change the representation of the state variables.

[6] For an example of how this is performed with the Alloy analyzer, see the complete model in the online website [1].

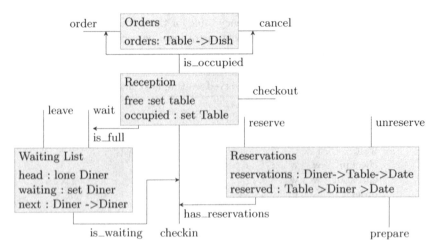

Fig. 5. A subsystem diagram of the restaurant system. Each subsystem box contains a subset of the system's state variables and operations. All the system operations must appear in the diagram. When a system operation is supported by a single subsystem, we draw a line on the border of the subsystem labeled with the operation's name. When several subsystems collaborate to support a system operation, we connect the subsystem operations to the system operation's line segment.

that are weakly connected to other clusters. Each such cluster is a good candidate for a subsystem for two reasons: (i) the amount of information it shares with the rest of the system is small, thus it is protected from changes in the rest of the system and vice versa, and (ii) its internal relationships are relatively dense which in most cases indicates a cohesive unit of functionality.

To create the visualization, we record in an *operation/relation table* the relationships between the system operations and the state variables that they read and write.[7] For example, Table 2 records the operation/relation dependencies in the restaurant system. An operation reads a variable if it refers to the variable only at the current system state. It writes to a variable if the variable is referenced in the next system state. For example, the operation *wait* only reads the variable *free* because it uses this variable to check that the restaurant is not full, but does not change its value (in fact it insists that it remains the same). In contrast, the operation changes the variable *head* because it sets *head* to the new diner in the next system state (see Fig. 2). Currently we produce the table by hand, however, it should not be difficult to write a tool that will generate the table from an Alloy model that follows our specification style.

We now use the table to build[8] an undirected bipartite graph whose vertices are the system's state variables and operations. An edge connects operation p to variable v if and only if p uses v (either reads or writes to v). In addition, we assign a weight to each edge, depending on the nature of the connection. A

---

[7] The information for this table is taken from the functional specification of the system.
[8] Building the graph could be easily automated.

Table 2. An operation/relation dependency table for the restaurant system. Columns represent state variables and rows represent operations ('w' write, 'r' read).

Operation	State variable						
	free	occupied	reserved	waiting	next	head	orders
reserve			w				
unreserve	w		w				
leave				w	w	w	
wait	r			w	w	w	
checkin	w	w	r	r			
checkout	w	w					
order		r					w
cancel		r					w
prepare	w		w				

read connection has the lowest weight (currently 1) and a write connection has the highest weight (currently 2). This choice tends to cluster together data with operations that change the data, thus preferring read interfaces between clusters. A write interface has a stronger coupling than a read interface because it actively engages both subsystems whereas a read interface affects only the reader. Finally, we use a spring model based drawing algorithm [16] to visualize the graph.[9] The algorithm draws undirected graphs such that nodes that are close to each other in graph theoretic space (i.e. shorted weighted path) are drawn closer to each other (see Fig. 6). The result clearly visualizes the dependencies between the system's operations and state variables. For example, we can see that the *orders* state variable is used by just 2 operations: *cancel*, and *order*. No other operation needs this variable. Similarly, the *waiting* state variable is used only by *wait*, *leave*, and *checkin*. We can use this visualization in three ways: (i) to suggest low dependency partitions, (ii) to evaluate partitions that are dictated by non-functional constraints, and (iii) to explore changes to the system model that reduce the dependencies between areas that we consider as good subsystem candidates. Figure 7 shows a partition based on the visualized graph, illustrating the first usage. We now illustrate the other two.

Exploring Alternative Decompositions. The partition we have selected in the previous section is not the only reasonable choice. Figure 8 shows two additional partitions. We can reason about which partition yields weaker dependencies by comparing the number and weight of the edges that cross the partitions. We can see that the right hand version connects two subsystems that are unconnected in the left hand version. Thus it may be better to use the one on the left.[10]. Adding non-functional requirements may force a different decomposition (e.g. some subsystems must run on specific hosts). In such cases we can use

---

[9] More specifically, we use neato [23].

[10] Note that Fig. 5 is the diagram that corresponds to this partition.

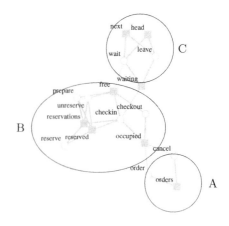

Fig. 6. A dependency diagram of the restaurant model. Thin (thick) edges are read (write) relationships; Circles are operations; squares are variables.

Fig. 7. A dependency diagram with a suggested partition. Each subsystem candidate is enclosed in an ellipse.

the diagram to assess the impact of the decision on the interfaces between the subsystems.

Partitioning the diagram facilitates the specification of the subsystems' operations. E.g., we can see that each of the operations *prepare*, *unreserve*, *reserve*, and *leave* can be supported by a single subsystem, while the operations *wait* and *checkin* require the cooperation of several subsystems. The *checkin* operation, for instance, requires the cooperation of three subsystems: reception, waiting list, and reservations. It must check if the incoming diner has a reservation, or if she is at the head of the waiting list, and it must allocate her a table.

Automatically Suggesting Decompositions. So far we have seen how to use the diagrams to manually look for good decompositions. But it is also possible to detect good decompositions automatically. Our criteria for a good decomposition is identical to that of a community, as defined in [8]: *"The problem of community detection requires the partition of a network into communities of densely connected nodes, with the nodes belonging to different communities being only sparsely connected."* This problem has received much interest recently and several algorithms were developed to solve it. We have applied[11] the algorithm described in [8] to the graphs of several systems, with good results.[12] For example, when applied to the restaurant system the algorithm selects exactly the same partition that we have selected (the left hand side of Fig. 8). For details on the results of applying the algorithms to commercial case studies see Section 4.

---

[11] We have used the modularity report feature of Gephi [5].
[12] The online website [1] includes models and diagrams of additional examples.

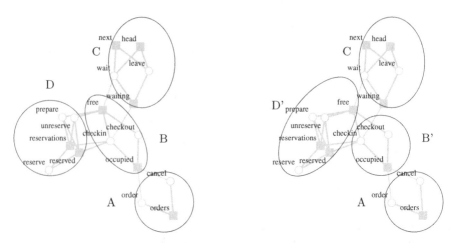

Fig. 8. Two additional partitions of the restaurant system. The difference in the partitions is in the location of the variable *free*. In the left version, *free* becomes a part of subsystem B while in the right version *free* becomes a part of subsystem D. The left version corresponds to the subsystem diagram in Fig. 5. We have used generic names to avoid bias in the decomposition.

Application to Informal Models. As illustrated earlier, a formal subsystem model has two powerful merits: it facilitates a rigorous analysis of correctness, and it increases our confidence in the validity of the decomposition. Unfortunately, most software engineers are either not familiar with or reluctant to use formal methods. Instead, they create semi formal models, using a mixture of diagrams and textual notations, for example with UML class diagrams and use cases. In such a case we may use parts of our technique to achieve some of its benefits. The idea is to consider the UML class model as a visual description of a relational model. Each class represents the set of all of its instances, inheritance is a subset relation and attributes and associations are functions and relations between the corresponding sets. We assume that the system model does not yet contain methods and that the functionality of the system is described at the level of the entire system (e.g., with use cases). The reason is that we consider the assignment of methods to objects to be a later task of the design activity, a task that depends on the subsystem decomposition model and follows from the discovery and assignment of operations to the subsystems. For instance, the UML class diagram in Fig. 9 represents the static structure of our restaurant system. We may then create the operation/relation dependency table by analyzing the use cases and recording how each use case manipulates the class diagram's attributes and associations. We can then perform the visualization as before.

4   Case Studies

In addition to smaller case studies, we have applied our technique to two non-trivial systems. The first is XOXO — a commercial mobile location-based

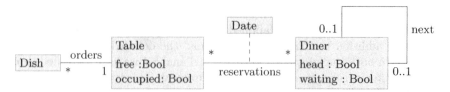

Fig. 9. A UML class diagram of the restaurant system, corresponding to the relational model of Section 3. E.g., the *next* association corresponds to the binary relation that models the queue of diners waiting outside. The *reservations* association corresponds to the reservations relation between the tables, the diners that have reserved them, and the reservation date. Because UML has no explicit representation of system state, we model the *free*, *occupied*, *head*, and *waiting* relations as boolean attributes.

chat application, and the second is the common component modeling example (CoCoME) [13], a system developed to evaluate and compare the practical application of component modeling approaches. this section we describe the results of applying our approach to each system. For more details of CoCoME, see [1].

XOXO was a commercial system for the iPhone that facilitated chatting between people based on common location and interests. It consisted of a chat server and an iPhone application. During its three years of active service, XOXO served tens of thousands of people. The system was specified in Z (available in the online website) by one of the authors. We have used this specification to generate the dependency diagram[13] for the system and compared the result with the system's actual design. The clustering algorithm suggests the following subsystems: profile management, search, photo capture, location management, chatterer blocking, and messaging. This partition appears reasonable and not too surprising. However, in practice, the system design did not decompose the system along these functional areas at all, with the exception of photo capturing. Instead the actual design focused on technological, non-functional constraints, and entirely neglected the functional decomposition. The system was partitioned into a client and a server, with the client being further partitioned into communication, entity and user interface layers. As a result, the functional areas identified by our technique are intertwined in the client and server code, making it difficult to understand and modify. Clearly, in this case, our technique would have significantly improved the system's design.

We now discuss the results of applying our technique to the CoCoME system. Briefly, this is a system for managing a commercial enterprise consisting of a set of stores and a set of product providers. Its specification includes operations for selling products, for ordering products from providers, and for managing the stocks in each store. The CoCoME reference implementation has 9,521 lines of code, 126 classes, and 21 interfaces. For more details see [6]. The specification is informal, given as a set of use cases and a UML class diagram. We have first used the informal specification to generate a dependency diagram, and compared the

---

[13] All the artifacts are available in the online website [1].

result with the reference implementation. In addition, we have created a formal model of the system and again applied our technique. The formal model has given us (in addition to the major subsystems) the detailed interfaces of each subsystem. In both the informal and the formal analysis we have identified three major subsystems: sales, inventory, and procurement. This is despite the considerable differences between the two models. This result gives us some confidence that our technique is not too sensitive to variations in the model.[13]

A particularly interesting option that our technique suggests, is to manage the price attribute of a stock item in the sales subsystem separately from the item's amount and product attributes (which are managed by the inventory subsystem). At first it seems wrong, as (especially from an object-oriented point of view) all these attributes belong to the same problem domain object (Stock-Item). However, upon further reflection, it becomes clear that the price of an item has nothing to do with its inventory status. Changing the price of an item, e.g., does not affect the number of items in the inventory. In fact, by managing the price in the sales subsystem, we have discovered the price-list, a problem domain concept that is separate from that of inventory.

The suggested partition appears reasonable. Yet, neither the reference model nor any of the other 13 models in the CoCoME site (http://www.cocome.org) have discovered it. Most models partitioned the system into an inventory and cash-desk-line components. None has identified procurement as a separate concern. Indeed, as in the XOXO case study, the emphasis of the decomposition is on technological (problem related) aspects such as layering the application into user interface, logic, data, and database components.

Finally, we have intended to apply our approach to a large open source project, but looking at the top 100 projects in sourceforge.net, we could not find any that had specification documents (neither use cases nor conceptual class models). As our approach needs these documents, we could not apply it to any of the projects.

5   Related Work

Parnas [24] argued that modules should hide parts of the system that may change in the future, thus protecting the rest of the system from the effects of these changes. We consider information hiding to be orthogonal to our work, as in essence it argues for implementing systems using high level abstractions, while we consider the problem of decomposing a system model (i.e., already at a high level of abstraction) into coherent subsystems at the same level of abstraction. Both techniques are examples of the principle of separation of concerns. But while information hiding separates the concerns of purpose from implementation, we separate different functional concerns into separate subsystems.

Event-B supports a notion of process refinement, where an abstract atomic event is refined to a sequence of events at a more concrete level. It is possible to reason about subsystems in Event-B using events, but we show that they are not necessary, as simple propositional logic is enough. In addition, shared variables in Event-B are replicated in all the subsystems that use them, whereas in our approach every variable appears in exactly one subsystem [3].

UML component diagrams describe what services one subsystem requires from another, but they do not show how several subsystems collaborate to implement the system. In contrast, our subsystem diagram shows which subsystems (and which subsystem operations) collaborate to implement every system operation. In addition, our subsystem diagram can be formally derived from a formal model and thus serve as a guiding and organizing map of the model.

There exists much research in computing coupling and cohesion metrics for object oriented systems [4,10,14,20,22]. These works focus on assessing the quality of existing decompositions, by measuring properties of the code. As a result they cannot be used at the early design phase.

Subsystem decomposition is similar in many ways to component identification. Researchers have suggested several approaches for identifying components (See [7] for a survey). These approaches are essentially elaborations of the heuristic mentioned in the introduction. They define a metric for measuring the similarity between use cases [17] (or classes [18]) and use clustering algorithms to collect groups of similar use cases (or classes) into components. When a class participates in several use cases, a conflict resolution algorithm decides which component is allocated the class (no work considers the possibility of partitioning the class itself between the components). And none of these works discuss the problems that we have raised. Indeed it is not even clear what is meant by allocating a class to a component. Does it mean that the class is entirely hidden inside the component? if so, what happens to the components whose use cases (or objects) refer to instances of this class? and what happens when a use case requires the cooperation of several components (for example, sitting a guest at a table requires the cooperation of the checkin and reservation subsystems)? None of these works consider these problems. In fact, we could not compare these approaches with ours, because they either lack examples entirely (e.g. [17]) or use examples that lack key details such as the actual uses cases (e.g. [11,18]).

The work most relevant to ours is [19]. It is a clustering technique for software requirements based on how they reference common *attributes*, where an attribute is any descriptive property or object associated with a requirement. The requirements and the attributes are written in a table, then the requirements are clustered based on their similarity with respect to the attributes that they use. The result is displayed as a dendrogram — a tree whose leaves are the requirements and the degree of similarity is higher the deeper the nodes are in the tree. The requirements are then partitioned into subsystems by selecting subtrees of the dendrogram. Compared with our approach, only the functional requirements are clustered, there is no rule to cluster the attributes. This is problematic when attributes are shared between requirements from different components. Second, the technique does not consider relationships between the attributes. Next, it offers no way to check correctness. Finally, because the dependencies between the subsystems are not visible, it is more difficult to explore different alternatives.

6 Summary

We have described a simple formal technique to model and reason about subsystem decomposition. In addition, we have described a diagram for showing how the system state variables and operations are partitioned into subsystems, and how the subsystems collaborate to implement the system operations. Finally, we have described a technique for visualizing the relationships between system operations and state variables in order to facilitate the selection of a good (strong cohesion, weak coupling) decomposition. We have illustrated the approach using an example and explained how it can improve the structure of two commercial systems. The results so far look promising; we plan to apply this technique to more commercial systems to further assess its effectiveness.

Modeling a system in a particular style affects its design, regardless of the approach. Our technique makes it possible to explicitly assess the design choices.

How scalable is this approach? The tools that create the diagrams and to suggest decompositions are quite fast. For example, neato takes about 4 seconds on our PC (Intel Core i5, 3GHz, 8Gig) to layout a graph of about 800 nodes and 4000 edges; it takes gephi less than a second to partition this graph into communities. To put these numbers into perspective, the commercial application that we have analyzed, a system whose implementation consists of about 60,000 lines of code, has a graph of 47 nodes and 73 edges.

Acknowledgment. We would like to thank Jim Davies and Daniel Jackson for their helpful and insightful comments and suggestions.

References

1. Subsystem decomposition. http://goo.gl/m5gnW3. Accessed: June 2015
2. Abrial, J.: The B-book: Assigning programs to meanings. Cambridge Press (2005)
3. Abrial, J.-R., Hallerstede, S.: Refinement, decomposition, and instantiation of discrete models: Application to event-b. Fundam. Inf. **77**(1–2), 1–28 (2007)
4. Al-Dallal, J.: Measuring the discriminative power of object-oriented class cohesion metrics. Trans. on Software Engineering **37**(6), 788–804 (2011)
5. Bastian, M., Heymann, S., Jacomy, M.: Gephi: An open source software for exploring and manipulating networks. In: ICWSM. The AAAI Press (2009)
6. Becker, S., Hauck, M., Trifu, M., Krogmann, K., Kofron, J.: Reverse engineering component models for quality predictions. In: CSMR, pp. 194–197. IEEE (2010)
7. Birkmeier, D., Overhage, S.: On component identification approaches – classification, state of the art, and comparison. In: Lewis, G.A., Poernomo, I., Hofmeister, C. (eds.) CBSE. LNCS, vol. 5582, pp. 1–18. Springer, Heidelberg (2009)
8. Blondel, V., Guillaume, J., Lambiotte, R., Mech, E.: Fast unfolding of communities in large networks. J. Stat. Mech. **2008**(10) (2008)
9. Bruegge, B., Dutoit, A.: Object-Oriented Software Engineering. Pearson (2010)
10. e Abreu, F.B., Goulão, M.: Coupling and cohesion as modularization drivers: Are we being over-persuaded? In: CSMR, pp. 47–57. IEEE (2001)
11. Fan-Chao, M., Den-Chen, Z., Xiao-Fei, X.: Business component identification of enterprise information system: a hierarchical clustering method. In: ICEBE, pp. 473–480. IEEE (2005)

12. Fowler, M.: Reducing coupling. IEEE Software **18**(4), 102–104 (2001)
13. Heinrich, R., Gärtner, S., Hesse, T.-M., Ruhroth, T., Reussner, R., Schneider, K., Paech, B., Jürjens, J.: A platform for empirical research on information system evolution. In: SEKE, pp. 415–420 (2015)
14. Hitz, M., Montazeri, B.: Measuring coupling and cohesion in object-oriented systems. In: ISAAC, pp. 1–10 (1995)
15. Jackson, D.: Software Abstractions: Logic, Language, and Analysis. MIT Press (2012)
16. Kamada, T., Kawai, S.: An algorithm for drawing general undirected graphs. Information processing letters **31**(1), 7–15 (1989)
17. Kim, S.D., Chang, S.H.: A systematic method to identify software components. In: APSEC, pp. 538–545. IEEE (2004)
18. Lee, J.K., Jung, S.J., Kim, S.D., Jang, W.H., Ham, D.H.: Component identification method with coupling and cohesion. In: APSEC, pp. 79–86 (2001)
19. Lung, C.-H., Xu, X., Zaman, M.: Software architecture decomposition using attributes. Software Engineering and Knowledge Engineering **17**(5), 599–613 (2007)
20. Mayer, T., Hall, T.: Measuring OO systems: A critical analysis of the MOOD metrics. In: TOOLS, pp. 108–117. IEEE (1999)
21. Morgan, C.: Programming from Specifications. Prentice-Hall Inc (1990)
22. Moser, M., Misic, V.B.: Measuring class coupling and cohesion: A formal meta-model approach. In: APSEC, pp. 31–40. IEEE (1997)
23. North, S.C.: Drawing graphs with NEATO, 2004. NEATO User Manual
24. Parnas, D.L.: On the criteria to be used in decomposing systems into modules. Commun. ACM **15**(12), 1053–1058 (1972)
25. Roscoe, A.W.: The Theory and Practice of Concurrency. Prentice Hall (1997)
26. Woodcock, J., Davies, J.: Using Z: Specification, Refinement, and Proof. Prentice-Hall (1996)

From Requirements Engineering to Safety Assurance: Refinement Approach

Linas Laibinis[1](✉), Elena Troubitsyna[1], Yuliya Prokhorova[2], Alexei Iliasov[3], and Alexander Romanovsky[3]

[1] Åbo Akademi University, Turku, Finland
{linas.laibinis,elena.troubitsyna}@abo.fi
[2] Space Systems Finland, Espoo, Finland
yuliya.prokhorova@ssf.fi
[3] Newcastle University, Newcastle Upon Tyne, UK
{alexei.iliasov,alexander.romanovsky}@ncl.ac.uk

Abstract. Formal modelling and verification are widely used in the development of safety-critical systems. They aim at providing a mathematically-grounded argument about system safety. In particular, this argument can facilitate construction of a safety case – a structured safety assurance document required for certification of safety-critical systems. However, currently there is no adequate support for using the artefacts created during formal modelling in safety case development. In this paper, we present an approach and the corresponding tool support that tackles this problem in the Event-B modelling framework. Our approach establishes a link between safety requirements, Event-B models and corresponding fragments of a safety case. The supporting automated tool ensures traceability between requirements, models and safety cases.

1 Introduction

Formal techniques provide the designers with a rigorous mathematical basis for reasoning about the system behaviour and properties. Usually formal modelling helps in uncovering problems in requirements definition as well as deriving additional constraints for ensuring safety. Though formal modelling provide the designers with a valuable input for safety assurance, currently there is no adequate support for integrating the results of formal modelling into construction of safety argument – a safety case. In this paper, we propose a method and tool support for linking formal modelling in Event-B and safety case construction.

Event-B is a formal framework for correct-by-construction system development [1]. It has been extensively experimented with in the industrial setting [2,3]. The framework employs refinement as the main development technique and proofs to verify correctness of the system behaviour with respect to system-level properties, such as safety. The industrial-strength tool support – the Rodin platform [4] – provides the developers with highly automated environment for modelling and verification.

© Springer International Publishing Switzerland 2015
X. Li et al. (Eds.): SETTA 2015, LNCS 9409, pp. 201–216, 2015.
DOI: 10.1007/978-3-319-25942-0_13

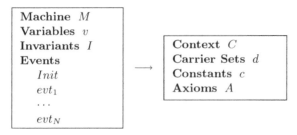

Fig. 1. Event-B machine and context

To efficiently exploit the benefits of formal modelling, in this paper we present an automated integrated approach that facilitates construction of safety cases from Event-B models. The approach spans over requirements engineering, formal modelling and safety argumentation via safety cases. While automating the proposed approach, we aim at creating a non-obtrusive tool support that nevertheless allows us to maintain the link between the dynamically changing requirements, models and safety cases. To achieve this goal, we relied on a novel industry-driven standard OSLC – *Open Services for Life Cycle Collaborations* [5]. The standard allows the engineers to achieve inter-operability between engineering tools by specifying the access to the external resources of these tools. We believe that the proposed approach has two main benefits: it supports co-engineering of requirements, models and safety cases, while the tool support ensures seamless interoperability and traceability across the domains.

The paper is structured as follows. In Section 2, we describe our chosen formal framework – Event-B as well as discuss classification and formalisation of safety requirements in Event-B. Section 3 presents our methodology for constructing safety cases from requirements and artefacts of formal modelling. In Section 4, we present the steam boiler case study demonstrating the proposed methodology. Section 5 presents our proposal on dynamic tool integration in a common information environment. Finally, in Section 6, we overview the related work and give some concluding remarks.

2   Modelling and Verification of Safety-Critical Systems in Event-B

Event-B: Background. Event-B is a state-based framework that promotes the top-down, correct-by-construction approach to system development and formal verification by theorem proving. In Event-B, a system model is specified as an *abstract state machine* [1]. An abstract state machine encapsulates the model state, represented as a collection of variables, and defines operations on the state, i.e., it describes the dynamic behaviour of a modelled system. The variables are strongly typed by the constraining predicates that together with other important properties of the systems are defined in the model *invariants*. Usually, a machine has an accompanying component, called *context*, which includes user-defined sets, constants and their properties given as a list of model axioms.

A general form for Event-B models is given in Fig. 1. The machine is uniquely identified by its name M. The state variables, v, are declared in the **Variables** clause and initialised in the *Init* event. The variables are strongly typed by the constraining predicates I given in the **Invariants** clause. The invariant clause might also contain other predicates defining properties (e.g., safety invariants) that should be preserved during system execution.

The dynamic behaviour of the system is defined by a set of atomic *events*. Generally, an event has the following form:

$$e \mathrel{\widehat{=}} \textbf{any } a \textbf{ where } G_e \textbf{ then } R_e \textbf{ end},$$

where e is the event's name, a is the list of local variables, the *guard* G_e is a predicate over the local variables of the event and the state variables of the system. The event body is defined by a *multiple* (possibly nondeterministic) assignment over the system variables. In Event-B, such an assignment represents the corresponding next-state relation R_e. The guard defines the conditions under which the event is *enabled*, i.e., its body can be executed. If several events are enabled at the same time, any of them can be chosen for execution nondeterministically.

Event-B development starts from an abstract specification that nondeterministically models most essential functional requirements. In a sequence of refinement steps, we gradually reduce nondeterminism and introduce detailed design decisions. In particular, we can add new events, split events as well as replace abstract variables by their concrete counterparts, i.e., perform *data refinement*.

The consistency of Event-B models, i.e., verification of well-formedness and invariant preservation as well as correctness of refinement steps, is demonstrated by discharging a number of verification conditions – proof obligations. Moreover, the Event-B formalism allows the developers themselves to formulate theorems to be proven. Full definitions of all the proof obligations are given in [1].

The Rodin platform [6] provides an automated support for formal modelling and verification in Event-B. In particular, it automatically generates the required proof obligations and attempts to discharge them. The remaining unproven conditions can be dealt with by using the provided interactive provers.

Formalisation of Safety Requirements in Event-B. Formal modelling is especially beneficial for requirements engineering. It helps to spot missing or contradictory requirements and rigorously define system properties and constraints. In a succession of EU projects [2,4,7], the most prominent of which is Deploy [2], we have gained significant experience in modelling safety-critical systems from different domains. It allowed us to identify a number of typical solutions for representing requirements in formal models. These solutions can be represented as classes of requirements (for more details, see [8]). Below we give a few examples of the classes of the requirements:

- *Class 1*: *Global properties* – contain invariant properties to be maintained;
- *Class 2*: *Local properties* – define effects of certain action in a particular system state;
- *Class 3*: *Causal order* – define the required order of system events;
- *Class 4*: *Absence of system deadlock* – require that execution of safety actions should not be prevented by a deadlock.

Table 1. Formalisation of safety requirements

Safety requirement	Model element expressions	Associated verification theorem(s)
SR of Cl. 1	invariants	group of invariance theorems for each event
SR of Cl. 2	event, state predicate	theorem about a specific post-state of an event
SR of Cl. 3	pairs of events, event control flow	group of theorems about enabling relationships between events
SR of Cl. 4	all events	theorem about the deadlock freedom

Table 1 summarises typical representation of the above classes in an Event-B model. Formally, the described relationships can be defined as a function F_M mapping safety requirements (SRs) into a set of the related model expressions:

$$SRs \rightarrow \mathcal{P}(MExpr),$$

where $\mathcal{P}(T)$ corresponds to a power set on elements of T and $MExpr$ stands for a generalised type for all possible expressions that can be built from the model elements, i.e., *model expressions*. Here *model elements* are basic elements of Event-B models such as *axioms*, *variables*, *invariants*, *events*, and *attributes*. Such defined mapping allows us to trace the system safety requirements given in an informal manner into formal specifications in Event-B.

Formal modelling and verification allow the designers to not only achieve a high confidence in system design, but also justify system safety during certification. The increasing reliance on safety cases in the certification process has motivated our work on linking formal modelling in Event-B with safety case construction – the work that we describe next.

3   From Event-B Models to Safety Cases

Safety Cases: Background. A *safety case* is *"a structured argument, supported by a body of evidence that provides a convincing and valid case that a system is safe for a given application in a given operating environment"* [9]. The construction, review and acceptance of safety cases are valuable steps in the safety assurance process of critical systems. Several industrial standards, e.g., ISO 26262 [10] and EN 50126 [11], prescribe production and evaluation of safety cases for system certification.

In general, safety cases can be documented either textually or graphically. Currently, the graphical notation called *Goal Structuring Notation (GSN)* [12,13] is gaining popularity for presenting safety arguments within safety cases. GSN aims at graphical representation of safety case elements as well as the relationships between them. The building blocks of GSN are shown in Fig. 2. Essentially, such a constructed safety case consists of *goals*, *strategies* and *solutions*. Here *goals* are the requirements, targets or constraints to be met by a system. *Solutions* contain the information extracted from analysis, verification or simulation of a system (i.e., evidence) to show that the goals have been met. Finally, *strategies* are reasoning steps describing how goals are decomposed into sub-goals.

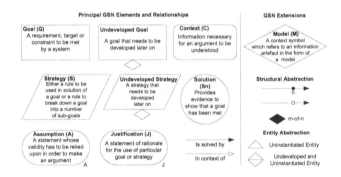

Fig. 2. Elements of GSN

Safety case elements can be in two types of relationships: *"Is solved by"* and *"In context of"*. The former is used between goals, strategies and solutions. The latter links a goal (a strategy) to a context, an assumption or a justification.

GSN has been extended with generic argument patterns [12], supporting structural and entity abstraction. The examples of structural abstraction are *multiplicity* and *optionality*. Multiplicity is a generalised n-ary relationship between the GSN elements, while optionality stands for optional and alternative relationship between them. There are also two extensions for entity abstraction: uninstantiated entity as well as undeveloped and uninstantiated entity. The former one specifies that the entity requires to be instantiated, i.e., to be replaced with a more concrete instance. In Fig. 2, this is depicted as a hollow triangle. The latter one indicates that the entity needs both further development and instantiation. This is displayed as a hollow diamond with a line in the middle.

From Requirements to Safety Cases via Event-B Models. The approach proposed at this paper should create an information continuum that spans requirements engineering, formal modelling and safety case construction as shown in Fig. 3. Problems with defining a safety argument during safety case construction might indicate that some safety requirements are overlooked or a formal specification is not sufficiently constrained. Such a feedback should invoke the corresponding corrective actions (a dashed line in Fig. 3).

The proposed approach encompasses two main activities : (1) representation of safety requirements in Event-B models, and (2) derivation of safety cases from the associated Event-B specifications. The activities are tightly connected with each other. They depend on several factors such as adequacy of representation of the system behaviour by a formal model and availability of modelling and verification artefact to substantiate safety argument.

To facilitate the first activity – representation of safety requirements in Event-B models – we rely on our classification and mapping rules defined above. To simplify the task of linking the formalised system safety requirements with the constructed safety case, we propose a set of classification-based argument patterns. In addition, a special pattern is created to provide the argumentation that the formal model we rely on is by itself correct and well-defined.

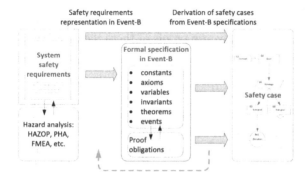

Fig. 3. High-level representation of the overall approach

The patterns have been developed using the described above GSN extensions. Some parts of an argument pattern may remain the same for any instance, while others need to be further instantiated (those are labelled with a hollow triangle). The text highlighted by braces { } should be replaced by a concrete value.

A generic representation of a classification-based argument pattern is given in Fig. 4. Here, a safety requirement *Requirement* of some class *Class* {X} is reflected in the goal **GX**. According to the proposed approach, the requirement is verified within a formal model M in Event-B (the model element **MX.1**).

In order to obtain the evidence that a specific safety requirement is met, different construction techniques might be undertaken. The choice of a particular technique influences the argumentation strategies to be used in each pattern.

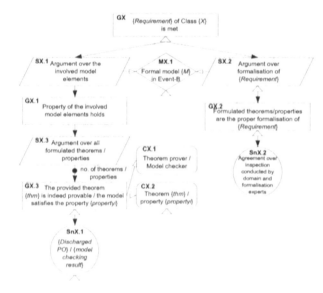

Fig. 4. Generic argument pattern

For example, if a safety requirement can be associated with a model invariant property, the corresponding theorem for each event in the model M is required to be proved. Correspondingly, the proofs of these theorems are attached as the evidence for the constructed safety case.

To bridge a semantic gap in the mapping associating an informally specified safety requirement with the corresponding formal expression in Event-B, we need to argue over a correct formalisation of the requirement (**SX.2** in Fig. 4). We rely on a joint inspection conducted by domain and formalisation experts (**SnX.2**) as the evidence that the associated model elements (via the defined mappings) are proper formalisations of the requirement under consideration.

As soon as all safety requirements are assigned to their respective classes and their mapping into Event-B elements is performed, we can construct the part of a safety case corresponding to assurance of these requirements. To make this construction generic, we associate each class with the corresponding safety case argument pattern that can be instantiated in different ways. Note that the process of safety requirements elicitation is left outside of consideration in this paper. We assume that the given list of these requirements is completed beforehand by applying safety analysis techniques.

In the next section, we will illustrate such safety case construction by a case study. More details of the proposed arguments patterns can be found in [14].

4 Case Study: A Steam Boiler System

In this section, we demonstrate our approach by a case study – a steam boiler control system [15]. Due to lack of space, we only give a brief overview of system requirements, constructed formal models and fragments of the safety case. The complete description can be found in [16].

Steam Boiler: Requirements and Development Strategy. The steam boiler is a safety-critical control system that produces steam and adjusts the quantity of water in the steam boiler chamber to maintain it between the lower safety boundary $M1$ and upper safety boundary $M2$. The situations when the water level is too low or high are hazardous and must be avoided.

The system consists of the following units: a chamber, a pump, a valve, a sensor to measure the water quantity in the chamber, a sensor to measure the steam quantity out of the chamber, a sensor to measure water input through the pump, and a sensor to measure water output through the valve.

After being powered on, the system enters the **Initialisation** mode. At each control cycle, the system reads sensors and performs failure detection. If no failure detected, the system may enter one of its operational modes **Normal**, **Degraded** or **Rescue**. In the **Normal mode**, the system attempts to maintain the water level in the chamber between the normal boundaries N1 and N2 (such that N1 < N2) providing that no failures of the system units have occurred. In the **Degraded mode**, the system tries to maintain the water level within the normal boundaries despite failures of some physical non-critical units. In the **Rescue mode**, the system attempts to maintain the normal water level in the

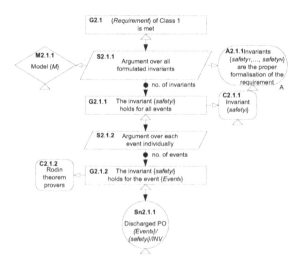

Fig. 5. Argument pattern for safety requirements of Class 1

presence of a failure of the critical unit – the water level sensor. If failures of the system units and the water level sensor occur simultaneously or the water level is outside of the predefined safety boundaries M1 and M2 (such that M1 < M2), the system enters the non-operational mode **Emergency_Stop**.

The failure of the steam boiler control system is detected if either the water level in the chamber is outside of the safety boundaries or the combination of a water level sensor failure and a failure of any other system unit (the pump or the steam sensor) is detected. The water level sensor is considered as failed if it returns a value which is outside of the nominal sensor range or the estimated range predicted in the last cycle. In a similar way, a steam output sensor failure is detected. The pump fails if it does not change its state when required.

Our Event-B development of the steam boiler case study consists of an abstract specification and its four refinements [16]. The abstract model (MACHINE **M0**) implements a basic control loop. The first refinement (MACHINE **M1**) introduces an abstract representation of the activities performed after the system is powered on and during system operation. The second refinement (MACHINE **M2**) introduces a detailed representation of the system failure conditions. The third refinement (MACHINE **M3**) models the system physical environment as well as elaborates on more advanced failure detection procedures. Finally, the fourth refinement (MACHINE **M4**) introduces a representation of the required execution modes. Each machine has the associated context where the necessary data structures are introduced and their properties are postulated as axioms.

From an Event-B Model to a Safety Case. The steam boiler control system should adhere to a number of safety requirements. Let us illustrate construction of fragments of a safety case for some given safety requirements.

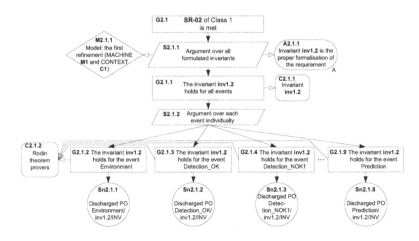

Fig. 6. A fragment of the safety case corresponding to assurance of SR1

The main safety requirement – **SR-02**: *During the system operation the water level shall not exceed the predefined safety boundaries* belongs to requirements Class 1. A natural way to formalise these requirements is by associating them with the corresponding invariant properties in the associated Event-B model. Therefore, the proposed form of the mapping function for *Class 1* is

$$Req_i \mapsto \{safety\_inv_{i1}, \ldots, safety\_inv_{iN}\}$$

for each such requirement Req_i and its associated invariants.

To formally verify the requirement, we have to prove the invariant preservation for all the affected model events.[1] The discharged proof obligations can be used then as the safety case evidence that the requirement holds. This is reflected in the associated safety case argument pattern for *Class 1* (see Fig. 5).

We formalise the requirement **SR-02** as the invariant **inv1.2** at the first refinement step of the Event-B development (MACHINE **M1**):

$$\mathbf{inv1.2:}\ failure = FALSE \land phase \in \{CONT, PRED\} \Rightarrow$$
$$min\_water\_level \geq M1 \land max\_water\_level \leq M2,$$

where the variable *failure* represents a system failure, the variable *phase* models the stages of the steam boiler controller behaviour (i.e., the stages of its control loop), and finally the variables *min_water_level* and *max_water_level* represent the estimated interval for the sensed water level.

The (fragment of) mapping function F_M for this case is

$$\mathbf{SR\text{-}02} \mapsto \{\mathbf{inv1.2}\},$$

which is a concrete instance of its general form given above.

Finally, we instantiate the argument pattern for *Class 1* as shown in Fig. 6. To support the claim that **inv1.2** holds for all the affected events, we attach the discharged proof obligations as the evidence.

---

[1] The affected model events are those that change any variables appearing in the considered invariant(s).

Since the steam boiler system is a failsafe system, whenever an unrecoverable system failure occurs, the system should be stopped. In our model, such a failure is associated with raising the corresponding flag *stop*. The overall condition is defined by the safety requirement **SR-01**: *When a system failure is detected, the steam boiler control system shall be shut down and an alarm shall be activated.*

The requirements belonging to *Class 2* that represents local properties, i.e., the properties that need to be true at particular points of system execution. In terms of Event-B, the particular system states we are interested in are usually associated with some desired post-states of specific model events. Hence, the proposed form of the mapping function for *Class 2* is

$$Req_i \;\mapsto\; \{(event_{i1}, q_1), \, ..., \, (event_{iN}, q_N)\},$$

where Req_i is a requirement, $event_{ij}$ are the associated events, and q_j are the desired post-conditions for those events. For each pair of an event and a predicate, it is rather straightforward in Event-B to generate the corresponding theorem, which becomes an additional proof obligation. In its turn, the proved theorem becomes the evidence for the constructed safety case (see [14] for details).

The corresponding instance of the mapping function F_M for **SR-01** is

$$\textbf{SR-01} \mapsto \{(EmergencyStop, stop = TRUE)\}.$$

Thus, we formalise the requirement by associating it with the desired post-condition $stop = TRUE$ of the event *EmergencyStop*. To verify it, we construct and prove the following theorem:

Thm1.1: $\forall stop' \cdot stop' \in BOOL \;\wedge\; (\exists phase, stop \cdot phase \in PHASE \;\wedge\;$
$\quad\quad stop \in BOOL \;\wedge\; phase = CONT \;\wedge\; stop = FALSE \;\wedge\; stop' = TRUE)$
$\quad \Rightarrow\; stop' = TRUE,$

The theorem is trivially true (i.e., automatically discharged by the Rodin provers).

The instantiated fragment of the safety case is presented in Fig. 7. The proof obligation *thm1.1/THM* serves as the evidence that this requirement holds.

The steam boiler is a typical control system that cyclically executes a predefined sequence of actions: reading sensors, detecting failures, executing control actions or error recovery, and predicting the next system state. We can formulate that sequence of events as a corresponding requirement belonging to *Class 3*.

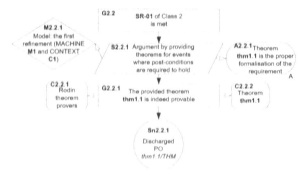

Fig. 7. A fragment of the safety case corresponding to assurance of **SR-01**

Formally, the ordering between system events can be expressed as a particular relationship amongst possible pre- and post-states of the corresponding model events. We rely on flow Event-B extension proposed by Iliasov [17] to verify that the required order of events is enforced. The Flow plug-in for the Rodin platform allows us to express all these relationships in a diagrammatic way, generating the corresponding theorems automatically.

In this paper, we omit further illustration of safety case construction for different classes of requirements. However, let us note that to ensure that the constructed safety arguments are valid, we also have to define a special argument pattern that demonstrates well-definedness of the formal models themselves as described in the accompanying technical report[14].

The use of the Rodin platform and accompanying plug-ins has facilitated derivation of formal evidence that the given safety requirements hold for the modelled system. The proof-based semantics of Event-B (a strong relationship between model elements and the associated proof obligations) has given us a direct access to the corresponding proof obligations, which in turn allowed us to explicitly refer to their proofs in the resulting safety case.

In this section, we demonstrated how models and proofs in Event-B can be used in construction of a safety case. Though the resultant development appears as a linearly constructed refinement chain, in practice it is a result of several iterations of trials and errors. To maintain traceability between the requirements, models and safety case fragments, we need to create an automated integrated engineering environment – the problem that we discuss next.

5   Integrated Automated Tool Support

Development of safety-critical systems is a joint effort of engineers from diverse domains, including electro-mechanical, hardware, software, safety etc. Each of the engineering teams applies domain-specific analysis and design methods and correspondingly uses the dedicated engineering tools. Though the engineering environment is inherently heterogenous, productivity of the development process and safety per se depend on how seamlessly the information about design decisions and constraints propagates across domains.

Let us consider the interactions between requirements engineering and formal modelling. Formal modelling typically results in identifying problems in given requirements (e.g., missing or contradictory ones) as well as deriving the constraints for the requirements to be satisfied. Hence, requirements definition and model creation co-evolve, and changes in one domain should invoke changes in the other. In its turn, these changes should be reflected in a safety case. Since the safety case construction should proceed alongside the development, the inability to produce safety argument may trigger the whole chain of requirement re-definition, formal model change and safety case re-construction.

Therefore, to address establishing an information continuum from requirements to safety cases, we should create a platform for non-obtrusive integration of tools in an integrated tool chain. The work presented in the paper is a part of a more general ongoing effort of tool integration as well as formalisation and mechanisation of rules that turn a collection of disparate tools into a tool chain.

We believe that dynamic tool integration enabling real-time sharing of data is the way to build tool chains of tomorrow. There is enough technological context to make such integration relatively cheap and painless, even for pre-existing tools not meant to operate in a dynamic setting. The enabling technologies we consider crucial are the structured data representation with stable identifiers and the actor paradigm. The former gives a common syntactic base for all the tools without enforcing unreasonable restrictions. An example of such a technology is OSLC [5] described below. The actor model provides a simple and flexible integration framework detached from the logic and code of integrated tools.

Before describing our solution in more detail, let us give a brief overview of a new industry-driven interoperability standard – OSLC – that we rely on.

OSLC: Background. *Open Services for Lifecycle Collaboration* (OSLC) [5] is an open community, the goal of which is to create specifications for integrating tools, their data and workflows to support lifecycle processes. OSLC address integration scenarios for individual topics such as change management, test management, requirements management and configuration management.

In simple terms, OSLC specifications focus on how the external resources of a particular tool can be accessed, browsed over, and specific change requests can be made. OSLC is not trying to standardise the behaviour of any tool. Instead, OSLC specifies a minimum amount of protocol and a small number of resource types to allow two different tools to work together relatively seamlessly.

To ensure coherence and integration across these domains, each workgroup builds on the concepts and rules defined in the OSLC Core specification [5]. OSLC Core consists mostly of standard rules and patterns for using HTTP and RDF (Resource Description Framework) that all the domains must adopt.

In OSLC, each artefact in the lifecycle – a requirement, test case, source file etc. – is an HTTP resource that is manipulated using the standard HTTP methods (GET, POST, etc.). Each resource has its RDF representation, which allows statements about resources in the form of subject/predicate/object expressions, i.e., as linked data. Other formats, like JSON or HTML, are also supported.

OSLC Requirements Management (RM) specification is built on the top of OSLC Core. It supports key REST APIs for software Requirements Management systems. The additionally specified properties describe the requirements-related resources and the relationships between them.

There are several different approaches to implementing an OSLC provider for software. For this work, we rely on so called the *Adapter* approach. It proposes to create a new web application that acts as an OSLC adapter, runs along-side of the target application, provides OSLC support and "under the hood" makes calls to the application web APIs to create, retrieve, and update external resources.

OSLC Tool Bus. To enable tool interconnection, we require that each tool has an OSLC adapter. The adapter offers a web service style API for traversing as well as changing tool data in real time. Generally, all well designed tools following

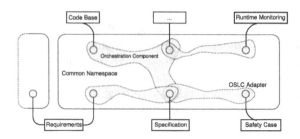

Fig. 8. OSLC-based tool bus.

the model-view-controller design pattern (e.g., based on Eclipse GMF) can be easily extended with an OSLC adapter.

An OSLC adapter is purely passive: it offers access to structured data that may be rendered in differing formats. It does not by itself link two tools together. The linking, or as we call it, tool orchestration, requires an additional piece of logic to define how and when the tools need to exchange information as illustrated in Fig. 8. An orchestration solution must (i) ensure that common names refer to same concepts, and (ii) manage the information flow between the tools.

To address this, we propose to use the agent paradigm [18], where each tool comes with one or more agents necessary for tool coordination. A collection of agents working together coordinating several tools is called an orchestration component. A tool may be a part of several interactions (see Fig. 8). Thus, e.g., a specification may be interlinked with code base, a safety case and requirements.

The role of an agent is to represent the interests of a respective tool by notifying other agents of any relevant new data and also acting on any such updates from other agents. The underlying communication framework implements a *federated tuple space* [19] - a distributed implementation of a shared blackboard with Linda coordination primitives [20]. To simplify agent implementation, we also offer the publisher/subscriber and mailbox communication styles realised on top of the tuple space API. Asynchronous message passing is a good fit for real-time coordination of a distributed tool chain, while federated tuple space is especially well-suited to loosely coupled parties that at times may be disconnected from some or all of peers. It is possible to construct generic agents able to handle simple tasks like synchronising certain data of some two tools or constantly broadcasting changes to a certain part of tool data. This enables, in principle, a compositional approach to agent design where complex orchestration logic is built, brick by brick, from the predefined agents.

A logical extension of this idea is fusion of an agent specification and the tool OSLC interface. Recall that OSLC is primarily a gateway to the tool data. It does not span across several tools. We are working on a way to extend an OSLC specification with the coordination meta-data defining the logic of orchestration components via static documents serialised in, e.g., XML or RDF form.

Prototype Tool Chain. In our prototype implementation, we aim at building an environment that integrates requirements engineering, formal modelling and verification, and safety case development. We strive to retain flexibility and notation that is native for each domain. For instance, requirements are defined in natural language. To maintain the link between the dynamically changing requirements and the associated formal models, we have created a prototype Requirements-Rodin adapter [21]. Formal modelling is done using the Event-B language, while safety cases are generated in a goal-structuring notation.

Our requirements tool uses the generic principle of organising requirements into a tree with further optional cross-links between them, and their classifications (by taxonomy, component, developer, etc.). The tool provides a simple form-based user interface. It embeds a web-service that provides OSLC-compliant RDF descriptions of requirements. Every requirement may be referred to by the project name and requirement id.

The second part of the prototype achieves a similar goal for the Rodin Platform. We have developed a Rodin plug-in that exposes the Event-B model database and proofs as externally referable OSLC resources. Once again, each model element (variable, invariant, refinement) has a unique global identifiers that can be used to cross-link with other OSLC and RDF resources.

The third part of the environment facilitates generation of safety case. It maps relevant elements of requirements and models into the corresponding parts of safety case, i.e., allows to reuse the results of formal modelling and verification to construct a safety argument.

6   Related Work and Conclusions

Related Work. The relationships between formal methods and safety cases have been studied along two main directions: to prove soundness of safety argument and gather evidences from formal modelling to substantiate safety argument. The most prominent work on the former is by Rushby [22], in which he formalises the top-level safety argument to support automated soundness checking. The obtained theorem can be then verified by a theorem prover or a model checker.

Our work is closer to the second research direction. Hawkins et al. [23] propose an approach that relies on static analysis of program code to demonstrate that the software does not contain hazardous errors. In [24], the authors automate generation of heterogeneous safety cases, starting from a (manually developed) top-level system safety case, while lower-level fragments are automatically generated from formal verification of safety requirements. In [25], to ensure that a model derived during model-driven development of a safety critical system satisfies all the required properties, the authors use the obtained model checking results. Our approach follows a similar idea. The main difference is in the reliance on the introduced requirements classification to construct both associated formal model and resulting safety argument. Moreover, the automatic tool support created for the proposed approach significantly improves its usability.

Conclusions. In this paper, we have presented an approach and a prototype tool implementation for integrating formal modelling in Event-B into the process of development and assurance of safety-critical systems. We aimed at providing support for linking requirements and formal models as well as efficient reuse of formal modelling and verification artefacts in safety case construction. The prototype tool implementation provides a platform for dynamic information sharing between safety engineers and verification team. It relies on the idea of linked data promoted by the OSLC standard, which is now rapidly spreading in industry.

To validate the approach, we have undertaken formal development and safety case construction of the steam boiler system. In our work, to test the approach scalability and usability, we have deliberately aimed at representing a large set of complex requirements of the system and then constructing the safety case.

We believe that the proposed approach is beneficial for the development of complex safety-critical systems because it allows the engineers to establish an information continuum between different involved domains. As a future work, we are planning to continue our work on integration by focusing on the integration with techniques for safety analysis as well as different verification tools.

Acknowledgement. The presented work is partially supported by the TEKES project Cyber Trust.

References

1. Abrial, J.R.: Modeling in Event B. Cambridge University Press (2010)
2. (EU-project DEPLOY). http://www.deploy-project.eu/
3. Romanovsky, A., Thomas, M. (eds.): Industrial Deployment of System Engineering Methods. Springer, Heidelberg (2013)
4. (EU-project RODIN). http://rodin.cs.ncl.ac.uk/
5. OSLC: (Open Services for Lifecycle Collaboration.). http://open-services.net/
6. RODIN: Event-B Platform (2009). http://www.event-b.org/
7. (EU-project ADVANCE). http://www.advance-ict.eu
8. Prokhorova, Y., Laibinis, L., Troubitsyna, E.: Towards rigorous construction of safety cases. Technical Report 1110 (2014)
9. Bishop, P., Bloomfield, R.: A methodology for safety case development. In: Safety-Critical Systems Symposium, Birmingham, UK. Springer (1998)
10. International Organization for Standardization: ISO 26262 Road Vehicles Functional Safety (2011)
11. European Committee for Electrotechnical Standardization: EN 50126 Railway applications - The Specification and Demonstration of Reliability. Availability, Maintainability and Safety (RAMS) (2011)
12. Kelly, T., McDermid, J.: Safety case construction and reuse using patterns. In: Daniel, P. (ed.) Proceedings of the 16th International Conference on Computer Safety, Reliability and Security (SAFECOMP 1997), pp. 55–69. Springer (1997)
13. Goal Structuring Notation Working Group: Goal Structuring Notation Standard (2011). http://www.goalstructuringnotation.info/
14. Prokhorova, Y., Laibinis, L., Troubitsyna, E.: Facilitating construction of safety cases from formal models in Event-B. Information and Software Technology **60**, 51–76 (2015)
15. Abrial, J.R.: Steam-Boiler control specification problem. In: Formal Methods for Industrial Applications, Specifying and Programming the Steam Boiler Control, London, UK, pp. 500–509. Springer (1996)

16. Prokhorova, Y., Troubitsyna, E., Laibinis, L.: A Case Study in Refinement-Based Modelling of a Resilient Control System. TUCS Technical Report 1086 (2013)
17. Iliasov, A.: Use case scenarios as verification conditions: event-B/Flow approach. In: Troubitsyna, E.A. (ed.) SERENE 2011. LNCS, vol. 6968, pp. 9–23. Springer, Heidelberg (2011)
18. Wooldridge, M.: An Introduction to MultiAgent Systems. Wiley Publishing (2009)
19. Iliasov, A., Romanovsky, A.: Structured coordination spaces for fault tolerant mobile agents. In: Cheraghchi, H.S., Lindskov Knudsen, J., Romanovsky, A., Babu, C.S. (eds.) Advanced Topics in Exception Handling Techniques. LNCS, vol. 4119, pp. 181–199. Springer, Heidelberg (2006)
20. Gelernter, D.: Generative communication in linda. ACM Transactions on Programming Languages and Systems **7**(1), 80–112 (1985)
21. Rodin OSLC Adapter: (Using Instructions). http://iliasov.org/oslc/
22. Rushby, J.: Formalism in safety cases. In: Dale, C., Anderson, T. (eds.) Making Systems Safer: Proceedings of the Eighteenth Safety-Critical Systems Symposium, pp. 3–17. Springer, Bristol (2010)
23. Hawkins, R., Habli, I., Kelly, T., McDermid, J.: Assurance cases and prescriptive software safety certification: a comparative study. Safety Science **59**, 55–71 (2013)
24. Denney, E., Pai, G., Pohl, J.: Automating the Generation of Heterogeneous Aviation Safety Cases. NASA Contractor Report NASA/CR-2011-215983 (2011)
25. Jee, E., Lee, I., Sokolsky, O.: Assurance cases in model-driven development of the pacemaker software. In: Margaria, T., Steffen, B. (eds.) ISoLA 2010, Part II. LNCS, vol. 6416, pp. 343–356. Springer, Heidelberg (2010)

Pareto Optimal Scheduling of Synchronous Data Flow Graphs via Parallel Methods

Yu-Lei Gu[1,2]([✉]), Xue-Yang Zhu[2], and Guangquan Zhang[1]

[1] State Key Laboratory of Computer Science, Institute of Software, Chinese
Academy of Sciences, Beijing, China
{guyl,zxy}@ios.ac.cn

[2] School of Computer Science and Technology, Soochow University, Suzhou, China
gqzhang@suda.edu.cn

Abstract. Synchronous data flow graphs (SDFGs) are widely used to model streaming applications such as multimedia and digital signal processing applications. They usually run on multicore processors and are required a high throughput, which in turn may increase the energy consumption. In this paper, we present a parallel framework to explore the Pareto space of energy consumption and throughput of SDFGs and to find the schedule of each Pareto point. The considered multicore platforms are heterogeneous. We present an exact method pruning the state space according to the properties of SDFGs and two approximate solutions to make the processes faster. Our experimental results show that our methods can deal with large scale models within reasonable execution time, and perform better than the existing methods.

Keywords: Synchronous data flow graphs · Multicore · Pareto optimization · Scheduling · Parallel

1 Introduction and Related Work

Embedded systems are everywhere today. They are in smart phones, e-book readers, portable media players and digital printers, etc. Streaming applications like audio and video processing, usually modeled by *Synchronous data flow graphs* (SDFGs) [5], are an important class of applications in these electronic devices. Energy efficiency is an essential issue in these devices, for reasons like the increasing demand for portable devices or the heat dissipation.

Streaming applications are usually required to reach a high throughput. The use of heterogeneous multicore processors to improve the throughput of streaming applications has become a feasible solution. However, a higher throughput is usually achieved at the cost of the increase of energy consumption. Designers have to carefully tune the mapping of applications on the platforms to meet performance requirement.

This work is partially supported by 973 program (No. 2014CB340701) and the National Natural Science Foundation of China (Nos. 61472406 and 61472474).

© Springer International Publishing Switzerland 2015
X. Li et al. (Eds.): SETTA 2015, LNCS 9409, pp. 217–223, 2015.
DOI: 10.1007/978-3-319-25942-0_14

Most mapping methods reported in the literature fall under design-time mapping [7]. The optimization goal of the mapping includes timing, energy consumption and reliability, etc. [6] and [2] present methods to achieve significant energy savings. [1] and [4] perform optimization for both energy consumption and execution time. However, these methods only consider homogeneous architectures. [9] works on heterogeneous architecture but only take energy consumption into consideration.

In this paper, we are concerned with constructing throughput and energy efficient static (compile-time) schedules of SDFGs on a heterogeneous multiprocessor platform. For a given platform, even we consider only one optimization criterion, e.g. throughput, the scheduling and mapping problem is already NP-complete [7]. [10] uses model checking to address the same problem and provides exact solutions. In this paper, we try to prune the state space and present a more efficient parallel algorithm which returns exact results. Two approximative methods are provided for larger models.

2   System Model and Problem Formulation

An *execution platform* P is a set of heterogeneous processors. For each processor p, the power consumption is defined by the consumption rates when p is used and when it's idle. The power consumption of processor p_1 shown in Fig. 1(b) is 90 when it's in use, for example.

A simple SDFG is depicted in Fig. 1(a). The nodes are called *actors*, modeling the computations of a system. The edges are FIFO channels, transferring the data items, called *tokens*. An essential property of SDFG is that when an actor starts an execution, also called *firing*, it consumes the same amount of tokens from its incoming edges, and when an actor ends a firing, it produces the same amount of tokens to its outgoing edges. The numbers of tokens are called consumption rate and production rate of edges, respectively. They are labeled on each edge. Each actor is weighted with a set of computation times, corresponding to processors. For example, actor a of G_1 in Fig. 1(a) need 1 unit of time to finish on p_1 and 2 units of time on p_2, respectively.

A *System model* $\mathcal{M} = (G, P)$ includes an SDFG G and its execution platform P. A simple system model $\mathcal{M}_1$ is shown in Fig. 1(a) and Fig. 1(b).

An SDFG G is *sample rate consistent* [5] if and only if there exists a positive integer vector q. After any sequence of actor firings conforming to q, the number of tokens in the channels are equal to their initial state values. The repetition vector of G_1 is $q = [3, 2, 1]$ for example. An *iteration* is a firing sequence in which each actor α occurs exactly $q(\alpha)$ times. We consider only sample rate consistent SDFGs. Only such SDFGs are meaningful in practice. A *static schedule* arranges computations of an algorithm to be executed repeatedly. An f-*schedule* of system model $\mathcal{M} = (G, P)$ is a static schedule arranging f consecutive iterations of G running on P.

The *throughput* (denoted by *thr*) of f-schedule S is the average number of iterations per unit time, that is, $thr = \frac{f}{T}$, where T is the total execution time of S. The throughput of schedule S_1 shown in Fig. 1(c) is $1/8 = 0.125$ for example.

The total energy consumption(denoted by tec) of f-schedule S is the sum energy of all processors. For each processor, it includes the energy consumed while it's in idle and in use. The *energy consumption*(denoted by ec) of S is $ec = \frac{tec}{f}$. For schedule S_1, for example, $ec = [(2*10+6*90)+(2*20+6*30)]/1 = 780$. A *Pareto point* is a tuple (thr, ec) of S in which one element (thr or ec) becomes better must make another element worse. Fig. 1(d) shows two Pareto points of the system model $\mathcal{M}_1$, which are $(0.1, 720)$ and $(0.125, 780)$. Schedule S is a *Pareto schedule* when (thr, ec) of S is a *Pareto point*.

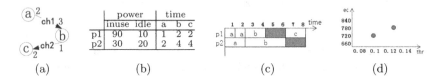

(a)   (b)   (c)   (d)

Fig. 1. The system model $\mathcal{M}_1$ and its schedules. (a) The SDFG G_1; (b) the execution platform P_1 and the execution time of actors in G_1 on different processors; (c) a periodic schedule S_1 with thr=0.125 and ec=780;(d)Pareto points diagrams of $\mathcal{M}_1$

Given a system model $\mathcal{M} = (G, P)$ and the number of iterations f, the problems we address are to find all Pareto f-schedules.

3 Pareto Optimal Scheduling and Mapping

We use a parallel framework to find all Pareto f-schedules from a system model. We use a map table to store the constructing schedules at each step. Initially, a constructing schedule includes one firing. The number of firings of schedules in the map table is increased by one at each step until all $f * qSum$ firings have been allocated, where $qSum$ is the sum of elements of the repetition vector q. That means the execution of f iterations of an SDFG has been mapped and scheduled. A map table is created by producer-consumer threads extending its previous map table.

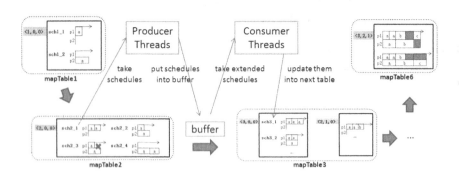

Fig. 2. The framework of our parallel method

Taking Pareto 1-schedules of $\mathcal{M}_1$ for example, we show our method framework in Fig. 2. The *key* of a map table is a vector contains the scheduled number of firings of each actor. Taking $key < 1, 0, 0 >$ in *mapTable*1 for example, it means actor a has already be executed once while other actors none. The *value* of a map table is a set of constructing schedules. The number of firings of each actor of each schedule equals the corresponding element of the *key*. Taking *value* with $key < 1, 0, 0 >$ in *mapTable*1 for example, it contains two constructing schedules, in which a firing of actor a is allocated on $p1$ and $p2$, respectively. We allocate one enable actor on one processor each time, called *extension*, based on the constructing schedules in previous map table. It finally stores all the Pareto schedules when the algorithm finishes. And we finally get two Pareto schedules in the *mapTable*6.

Producer-consumer mode is used in each extension. Producer threads take each constructing schedule from previous table, extend the schedule and put the extended schedule set into buffer queue. The start time of each actor can be obtained via max-plus algebra [3] by simply calculating $max(maxT, maxP)$, where $maxT$ is the max produced time of tokens that actors need to consume and $maxP$ is the max end time of the last actor on each processor. Taking the extension

---
Algorithm 1 Judge

Input: two compared schedule A,B
Output: judge result of A and B
1: **if** A $\preceq$ B **then**
2:     **return** -1 // A is not worse than B
3: **else**
4:     **if** B $\preceq$ A **then**
5:         **return** 1 // A is worse than B
6:     **else**
7:         **return** 0 // can't judge
8:     **end if**
9: **end if**
---

between *mapTable*2 and *mapTable*3 for example, one producer thread may take schedule *sch*2_1 in *mapTable*2, and extend it to two schedules by allocating a third firing of actor a on $p1$ and $p2$, respectively. This producer thread puts the two schedules into buffer. Then one consumer thread takes these two schedules and put them into *mapTable*3 which are *sch*3_1 and *sch*3_2, respectively.

Consumer threads take schedules from buffer queues and insert them into the next map tables. For pruning the state space, we compare the new schedule with those in the map table to decide whether to insert it. By judging schedule B in buffer queue with each schedule A with same key in that next map table via Algorithm 1, we insert B when we can't judge, discard it when A is not worse , insert B and remove A when A is worse. Taking the extension between *mapTable*1 and *mapTable*2 for example, *sch*2_2 is extended by *sch*1_1 through allocating a firing of a on processor $p2$. We discard *sch*2_3 because it's the same as *sch*2_2.

Let $sch[p]$ be the end time of the last firing on processor p and $occT[p]$ be the total occupied time of processor p. Schedule A **dominate**($\preceq$) schedule B is defined as following.

1. $A.sch[p] \leq B.sch[p]$,
2. $A.occT[p] \leq B.occT[p]$, and
3. the start time of each next enable actor of A is earlier than that of B.

Proposition. Method above is an exact pruning policy. We can always find a schedule extended by A which is not worse than that of B if $A \preceq B$.

Proof: According to condition 1 and 3, for any f-schedule B' extended by the constructing schedule B, we can move the firings after B to extend A. The procedure is illustrated in Fig. 3 with shadow boxes. The resulting f-schedule A' has the same thr as B'. According to condition 2, ec of A is apparently not worse than B. So it's proved.

The state space of scheduling an SDFG can be very large. To further prune the state space, approximate methods can be obtained by replacing the definition of dominate($\preceq$) but may lose accuracy at different degree. The first approximate method we proposed , named $appr1$, is obtained by removing the third condition in the accurate dominate($\preceq$) definition. The second approximate method, named $appr2$, is less accurate than $appr1$. Its dominate($\preceq$) definition is defined as: both of the temporary throughput and energy consumption of constructing schedule A are not greater than that of B.

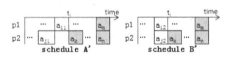

Fig. 3. dominate ($\preceq$) illustration

4   Experiments

We have implemented our algorithms and tested them on two sets of system models on a 2.9GHz server with 32 logical cores, 24M Cache and 384GB RAM. The platforms in system models we considered are 2 processors with different type and 4 processors with two processors per type.

Table 1. Experimental results for MPEG-4 Decoder

info		P5	P10	P30	P5	P10	P30
f	#P	model checking [10]			parallel(exact)		
1	2	2/0.1[a]	2/0.2	3/8.1	2/0.3	2/0.3	3/0.5
	4	1/17.8	1/1221	0/N[b]	1/0.4	1/5.5	0/N
2	2	2/1.2	3/8.3	2/235.5	2/0.4	3/0.6	2/4.3
	4	1/1902	0/N	0/N	1/55.6	2/28479	0/N
		parallel(appr1)			parallel(appr2)		
1	2	2/0.2	2/0.3	3/0.5	2/0.3	2/0.3	3/0.5
	4	1/0.4	1/2.1	2/6978	1/0.3	1/0.3	2/0.5
2	2	2/0.4	3/0.5	2/3.1	2/0.3	3/0.5	2/2.5
	4	1/3.9	2/270	0/N	1/0.3	2/0.5	1/2.6

[a] number of Pareto points/execution time(s).
[b] not finished after 10 hours or running out of memory.

The first case is an MPEG-4 decoder [8] with different parameters. We consider three scenarios, P5, P10 and P30. For each scenario Px, the sum of elements of their q is $3 + 2x$, which means the problem scale grows when x is larger. We compare the model checking methods in [10] with our parallel methods.

The results are shown in Table 1. Each cell is filled with the number of Pareto points the corresponding method returns and its execution time in seconds. For small scale problems, model checking method performs as well as the parallel method, while it takes a lot of time or even can't work when problem scale grows. The results show that even our approximate methods hit all the Pareto points while the execution time is much less than the model checking methods for large scale problems.

The second set of case includes some large SDFGs. It is mainly used to show the scalability of our methods. We randomly generate 30 SDFGs using SDF3 tool (http:// www.es.ele.tue.nl/sdf3) with the

	500s	5000s	15000s	10hours	timeout
appr2	12	7	2	3	6
[10]	0	0	0	6	24

Fig. 4. Experimental results for large models

sum of elements of their q nearly 1000. The system models we considered are these 30 SDFGs with a platform with two processors. The experimental results illustrated in Fig. 4 present the execution time of the model checking method and our parallel method $appr2$. The number in cell indicates the number of cases solved within these duration. Method $appr2$ can solve 7 cases in 500∼5000 seconds, for example. The results show method $appr2$ can solve 24 of the 30 cases while model checking method solves only 6 cases.

5   Conclusion

In this paper, we have presented a parallel framework for scheduling SDFGs on heterogenous multiprocessor platforms considering the optimization of both throughput and energy consumption. An exact method can be used to obtain all exact Pareto-optimal schedules and two approximate methods have provided a trade-off between accuracy and execution time. Our experimental results show that the execution time of our algorithm is much less than the existing methods for large models while hits all Pareto points for the MPEG-4 decoder case. We will conduct more comparative studies, comparing our methods with other heuristics like list scheduling, in the future.

References

1. Ascia, G., Catania, V., Palesi, M.: Multi-objective mapping for mesh-based noc architectures, pp. 182–187. IEEE (2004)
2. Chen, G., Li, F., Son, S., Kandemir, M.: Application mapping for chip multiprocessors, pp. 620–625. IEEE (2008)
3. Heidergott, B., Olsder, G.J., Woude, J.v.d.: Max Plus at Work: Modeling and Analysis of Synchronized Systems. Princeton University Press (2005)
4. Hu, J., Marculescu, R.: Energy- and performance-aware mapping for regular noc architectures. Computer-Aided Design of Integrated Circuits and Systems 4(24), 551–562 (2005)
5. Lee, E., Messerschmitt, D.: Static scheduling of synchronous data flow programs for digital signal processing. IEEE Trans. Comput. 36(1), 24–35 (1987)

6. Murali, S., Coenen, M., Radulescu, A., Goossens, K., Micheli, G.D.: A methodology for mapping multiple use-cases onto networks on chips. In: DATE, pp. 118–123. IEEE (2006)
7. Singh, A.K., Shafique, M., Kumar, A., Henkel, J.: Mapping on multi/many-core systems: Survey of current and emerging trends. In: Proc. of the 50th Ann. Design Automation Conf. (DAC), pp. 1–10 (2013)
8. Theelen, B., Katoen, J.P., Wu, H.: Model checking of scenario-aware dataflow with CADP. In: Proceedings of the Conference on Design, Automation and Test in Europe, pp. 653–658 (2012)
9. Wu, D., Al-Hashimi, B., Else, P.: Scheduling and mapping of conditional task graph for the synthesis of low power embedded systems. Computers and Digital Techniques **150**(5), 262–273 (2003)
10. Zhu, X.-Y., Yan, R., Gu, Y.-L., Zhang, J., Zhang, W., Zhang, G.: Static optimal scheduling for synchronous data flow graphs with model checking. In: Bjørner, N., de Boer, F. (eds.) FM 2015. LNCS, vol. 9109, pp. 551–569. Springer, Heidelberg (2015)

Symbolic Execution and Invariants

PathWalker: A Dynamic Symbolic Execution Tool Based on LLVM Byte Code Instrumentation

Zhang Jun-xian[1]([⊠]), Li Zhou-jun[1], and Zheng Xian-chen[2]

[1] School of Computer Science & Engineering, Beihang University, Beijing 100191, China
LoongWalker@163.com, lizj@buaa.edu.cn
[2] School of Electrical Engineering, University of Jinan, Jinan 250022, Shan Dong, China
zxcwin@163.com

Abstract. Dynamic symbolic execution (or concolic execution) is a powerful method for program analysis and software testing by attaching symbolic execution to the concrete running of a program. This paper proposes an approach to handle aggregate types (e.g., pointers, arrays, structures) and their complex combinations for the dynamic symbolic execution of C programs. The main idea of the approach is splitting a complex type program variable into a series of primitive type variables. During the concrete execution of a program, a concolic execution engine is provided to observe the operations on every program variable at the level of primitive types, and then the symbolic state of the program is updated. The path constraints which must be satisfied to drive the program running along the current execution path are collected to generate new test data for other paths. Our approach guarantees that only primitive type variables can appear in the symbolic states and path constraints. Based on LLVM byte code instrumentation, we present a new tool, called PathWalker, which implements this approach. Experimental results reveal that PathWalker is effective to deal with complex types in C codes.

Keywords: Dynamic symbolic execution · Program instrumentation · LLVM aggregate type

1 Introduction

Software testing is indispensable for software development. It is a necessary part of the software engineering discipline. However, testing is labor-intensive and expensive. It often accounts for more than 50% of total development costs [1]. Thus, there are clearly visible benefits in reducing the cost and improving the effectiveness of software testing by making the process automatic. In fact, there has been a rapid growth of practice in using automated software testing tools. Currently, a large number of software test automation tools or prototypes have been developed and already available.

Random Fuzz Testing plays an important role to guarantee the safety quality of software. Yet, in practice, in fuzz testing it is quite hard to randomly choose all the values within the domain of potential inputs [2] as many sets of values may lead to the same

© Springer International Publishing Switzerland 2015
X. Li et al. (Eds.): SETTA 2015, LNCS 9409, pp. 227–242, 2015.
DOI: 10.1007/978-3-319-25942-0_15

runtime behavior, which means most of them are unnecessary. To select particular inputs that can hit the bug the program under test may need to be executed for thousands of times.

Static symbolic execution that aims to represent the path's computations, as opposed to concrete execution, is a traditional program analysis method. It was proposed by Balzer for "extensible debugging and monitoring system" in 1969[3]. The key idea behind this method is to use symbolic values instead of actual values as program input data, and to replace concrete states of program variables with symbolic expressions which only consist of input symbolic variables. As a result, at every step during the running of the program, a variable can be expressed as a function of the symbolic inputs. Once a specific execution is over, symbolic path constraints are generated. These constraints limit what conditions the input data must satisfy to guide the program to run along the same path.

In this paper, we propose a new tool to automatically generate test cases for C codes that can drive the program under test to run time and time again in order to achieve a high rate of branch coverage. It recognizes complex data structures used in the program and builds the test driver code. We use a mechanism which is referred to as dynamic symbolic or concolic execution [2] that consists in performing tests, i.e. a concrete execution, mirrored by a symbolic execution following the same path.

1.1   Background

The main limitation of static symbolic execution method is that when the decision procedure fails to solve the path constraints, the symbolic execution engine will get stuck and have to drop the current path. This leads to the reduction of the code coverage rate and may miss some potential bugs. To cope with this problem, P. Godefroid, etc. proposed a dynamic symbolic execution method named concolic execution [4][2]. It improves classical symbolic execution by making a distinction between the concrete and the symbolic state of a program. The code is essentially run unmodified, and only statements that depend on the symbolic inputs are treated differently, adding constraints to the current path condition [5]. When the decision procedure fails, concolic execution will find out which part of the path constraints results in this failure and try to replace this symbolic expression with its concrete value. This allows concolic execution to continue to run through the current path and bypass the limitation of the decision procedure.

The concolic execution method was proposed about a decade ago. Since then researchers have spent a great amount of efforts in this area, and a significant number of different techniques, prototypes and tools for test case generation using this method have been proposed. All these works could be roughly divided into two groups by whether they aim to process source code like DART [4], CUTE [2] and KLEE [6], or binary code like SAGE [1], and MergePoint [7]. A tool that works on binary code has the advantage of being more direct and precise; however, it has to suffer the loss of type information of the tested program. On the other hand, a tool that handles source code can take full advantage of type information of the analyzed code; however, until now to our knowledge, few of such tools pay attention to generate input data for complex types.

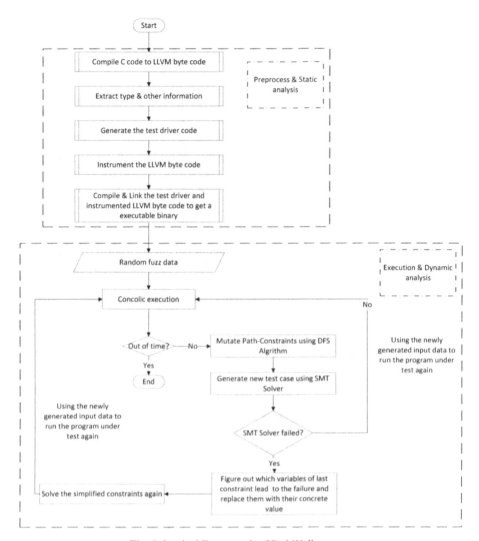

Fig. 1. Logical Framework of PathWalker

1.2   Overview

Fig. 1 shows the overall framework of PathWalker which consists of two main parts. In the static stage, we compile C source code to LLVM [8, 9] byte code using Clang [10], a compiler front-end which is a part of LLVM compile framework. Then Path-Walker extracts type information and other static information of the byte code to generate the test driver. This test driver is a C++ program that performs the random initialization of the input data for the testee function, and then it reads the results of the SMT solver and feeds them back to the testee function again.

The instrumentation procedure reads the byte code and inserts additional function calls into the concolic execution engine, where we implement the concolic execution logic. Finally, we compile the instrumented LLVM byte code to a dynamic link library, and link it with the compiled test driver and our concolic execution engine library to form an executable binary.

In the dynamic stage, the preprocessed program is executed symbolically. The process of this stage can be explained as follows:

- The Test Driver performs the random initialization of the input data for the testee function, and calls the testee function.
- During the actual execution of the program, the concolic execution engine observes the dynamic behaviors of the program under test and updates the symbolic states of the symbolic variables.
- After a path is executed, the outcome is a sequence of path constraints. PathWalker negates one of them in depth first order to form a set of mutated path constraints.
- PathWalker feeds the mutated constraints to the SMT Solver to generate new input data which should drive the program to run along an unexecuted path.
- If the solver succeeds, the test driver will use these new input data to call the testee function.
- If the solver fails, PathWalker will replace the symbolic values of last constraint with their concrete values and resolve the simplified path constraints again.

1.3   Contributions

The main contributions of this paper are as follows:

- Extraction of structure information from complex types: How to deal with complex type variables effectively is one of the challenges of symbolic execution. We proposed an approach in this paper to decompose the combination of array, struct and pointer types in C codes, and scatter an aggregate type variable to a series of primitive type variables.
- Generating test drivers automatically: To save the laborious work to write the test driver code, PathWalker exploits the information extracted from complex types to generate test drivers automatically.
- Implementation and Evaluation: Based on LLVM byte code instrumentation, we develop a tool, called PathWalker, using the concolic execution method to generate test data for complex types. The experimental results show that our approach is effective.

1.4   Structure of the Paper

The rest of this paper is organized as follows. In the following section, a motivating example is presented to illustrate our brief idea. The framework of our approach is discussed in Section 3 and its implementation is introduced in Section 4. Experiments are performed to show the efficiency of our approach, and the results are demonstrated in Section 4. Section 5 discusses the related work and Section 6 concludes this paper.

2   Example

We use a simple example to illustrate how PathWalker   recognizes input data with complex types as symbolic variables and performs concolic execution. PathWalker can only process C source code for now; but we will extend it to other programming languages in the future. Consider the C function *testee* shown in Fig. 2a, it accepts two formal arguments: an array of struct *s* and an unsigned integer *index*. The error at line 15 will occur if the input arguments satisfy the constraint $s[0].arr[3] == 3*s[1].a$. In this case, a concolic execution tool that cannot handle pointer reference, aggregate type, or address calculations may just drop the symbolic execution and only perform the concrete execution or even abort the current running, which misses the chance to hit the error.

```
typedef struct
{
    int a;
    int arr[4];
}myStruct;

int triple(int a)
{
    return 3*a;
}

void testee(myStruct s[], unsigned index)
{
    if(s[index].arr[3] == triple(s[index+1].a)
        assert(false); //Hit an error
}
```

Fig. 2a. An Example of C Code

a	9	a	8
arr[0]	0	arr[0]	7
arr[1]	1	arr[1]	6
arr[2]	2	arr[2]	5
arr[3]	3	arr[3]	4
S[0]		S[1]	

Fig. 2b. Memory Layout of array *s*

To deal with this problem, PathWalker will first extract the structure information of the array variable *s* which is in fact transformed into a pointer that refers to the address of the first element in the struct array *s*[0], and then it labels out all child primitive variables contained in the struct array *s* and saves all these information. Path-Walker performs this task in the static analysis stage. After that, the test driver which is generated automatically will randomly initialize the input data, and uses them as arguments to make a call into function *testee*.

Suppose there are two elements in array *s* which is passed to *testee* and the actual argument *index* equals 0, Fig. 2b shows the memory layout of *s*.

In the first iteration of the execution, when function testee reaches the branch, it will first make a call to function *triple*, passing the concrete value of *s*[1].*a*, which is the actual argument and equals 8, and also the symbolic value of *s*[1].*a* to the function. When function *triple* returns, we will get 24 as its return value and a symbolic expression 3*$*$s[1].*a* as its symbolic value. According to the current program state, we have the path constraints which is *index*=0∧*s*[0].*arr*[3]=3∧*triple*(*s*[1].*a*)=24. As 3≠24, the branch condition fails, thus the function *testee* takes the false branch and has the error missed. Then PathWalker will negate the last part of the path constraints and query the SMT Solver again. Now we may have *index*=0∧*s*[0].*arr*[3]=3∧*s*[1].*a*=1. In the second iteration of execution, the test driver feeds these new input data to function *testee*, and this time the execution will cover the other branch of the condition statement and hit the error successfully.

3   Our Approach

In this section, we present our approach in details. Firstly, we introduce the concolic execution method by a simple example. Then we explain how our approach splits variables of complex types into series of primitive type variables. Finally, we describe how to instrument the program under test based on LLVM byte code, and automatically generate a test driver.

3.1   Concolic Execution

PathWalker firstly establishes a logical memory model mapping every program variable at the level of primitive type to a pair of concrete and symbolic value. We define this pair as the concolic state of a specific program variable. All these concolic states of the program variables constitute the concolic state of the program.

With the given input data, the program under test is executed concretely while being observed by a concolic engine which updates the concolic states of program's variables at every execution step and collects path constraints at every branch it encounters.

```
void testee(int a, int b)
{
    int c = a + 2*b;
    int d = a * b;

    a = c;
    if(a > d)
        printf("1\n");
    else
    {
        b = d - b;
        if(a > b)
            assert(false);
    }
}
```

Fig. 3. An Example of C Code

Consider the C function *testee* shown in Fig. 3, we give the input data as $a=3$, $b=5$. Once an assignment statement is executed, the concolic program state of the function *testee* will be correspondingly updated. Thus we could have a concolic state transition trace as shown in Fig. 4.

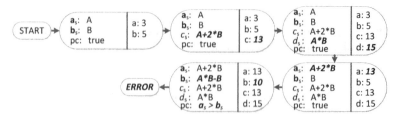

Fig. 4. A Concolic State Transition Trace

We label out both the concrete and symbolic variable states updated using red color in every program state. For a specific function, there are three types of symbolic variables, including global variable, local variable and arguments.

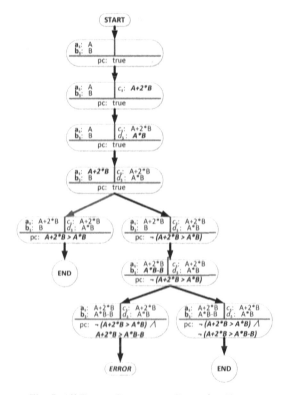

Fig. 5. All Traces Compose an Execution Tree

After an assignment statement is executed, a symbolic variable should be assigned a new symbolic expression; if there appear local symbolic variables in the right hand of this assignment statement, PathWalker uses their symbolic values to replace their occurrences. Obviously, in every symbolic expression, there can only appear symbolic global variables and symbolic arguments. This can be proved inductively.

In every symbolic state shown in Fig. 5, the up-left corner shows the symbolic arguments, the up-right corner shows the symbolic local variables, and the bottom shows the path constraints. Every updating is labeled in red color.

Using different input data, function *testee* can come out with different concolic state transition traces; all possible traces can be organized as an execution tree as shown in Fig. 5. Two traces may have a common prefix until they fork to two suffixes after a branch condition. PathWalker tries to explore the execution tree of the program under test dynamically, and it uses DFS algorithm which is similar with DART [4].

3.2   Splitting Complex Type Variable

In source code written in C programming language, there are amount of pointers, structures, arrays, and their combinations are frequently used. The type system of the C language is powerful to represent complicated data structures while it also results in the difficulty that has to be faced by a program analysis tool. Fig. 6 models the cross-references among variable types in the C language.

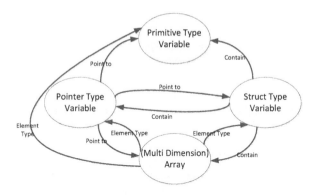

Fig. 6. Cross-references among Variable Types in C

Our goal is to scatter any complex type variable into a series of primitive variables which would be labeled as symbolic variables at runtime. For an example as shown in Fig. 2, the results of scattering variable struct array *s* will be 14 variables including: *s*[0], *s*[0].*a*, *s*[0].*arr*, *s*[0].*arr*[0], *s*[0].*arr*[1], *s*[0].*arr*[2], *s*[0].*arr*[3], *s*[1], *s*[1].*a*, *s*[1].*arr*, *s*[1].*arr*[0], *s*[1].*arr*[1], *s*[1].*arr*[2], *s*[1].*arr*[3].

LLVM has a sufficient type system to represent the type information in C codes completely. Unfortunately, this information will no longer exist when the program is concretely executed. Thus before PathWalker concolicly executes the tested program, it will at first extract the type information of every program variable including global variables, local variables and function arguments. For aggregate types like (multi dimension) array, structure, pointer and any possible combination of them, the structural information must also be extracted. All these information will be saved and can be accessed at runtime.

To save the type information, we design a set of classes to represent the relationships of concolic variables with different types as illustrated in Fig. 7a; we also develop an algorithm to extract type information, as shown in Fig. 7b.

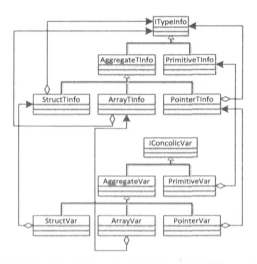

Fig. 7a. Relationships of Concolic Variables with Different Types

The procedures shown in Fig. 7b make calls into each other and thus form indirect recursive calls. These indirect recursive calls will terminate ultimately for sure. The key insight is that any variable that appears in program P can only possess limited memory which can always be treated as a series of primitive type variables. When a sequence of calls meets such a deep-most primitive variable, it will execute a return instruction definitely.

3.3   Generation of Test Driver

After the type information has been extracted, PathWalker automatically generates a test driver for the C program under test. This test driver is a readable C++ program which can be easily modified or extended. Once the test driver has been generated, it can be compiled to an executable program combined with the C program under test. All these works are performed automatically.

This test driver simulates the general environment visible to the program. In the first execution it performs the random initialization and feeds these data to the program under test. After one execution, a path constraints file will be generated. We use the Z3 SMT Solver [12] to solve these constraints and get a solution file, and then the test driver reads this solution to rebuild input data and calls the program again.

Input: an LLVM variable object *v*, Program *P*
Output: type information

FOR EACH *v* in Program *P*
  t = typeof (*v*)
  ExtractTypeInfo (*t*)
END

ExtractTypeInfo (*t*)
  IF *t* Has Been Recorded RETURN
  IF *t* is Primitive
    ExtractPrimitiveType (*t*)
  IF *t* is Array
    ExtractArrayType (*t*)
  IF *t* is Struct
    ExtractStructType (*t*)
  IF *t* is Pointer
    ExtractPointerType (*t*)
END

ExtractArrayType (*t*)
  Retrieve Dimension information of *t*
  IF *t* is Multi Dimension
    For EACH ELEMENT ARRAY TYPE *subt*
      ExtractArrayType (*subt*)
    END
  ELSE
    t_1= typeof (First element of *t*)
    ExtractTypeInfo (t_1)
  END

ExtractStructType (*t*)
  FOR EACH field *f* of Struct *t*
    ExtractTypeInfo (*f*)
  END
END

ExtractPointerType (*t*)
  Retrieve the Level of *t*
  t_2 = typeof (referenced type of *t*)
  ExtractTypeInfo (t_2)
END

Fig. 7b. Type Information Extraction Algorithm

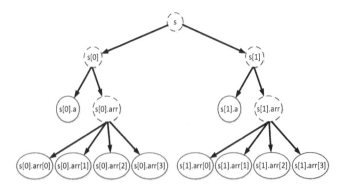

Fig. 8. Tree Structure of Struct Array *s*

The structure of a complex type variable can be represented as a tree, in which the root node is the variable and all the leaf nodes are primitive types. For each primitive type that LLVM supports we design a specific loader. To generate these loaders we use a DFS algorithm to explore the structure tree. Fig. 8 shows the structure tree of the struct array *s* shown in Fig. 2a, and the loaders read data from the solution file in the depth first order which is:

$$s[0].a \rightarrow s[0].arr[0] \rightarrow s[0].arr[1] \rightarrow s[0].arr[2] \rightarrow s[0].arr[3] \rightarrow$$
$$s[1].a \rightarrow s[1].arr[0] \rightarrow s[1].arr[1] \rightarrow s[1].arr[2] \rightarrow s[1].arr[3].$$

3.4   Program Instrumentation Based on LLVM Byte Code

LLVM is a compiler infrastructure which supports effective optimization and analysis at compile time, link-time, run-time and offline. PathWalker utilizes some useful features and interfaces provided by LLVM to instrument the tested program which has been compiled into LLVM byte code before. Klee is another concolic execution tool based on the LLVM interpreter, lli, which is a general purpose LLVM execution tool. It directly interprets compressed LLVM byte code without a code generation pass, just like Java VM does. lli is very slow (approximately 1000 times slower than native execution), because it is designed for flexibility and ease of implementation, not performance [11]. For performance consideration, we instrument the tested program based on LLVM byte code, and then compile it to an executable binary which can be directly executed.The instrumentation of LLVM instructions is straightforward. For example, to instrument an LLVM add instruction:

```
%dst = add i32 %src0, %src1
```

PathWalker inserts an LLVM call instruction that invokes ConcolicAdd function which has been implemented in our concolic execution engine. Six arguments are passed to the function ConcolicAdd, including the two addends from the *%src0* and *%src1* registers, the return register *%dst* and three IDs of concolic variables representing them.

In LLVM, everything is an LLVM value object; that is, a value representing an instruction can be treated as the returned register variable of the instruction.

This implies that such a value could be used as the operand of another instruction, thus we use the value object representing the *add* instruction to label the return register *%dst*. Besides, the two operands *%src0* and *%src1* of the *add* instruction must have already been loaded by two LLVM *load* instructions before, and these two *load* instructions are used to represent the two operands passing to ConcolicAdd function. Then we have the instrumented code:

```
%dst = add i32 %src0, %src1
call void @ConcolicAdd(i32 24677784, %dst
                       i32 24677564, %src0,
                       i32 24677668, %src1)
```

The three integer constants are identifiers labelling the three concolic variables. Function ConcolicAdd assigns a new expression Add(24677564, 24677668) to the concolic variable whose ID is 24677784.

4   Implementation and Evaluation

This section presents the experimental evaluation of our developed tool PathWalker for test case generation. The main part of PathWalker is implemented in C++ language. Program instrumentation is performed by using llvm-2.8. To solve path constraints, we use the Z3 SMT solve, which is developed by Microsoft Corporation. We have performed the experiments on a machine with an Intel(R) Core(TM) 2 Duo CPU @ 2.40GHz with 3GB allocated memory running Windows XP OS.

4.1   Implementation

As shown in Fig. 9, PathWalker consists of 4 main modules including a symbolic standard C library, a program instrumenter, a test driver generator and a concolic execution engine. Particularly we instrument the most frequently used part of the standard C library to generate correct and precise constraints.

4.2   Evaluation

We use the benchmark provided by K. Kratkiewicz [16] to test the effectiveness of PathWalker. This benchmark is originally designed to evaluate static analysis tools for detecting buffer overflow vulnerabilities in C codes, while we only aim to test the branch coverage of our tool.

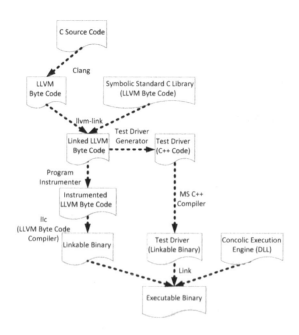

Fig. 9. Physical Architecture of PathWalker

Table 1. Experiment Result of PathWalker

Prog	Vul-ID	Iters	Time(s)	Cov
wu-ftpd	CVE-1999-0368	7	5	100%
sendmail	CVE-2002-0906	6	3	100%
wu-ftpd	CVE-2003-0466	7	8	100%
sendmail	CVE-2003-0681	9	12	91%
apache	CVE-2004-0940	14	82	77%
apache	CVE-2006-3747	10	25	100%
MADWiFi	CVE-2006-6332	6	13	100%
OpenSER	CVE-2006-6876	8	11	100%
gxine	CVE-2007-0406	5	4	100%
samba	CVE-2007-0453	6	7	100%

The result is shown in Table 1. The first column shows the name of the code sample; the second column shows the vulnerability ID; the third column shows the iteration times PathWalker runs the program under test; the fourth column shows the time that is used; and the last column shows the branch coverage reached by our tool finally.

In some cases, PathWalker fails to cover all branches in the program under test. There are two main reasons. First, PathWalker doesn't yet symbolically execute all library functions while this can lead to a loss of precision. Second, there exist dead codes in the program being tested which can never be reached.

5   Related Work

Up to now, how to build new tools for properly making the testing tasks automatic is still a problem worth more research effort. One of the key challenges is how to generate appropriate test input adapting to complex types. Many methods and tools have been proposed in the past decades. Following are some representative tools that generate test cases for C source code.

DART [4] (Directed Automated Random Testing) is one of the first tools to use dynamic symbolic execution. It aims to systematically executing all feasible program paths to detect latent runtime errors. Yet it pays little attention to handle aggregate types.

CUTE [2] is a concolic unit testing engine for C which proposed the concept "Concolic Execution" for the first time which could handle multi-threaded programs and pointer operations.

EXE [13] is a bug-finding tool that uses symbolic and concrete execution by turns. EXE was later redesigned in KLEE [6] which can automatically generates tests that achieve high coverage on a diverse set of complex and environmentally-intensive programs. However, to analyze the target program, it must run the program by using an LLVM interpreter, which is very slow compared to concrete execution [11].

CREST [14] is an automatic test generation tool for C. It instruments the source code to perform symbolic execution, and uses a constraint solver to search for unexplored program paths.

6   Conclusion and Future Work

We propose an approach to generate test data for C code in this paper; furthermore, we also implement a prototype tool named PathWalker. This tool can generate test data for (multi dimension) arrays, pointers, structs and any possible combination of them. Experiments show that our tool is effective, but still, the development is in the prototype stage. We plan to improve the tool on several aspects in the future work including:

A. Performance

PathWalker heavily depends on the SMT Solver which becomes the bottleneck of performance. We intend to use some constraints optimization algorithm to simplify the constraint set in order to alleviate the heavy load of the SMT Solver. Moreover, we plan to leverage the ability of parallel computing to solve multiple constraints simultaneously.

B. Environment Modeling

A large portion of research has practically ignored the possible issues of test data generation when the system under test interacts with its environment [15]. In the real world, data from files or sockets is an important input source for a program. To expand the range of the application of our tool, we plan to symbolically simulate the running environment that the program under test interacts with.

C. Safety Property Checker

Detection of vulnerabilities including memory overrun, integer overflow and so forth, hidden in C codes is our ultimate goal to develop PathWalker. To achieve this goal we may provide some safety property checkers and insert them to proper check points in the C program.

D. Extending to Other Programming Languages

Various LLVM front-ends have been developed to compile C++, FORTRAN, Java, PHP, JavaScript, Python and Haskell source code to LLVM byte code. In the future, we plan to extend PathWalker in order to deal with programs written in these programming languages.

Acknowledgments. This work was supported by the National Natural Science Foundation of China under Grant No.90718017, 60973105, 61170189 and the Research Fund for the Doctoral Program of Higher Education of China under Grant No.20111102130003.

References

1. Godefroid, P., Levin, M., Molnar, D.: Automated whitebox fuzz testing. In: 16th Annual Network & Distributed System Security Symposium, pp. 6–79. THE INTERNET SOCIETY, San Diego, California, USA (2008)
2. Sen, Koushik, Agha, Gul: CUTE and jCUTE: Concolic unit testing and explicit path model-checking tools. In: Ball, Thomas, Jones, Robert B. (eds.) CAV 2006. LNCS, vol. 4144, pp. 419–423. Springer, Heidelberg (2006)
3. Clarke, L.A.: A system to generate test data and symbolically execute programs. J. IEEE Trans on Software Engineering. 2(3), 215–222 (1976)
4. Godefroid, P., Klarlund, N., Sen, K.: DART: directed automated random testing. In: 26th ACM SIGPLAN Conference on Programming Language Design and Implementation, pp. 213–223. ACM Press, Chicago, Illinois, USA (2005)
5. Cadar, C., Godefroid, P., Tillmann, N., Visser, W.: Symbolic execution for software testing in practice preliminary assessment. In: 33th International Conference on Software Engineering, pp. 1066–1071. ACM Press, Waikiki, Honolulu, HI, USA (2011)
6. Cadar, C., Dunbar, D., Engler, D.: KLEE: unassisted and automatic generation of high-coverage tests for complex systems programs. In: 8th USENIX Symposium on Operating Systems Design and Implementation, pp. 209–224. IEEE Press, San Diego, California, USA. (2008)
7. Avgerinos, T., Rebert, T., Cha, S.K., Brumley, D.: Enhancing symbolic execution with veritesting. In: 36th International Conference on Software Engineering, pp. 1083–1094. IEEE Press, New York, USA (2014)

8. Lattner, C., Adve, V.: LLVM: a compilation framework for lifelong program analysis and transformation. In: 2nd International Symposium on Code Generation and Optimization, pp. 75–88. IEEE Press, San Jose, CA, USA (2004)

9. Lattner, C.: LLVM: an Infrastructure for Multi-Stage Optimization. Masters Thesis, Computer Science Dept., University of Illinois at Urbana-Champaign (2002)

10. Clang: a C language family frontend for LLVM. http://clang.llvm.org/

11. Lattner, C., Adve, V.: The LLVM Instruction Set and Compilation Strategy. Technical report, University of Illinois at Urbana-Champaign (2002)

12. de Moura, Leonardo, Bjørner, Nikolaj S.: Z3: an efficient SMT solver. In: Ramakrishnan, C.R., Rehof, Jakob (eds.) TACAS 2008. LNCS, vol. 4963, pp. 337–340. Springer, Heidelberg (2008)

13. Cadar, Cristian, Engler, Dawson: Execution generated test cases: how to make systems code crash itself. In: Godefroid, Patrice (ed.) SPIN 2005. LNCS, vol. 3639, pp. 2–23. Springer, Heidelberg (2005)

14. Burnim, J., Sen, K.: Heuristics for scalable dynamic test generation. In: 23rd IEEE/ACM International Conference on Automated Software Engineering, pp. 443–446. IEEE Press, L'Aquila, Italy (2008)

15. Fraser, G., Arcuri, A.: Sound empirical evidence in software testing. In: 34th International Conference on Software Engineering, pp. 178–188. IEEE Press, Zurich, Switzerland (2012)

16. Kratkiewicz, K.: Evaluating Static Analysis Tools for Detecting Buffer Overflows in C Code. Harvard University, USA (2005)

Generating Specifications for Recursive Methods by Abstracting Program States

Nathan Wasser[(⊠)]

Department of Computer Science, TU Darmstadt, Darmstadt, Germany
wasser@informatik.tu-darmstadt.de

Abstract. In this paper we present a novel approach to automatically generate sound specifications for recursive methods. These specifications can help prove the absence of undesired behavior, provide programmers with a foundation to build upon and help locate implementation bugs. Our approach is based on symbolic execution which we use to determine the states of re-entry and exit points. From these we generalize the necessary pre- and postconditions using techniques from abstract interpretation. The presented approach has been prototypically implemented by integration into a faithful and precise program logic for sequential Java programs.

Keywords: Program verification · Abstract interpretation · Specification generation · Method contracts · Recursion

1 Introduction

Program verification and deductive program analysis for non-trivial properties must choose a trade-off between automation and exactness. There has been much research on the topic of automatic generation of loop invariants: starting in the 1970s with abstract interpretation [1], much new research has appeared in the last 15 years: counterexample-guided abstraction refinement [2], linear [3] and non-linear [4] invariants, using postconditions to generate invariants [5], dynamic invariant generation [6] and more. The automatic generation of specifications for recursive methods in imperative programs has also received some attention, for example in the form of Boolean program models [7–9]. While some form of recursion analysis is obviously required when dealing with functional languages, recursion is also used in modern imperative languages. Furthermore, some of the most fundamental code is recursive in nature: for example *quicksort*, *mergesort* and *recursive descent parsers*; while other code can often be expressed in a much more natural way using recursion, even if the optimized code would usually be iterative: for example the calculation of Fibonacci numbers.

The work has been funded by the DFG priority program 1496 *Reliably Secure Software Systems*.

© Springer International Publishing Switzerland 2015
X. Li et al. (Eds.): SETTA 2015, LNCS 9409, pp. 243–257, 2015.
DOI: 10.1007/978-3-319-25942-0_16

In this paper we concentrate on the automatic generation of specifications for method calls, i.e. method contracts. Based on previous work [10] in which a theoretical framework combining deductive reasoning with abstract interpretation was introduced in order to automatically generate loop invariants, we extend their framework with a novel approach for automatic specification generation for recursive method calls. In addition to generating a one-size-fits-all specification applicable to all recursive calls encountered while dealing with the initial method call, our approach can further refine this specification to produce additional, stronger specifications for some calls, resulting in a better approximation.

The ideal approach to writing code with specifications is to write the specifications first and base the code on the specification, trying to ensure that it is valid. Verification techniques can be used to try and prove this. We turn this on its head and generate specifications from the code, a practice fairly common in industry. Our generated specifications are valid by construction.

As a proof of concept we implemented our approach using the KeY verification system [11] as our theorem prover backend.

The paper has the following structure: Section 2 describes the overview of our approach, as well as how and why we use abstract interpretation. Some uses for our generated specifications are listed in Section 3. In Section 4 we introduce the logic framework, calculus rules to deal with method calls and how abstraction is integrated into the framework. Section 5 shows the general idea behind automatic specification generation alongside an example, before delving more deeply into the specifics. In Section 6 our implementation is described and results for some analyzed methods are shown. Related work is discussed in Section 7, while Section 8 shows our conclusions and future outlook.

2   Methodology

For a brief overview of our approach, we consider a method `fact` which calculates the factorial $n!$ for a non-negative input n through case distinction and recursion, similar to the declarative definition of factorial (see Fig. 1).

$$n! = \begin{cases} 1 & \text{, if } n = 0 \\ n * (n-1)! & \text{, if } n > 0 \end{cases}$$

Fig. 1. Factorial

Our approach finds a sound specification applicable for all calls to the method `fact` which can be reached by starting at the initial call `fact(n)`. I.e. for $n = 2$ it would generate a specification that at least holds for `fact(2)`, `fact(1)` and `fact(0)`. The specification contains a precondition and a postcondition. The precondition expresses what values the parameters may have, while the postcondition expresses what values the return values may have. In this case, therefore, the precondition must at least express that n may be in the set $\{2, 1, 0\}$, while the postcondition must at least allow return values in the set $\{2!, 1!, 0!\} = \{2, 1\}$. Relational postconditions, such as $\text{fact}(n) \geq n$, will be discussed at the end of section 5.

In order to calculate (overapproximations of) these sets, our approach starts with $PRE = \{2\}$ as initial precondition set and $POST = \emptyset$ as initial postcondition set, based on the initial call `fact(2)`. Until fixpoints for both sets are found, we gather all return statements and recursive calls reached by calling fact(*pre*), with *pre* $\in$ *PRE*. These new parameters/return values are then added to *PRE* and *POST*, as well as all recursive calls being replaced by *post*

Table 1. Fixpoint iteration starting with call to fact(2).

PRE	POST	Return Values	Recursive Calls
{ 2 }	$\emptyset$	-	fact(1)
{ 2, 1 }	$\emptyset$	-	fact(1), fact(0)
{ 2, 1, 0 }	$\emptyset$	1	fact(1), fact(0)
{ 2, 1, 0 }	{ 1 }	1, 2 * 1, 1 * 1	fact(1), fact(0)
{ 2, 1, 0 }	{ 1, 2 }	1, 2, 2 * 2, 1 * 2	fact(1), fact(0)
. . .	. . .	. . .	. . .
{ 2, 1, 0 }	{1, 2, 4, 8, . . .}	1, 2, 4, 8, . . .	fact(1), fact(0)

in order to reach new return statements (and possibly new recursive calls), with *post* $\in$ *POST*. As can be seen in Table 1, the postcondition is an overapproximation. We cannot stop at the optimal sets $PRE = \{2, 1, 0\}, POST = \{1, 2\}$ as a method contract stating that fact called with an element of $\{2, 1, 0\}$ returns an element of $\{1, 2\}$ is not provable using only induction. Based on this contract fact(1) = 2 could be possible and therefore fact(2) = 2 * fact(1) = 4 as well. Avoiding overapproximation is therefore not possible. Additionally, infinite steps are required in order to reach a fixpoint for *POST*. Our approach uses abstractions for the pre- and postcondition with abstract domains of finite height in order to reach a fixpoint in finite steps.[1] This abstraction can overapproximate pre- and postconditions, but as this is possible in any case it serves a good purpose with limited downside.

Section 5.1 has a more detailed description of this example.

3   Application Scenarios

Generating specifications directly from the code serves more as a supportive function, rather than a way to generate precise functional specifications. While the specification generated for fact by our approach will not express exactly what the method does (at least not without a highly specialized abstract domain supplied which would be useless in analyzing most other methods), it remains quite useful by, e.g., *i*) being strong enough to show that calculating $\binom{n}{k} = \frac{n!}{k!(n-k)!}$ for $n \geq k \geq 0$ will not cause division by zero, and *ii*) supplying a sound contract as a foundation upon which programmers can build by strengthening it where needed. In addition, the generated specifications can help find bugs in the implementation, as a specification which is stronger than it should be signals that the implementation is faulty and a specification much weaker than it should be could be a sign that the programmer has neglected corner cases.

In particular, the specifications we generate related to integers tend to be able to supply upper and/or lower bounds for these, which in turn can help prove the absence of Java ArithmeticExceptions and IndexOutOfBoundsExceptions.

---

[1] A widening operator could be used instead of abstract domains of finite height.

4 Background

4.1 Program Logic

Here we introduce our program logic and calculus, and explain our integration of value-based abstraction based on previous work [10].

Syntax. The program logic is a first order dynamic logic which is closely related to Java Card DL [11]. To define the logic, we need first to define its signature which is a collection of the symbols that can be used to construct formulas.

Definition 1 (Signature). *A signature $\Sigma = ((\mathcal{T}, \sqsubseteq), \mathcal{P}, \mathcal{F}, \mathcal{PV}, \mathcal{V})$ consists of a set of sorts $\mathcal{T}$ together with a type hierarchy $\sqsubseteq$, predicates $\mathcal{P}$, functions $\mathcal{F}$, program variables $\mathcal{PV}$ and logical variables $\mathcal{V}$. The set of sorts contains at least the sorts $\top$ and* int *with $\top$ being the top element and the other sorts being direct subsorts of $\top$.*

Our logic consists of terms *Trm*, formulas *For*, programs *Prog* and updates *Upd*. Besides some extension, which we elaborate on below, terms and formulas are defined as in standard first-order logic. Note, that there is a distinction between logical variables and program variables. Both are terms themselves, the difference is that logical variables must not occur in programs, but can be bound by a quantifier. On the other hand, program variables can occur in programs, but cannot be bound by a quantifier. Program variables are flexible function constants, whose value can be changed by a program.

Updates are discussed in [11] and can be viewed as generalized explicit substitutions. The syntax of updates is: $\mathcal{U} ::= (\mathcal{U} \,\|\, \mathcal{U}) \mid x := t$, where $x \in \mathcal{PV}$ and t is a term of the same type as x (or a subtype thereof). Updates can be applied to terms and formulas, i.e., given a term t then $\{\mathcal{U}\}t$ is also a term (analog for formulas). The only other non-standard operator for terms and formulas in our logic is the conditional term: let φ be a formula and ξ_1, ξ_2 are both terms of compatible type or formulas, then *if* (φ) *then* (ξ_1) *else* (ξ_2) is also a term or formula. There is a modality called box $[\cdot]\cdot$ which takes a program as first parameter and a formula as second parameter. Intuitively the meaning of $[p]\phi$ is that *if* program p terminates (uncaught exceptions are treated as non-termination) then in its final state the formula ϕ holds (our programs are deterministic). This means the box modality is used to express partial correctness. The formula $\phi \rightarrow [p]\psi$ has the exact same meaning as the Hoare triple $\{\phi\}$ p $\{\psi\}$. In contrast to Hoare logic, dynamic logic allows nested modalities. The grammar for programs is:

$$
\begin{aligned}
&\texttt{p}\ ::= \texttt{st where defs}\\
&\texttt{defs}\ ::= m(\texttt{x}_1, \ldots, \texttt{x}_n)\{\texttt{local l}_1, \ldots, \texttt{l}_k;\ \texttt{st return l}_i;\}\ \texttt{defs} \mid \epsilon\\
&\texttt{st}\ ::= \texttt{st st} \mid \texttt{if}\ (\varphi)\ \{\texttt{st}\}\ \texttt{else}\ \{\texttt{st}\} \mid \texttt{x}\ \texttt{=}\ t; \mid \texttt{x} = m(\texttt{x}_1, \ldots, \texttt{x}_n); \mid\\
&\qquad\quad \texttt{m-f(x)}\{\texttt{st return y;}\} \mid \epsilon
\end{aligned}
$$

where $\texttt{x}$, $\texttt{y}$, $\texttt{x}_i \in \mathcal{PV}$, m is a method name and t, φ are terms/formulas containing no method calls. The abbreviation m-f stands for *method frame* and signals a block being executed within a call to a method. Our calculus rules create method frames when expanding method calls and destroy them when returning; they are not allowed in user defined programs. The statement st in a method body may contain no variables other than the parameters x_i and the local variables l_i. Syntactically valid programs are well-typed and do not contain logic variables, quantifiers or modalities.

We write if (φ) {p} as an abbreviation for if (φ) {p} else {x = x}, where $x \in \mathcal{PV}$ is an arbitrary program variable.

Semantics. Terms, formulas and programs are evaluated with respect to a first order structure.

Definition 2 (First Order Structure, Variable Assignment). *Let D denote a non-empty domain of elements. A first order structure $M = (D, I, s)$ consists of*

1. *an interpretation I which assigns each*
   - *sort $T \in \mathcal{T}$ a non-empty domain $D^T \subseteq D$ s.t. for $S \sqsubseteq T \in \mathcal{T} : D^S \subseteq D^T$*
   - *$f : T_1 \times \ldots \times T_n \to T \in \mathcal{F}$ a function $I(f) : D^{T_1} \times \ldots \times D^{T_n} \to D^T$*
   - *$p : T_1 \times \ldots \times T_n \in \mathcal{P}$ a relation $I(p) \subseteq D^{T_1} \times \ldots \times D^{T_n}$*
2. *a state $s : \mathcal{PV} \to D$ assigning each program variable $v \in \mathcal{PV}$ of type T a value $s(t) \in D^T$. We denote the set of all states by States.*

We fix the interpretation of some sorts and symbols: $I(\text{int}) = \mathbb{Z}$, $I(\top) = D$ and the arithmetic operations $+, -, /, \%, \ldots$ as well as the comparators $<, >, \leq, \geq, \doteq$ are interpreted according to their standard semantics.

In addition we need the notion of a variable assignment $\beta : \mathcal{V} \to D$ which assigns to each logical variable an element of its domain.

Definition 3 (Evaluation). *Given a first order structure $M = (D, I, s)$ and a variable assignment β, we evaluate terms t (of sort T) to a value $val_{M,\beta}(t) \in D^T$, updates $\mathcal{U}$ to a function $val_{M,\beta}(\mathcal{U}) : States \to States$, formulas φ to a truth value $val_{M,\beta}(\varphi) \in \{tt, ff\}$, and programs p to a set of states $val_{M,\beta}(p) \in 2^{States}$ with $val_{M,\beta}(p)$ being either empty or a singleton set.*

A formula φ is called valid iff $val_{M,\beta}(\varphi) = tt$ for all interpretations I, all states s and all variable assignments β.

The evaluation of terms and formulas without programs and updates is almost identical to standard first-order logic and omitted for brevity. The evaluation of an elementary *update* with respect to a first order structure $M = (D, I, s)$ and variable assignment β is defined as follows:

$$val_{M,\beta}(x := t)(s') = \begin{cases} s'(y) & , y \neq x \\ val_{M,\beta}(t) & , otherwise \end{cases}$$

The evaluation of a parallel update $val_{M,\beta}(x_1 := t_1 \| x_2 := t_2)$ maps a state s' to a state s'' such that s'' coincides with s' except for the program variables x_1, x_2 which are assigned the values of the terms t_i in parallel. In case of a clash between two sub-updates (i.e., when $x_i = x_j$ for $i \neq j$), the rightmost update "wins" and overwrites the effect of the other. The meaning of a term $\{\mathcal{U}\}t$ and of a formula $\{\mathcal{U}\}\varphi$ is that the result state of the update $\mathcal{U}$ should be used for evaluating t and φ, respectively.

A *program* is evaluated to the set of states that it may terminate in when started in s. We only consider deterministic programs, so this set is always either empty (if the program does not terminate) or it consists of exactly one state. The semantics of a program formula $[p]\varphi$ is that φ should hold in all result states of the program p, which corresponds to partial correctness of p wrt. φ.

Calculus. We use a *sequent calculus* to prove that a formula is valid. A *sequent* is a tuple $\Gamma \Rightarrow \Delta$ where Γ (the *antecedent*) and Δ (the *succedent*) are finite sets of formulas. A sequent $val_{M,\beta}(\Gamma \Rightarrow \Delta)$ has the same meaning as the formula $val_{M,\beta}(\bigwedge \Gamma \rightarrow \bigvee \Delta)$. A sequent calculus

$$\frac{seq_1 \quad \cdots \quad seq_n}{seq}$$

Fig. 2. Rule Schema

rule is given by the rule schema in Fig. 2, where $seq_1, \ldots, seq_n$ (the *premisses*) and seq (the *conclusion*) are sequents. A rule is *sound* iff the validity of the conclusion follows from the validity of all its premisses.

A sequent proof is a tree of which each node is annotated with a sequent. The root node is annotated with the sequent to be proven valid. A rule is applied by matching its conclusion with a sequent of a leaf node and attaching the premisses as its children. If a branch of the tree ends in a leaf that is trivially true, the branch is called closed. A proof is closed if all its leaves are closed.

As the first order calculus rules are standard, we explain only selected rules which deal with formulas involving programs. Given a suitable strategy for rule selection, the sequent calculus implements a symbolic interpreter. For example, symbolic execution of *conditional statements* splits the proof into two branches:

$$\text{ifElse} \quad \frac{\Gamma, \{\mathcal{U}\}g \Rightarrow \{\mathcal{U}\}[\pi \ \text{p1}; \ \omega]\varphi, \Delta \qquad \Gamma, \{\mathcal{U}\}!g \Rightarrow \{\mathcal{U}\}[\pi \ \text{p2}; \ \omega]\varphi, \Delta}{\Gamma \Rightarrow \{\mathcal{U}\}[\pi \ \text{if } (g) \ \{\text{p1}\} \ \text{else} \ \{\text{p2}\}; \ \omega]\varphi, \Delta}$$

where π contains the opening method frames of all entered method calls and ω has the form *rest* where *defs*, with *rest* containing the rest of the program and closing method frames and *defs* containing method definitions. The assignment rule moves an assignment into an update. Updates are accumulated in front of modalities during symbolic execution of the program and can be simplified and applied to terms and formulas using the set of (schematic) rewrite rules given in [11,12]. Once the program has been symbolically executed, the update is applied to the formula behind the modality (using the emptyModality rule) computing its weakest precondition.

$$\text{assignment} \quad \frac{\Gamma \Rightarrow \{\mathcal{U}\}\{x := t\}[\pi \ \omega]\varphi, \Delta}{\Gamma \Rightarrow \{\mathcal{U}\}[\pi \ x = t; \ \omega]\varphi, \Delta} \qquad\qquad \text{emptyModality} \quad \frac{\Gamma \Rightarrow \{\mathcal{U}\}\varphi, \Delta}{\Gamma \Rightarrow \{\mathcal{U}\}[\ \text{where} \ defs]\varphi, \Delta}$$

For a *method call* the simplest approach is to *expand* it. However, this is only useful if the method is not recursive or the number of recursions required is bound.

$$\text{methodExpand} \quad \frac{\Gamma \Rightarrow \{\mathcal{U}\}[\pi \; \mathtt{z_1 = x_1; \ldots; z_n = x_n; \; m\text{-}f(x)\{\mathit{body'}\}} \; \omega]\varphi, \Delta}{\Gamma \Rightarrow \{\mathcal{U}\}[\pi \; \mathtt{x = m(x_1, \ldots, x_n);} \; \omega]\varphi, \Delta}$$

where $m(\mathtt{y_1}, \ldots, \mathtt{y_n})\{\mathtt{local} \; \mathtt{l_1}, \ldots, \mathtt{l_k};\; \mathit{body}\}$ is in the **where**-clause of ω, all $\mathtt{z}_i$ are fresh program variables and replacing all $\mathtt{y}_i$ in body with matching $\mathtt{z}_i$ and all $\mathtt{l}_j$ with matching fresh variables $\mathtt{g}_j$ results in $\mathit{body'}$. Returning from a method is dealt with by the **return** rule:

$$\text{return} \quad \frac{\Gamma \Rightarrow \{\mathcal{U}\}[\pi \; \mathtt{x = g;} \; \omega]\varphi, \Delta}{\Gamma \Rightarrow \{\mathcal{U}\}[\pi \; \mathtt{m\text{-}f(x)\{return \; g;\}} \; \omega]\varphi, \Delta}$$

There is also a rule for applying a method contract (requiring an additional proof obligation stating that the method contract is sound to be proven), instead of expanding the method body. In particular this allows recursive calls with unknown depth to be dealt with.

$$\text{useMethodContract} \quad \frac{\begin{array}{c} \Gamma \Rightarrow \{\mathcal{U}\}PRE', \Delta \\ \Gamma, POST' \Rightarrow \{\mathcal{U}\}[\pi \; \mathtt{x = result';} \; \mathit{rest} \; \mathtt{where} \; \mathit{defs}]\varphi, \Delta \end{array}}{\Gamma \Rightarrow \{\mathcal{U}\}[\pi \; \mathtt{x = m(x_1, \ldots, x_n);} \; \mathit{rest} \; \mathtt{where} \; \mathit{defs}]\varphi, \Delta}$$

where **result'** is a fresh program variable, defs contains $m(\mathtt{y_1}, \ldots, \mathtt{y_n})\{\mathit{body}\}$ and a method contract $PRE \Rightarrow [\mathtt{result} = m(\mathtt{y_1}, \ldots, \mathtt{y_n}); \; \mathtt{where} \; \mathit{defs}]POST$ exists, where $\mathtt{y}_i$ are the only program variables in PRE, the only program variables in $POST$ are $\mathtt{y}_i$ and **result**, and replacing all $\mathtt{y}_i$ with matching $\mathtt{x}_i$ and **result** with **result'** leads to PRE' and $POST'$. When proving a method contract, induction allows us to use the contract on all recursive calls.

4.2   Integrating Abstraction

We summarize from [10] how to integrate abstraction into our program logic. This integration provides the technical foundation for generating loop invariants.

Definition 4 (Abstract Domain). *Let D be a concrete domain (e.g., from a first order structure). An* abstract domain A *is a countable lattice with partial order $\sqsubseteq$ and join operator $\sqcup$ and without infinite ascending chains. It is connected to D with an abstraction function $\alpha : 2^D \to A$ and a concretization function $\gamma : A \to 2^D$ which form a Galois connection [1].*

Instead of extending our program logic by abstract elements, we use a different approach to refer to the element of an abstract domain:

Definition 5 ($\gamma_{\alpha,\mathbb{N}}$-symbols). *Given an abstract domain $A = \{\alpha_1, \alpha_2, \ldots\}$. For each abstract element $\alpha_i \in A$ there a) are infinitely many constant symbols $\gamma_{\alpha_i,j} \in \mathcal{F}$, $j \in \mathbb{N}$ and $I(\gamma_{\alpha_i,j}) \in \gamma(\alpha_i)$, and b) is a unary predicate χ_{α_i} where $I(\chi_{\alpha_i})$ is the characteristic predicate of set $\gamma(\alpha_i)$.*

The interpretation I of a symbol $\gamma_{\alpha_i,j}$ is restricted to one of the concrete domain elements represented by α_i, but it is not fixed. This is important for the following notion of weakening: with respect to the symbols occurring in a given (partial) proof P and a set of formulas C, we call an update $\mathcal{U}'$ (P,C)-weaker than an update $\mathcal{U}$ if $\mathcal{U}'$ describes at least all state transitions that are also allowed by $\mathcal{U}$. Formally, given a fixed D and β, then $\mathcal{U}$ is weaker than $\mathcal{U}'$ iff for any first order structure $M = (D, I, s)$ there is a first order structure $M' = (D, I', s)$ with I and I' being two interpretations coinciding on all symbols used so far in P and in C and for both structures $val_{M,\beta}(C) = tt$ and $val_{M',\beta}(C) = tt$ holds, for all program variables v the equation $val_{M,\beta}(\{\mathcal{U}\}v) = val_{M',\beta}(\{\mathcal{U}'\}v)$ must hold.

Example 1. An abstract domain for integers ($\mathbb{Z}$): The abstract domain is $A = (\top, \leq, \geq, neg, pos, \emptyset, 0, 1, -1, 2, -2, \ldots)$. The partial order between elements of A is shown in the graph below.

Let P be a partial proof with $\gamma_{\leq,3}$ not occurring in P. Then update i := $\gamma_{\leq,3}$ is $(P, \emptyset)$-weaker than update i := -5 or update i := c with a constant c (occurring in P) provided $\chi_{\leq}(c)$ holds, i.e. $c \leq 0$.

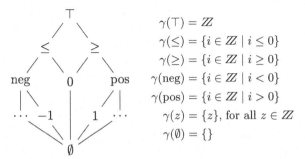

$\gamma(\top) = \mathbb{Z}$
$\gamma(\leq) = \{i \in \mathbb{Z} \mid i \leq 0\}$
$\gamma(\geq) = \{i \in \mathbb{Z} \mid i \geq 0\}$
$\gamma(neg) = \{i \in \mathbb{Z} \mid i < 0\}$
$\gamma(pos) = \{i \in \mathbb{Z} \mid i > 0\}$
$\gamma(z) = \{z\}$, for all $z \in \mathbb{Z}$
$\gamma(\emptyset) = \{\}$

The `weakenUpdate` rule from [10] allows abstraction in our calculus:

$$\text{weakenUpdate} \quad \frac{\Gamma, \{\mathcal{U}\}(\bar{x} \doteq \bar{c}) \Rightarrow \exists \bar{\gamma}.\{\mathcal{U}'\}(\bar{x} \doteq \bar{c}), \Delta \qquad \Gamma \Rightarrow \{\mathcal{U}'\}\varphi, \Delta}{\Gamma \Rightarrow \{\mathcal{U}\}\varphi, \Delta}$$

where $\bar{x}$ are all program variables occurring as left-hand sides in $\mathcal{U}$ and $\bar{c}$ are fresh skolem constants. The formula $\exists \bar{\gamma}.\psi$ is a shortcut for $\exists \bar{y}.(\chi_{\bar{a}}(\bar{y}) \wedge \psi[\bar{\gamma}/\bar{y}])$, where $\bar{y} = (y_1, \ldots, y_m)$ is a list of fresh first order variables of the same length as $\bar{\gamma}$, and where $\psi[\bar{\gamma}/\bar{y}]$ stands for the formula obtained from ψ by replacing all occurrences of a symbol in $\bar{\gamma}$ with its counterpart in $\bar{y}$.

Performing value-based abstraction thus becomes replacement of an update by a weaker update. In particular, we do not perform abstraction on the program, but on the *symbolic state*.

5   Generation of Method Contracts

In [10] loop unrolling is used to find an invariant for an `update invariant` rule. Similarly we expand a method's body in order to find precondition and postcondition invariants, allowing us to create, prove and use a method contract.

Note: The φ in a DL-formula [p]φ is required for the sequent calculus rules. However, we do not use φ in our analysis, as we generate a specification of the program, not of what may be wanted to be proven (as this could be false).

5.1   Example

Given the program p in Listing 1.1 and some property φ we can simplify the sequent $\Rightarrow [p]\varphi$, leading to two branches, of which we are interested in the open branch with the method call: $y > 0 \Rightarrow [x = \texttt{fact(y); where fact(n)}\{\dots\}]\varphi$

In order to be able to use a method contract for this call to fact, the contract's precondition must hold for y. In this case therefore the precondition cannot be stronger than $n > 0$ for the formal parameter n. This gives us a starting point for the precondition. At this point we have no knowledge of the postcondition. Expanding the method call gives us:

$y > 0 \Rightarrow [z = y; \texttt{m-f(x)}\{\texttt{if (z == 0) \{res = 1;\} else \{\dots\}\}} \text{ where } \dots]\varphi$

Performing some simplification results in a closed goal on one branch (as y cannot be both greater than and also equal to 0) and the sequent:

$y > 0, y \neq 0 \Rightarrow \{z := y \parallel arg := y - 1\}[\texttt{m-f(x)}\{\texttt{tmp = fact(arg);} \dots\}]\varphi$

Here we have another call to fact. If we want a method contract which is applicable not only for the initial call but for all recursive calls as well, we need to make sure the precondition is valid for all calls. As arg is not necessarily greater than 0, we need to refine our initial precondition. Using the abstract domain A from Example 1 we join the abstract elements $>$ (the abstraction of our initial argument y) and $\geq$ (the abstraction of the argument arg to the recursive call) to get $\geq$ and create the weaker precondition $n \geq 0$.

Listing 1.1. Factorial

```
if (y > 0) {
    x = fact(y);
} where fact(n) {
    local res,arg,tmp;
    if (n == 0) {
        res = 1;
    } else {
        arg = n - 1;
        tmp = fact(arg);
        res = n * tmp;
    }
    return res;
}
```

In order to analyse what effect this new precondition has on the execution of the method call, we incorporate the precondition in an update, which is placed before a call to fact in an otherwise empty sequent with an uninterpreted predicate ψ:

$\Rightarrow \{y := \gamma_{\geq,1}\}[x = \texttt{fact(y); where fact(n) } \{\dots\}]\psi$

Performing methodExpand and simplification once more results in two open branches with the sequents:

$\gamma_{\geq,1} \doteq 0 \Rightarrow \{y := \gamma_{\geq,1} \parallel z := \gamma_{\geq,1} \parallel res := 1\}[\texttt{m-f(x)}\{\texttt{return res;}\} \dots]\psi \qquad (1)$

$\gamma_{\geq,1} \neq 0 \Rightarrow \{y := \gamma_{\geq,1} \parallel z := \gamma_{\geq,1} \parallel arg := \gamma_{\geq,1} - 1\}$
$\qquad [\texttt{m-f(x)}\{\texttt{tmp = fact(arg); res = z * tmp; return res;}\} \dots]\psi \qquad (2)$

The return statement in sequent (1) is used to refine the postcondition, which now states that the return value is always 1. This can be expressed by the method contract $\chi_{\geq}(n) \Rightarrow [\texttt{result} = \texttt{fact(n); where } \dots]\chi_1(\texttt{result})$, which is not yet guaranteed to be valid as it is still being generated. Sequent (2) once again requires a method contract fulfilling the precondition $arg \geq 0$, but this time our generated precondition holds. We can therefore use our method contract and simply replace the method call with a fresh γ-term matching our generated postcondition:

$$\gamma_{\geq,1} \neq 0 \Rightarrow \{\texttt{y} := \gamma_{\geq,1} \parallel \texttt{z} := \gamma_{\geq,1} \parallel \texttt{arg} := \texttt{z} - 1\}$$
$$[\texttt{m-f(x)\{tmp = } \gamma_{1,2}\texttt{; res = z * tmp; return res;\}} \ldots]\psi$$

Simplification leads to:

$$\gamma_{\geq,1} \neq 0 \Rightarrow \{\texttt{y} := \gamma_{\geq,1} \parallel \texttt{z} := \gamma_{\geq,1} \parallel \texttt{arg} := \texttt{z} - 1 \parallel \texttt{tmp} := 1 \parallel \texttt{res} := \gamma_{\geq,1}\}$$
$$[\texttt{m-f(x)\{return res;\}} \ldots]\psi$$

This return statement provides yet another postcondition which states that the return value is $\gamma_{\geq,1}$ and also unequal to 0. The abstract element expressing this is $>$, which when joined with 1 remains $>$. Our new partial method contract is therefore $\chi_{\geq}(\texttt{n}) \Rightarrow [\texttt{result} = \texttt{fact(n)}; \texttt{ where } \ldots]\chi_{>}(\texttt{result})$. With this new contract we can now reconsider sequent (2). Simplification leads to:

$$\gamma_{\geq,1} \neq 0 \Rightarrow \{\texttt{y} := \gamma_{\geq,1} \parallel \texttt{z} := \gamma_{\geq,1} \parallel \texttt{arg} := \texttt{z} - 1 \parallel \texttt{tmp} := \gamma_{>,3} \parallel \texttt{res} := \gamma_{\geq,1} * \gamma_{>,3}\}$$
$$[\texttt{m-f(x)\{return res;\}} \ldots]\psi$$

The abstract element for the return value remains $>$ while no calls to $\texttt{fact}$ can be reached where the parameter is not in $\chi_{\geq}$ so we have reached a fixpoint for both pre- and postconditions and therefore our partially generated method contract holds in each call to $\texttt{fact}$ originating from the initial call $\texttt{fact(y)}$ and therefore is guaranteed to be a sound contract:

$$\chi_{\geq}(\texttt{n}) \Rightarrow [\texttt{result} = \texttt{fact(n)}; \texttt{ where } \ldots]\chi_{>}(\texttt{result})$$

This contract states that if $\texttt{fact}$ is called with a non-negative parameter and terminates, its result will be positive. It makes no claim about whether or not $\texttt{fact}$ terminates on this input (which indeed it always does). The contract generated for $\texttt{fact}$ if called initially with a negative number states that $\texttt{fact}$ does not terminate when called with a negative parameter, as nothing is in the abstract class $\bot$:

$$\chi_{<}(\texttt{n}) \Rightarrow [\texttt{result} = \texttt{fact(n)}; \texttt{ where } \ldots]\chi_{\bot}(\texttt{result})$$

5.2   Gathering Partial Method Contracts

Definition 6 (Partial method contract stack). *A partial method contract stack is a stack of triples, with each entry containing:*

1. *an abstract update matching each parameter to an abstract element*
2. *the method call, i.e. method name and method parameters*
3. *an abstract element expressing our current knowledge of the return value.*

Given an initial sequent *seq* to generate method contracts for, we simplify *seq* until we reach a sequent $\Gamma \Rightarrow \{\mathcal{U}\}[\pi \texttt{ x = } m(\texttt{x}_1, \ldots, \texttt{x}_n); \ldots \texttt{ where } \textit{defs}]\varphi, \Delta$. In order to generate a method contract for m, we first find a_i, $i \in \{1, \ldots, n\}$, such that $\Gamma \cup !\Delta \to \{\mathcal{U}\}\chi_{a_i}(\texttt{x}_i)$ holds for all i. We now create a partial method contract stack with the only entry $(x_1 := \gamma_{a_1,z_1} \parallel \dots \parallel x_n := \gamma_{a_n,z_n}, m(x_1,\dots,x_n), \bot)$, where all z_i are chosen such that all γ_{a_i,z_i} are fresh. We then create the sequent $\Rightarrow \{x_1 := \gamma_{a_1,z_1} \parallel \dots \parallel x_n := \gamma_{a_n,z_n}\}[x = m(x_1,\dots,x_n); \text{ where } \textit{defs}]\psi$, with ψ an uninterpreted predicate, and simplify the sequent, allowing all rules except `methodExpand`, `useMethodContract` and `return`. Finally, we examine the following groups of resulting branches:

Closed branches. A branch is closed either due to a purely logical reason, which does not interest us for method contract generation, or due to an infeasibility introduced by the program, i.e. unreachable code. This is also not of interest for method contract generation. Therefore closed branches can be safely ignored.

Return statements. From $\Gamma' \Rightarrow \{\mathcal{U}'\}[\pi' \text{ return } z; \dots \text{ where } \textit{defs}]\psi, \Delta'$ we generate an abstract element a such that $\Gamma' \cup !\Delta' \rightarrow \{\mathcal{U}'\}\chi_a(z)$ holds. We look at the top stack entry $(\mathcal{V}, m(\dots), b)$ and check if $a \sqsubseteq b$. If so nothing more is done for this branch and we move on to the next open branch. Otherwise the stack entry is changed to $(\mathcal{V}, m(\dots), a \sqcup b)$ and we keep track of the fact that a fixpoint has not yet been found.

Recursive calls to m. We look at the top entry $(x_1 := \gamma_{a_1,z_1} \parallel \dots \parallel x_n := \gamma_{a_n,z_n}, m(x_1,\dots,x_n), b)$ of the stack and for each $i \in \{1,\dots,n\}$ set p_i initially to the value a_i. Now for each open branch containing a recursive call to m $\Gamma' \Rightarrow \{\mathcal{U}'\}[\pi' \text{ } y = m(y_1,\dots,y_n); \dots \text{ where } \textit{defs}]\psi, \Delta'$, we first check if the call fulfills the precondition, i.e. if $\Gamma' \cup !\Delta' \rightarrow \{\mathcal{U}'\}\chi_{a_i}(y_i)$ holds for all $i \in \{1,\dots,n\}$. If so, we replace $y = m(\dots)$ with $y = \gamma_{b,z}$, where $z \in \mathbb{Z}$ is chosen such that $\gamma_{b,z}$ is fresh. We then continue the simplification of this branch, adding any branches still open after simplification to the set of remaining branches to consider (returns or recursive calls). If the precondition is not fulfilled, we find abstract elements b_i such that $\Gamma' \cup !\Delta' \rightarrow \{\mathcal{U}'\}\chi_{b_i}(y_i)$ and set each p_i to $p_i \sqcup b_i$. Once all recursive calls have been dealt with, if any p_i has been changed, we add a new entry $(x_1 := \gamma_{p_1,z_1} \parallel \dots \parallel x_n := \gamma_{p_n,z_n}, m(x_1,\dots,x_n), b)$ to the stack and mark that a fixpoint has not yet been found.

If we have not yet found a fixpoint, the sequent $\Rightarrow \{\mathcal{V}\}[x = m(\dots); \text{ where } \textit{defs}]\psi$ is generated from the top entry of the stack $(\mathcal{V}, m(\dots), b)$, to be used in the next iteration. If a fixpoint has been found, i.e. neither pre- nor postcondition has been changed in an iteration, we generate (and are able to trivially prove, possibly with induction) a method contract based on the top stack entry $(x_1 := \gamma_{a_1,z_1} \parallel \dots \parallel x_n := \gamma_{a_n,z_n}, m(x_1,\dots,x_n), b)$:

$$\chi_{a_1}(x_1),\dots,\chi_{a_n}(x_n) \Rightarrow [\text{res} = m(x_1,\dots,x_n); \text{ where } \textit{defs}]\chi_b(\text{res})$$

While this method contract is a decent overapproximation, it relies on the precondition being valid for each and every recursive call and therefore could possibly be refined into multiple separate method contracts expressing more detailed postconditions for less vague preconditions. For this reason we have left some partially generated method contracts on the stack. From these we can re-run our contract generation, applying the partial contract where applicable while applying the weaker contract where required. In this way we can for example generate for the sequent $\Rightarrow [\mathtt{p}]\varphi$, where $\mathtt{p}$ is the Fibonacci program in Listing 1.2, not only the method contract

$$\chi_{\geq}(\mathtt{n}) \Rightarrow [\mathtt{result} = \mathtt{fib(n)}; \ \ldots]\chi_{\geq}(\mathtt{result})$$

which is applicable for all reachable calls to `fib`, but also the stronger method contract

$$\chi_{>}(\mathtt{n}) \Rightarrow [\mathtt{result} = \mathtt{fib(n)}; \ \ldots]\chi_{>}(\mathtt{result})$$

applicable, in particular, to the initial call.

Listing 1.2. Fibonacci

```
if (y > 0) {
  x = fib(y);
} where fib(n) {
    local res,arg,fib1,fib2;
    if (n == 0 || n == 1) {
      res = n;
    } else {
      arg = n - 1;
      fib1 = fib(arg);
      arg = n - 2;
      fib2 = fib(arg);
      res = fib1 + fib2;
    }
    return res;
}
```

There is one further possibility for an open branch resulting from simplification: a call to a method other than the one under consideration. This last option must be dealt with carefully, as it can lead to, among others, mutual recursion.

5.3   Dealing with Other Method Calls, Mutual Recursion

Our goal is to keep high precision whenever possible, abstracting only at points where this is needed to ensure termination of our analysis. For this reason we do not want to start abstracting the first time we reach a method call, but only once we reach a recursive call and are therefore forced to perform abstraction. This allows us not only to be able to expand method calls which are not recursive in nature, but also to turn some forms of mutual recursion into direct recursion, creating method contracts only for method calls that really require one. One such example is where `even` and `odd` are defined in a mutual recursive way (so, e.g., $\mathtt{even}(2) = \mathtt{odd}(1) = \mathtt{even}(0) = \mathtt{true}$), but by always expanding any call to `odd` it suffices to generate a method contract only for `even`.

Beginning with an initial sequent $\Gamma \Rightarrow [\mathtt{p}]\varphi, \Delta$ for some program $\mathtt{p}$, we need to generate all required method contracts, i.e. contracts for method calls reached by analysis of $\mathtt{p}$ which are called recursively. The basic idea is to simply expand a method call if it is not being called from within a call to itself and to keep track of all such methods so as to begin generating partial method contracts for these methods once a recursive call is reached. These partial contracts are iteratively refined until a fixpoint is found, based on new pre- and postconditions determined during further analysis. Once a fixpoint has been determined for a contract, it is stored in a set of sound contracts, both to be used for further analysis of other calls, as well as for the final result we are computing: all sound method contracts required in order to analyze the sequent $\Gamma \Rightarrow [\mathtt{p}]\varphi, \Delta$.

Relational Abstract Domains. While our approach does not explicitly allow relational abstract domains, we can simulate some of these by tracking, for example,

Table 2. Test results on an Intel Core i7 processor with 2.6 GHz.

Method Call	Constraints	Precondition	Postcondition (r is result)	Time (s)
fact(x)	$x > 0$	$x \geq 0$	$r > 0$	7.236
fact(x)	$x < 0$	$x < 0$	false	0.689
fib(x)	$x > 0$	$x \geq 0$ $x > 0$	$r \geq 0$ $r > 0$	10.465
hanoiCount(x)	$x > 0$	$x > 0$	$r > 0 \wedge r \geq x$	2.971
ackermann(x,y)	$x > 0, y > 0$	$x \geq 0, y \geq 0$	$r > 0 \wedge r > y$	15.879
gcd(x,y)	$x > y, y > 0$	$x > 0, y \geq 0$	$r > 0 \wedge r \leq x$	9.308
gcd2(x,y)	$x > y, y > 0$	$x > 0, y > 0$	$r > 0 \wedge r \leq x \wedge r \leq y$	7.511
gcd3(x,y)	$x > y, y > 0$	$x > 0, y \geq 0, x > y$	$r > 0 \wedge r \leq x$	8.986

the value of $x - y$. Knowing that $\chi_>(x-y)$ implies $x > y$ and so on for the other abstract elements. We use this to compare method parameters amongst one another and with the result to gain further pre- and postconditions.

6   Experimental Evaluation

Our implementation differs somewhat from the theoretical ideas discussed in the last section, as it is based on the KeY system which allows for full sequential Java, rather than the toy language described in this paper. Some aspects of the implementation are more powerfull: both pre- and postconditions additionally contain information about the state of the program heap, return statements can appear at any point in the code rather than only as the final method statement, etc. However, the implementation cannot yet deal with mutual recursion.

An extension of the framework with our approach to automatic specification generation is available at http://www.key-project.org/setta15-albia/ and has been used to generate method contracts for some recursive method calls with initial constraints as shown in Table 2. The abstract domain used is A from Example 1.

Even with this simple abstract domain, the postconditions generated can be used to show, for example, that calculation of x/gcd(x,y) will not divide by zero and the result will be greater than zero, given the initial constraints.

7   Related Work

The basics of interprocedural dataflow analysis stem from Sharir and Pnueli [13]. The tools Bebop [14], SLAM [7] and BLAST [8] all transform a program using Boolean program models before performing analysis on the resulting Boolean program. We do not abstract the program, but rather the program state and only at points where abstraction is needed to ensure termination. At all other points we keep full precision. The dynamic program analysis tool Daikon [6] can generate pre- and postconditions for methods reached in program runs, but it only generates likely invariants based on the actual runs it has performed, while our invariants are correct by construction. Chen et al. [15] use a tool which can analyze only non-recursive methods and reduce all recursive calls to a non-recursive under-approximation in order to re-use the existing tool. In our approach we deal more directly with recursion. Houdini [16] is an annotation assistant for ESC/Java which generates pre- and postconditions in a bottom up fashion from a large set of annotation candidates by iteratively dropping candidates that do not provably hold at some method call or return statement. SATURN [17] is a bug finding framework, which keeps full precision for loop-free code (like our approach) and generates method summaries from the bottom up, which is quite efficient provided the method call graph is acyclic. As we wish to be able to analyze programs with mutual recursion we use a top down approach.

8   Conclusion and Future Work

We have shown a novel approach to automate generation of specifications for (mutually) recursive methods. In addition to a single specification which is applicable at all reachable call sites, our approach can also deliver stronger specifications for some call sites. Our approach integrates easily into a framework combining deductive verification with abstract interpretation. The implementation shows this approach to be feasible. As future work we intend to extend the implementation by adding the ability to deal with mutual recursion as outlined in Section 5.3. In addition, integration with our extension of the framework for array abstraction [18] will enable more detailed automatic analysis of recursive array-manipulating methods, such as quicksort, mergesort and binary search implementations. Our approach will also be extended to generate total correctness specifications. We will investigate integrating our approach into the framework presented in [19], allowing their analysis to deal with recursive methods without the need for user specified method contracts. Finally, we will look into using the property φ in $[\text{p}]\varphi$ to help guide analysis.

Acknowledgments. We thank Richard Bubel and Reiner Hähnle for our many fruitful discussions, Eduard Kamburjan for his work on the implementation and the anonymous reviewers for their helpful comments.

References

1. Cousot, P., Cousot, R.: Abstract interpretation: A unified lattice model for static analysis of programs by construction or approximation of fixpoints. In: 4th Symposium on Principles of Programming Languages (POPL), pp. 238–252. ACM (1977)
2. Clarke, E., Grumberg, O., Jha, S., Lu, Y., Veith, H.: Counterexample-guided abstraction refinement. In: Computer Aided Verification, pp. 154–169. Springer (2000)
3. Colón, M.A., Sankaranarayanan, S., Sipma, H.B.: Linear invariant generation using non-linear constraint solving. In: Hunt Jr., W.A., Somenzi, F. (eds.) CAV 2003. LNCS, vol. 2725, pp. 420–432. Springer, Heidelberg (2003)

4. Sankaranarayanan, S., Sipma, H.B., Manna, Z.: Non-linear loop invariant generation using gröbner bases. In: Proceedings of the 31st ACM SIGPLAN-SIGACT Symposium on Principles of Programming Languages. POPL 2004, pp. 318–329. ACM (2004)

5. Furia, C.A., Meyer, B.: Inferring loop invariants using postconditions. In: Blass, A., Dershowitz, N., Reisig, W. (eds.) Fields of Logic and Computation. LNCS, vol. 6300, pp. 277–300. Springer, Heidelberg (2010)

6. Ernst, M.D., Perkins, J.H., Guo, P.J., McCamant, S., Pacheco, C., Tschantz, M.S., Xiao, C.: The daikon system for dynamic detection of likely invariants. Sci. Comput. Program. **69**(1–3), 35–45 (2007)

7. Ball, T., Rajamani, S.K.: The SLAM toolkit. In: Berry, G., Comon, H., Finkel, A. (eds.) CAV 2001. LNCS, vol. 2102, p. 260. Springer, Heidelberg (2001)

8. Henzinger, T.A., Jhala, R., Majumdar, R., Sutre, G.: Lazy abstraction. In: Proceedings of the 29th ACM SIGPLAN-SIGACT Symposium on Principles of Programming Languages. POPL 2002, pp. 58–70. ACM (2002)

9. La Torre, S., Parthasarathy, M., Parlato, G.: Analyzing recursive programs using a fixed-point calculus. In: Proceedings of the 2009 ACM SIGPLAN Conference on Programming Language Design and Implementation. PLDI 2009, pp. 211–222. ACM (2009)

10. Bubel, R., Hähnle, R., Weiß, B.: Abstract interpretation of symbolic execution with explicit state updates. In: de Boer, F.S., Bonsangue, M.M., Madelaine, E. (eds.) FMCO 2008. LNCS, vol. 5751, pp. 247–277. Springer, Heidelberg (2009)

11. Beckert, B., Hähnle, R., Schmitt, P.H. (eds.): Verification of Object-Oriented Software: The KeY Approach. LNCS, vol. 4334. Springer, Heidelberg (2007)

12. Rümmer, P.: Sequential, parallel, and quantified updates of first-order structures. In: Hermann, M., Voronkov, A. (eds.) LPAR 2006. LNCS (LNAI), vol. 4246, pp. 422–436. Springer, Heidelberg (2006)

13. Sharir, M., Pnueli, A.: Two approaches to interprocedural data flow analysis. In: Muchnick, S., Jones, N., (eds.) Program Flow Analysis: Theory and Applications. pp.189–233, Prentice-Hall (1981)

14. Ball, T., Rajamani, S.K.: Bebop: A symbolic model checker for boolean programs. In: Proceedings of the 7th International SPIN Workshop on SPIN Model Checking and Software Verification, pp. 113–130. Springer (2000)

15. Chen, Y.-F., Hsieh, C., Tsai, M.-H., Wang, B.-Y., Wang, F.: Verifying recursive programs using intraprocedural analyzers. In: Müller-Olm, M., Seidl, H. (eds.) Static Analysis. LNCS, vol. 8723, pp. 118–133. Springer, Heidelberg (2014)

16. Flanagan, C., M. Leino, K.R.: Houdini, an annotation assistant for ESC/Java. In: Oliveira, J.N., Zave, P. (eds.) FME 2001. LNCS, vol. 2021, p. 500. Springer, Heidelberg (2001)

17. Xie, Y., Aiken, A.: Saturn: A scalable framework for error detection using boolean satisfiability. ACM Trans. Program. Lang. Syst. 29(3), May 2007

18. Wasser, N., Bubel, R., Hähnle, R.: Array abstraction with symbolic pivots. Technical report, Department of Computer Science, Technische Universität Darmstadt, Germany August 2015. URL: https://www.se.tu-darmstadt.de/fileadmin/user_upload/Group_SE/Publications/ALBIA/TR_Symbolic_Pivots.pdf

19. Hentschel, M., Käsdorf, S., Hähnle, R., Bubel, R.: An interactive verification tool meets an IDE. In: Albert, E., Sekerinski, E. (eds.) IFM 2014. LNCS, vol. 8739, pp. 55–70. Springer, Heidelberg (2014)

Assertion-Directed Precondition Synthesis for Loops over Data Structures

Juan Zhai[1,2]($\boxtimes$), Hanfei Wang[1,3], and Jianhua Zhao[1,3]

[1] State Key Laboratory for Novel Software Technology,
Nanjing University, Nanjing, China
{zhaijuan,wanghaifei1988}@seg.nju.edu.cn, zhaojh@nju.edu.cn
[2] Software Institute, Nanjing University, Nanjing, China
[3] Department of Computer Science and Technology,
Nanjing University, Nanjing, China

Abstract. Program verification typically generates verification conditions for a program to be proven and then uses a theorem prover to prove their correctness. These verification conditions are normally generated by means of weakest-precondition calculus. Nevertheless, the weakest-precondition calculus faces a big challenge when dealing with loops. In this paper, we propose a framework that automatically generates preconditions for loops that iterate over commonly-used data structures. The preconditions are generated based on given assertions of loops and they are proved to be strong enough to ensure those given assertions hold. The data structures dealt with in our framework include one-dimensional arrays, acyclic singly-linked lists, doubly-linked lists and static lists. Such loops usually achieve their final results by focusing on one element in each iteration. In many such cases, the given assertion and the corresponding precondition of the loop separately reflect the part and the whole or vice versa. Inspired by this, our framework automatically generates precondition candidates for loops by transforming a given assertion. Then the framework uses the SMT solver Z3 and the weakest-precondition calculator for non-loop statements provided in the interactive code-verification tool Accumulator to check whether they are strong enough to prove the given assertion. The framework has been integrated into the tool Accumulator to generate suitable preconditions for loops, which greatly relieves the burden of manually providing preconditions for loops.

1 Introduction

Program verification is a classic approach to improve software reliability by verifying program correctness. A standard method for program verification is to generate weakest-preconditions for assertions of a program and then prove these weakest-preconditions using theorem provers. The generation of weakest-preconditions is of great significance in the research field of program verification and has been explored in many literatures, see e.g., [1–5]. Weakest-preconditions for simple program statements can be obtained easily by weakest-precondition calculus techniques while weakest-preconditions for loop statements are difficult

© Springer International Publishing Switzerland 2015
X. Li et al. (Eds.): SETTA 2015, LNCS 9409, pp. 258–274, 2015.
DOI: 10.1007/978-3-319-25942-0_17

to generate. In order to verify programs containing loop statements, programmers are required to provide weakest-preconditions for loops, which increases the burden for programmers. Automatic generation of weakest-preconditions for loops will facilitate the formal verification of programs containing loops.

However, it is challenging to calculate weakest-preconditions for loop statements due to two main factors: (1) there are a great many kinds of loops which makes it difficult to find a uniform way to automatically gain weakest-preconditions for all kinds of loop statements. (2) It is difficult to determine whether the loop terminates and obtain the exact number of loop iterations. In this paper, we present a framework to automatically generate preconditions for the kind of loops that manipulate commonly-used data structures. These data structures include one-dimensional arrays, acyclic singly-linked lists, doubly-linked lists and static lists. The data stored in these data structures can be modified in the loop, but the shapes of these data structures cannot be modified. We generate preconditions for such loops with respect to both intermediate assertions inside the loops and post-conditions of the loops. Although the preconditions generated using our framework may not be the weakest-preconditions, they are proved to be practically useful to prove the given assertions of the kind of loops that operate frequently-used data structures.

The framework proposed in this paper is inspired by our statistic analysis on loops that operate frequently-used data structures occurring in several open-source softwares. These softwares include *memcached*, *Apache httpd* and *nginx*. The inspiring observations are as follows:

1. We found that about eighty percent of loops manipulate a data structure by iterating over its elements. From a practical standpoint, automatic generation of preconditions for this kind of loops would cover a great number of real-world cases and make the task of verifying such loops much easier.
2. This kind of loops usually achieves the final goals by concerning one element in each iteration. In this sense, a precondition of such loops with respect to an intermediate assertion inside the loop is usually a quantified result of the intermediate assertion. On the contrary, a precondition of such loops with respect to a post-condition of the loop usually applies the property in the post-condition to some specific elements. This leads us to believe that we are able to generate practical preconditions for such loops by transforming given assertions of these loops.

Our research is based on Scope Logic [6], though the core idea presented in this paper can be applied in code verifications using other logics. Scope Logic is an extension of Hoare Logic for verification of pointer programs with recursive data structures. An interactive tool named Accumulator(Available at http://seg.nju.edu.cn/scl.html) has been implemented to support code verification in Scope Logic. The weakest-precondition calculation for assignments and conditionals is well-supported in this logic, which greatly eases the verification tasks of programs without loops. However, loop statements cannot benefit from this calculation. This motivates us to provide an automatic framework to generate preconditions for loops to relieve the burden of verify loops.

Given a loop, we first collect information like names/types of the loop control variable, and check whether the loop can be handled by our approach. Then we generate precondition candidates of the loop based on a given assertion, which are subsequently checked to see whether they are strong enough to prove the given assertion. The checking process uses the high-performance SMT solver Z3 [7] and the weakest-precondition calculator for non-loop statements in Accumulator. For an intermediate assertion inside a loop, we first compute the weakest-precondition of the loop body with respect to the intermediate assertion using the weakest-precondition calculator provided in Accumulator. Then precondition candidates are obtained by transforming the generated weakest-precondition according to whether it contains the loop control variable. By contrast, we generate preconditions of the loop for a post-condition by transforming the post-condition itself based on whether it contains loop variables.

The main contribution of this paper is a novel framework that automatically generates preconditions for loops that manipulate commonly-used data structures, including one-dimensional arrays, acyclic singly-linked lists, doubly-linked lists and static lists. The framework has been implemented as a module of the tool Accumulator. We have evaluated it on several programs and the results show that the framework is capable of generating suitable preconditions to prove the partial correctness of the loops manipulating commonly-used data structures.

The remainder of the paper is organized as follows. Section 2 makes a brief introduction to Scope Logic and its weakest-precondition calculus. Section 3 gives a motivating example to show why automatic generation of preconditions for loops are necessary in code verification. Section 4 gives the details of generating preconditions for while-loops by dealing informally with an example program. Section 5 sketches the implementation and application of the framework. Section 6 lists the limitations of our approach together with the future work. Section 7 surveys related work and, finally, Section 8 concludes the paper.

2   Preliminary

In this section, we present a brief overview of Scope Logic and the weakest-precondition calculus in Scope Logic.

2.1   Scope Logic

Scope Logic is an extension of Hoare Logic for verification of pointer programs with recursive data structures. For details, please refer to [6]. The basic idea of Scope Logic is that the value of an expression e depends only on the memory units which are accessed during the evaluation of e. The set of these memory units are called the memory scope of e, denoted as $\mathfrak{M}(e)$. If no memory unit in the set $\mathfrak{M}(e)$ is modified by program statements, the value of e keeps unchanged.

$$isSL(x : P(Node)) : bool \triangleq (x == null)?true : isSL(x \rightarrow link)$$

$$Nodes(x : P(Node)) : SetOf(P(Node)) \triangleq (x == null)?\emptyset : (\{x\} \cup Nodes(x \rightarrow link))$$

$$isSLSeg(x : P(Node), y : P(Node)) : bool \triangleq (x == null)?false :$$
$$((x == y)?true : isSLSeg(x \rightarrow link, y))$$

$$NodesSeg(x : P(Node), y : P(Node)) : SetOf(P(Node)) \triangleq (x == null)?\emptyset : ((x == y)?\emptyset :$$
$$(\{x\} \cup NodesSeg(x \rightarrow link, y)))$$

Fig. 1. A set of recursive functions of singly-linked lists

User-Defined Recursive Functions.   Scope Logic allows users to define recursive functions to describe properties of recursive data structures. For example, four user-defined recursive functions are given in Fig. 1 to specify properties of acyclic singly-linked lists. Here an acyclic singly-linked list node contains two fields: the data field d and the link field $link$. These functions will be used in the rest of this paper to verify code manipulating acyclic singly-linked lists.

Example 1. In Fig. 1, the function $isSL(x)$ asserts that if a node x is a null pointer or $x \rightarrow link$ points to an acyclic singly-linked list, then x is an acyclic singly-linked list. The function $Nodes(x)$ yields the node set of the singly-linked list x. The function $isSLSeg(x, y)$ asserts that if the node x can reach node y along the field $link$, then the segment from x to y is an acyclic singly-linked list segment. The function $NodesSeg(x, y)$ yields the set of nodes from node x to node y (excluded) along the filed $link$.   □

Nevertheless, some properties should be provided to support local reasoning because first-order logic cannot handle recursive functions directly. Some selected properties of the user-defined functions in Fig. 1 are listed in Table 1. Take the first property as an example, it describes that if the expression x is null, then x is an acyclic singly-linked list and the node set of x is empty.

Table 1. Properties of user-defined acyclic singly-linked list functions

ID	Property
1	$\forall x(x == null) \Rightarrow (isSL(x) \wedge Nodes(x) == \emptyset)$
2	$\forall x(x \neq null \wedge isSL(x)) \Rightarrow (Nodes(x) == \{x\} \cup Nodes(x \rightarrow link) \wedge x \notin Nodes(x \rightarrow link))$
3	$\forall x \forall y(x == y) \Rightarrow (NodesSeg(x, y) == \emptyset)$
4	$\forall x \forall y(x \neq null \wedge y == null) \Rightarrow (NodesSeg(x, y) == Nodes(x))$
5	$\forall x \forall y(isSL(y) \wedge isSLSeg(x, y)) \Rightarrow (isSL(x) \wedge Nodes(x) == NodesSeg(x, y) \cup Nodes(y))$

Program-Point-Specific Expressions.   In Scope Logic, assertions and verifications are written in the proof-in-code form. Formulas are written at program points which are places before and after program statements. All the program points are uniquely numbered. A formula at a program point is used to describe a property that the program satisfies. If a program runs into the program point j before it runs into the program point i, $e@j$ can be written at the program point

```
{1:  sl ≠ null ,  isSL(sl) ,  ∀x ∈ Nodes(sl).x → d > 0}
min  =  sl→d ;
{2:  sl ≠ null ,  isSL(sl) ,  min == sl → d ,  min > 0 ,  ∀x ∈ Nodes(sl).x → d > 0 ,
     min ∈ (λx.x → d)[Nodes(sl)]}
p  =  sl→link ;
{3:  sl ≠ null ,  isSL(sl) ,  p == sl → link ,  isSL(p) ,  ∀x ∈ Nodes(sl).x → d > 0 ,  min > 0 ,
     p ∈ Nodes(sl)}
while (p ≠ null){
        {4:  p ≠ null ,  p ∈ Nodes(sl) ,  ∀x ∈ Nodes(sl).x → d > 0}
        if (p→d < min)
               {5:  p ≠ null ,  p → d < min}
               min = p→d ;
               {6:  p ≠ null ,  min == p → d ,  min > 0 ,  min ∈ (λx.x → d)[Nodes(sl)]}
        else
               {7:  p ≠ null ,  not(p → d < min)}
               skip ;
               {8:  p ≠ null }
        {9:  p ≠ null }
        p = p→link ;
        {10:  isSL(sl) }
}
{11:  p == null ,  ∀x ∈ Nodes(sl).x → d > 0 ,
     (λx.x → d)[Nodes(sl)] == (λx.x → d)[Nodes(sl)]@1 ,
min ∈ (λx.x → d)[Nodes(sl)] ,  ∀x ∈ Nodes(sl).x → d ≥ min}
```

Fig. 2. Find the minimum value of an acyclic singly-linked list

i to represent the value of e evaluated at the program point j. Expressions like $e@j$ are called program-point-specific expressions. With this kind of expressions, the relations between different program states can be specified.

Set-Image Expression. Set-image expression is of the form $\lambda x.exp[setExp]$, which means the set of values derived by applying the anonymous function defined by $\lambda x.exp$ to the elements in the set $setExp$.

Restricted Quantifier Expression. Restricted quantifier expression is of the form $\forall x \in setExp.exp$, which asserts that for each element x in the set $setExp$, exp is satisfied.

Example 2. A program written in the proof-in-code form is given in Fig. 2 where the numbered program points and some formulas are also shown. This program finds the minimum element in the acyclic singly-linked list sl. The entrance program point and the exit point are respectively 1 and 11. The preconditions of this program are shown at the program point 1 while the post-conditions are written at the program point 11.

2.2 Weakest-Precondition Calculus in Scope Logic

The weakest-precondition was introduced by Dijkstra in [8]. For a statement S and a predicate Q on the post-state of S, the weakest-precondition of S with respect to Q, written as $wp(S, Q)$, is a predicate that characterizes all the pre-states of S from which no execution will go wrong and from which every terminating execution ends in a state satisfying Q. In program verification, weakest-preconditions are often used to prove the correctness of programs in regard to assertions represented by preconditions and post-conditions. Here we assume that P stands for the predicates on the pre-state of S, we can verify $\{P\}S\{Q\}$ by proving $P \Rightarrow wp(S, Q)$.

The calculation of weakest-preconditions for assignments and conditionals are well-supported in Scope Logic. Suppose that we have an assignment $e_1 = e_2$ and the program points before/after this assignment are i and j respectively. The differences between the program state at i and the program state at j result from the modification of the contents in the memory unit $(\&e_1)@j$. The basic idea of generating weakest-preconditions is that for an arbitrary x of a memory unit, the value of $((x \neq (\&e_1)@i)? * x : e_2@i)$ at the program point i is equivalent to the value of $*x$ at the program point j. Firstly, an expression $exp(\&e)$ is constructed. The value of $exp(\&e)$ at i equals to the value $\&e$ at j. After that, $exp(e')$ is constructed as $(exp(\&e) \neq (\&e_1)@i)? * exp(\&e) : e_2@i$. As discussed earlier, the value of $exp(e)$ at i and the value of $*(\&e)$ at j are equivalent. The detailed rules for generating weakest-preconditions are omitted here. Interested readers can refer to the paper [6].

3   Motivating Example

The program *findMin* in Fig. 2 finds the minimum element in the list sl. It is used as an example here to show why preconditions of loops are necessary and helpful to verify this program.

Proving that no null-pointer dereference occurs requires that $p \neq null$ holds in some program points. Take the assertion $p \neq null$ at program point 5 as an example, we can compute the weakest-precondition at program point 4 with respect to it and we get $(p \to d < min) \Rightarrow (p \neq null)$. At program point 4, this weakest-precondition can be implied by $p \neq null$ which is surly true because of the loop condition.

The above is a simple assertion which can be proved inside the loop. There are many other assertions that cannot be proved without preconditions of the loop, for example, $min > 0$ at program point 6. Just like $p \neq null$, the weakest-precondition

$$(p \to d < min) \Rightarrow (p \to d > 0) \tag{1}$$

at program point 4 is first generated for $min > 0$ at program point 6. Proving this weakest-precondition requires ingenuity in generating the precondition of the loop for it.

Based on the weakest-precondition (1), the following precondition of the loop is generated using our framework.

$$\forall x \in Nodes(sl).((x \to d < min) \Rightarrow (x \to d > 0)) \tag{2}$$

Fig. 3. Overview of our approach

The precondition (2) is proved to be a loop invariant of this loop, thus it holds at the program point 4. The weakest-precondition (1) at program point 4 is implied by (2) together with $p \neq null$ and $p \in Nodes(sl)$. In this way, the assertion $min > 0$ at program point 6 is proved to be true.

Preconditions of loops are also necessary to prove post-conditions of loops. Take the post-condition

$$\forall x \in Nodes(sl).x \rightarrow d \geq min \tag{3}$$

as an example. Our framework generates the precondition of the loop for it and the precondition is

$$\forall x \in NodesSeg(sl, p).x \rightarrow d \geq min \tag{4}$$

This precondition is proved to be a loop invariant and the post-condition (3) can be implied by this precondition (4) together with the loop exit condition $p == null$, the precondition of the loop $l \neq null$ and Property 4 in Table 1.

From this, we can see that automatically generating preconditions for loops is useful and practical in verifying programs.

4   Design

In this section, we present our approach of automatically generating preconditions for the kind of loops that manipulate commonly-used data structures. Fig. 3 gives the overview of our approach, which takes the program annotated with assertions as input, and uses information extractor, pre-processor, pre-condition generator and pre-condition validator to generate pre-conditions for the loop in this program. The information extractor takes the program as input, and extracts necessary information to generate pre-conditions and checks whether the loop can be handled by our approach. The pre-processor derives some simple but useful loop invariants used as the premises to check the generated preconditions. The pre-condition generator generates pre-conditions from a given assertion and the information extracted before. The pre-condition validator makes use of the SMT solver Z3 and the weakest-precondition calculator to check whether the generated pre-condition is strong enough to prove the correctness of the assertion based on which to generate the pre-conditions.

In the rest of this section, we discuss the details of our approach. The discussion is driven by the example shown in Fig. 2.

4.1   Information Extractor

The information extractor mainly performs the following two tasks:

Information Collector. Our approach collects different kinds of information of the loop, which include names, types, initial values and final values of the loop control variables, the loop condition, and the data structure manipulated by the loop. If the data structure manipulated by the loop is a one-dimensional array, the size of the array and the traverse pattern are also needed to be gathered. Here the traverse pattern means whether the loop iterates over the array elements from left to right or the other way.

Loop Checker. Our approach is capable of generating pre-conditions for while-loops that iterate over elements stored in a data structure without modifying the shape of this data structure. These loops should conform to our pre-defined loop patterns. Because of space limitation, we only gives the patterns for loops manipulating acyclic singly-linked lists and one-dimensional arrays.

```
{i:  isSL(first),  cur == first}
while (cur ≠ null) {
        {j: }
        S
        {m:  cur == (cur → link)@j}
}
{n:  ψ}
```

```
{i:  index == low_exp}
while (index # up_exp) {
        {j: }
        S
        {m:  index == index@j + 1}
}
{n:  ψ}
```

(a)   (b)

Fig. 4. The loop patterns for acyclic singly-linked lists and one-dimensional arrays

(1) Pattern of Loops Manipulating Acyclic Singly-Linked Lists. The pattern of the while-loops that manipulate an acyclic singly-linked list in C syntax is given in Fig. 4a. Here $first$ represents the acyclic singly-linked list traversed in the loop and cur represents the expression used to access each list node. In this pattern, cur is also the loop control variable. This is often the case when an acyclic singly-linked list is iterated over in practice. For example, in Fig. 2, p is the loop control variable and the loop body accesses each data stored in the list node referred to by p.

For the loop to be handled by our approach, the following are also required:

1) $isSL(first)$ and $cur == first$ hold at the program point i.
2) The loop control condition is either $cur \neq null$ or $null \neq cur$.
3) $cur == (cur \rightarrow link)@j$ holds at the program point m, which guarantees that the value of cur after the loop body equals to the value of $cur \rightarrow link$ before the loop body.

4) For each assignment $e_1 = e_2$ in the loop body, $\&e_1 \notin \mathfrak{M}(isSL(first))$ holds at the point before the assignment statement, which guarantees that the loop does not modify the field $link$ of all the nodes. Hence the shape of the singly-linked list is not modified.

Together with the definition of an acyclic singly-linked list in Fig. 1 and the loop control condition, the condition 3) listed above can guarantee that the loop will terminate.

(2)Pattern of Loops Manipulating One-Dimensional Arrays. The pattern of the while-loops that iterate over a one-dimensional array from left to right in C syntax is shown in Fig. 4b. The pattern of the while-loops that iterate over a one-dimensional array from right to left is symmetrical, which is omitted here. In this pattern, *index* represents the subscript used to access each element of the array being traversed. The expressions *low_exp* and *up_exp* respectively represent the lower/upper bound expressions of *index*. In this pattern, *index* is also the loop control variable. The expression *index#up_exp* represents the loop control condition where $\#$ can be operators $<$, $\leq$ or $\neq$.

For the loop to be handled by our approach, the following are also required:

1) $up\_exp == up\_exp@j$ holds at the program point m.
2) The loop control condition is one of the following six forms: $index < up\_exp$, $index \neq up\_exp$, $up\_exp > index$, $up\_exp \neq index$, $index \leq up\_exp$ and $up\_exp \geq index$.
3) $index == index@j + 1$ holds at the program point m.

Together the loop control condition, the condition 3) listed above can guarantee that the loop will terminate.

4.2   Pre-processor

The pre-processor makes an attempt to generate some simple but useful loop invariants which are used to check the generated preconditions. These loop invariants are verified via Z3 and the weakest-precondition calculator. For example, in Fig. 2, the loop invariant $(p \neq null) \Rightarrow (p \in Nodes(sl))$ is generated.

4.3   Pre-condition Generator

In this section, we describe in details how to generate preconditions candidates based on a given intermediate assertion inside a loop and a post-condition of a loop.

Generating Precondition Candidates from an Intermediate Assertion. Generating preconditions based on an intermediate assertion inside a loop is given in Algorithm 1. The algorithm takes as arguments a loop program *loop*, a given intermediate assertion *assertion* of *loop* and the information *info* of *loop*. This algorithm returns a set of precondition candidates with respect to *assertion*.

Algorithm 1. Generating Preconditions from an Intermediate Assertion

---

Input: a loop program *loop*; an intermediate assertion *assertion* of *loop*; loop information *info*;

Output: a set of precondition candidates with respect to *assertion*;

1: $set \leftarrow \emptyset$;
2: let i be the program point before the loop body of *loop*
3: let j be the program point of *assertion* inside *loop*
4: $wp \leftarrow compute\_wp(assertion, j, i)$;
5: $swp \leftarrow simplify(wp)$;
6: **if** swp contains the loop control variable **then**
7: $\quad qwp = quantify(swp, info)$;
8: $\quad set \leftarrow set \cup qwp$;
9: **else**
10: $\quad set \leftarrow set \cup swp$;
11: **end if**
12: let *cond* be the loop control condition of *loop*
13: **for** each $exp \in set$ **do**
14: $\quad exp' = transform(exp, cond)$;
15: $\quad set \leftarrow set \cup exp'$;
16: **end for**
17: **return** set;

To start with, the variable *set* used to store precondition candidates of *loop* is initialized to an empty set. In line 4, the algorithm invokes the procedure *compute_wp* to obtain the weakest-precondition at program point i with respect to the intermediate assertion *assertion* at program point j. Since wp may contain redundant information, this algorithm simplifies it via the procedure *simplify* in line 5 and the simplified result is stored in swp. Then the algorithm analyzed swp to see whether swp contains the loop control variable. If so, what swp reflects is the property which holds by a set of elements. In this case, swp is universally quantified via the procedure *quantify* in line 7. The quantified result qwp is added to *set* as a precondition candidate. Otherwise, we simply regard swp as a precondition candidate and add it to *set* in line 10. Lines 13-16 make a transformation of each expression in *set* and add the transformation result to *set*. The procedure *tranform* in line 14 construct a new expression $(cond) \Rightarrow (exp)$ where *cond* represents the loop control condition of *loop*. Eventually, *set* which contains all the precondition candidates is returned in line 17.

Example 3. Consider the intermediate assertion $isSL(l)$ at program point 10 of the program in Fig. 2. Firstly, Algorithm 1 computes the weakest-precondition at program point 4 for $isSL(l)$ and we get $p \rightarrow d < min?(isSL(l)) : (isSL(l))$ which can be simplified to $isSL(l)$. Since $\&p \notin \mathfrak{M}(isSL(l))$ holds at program point 4, the algorithm simply adds $isSL(l)$ to the set containing precondition candidates. After that, the pre-condition $(p \neq null) \Rightarrow (isSL(l))$ is constructed via the procedure *transform* in line 14 and added to the candidate set. □

Universal Quantification. It is obvious that when a formula at the program point before the loop body contains the loop control variable, this formula actually describes some property that should be held by the set of elements which are manipulated in the loop. For this reason, our framework universally quantifies the weakest-precondition at the program point before the loop body with respect to an intermediate assertion inside the loop body to generate a precondition candidate of the loop if this weakest-precondition contains the loop control variable. We achieve this by introducing a fresh variable which does not appear elsewhere in the program or in the weakest-precondition. The details of quantifying for loops manipulating singly-linked lists and one-dimensional arrays are given below. Doubly-linked lists and static lists are also dealt with in this paper, but the details are omitted here because of space limitation.

(1) Acyclic Singly-Linked List. Suppose that $first$ represents an acyclic singly-linked list and cur represents the loop control variable used to access each list node of $first$. The concrete expressions of $first$ and cur are obtained through a static analysis. Besides, we assume that the expression exp represents the weakest-precondition at the program point before the loop body. Note that exp contains the loop control variable cur. By universally quantifying over cur which appears in exp, we get the following precondition candidate of the loop:

$$\forall x \in Nodes(first).(exp[cur \longmapsto x])$$

Example 4. In Fig. 2, the weakest-precondition at program point 4 with respect to the intermediate assertion

$$min \in (\lambda x.x \to d)[Nodes(sl)] \tag{5}$$

at program point 6 is as follows:

$$(p \to d < min) \Rightarrow (p \to d \in (\lambda x.x \to d)[Nodes(sl)]) \tag{6}$$

where p is the loop control variable used to access each list node. Our framework universally quantifies the weakest-precondition (6) by introducing a new variable y to substitute p. The quantified result is the following precondition candidate:

$$\forall y \in Nodes(sl).((y \to d < min) \Rightarrow (y \to d \in (\lambda x.x \to d)[Nodes(sl)])) \tag{7}$$

The precondition candidate (7) is proved to be strong enough to guarantee (6) holds at program point 4. Thus the assertion (5) is verified to be true at program point 6. □

(2) One-Dimensional Arrays. Suppose that arr represents a one-dimensional array, $index$ represents the loop control variable used as the subscript to access each element of arr, low and $high$ respectively represent the lower/upper bound expressions of $index$. The concrete expressions of arr, $index$, low and $high$ are obtained through a static analysis. Besides, we assume that the expression exp represents the weakest-precondition at the program point before the loop body.

```
{ 1:  a ≠ null ,  b ≠ null ,  ∀x ∈ [0, 99].a[i] ≥ 0}
size  =  100;
{ 2:  a ≠ null ,  b ≠ null ,  ∀x ∈ [0, 99].a[i] ≥ 0 ,  size == 100}
i  =  0;
{ 3:  a ≠ null ,  b ≠ null ,  ∀x ∈ [0, 99].a[i] ≥ 0 ,  size == 100 ,  i == 0}
while ( i  <  size ) {
       { 4:  i ≥ 0 ,  i < size ,  a ≠ null ,  a[i] ≥ 0}
       b [ i ]  =  a [ i ];
       { 5:  b ≠ null ,  b[i] == a[i] ,  b[i] ≥ 0}
       i  =  i  +  1;
       { 6:  b[i − 1] ≥ 0}
}
{ 7:  ∀x ∈ [0, 99].b[x] == a[x] ,  (λx.a[x])[0, 99] == (λx.b[x])[0, 99]}
```

Fig. 5. Array Copy

Here exp contains the loop control variable $index$. By universally quantifying over $index$, we get the following precondition candidate of the loop:

$$\forall x \in [low, high].(exp[index \longmapsto x])$$

Example 5. We now illustrate the quantifying process for programs operating one-dimensional arrays using the program $arrayCopy$ in Fig. 5. This program copies each element of the array a to the corresponding position of the array b. The subscript expression i is the loop control variable. The lower bound expression of i is 0 while the upper bound of i is 99.

The weakest-precondition at program point 4 with respect to the intermediate assertion $b[i − 1] \geq 0$ at program point 6 is $a[i] \geq 0$. Our framework universally quantifies $a[i] \geq 0$ by introducing a new variable x to substitute i and get the following quantified result:

$$\forall x \in [0, 99].a[i] \geq 0 \tag{8}$$

The precondition candidate (8) is proved to be strong enough to guarantee $a[i] \geq 0$ holds at program point 4. Thus $b[i − 1] \geq 0$ is verified to be true at program point 6.   □

Generating Precondition Candidates from a Post-condition. Algorithm 2 illustrates the process of generating preconditions based on a post-condition of a loop. The algorithm takes as arguments a loop program $loop$, a given post-condition $post$ of $loop$ and the information $info$ of $loop$. This algorithm returns a set of precondition candidates with respect to $post$.

This algorithm divides post-conditions of loops into two distinct categories. The classification criteria is whether the post-condition contains loop variables.

If the post-condition contains loop variables, the algorithm invokes the procedure gen_equiv_exps in line 3 to get a set of expressions which are equivalent to $post$ at the loop exit point. These expressions are regarded as precondition candidates and they are added to set in line 4. The core idea of gen_equiv_exps

---

Algorithm 2. Generating Preconditions from a Post-condition

Input: a loop program *loop*; a post-condition *post* of *loop*; loop information *info*;
Output: a set of precondition candidates with respect to *post*;
1: *set* ← ∅;
2: **if** post contains loop variables **then**
3:     *exps* = *gen_equiv_exps*(*post, info*);
4:     *set* ← *set* ∪ *exps*;
5: **else**
6:     *set* ← *set* ∪ *post*;
7: **end if**
8: **return** *set*;

---

is to substitute some sub-expressions of a given expression with some new sub-expressions which equals to the original one at the loop exit point. The substitution follows the heuristics given in our previous paper [9]. Further details of *gen_equiv_exps* can also be found in [9]. As stated in that paper, when the argument of the procedure *gen_equiv_exps* is a post-condition of a loop, the generated expressions are very likely to be loop invariants which can be used to imply the post-condition. Consequently, these expressions can be regarded as preconditions of the loop to guarantee that the post-condition holds at the loop exit point.

Example 6. The post-condition

$$min \in (\lambda x.x \to d)[Nodes(sl)] \tag{9}$$

at program point 11 of the loop in Fig. 2 contains a loop variable *min*. Algorithm 2 generates some precondition candidates for it by invoking the procedure *gen_equiv_exps*. One of the candidates is

$$(l \neq p) \Rightarrow (min \in (\lambda x.x \to d)[NodesSeg(sl, p)]) \tag{10}$$

and it is proved to be a loop invariant. The post-condition (9) can be implied by (10) together with $l \neq null$, $p == null$ and Property 4 in Table 1. Thus (10) is a precondition that is strong enough to prove the post-condition (9).   □

If the post-condition does not contain any loop variable, there is a great possibility that the execution of the loop has no influence on the post-condition. Considering this, Algorithm 2 thinks of the post-condition itself as a precondition candidate and adds it to *set* in line 6.

Example 7. The post-condition

$$\forall x \in Nodes(sl).x \to d > 0 \tag{11}$$

at program point 11 of the loop in Fig. 2 does not contain any loop variable. Algorithm 2 regards (11) as a precondition. The candidate (11) is proved to be a loop invariant and holds at program point 11. Apparently the post-condition (11) can be proved with the presence of itself as the precondition of the loop.   □

4.4   Checking Precondition Candidates

After the precondition candidates are generated, we check their validity utilizing the SMT solver Z3 and the weakest-precondition calculator for non-loop statements provided in the tool Accumulator.

Checking Precondition Candidates for an Intermediate Assertion.
Suppose that *assertion* is an intermediate assertion of a loop, *wp* is the weakest-precondition of *assertion* at the program point before the loop body and *pre* is the generated precondition of the loop. To guarantee *assertion* holds, *wp* at the program point before the loop body must be true each time the program runs into this point. If *pre* is a loop invariant and it is strong enough to imply *wp*, then *assertion* can be proved. For *pre* to be our desired precondition of the loop, it must satisfy the following conditions:

1. The known preconditions imply *pre* at the loop entry point;
2. *pre* holds at the points before/after the loop body;
3. *pre* holds at the loop exit point;
4. *pre* and the proven properties at the program point before the loop body imply *wp* with respect to the intermediate assertion *assertion*.

If *pre* satisfies the first three conditions, it is a loop invariant. If the fourth condition is also met, it means that *pre* is strong enough to ensure the intermediate assertion *assertion* holds.

In our framework, the first condition and the last condition are checked using the SMT solver Z3.

The correctness of *pre* at the point after the loop body is checked using the following steps. Firstly, we use Z3 to check whether *pre* holds at the point after the loop body. If not, we compute the weakest-precondition of the loop body with respect to *pre* and check whether this weakest-precondition can be implied by *pre* together with the proven properties at the point before the loop body and the loop control condition. If so, it means *pre* holds at the point after the loop body.

As long as *pre* holds at the loop entry point and the point after the loop body, it surely holds at the point before the loop body and the loop exit point. As a result, the condition 2 and the condition 3 are satisfied.

If *pre* passes all these validation steps, it is a suitable precondition of the loop with respect to the given intermediate assertion.

Checking Precondition Candidates for a Post-condition. Suppose that *post* is a post-condition of a loop and *pre* is the generated precondition of the loop based on *post*. If *pre* is true both at the loop entry point and the loop exit point, *post* is sure to hold. To ensure *pre* holds at the loop exit point, it must be true at the program point after the loop body in addition to the loop entry point. In this case, *pre* is actually a loop invariant according to the definition of loop invariant. Thus if the precondition *pre* of the loop is a loop invariant and it is strong enough to imply *post*, it is the desired precondition. To be more specific, if the following conditions are satisfied, the generated precondition *pre* is strong enough to ensure *post* holds at the loop exit point.

1. The preconditions imply *pre* at the loop entry point;
2. *pre* holds at the points before/after the loop body;
3. *pre* holds at the loop exit point;
4. *pre* and the proven properties at the loop exit point imply the given post-condition of the loop.

Our framework checks these conditions similarly in the way it deals with the precondition generated from an intermediate assertion.

5   Implementation and Application

We have implemented the proposed framework as part of the interactive code-verification tool Accumulator. The framework has been evaluated using various programs. The results show that by automatically generating suitable preconditions of loops, our framework can be fully leveraged to help prove some assertions of loops that manipulate commonly-used data structures. In this way, the tasks of proving the partial correctness of programs can be greatly eased. For details of these examples, please visit http://seg.nju.edu.cn/toolweb/casestudy.html.

6   Limitations

Our framework currently can deal with while-loops that manipulate commonly-used data structures including one-dimensional arrays, two-dimensional arrays, acyclic singly-linked lists and static lists. We plan to deal with more types of loops to cover a greater variety of real-world programs, such as foreach loops and loops that contain break and continue statements. Programs with nested loops would be another interesting extension since we deeply believe that the same techniques can be applied. In addition, it is possible that similar techniques can be developed for loops that manipulate data structures like binary search trees, heaps and multi-dimensional arrays.

Furthermore, the loops dealt with in our framework iterate over each element without modifying their shapes, which limits the scope of programs that can be handled. We will attempt to handle loops that modify the shape of singly-linked lists, such as inserting or removing a node from the original list.

7   Related Work

As always, automatic inference of preconditions for loops is a critical challenge. In recent years, there is a plenty of research on the automatic generation of preconditions for loops.

The majority of the existing works compute preconditions for loops by transforming loops into acyclic forms. In this way, they are able to use the techniques for successive sequential statements to compute preconditions for loops. Some works like [4,5] achieve transforming loops by bounding the number of loop iterations. Other papers, such as [2,3], work by de-sugaring loops with loop invariants. Some works attempt to automatically derive the necessary loop invariants while others expect programmers to provide loop invariants. Although our work uses the concept of loop invariant when we generate preconditions for loops, no transformations of loops are needed in our work.

Another approach is proposed in [10] and this approach computes preconditions for loops based on invariant relations [11]. Intuitively, an invariant relation is a pair of states (s, s') in which s' can be derived from s by application of an arbitrary number of iterations of the loop body. This work focuses on numeric computations while our work can identify more types of preconditions, such as the shape of a recursive data structure and quantifying information.

The works [9,12,13] share the similarities with our work in that user-defined predicates and lemmas are used to allow programmers to describe a wide range of data structures. The work [12] aims at generating post-conditions while our work focuses on generating pre-conditions. The goals of the works [9,13] are to synthesize loop invariants which is different from our pre-condiiton generation goal.

8   Conclusion

An automatic framework of generating preconditions for loops is presented in this paper, which deals with loops manipulating commonly-used data structures by iterating over the elements. We first generate precondition candidates for a loop by transforming a given assertion of the loop or the weakest-precondition of the loop body with respect to a given assertion inside the loop. Then we check the validity and the effectiveness of these precondition candidates via the SMT solver Z3 and the weakest-precondition calculator for non-loop statements in Accumulator. Whether the precondition generated is strong enough to imply the given assertion is checked since it is the ultimate goal of generating preconditions.

The key novelty of our framework is that we focus on loops that manipulate heavily-used data structures. This kind of loops appears frequently in real-world programs according to our statistic analysis. Thus our framework is of great use to boost automation and efficiency in the code verification of many practical programs. Though in actual programs, some loops iterate over elements of a container data structure via an iterator, this kind of loops is essentially the same with the loops studied in this paper. When we can handle these interfaces well, we will be able to generate preconditions for these kinds of complex loops using the idea presented in this paper.

The framework has been implemented as part of the verification tool Accumulator. Its effectiveness and practicability have been validated by several programs. By generating useful preconditions for loops manipulating commonly-used data structures, our framework significantly reduces the burden of providing appropriate preconditions for loops manually.

J. Zhai et al.

References

1. Berghammer, R.: Soundness of a purely syntactical formalization of weakest preconditions. Electronic Notes in Theoretical Computer Science 35 (2000)
2. Flanagan, C., Saxe, J.B.: Avoiding exponential explosion: Generating compact verification conditions. In: ACM SIGPLAN Notices. Volume 36, ACM (2001)
3. Barnett, M., Leino, K.R.M.: Weakest-precondition of unstructured programs. In: ACM SIGSOFT Software Engineering Notes. Volume 31, ACM (2005)
4. Leino, K.R.M.: Efficient weakest preconditions. Information Processing Letters 93(6), 281–288 (2005)
5. Jager, I., Brumley, D.: Efficient directionless weakest preconditions. Technical report, CMU-CyLab-10-002, CMU, CyLab (2010)
6. Jianhua, Z., Xuandong, L.: Scope logic: an extension to hoare logic for pointers and recursive data structures. In: Liu, Z., Woodcock, J., Zhu, H. (eds.) ICTAC 2013. LNCS, vol. 8049, pp. 409–426. Springer, Heidelberg (2013)
7. de Moura, L., Bjørner, N.S.: Z3: an efficient SMT solver. In: Ramakrishnan, C.R., Rehof, J. (eds.) TACAS 2008. LNCS, vol. 4963, pp. 337–340. Springer, Heidelberg (2008)
8. Dijkstra, E.W.: Guarded commands, nondeterminacy and formal derivation of programs. Commun. ACM 18(8), 453–457 (1975)
9. Zhai, J., Wang, H., Zhao, J.: Post-condition-directed invariant inference for loops over data structures. In: 2014 IEEE Eighth International Conference on Software Security and Reliability-Companion (SERE-C), IEEE (2014)
10. Mraihi, O., Ghardallou, W., Louhichi, A., Labed Jilani, L., Bsaies, K., Mili, A.: Computing preconditions and postconditions of while loops. In: Cerone, A., Pihlajasaari, P. (eds.) ICTAC 2011. LNCS, vol. 6916, pp. 173–193. Springer, Heidelberg (2011)
11. Mraihi, O., Louhichi, A., Jilani, L.L., Desharnais, J., Mili, A.: Invariant assertions, invariant relations, and invariant functions. Volume 78, 1212–1239 Elsevier (2013)
12. Chin, W.N., David, C., Nguyen, H.H., Qin, S.: Automated verification of shape, size and bag properties via user-defined predicates in separation logic. Sci. Comput. Program. 77(9), 1006–1036 (2012)
13. Qin, S., He, G., Luo, C., Chin, W.N., Chen, X.: Loop invariant synthesis in a combined abstract domain. Journal of Symbolic Computation 50, 386–408 (2013)

Verification and Case Studies

Automatic Fault Localization for BIP

Wang Qiang[1]([✉]), Lei Yan[2], Simon Bliudze[1], and Mao Xiaoguang[3,4]

[1] École Polytechnique Fédérale de Lausanne, Lausanne, Switzerland
wenjunwang.nudt@gmail.com
[2] Logistical Engineering University of PLA, Chongqing, China
[3] College of Computer, National University of Defense Technology, Changsha, China
[4] Laboratory of Science and Technology on Integrated Logistics Support,
National University of Defense Technology, Changsha, China

Abstract. This paper presents a novel idea of automatic fault localization by exploiting counterexamples generated by a model checker. The
key insight is that, if a candidate statement is faulty, it is possible to
modify (i.e. correct) this statement so that the counterexample is eliminated. We have implemented the proposed fault localization algorithm
for component-based systems modelled in the BIP (Behaviour, Interaction and Priority) language, and conducted the first experimental evaluation on a set of benchmarks with injected faults, showing that our
approach is promising and capable of quickly and precisely localizing
faults.

1 Introduction

The rigorous system design process in BIP starts with the high-level modelling
of application software. The final system implementation is then derived from
the high-level system model by a series of property preserving model transformations, taking into account the architectural features of execution platform.
Thus, correctness of the system implementation with respect to essential safety
properties follows from the correctness of high-level system models, which can be
guaranteed by applying verification techniques [2, 12]. When a counterexample is
found, showing that the system model violates the required properties, designers
manually investigate it in order to fix the model. However, the counterexample
generated by a model checker can be large, requiring considerable effort to localize the fault. It is thus desirable to provide a method for automatic localization
of faults to streamline the rigorous system design process.

Existing fault localization techniques [10] are mostly statistical. They are generally referred to as Spectrum-based Fault Localization (SFL) [11]. In order to
identify suspicious locations, they require a considerable number of test cases,
including both passed and failed ones. When only a few tests are available,
these techniques become imprecise. In [1], the authors exploit the difference
between counterexamples and successful traces to localize faults in the program.

This work was partially funded by National Natural Science Foundation of China
(61379054).

X. Li et al. (Eds.): SETTA 2015, LNCS 9409, pp. 277–283, 2015.
DOI: 10.1007/978-3-319-25942-0_18

The faults are those transitions that do not appear in the correct traces. In [7], the authors propose to instrument the program with additional diagnosis variables and perform model checking on this modified program. The valuation of diagnosis variables indicates the location of a fault, when a counterexample is found. In [8], the authors propose a reduction of the fault localization problem to the maximum Boolean satisfiability problem extracted from the counterexample trace. The solution of the satisfiability problem provides a set of locations that are potentially responsible for the fault.

In this paper, we focus on component-based systems modelled in BIP. In contrast with the work cited above, our approach does not require neither test inputs, nor instrumentation of the model. Instead, it exploits the counterexample generated by a model checker. It reports the exact location, where the fault could be corrected instead of a set of suspicious locations.

The key insight of our approach stems from the observation that a statement in the counterexample is faulty if it is possible to modify (i.e. correct) this statement so that the counterexample is eliminated. Given a counterexample—that is an execution trace that violates the desired property—we first assume that this counterexample is spurious, meaning that its postcondition is *false*.[1] Our algorithm then proceeds by propagating this postcondition backwards, computing the weakest preconditions of the statements that form the execution trace, until it reaches a statement that interferes with the propagated postcondition. We mark this statement as a candidate fault location. In the second phase, the algorithm symbolically executes the counterexample trace from the initial state to the candidate faulty statement, which results in a symbolic state. This symbolic state, together with the candidate faulty statement and the propagated postcondition form a Hoare triple. We say that the candidate faulty statement is a fault if this statement can be modified to make the Hoare triple valid. Since the postcondition of the resulting trace is *false*, the counterexample is eliminated.

We remark that BIP is an expressive intermediate modelling language for component-based software. Industrial languages, used, for instance, for the design of Programmable Logic Controller software [5], can be encoded into BIP. This opens the possibility of applying our fault localisation approach to real-life industrial programs.

2   The BIP Language

The BIP framework advocates strong separation of computation and coordination concerns. To this end, the BIP language provides a modelling formalism based on three layers: Behaviour, Interaction and Priority. Behaviour is characterised by a set of atomic components, modelled by automata extended with linear arithmetic. Transitions are labelled by ports, used for synchronization and data transfer with other components. Coordination is specified by interaction and priority models. An interaction model is a set of *interactions*, representing

---

[1] We assume the readers to be familiar with the notions of Hoare triple and weakest precondition.

guarded strong synchronizations of transitions of atomic components. An interaction is a triple, consisting of a sets of ports to be synchronized, a Boolean
guard and an assignment statement updating the variables of the participating
components. When several interactions are enabled simultaneously, priority can
be used to reduce non-determinism and decide which interaction will be executed. We refer to [2,4] for the formal presentation of the BIP framework and
operational semantics.

Example 1. We model in BIP the ticket mutual exclusion algorithm [9] with
two processes. A graphical representation is shown in Fig. 1. Each process gets
a ticket from the controller by taking its corresponding **request** transition (e.g.
request1 in the leftmost component in Fig. 1), and stores it in its *buffer* variable
(e.g. *buffer1*). When the ticket held by the process is equal to the number to be
served (represented by the guards [*ticketN* = *next*], with $N = 1, 2$, on the
interactions in Fig. 1), the process can enter the critical location (i.e. *S3*) by
taking the **enter** transition. The controller keeps track of the latest ticket it
issues in the *number* variable and the next ticket to be served in the *next* variable.
These variables are increased by one when a process requests a ticket or leaves
the critical location, respectively. The mutual exclusion property requires that
the two processes never be in the critical locations simultaneously.

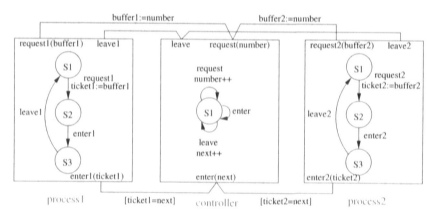

Fig. 1. Ticket mutual exclusion algorithm in BIP

For the sake of conciseness, in Section 3, we will denote the **request** ports
of the controller and the two process components r, r_1 and r_2, respectively.
Similarly, we will use e, e_1, e_2 for the **enter** ports; t_1, b_1, t_2, b_2 for the variables
of the two process components; n and x for the *number* and *next* variables of the
controller component.

3   Overview of the Algorithm

We inject a fault in the model presented in Example 1 by modifying the assignment of transition r_2 to be $t_2 := b_2 - 1$. The mutual exclusion property

is then violated by the sequence of interactions $\langle \gamma_1, \gamma_2, \gamma_3, \gamma_4 \rangle$, where $\gamma_1 = (\{\mathbf{r}, \mathbf{r}_1\}, true, b_1 := n)$, $\gamma_2 = (\{\mathbf{r}, \mathbf{r}_2\}, true, b_2 := n)$, $\gamma_3 = (\{\mathbf{e}, \mathbf{e}_1\}, t_1 = x, skip)$, $\gamma_4 = (\{\mathbf{e}, \mathbf{e}_2\}, t_2 = x, skip)$. We first build a sequential execution of this counterexample by serializing the statements associated with interactions and their participating transitions: $cex = \langle b_1 := n;\ t_1 := b_1;\ n := n+1;\ b_2 := n;\ t_2 := b_2 - 1;\ n := n+1;\ \texttt{assume}(t_1 = x \wedge t_2 = x) \rangle$.

Our first observation is that if a statement is faulty, it is possible to modify it so that the counterexample is eliminated. However, this can also be the case for a correct statement: e.g. replacing $n := n+1$ in the transition $\mathbf{r}$ of the controller component by $n := n$ eliminates the above counterexample. To avoid this, we use the following characterisation of faults. We say that a statement s *interferes* with a predicate φ if the Hoare triple $\{\varphi\}s\{\varphi\}$ is invalid. Given a counterexample cex, we call a statement s *faulty*, if 1) it interferes with the predicate φ obtained by backward propagation of *false* along cex through the computation of weakest preconditions and 2) it is possible to eliminate cex by modifying s. We explain the idea by applying our algorithm to the counterexample above.

We start by computing the weakest precondition of *false* for the $\texttt{assume}$ statement: $wp(false, \texttt{assume}(t_1 = x \wedge t_2 = x)) = (t_1 \neq x \vee t_2 \neq x)$. According to our fault model for BIP (Section 4), an $\texttt{assume}$ statement cannot be a fault candidate. Therefore, we proceed to the statement $n := n+1$, which is a fault candidate. Since $wp(t_1 \neq x \vee t_2 \neq x, n := n+1) = (t_1 \neq x \vee t_2 \neq x)$, $n := n+1$ does not interfere with the predicate $(t_1 \neq x \vee t_2 \neq x)$. Hence it is not faulty and we proceed to the next statement. Since $wp(t_1 \neq x \vee t_2 \neq x, t_2 := b_2 - 1) = (t_1 \neq x \vee b_2 - 1 \neq x)$ is not implied by $t_1 \neq x \vee t_2 \neq x$, we conclude that $t_2 := b_2 - 1$ interferes with this latter predicate.

To check if this statement is the fault, we replace it by $t_2 := v$, where v is a fresh variable, and compute its precondition by symbolically executing the fragment preceding $t_2 := b_2 - 1$, (i.e. $\langle b_1 := n;\ t_1 := b_1;\ n := n+1;\ b_2 := n \rangle$), which results in $b_1 = 1 \wedge t_1 = 1 \wedge n = 2 \wedge x = 1 \wedge b_2 = 2 \wedge t_2 = 0$. We now have to check whether there exists a valuation of v that makes the Hoare triple $\{b_1 = 1 \wedge t_1 = 1 \wedge n = 2 \wedge x = 1 \wedge b_2 = 2 \wedge t_2 = 0\} t_2 := v \{t_1 \neq x \vee t_2 \neq x\}$ valid, which would ensure the elimination of the counterexample cex. This is, indeed, the case, since the implication $b_1 = 1 \wedge t_1 = 1 \wedge n = 2 \wedge x = 1 \wedge b_2 = 2 \wedge t_2 = 0 \rightarrow wp(t_1 \neq x \vee t_2 \neq x, t_2 := v)$ is satisfiable. Thus we conclude that the statement $t_2 := b_2 - 1$ associated with the transition $\mathbf{r}_2$ is the fault responsible for the counterexample cex.

4   Fault Localization Algorithm for BIP

Since the synchronization aspect of interaction models is memoryless and can be synthesized from high-level properties [3], it is reasonable to assume that coordination is correct and focus on the faults in the assignment statements. We assume that there is at most one fault, which can occur in the right-hand side of an assignment, and we do not consider missing-code faults. Although these assumptions are quite strong, they are satisfied by a considerable number of

Algorithm 1. Automatic fault localization algorithm

Input: A BIP model B with the encoding of safety property
Output: Either no counterexample is found or potential fault is suggested
1: $cex \leftarrow CounterexampleDetection(B)$
2: **if** cex is Null **then**
3:     **return** 'No counterexamples found'
4: **else**
5:     $tr \leftarrow SequentialExecution(cex)$
6:     $post \leftarrow false$
7:     **for** each s in tr **do**
8:         $pre \leftarrow WeakestPrecondition(post, s)$
9:         **if** s is suspicious and $post \rightarrow pre$ is invalid **then**
10:             $s' \leftarrow Modify(s)$
11:             $prefix \leftarrow PrefixExecution(tr, s)$
12:             $st \leftarrow SymbolicExecute(prefix, s)$
13:             $pre' \leftarrow WeakestPrecondition(post, s')$
14:             **if** $st \rightarrow pre'$ is satisfiable **then**
15:                 **return** 's is the fault location'
16:             **else**
17:                 $post \leftarrow pre$
18:         **else**
19:             $post \leftarrow pre$

realistic models. In fact, our fault model is quite similar to the faulty expression model widely used for fault localization in C programs [7], where the control flow of the program is assumed to be correct, but the expressions may be wrong.

Our algorithm (Algorithm 1) utilizes a model checker or a symbolic executor as a subroutine to detect a counterexample (line 1). When a counterexample is generated, a sequential execution trace tr is constructed (line 5). Then for each statement s in tr, we compute the weakest precondition pre of s with respect to $post$, initially set to $false$ (lines 6, 8, 17, 19). If s is suspicious (i.e. it is admitted by our fault model) and interferes with its postcondition (line 9), we check whether it is possible to modify it to eliminate cex. To this end, we compute $s' = Modify(s)$ (line 10), which replaces the right-hand side of s by a fresh variable. We symbolically execute the counterexample until s (lines 11–12). Notice that the same statement may appear in the prefix due to the presence of a loop. Finally, we check whether the symbolic state st implies the weakest precondition pre' of s' (lines 13–14). If the implication is satisfiable, there exists a replacement s' of s that eliminates cex and s is the fault (line 16). Otherwise, we propagate the postcondition backwards and proceed to the next statement.

5   Experimental Evaluation

We have implemented the proposed algorithm based on an existing model checker [2], and adopted several benchmarks from the same work for the experimental evaluation. We also used industrial benchmarks [5] and the TCAS test suite [6], which is widely used by the fault localization community. Faults are injected into all benchmarks by modifying some assignments in the transitions of atomic components. Due to the space limitation, we refer the reader to our website[2] for further detail.

All the experiments have been performed on a 64-bit Linux PC with a 2.8 Ghz Intel i7-2640M CPU, with a memory limit of 4Gb and a time limit of 300 seconds. The results are listed in Table 1, which shows that our algorithm has quickly and precisely localized the faults in all considered benchmarks. The second column of Table 1 shows the number of lines of the BIP model; the third shows the exact location (i.e. line number) of the fault in the program; in the forth, $\sqrt{}$ indicates that our algorithm has localized the fault successfully; the fifth shows the time of performing fault localization, which remains stable with the size of the benchmarks. This can be explained by the fact that our algorithm uses counterexamples, rather than the models themselves. The last column shows the total time of detecting and localizing the fault.

Table 1. Experimental results

Benchmark	LOC	Fault Location	Result	FaultLoc Time (s)	Total Time (s)
atm_transaction_system	90	L57	$\sqrt{}$	0.004	0.036
ticket_algorithm	89	L54	$\sqrt{}$	0.008	0.024
gate_control_system	80	L51	$\sqrt{}$	0.004	0.244
bakery_algorithm	77	L41	$\sqrt{}$	0.004	0.048
plc_code1	162	L98	$\sqrt{}$	0.004	0.040
plc_code2	76	L46	$\sqrt{}$	0.004	0.016
plc_code3	133	L96	$\sqrt{}$	0.008	1.144
simple_c_code	68	L32	$\sqrt{}$	0.004	0.020
tcas	197	L140	$\sqrt{}$	0.008	0.700

6   Conclusion

Fault localization techniques based on formal methods are attracting attention. In this short paper, we have presented a novel automatic fault-localization algorithm for single assignment faults in BIP models. Our first experimental evaluation shows that the algorithm is promising: under some admittedly strong, but realistic assumptions, it is capable of quickly and precisely localizing faults. In the future work, we are planning to explore the possibilities of relaxing these assumptions, perform further experimental evaluation, and investigate the possibilities of automatically repairing the detected faults.

References

1. Ball, T., Naik, M., Rajamani, S.K.: From symptom to cause: Localizing errors in counterexample traces. In: POPL (2003)
2. Bliudze, S., Cimatti, A., Jaber, M., Mover, S., Roveri, M., Saab, W., Wang, Q.: Formal verification of infinite-state BIP models. In: ATVA (2015, to appear)

---

[2] http://risd.epfl.ch/fault-localisation

3. Bliudze, S., Sifakis, J.: Synthesizing glue operators from glue constraints for the construction of component-based systems. In: Apel, S., Jackson, E. (eds.) SC 2011. LNCS, vol. 6708, pp. 51–67. Springer, Heidelberg (2011)

4. Bliudze, S., Sifakis, J., Bozga, M.D., Jaber, M.: Architecture internalisation in BIP. In: Proceedings of the 17th International ACM Sigsoft Symposium on Component-based Software Engineering, CBSE 2014, pp. 169–178. ACM, New York (2014)

5. Darvas, D., Fernández Adiego, B., Vörös, A., Bartha, T., Blanco Viñuela, E., González Suárez, V.M.: Formal verification of complex properties on PLC programs. In: Formal Techniques for Distributed Objects, Components and Systems (2014)

6. Do, H., Elbaum, S., Rothermel, G.: Supporting controlled experimentation with testing techniques: An infrastructure and its potential impact. Empirical Software Engineering (2005)

7. Griesmayer, A., Staber, S., Bloem, R.: Automated fault localization for C programs. Electron. Notes Theor. Comput, Sci (2007)

8. Jose, M., Majumdar, R.: Cause clue clauses: Error localization using maximum satisfiability. In: PLDI (2011)

9. Lynch, N.A.: Distributed Algorithms (1996)

10. Mao, X., Lei, Y., Dai, Z., Qi, Y., Wang, C.: Slice-based statistical fault localization. Journal of Systems and Software (2014)

11. Naish, L., Lee, H., Ramamohanarao, K.: A model for spectra-based software diagnosis. ACM Transactions on Software Engineering and Methodology (2011)

12. Sifakis, J.: Rigorous system design. Foundations and Trends in Electronic Design Automation (2013)

Formal Verification of the Pastry Protocol Using TLA$^+$

Tianxiang Lu$^{(\boxtimes)}$

Department of Computer Science,
Technische Universität Darmstadt, Darmstadt, Germany
contact@tiit.lu

Abstract. As a consequence of the rise of cloud computing, the reliability of network protocols is gaining increasing attention. However, formal methods have revealed inconsistencies in some of these protocols, e.g., Chord, where all published versions of the protocol have been discovered to be incorrect. Pastry is a protocol similar to Chord. Using TLA$^+$, a formal specification language, we show that LuPastry, a formal model of Pastry with some improvements, provides correct delivery service. This is the first formal proof of Pastry where concurrent joins and lookups are simultaneously allowed. In particular, this article relaxes the assumption from previous publication to allow arbitrary concurrent joins of nodes, which reveals new insights into Pastry through a final formal model in TLA$^+$, LuPastry. Besides, this article also illustrates the methodology for the discovery and proof of its invariant. The proof in TLA$^+$ is mechanically verified using the interactive theorem prover TLAPS.

Keywords: Formal verification · Interactive theorem proving · Network protocols

1 Introduction

1.1 The Pastry Protocol

Pastry ([16], [3], [4]) is a structured *P2P* algorithm realizing a Distributed Hash Table (*DHT*, by [5]) over an underlying virtual ring. The network nodes are assigned logical identifiers from an ID space of naturals in the interval $[0, 2^M - 1]$ for some M. The ID space is considered as a ring^1 as shown in Fig. 1, i.e. $2^M - 1$ is the neighbor of 0.

The IDs are also used as object keys, such that an overlay node is responsible for keys that are numerically close to its ID, i.e. it provides the primary storage for the hash table entries associated with these keys. Key responsibility is divided equally according to the distance between two adjacent nodes. If a node is responsible for a key we say it *covers* the key.

The most important sub-protocols of Pastry are *join* and *lookup*. The join protocol eventually adds a new node with an unused network ID to the ring.

---

^{1} The ring here does not refer to algebraic group structure with operation.

© Springer International Publishing Switzerland 2015
X. Li et al. (Eds.): SETTA 2015, LNCS 9409, pp. 284–299, 2015.
DOI: 10.1007/978-3-319-25942-0_19

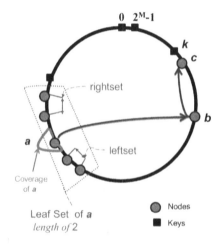

Fig. 1. Pastry ring.

The lookup protocol delivers the hash table entry for a given key. This paper focuses on the correctness property *CorrectDelivery* (mentioned as dependability in algorithm paper [3]), requiring that there is always at most one node responsible for a given key. This property is non-trivial to obtain in the presence of concurrent join or departure of nodes, i.e., *churn*. To cope with that, each Pastry node maintains a local state of a set of nodes called *leaf sets*, as shown in Fig. 1, consisting of a left set and a right set of the same length, which is a parameter of the algorithm. The nodes in leaf sets are updated when new nodes join or failed nodes are detected using a maintenance protocol. A Pastry node also maintains a routing table to store more distant nodes, in order to achieve efficient routing.

In the example of Fig. 1, node a received a lookup message for key k. The key is outside node a's coverage. Moreover, it doesn't lie between the leftmost node and the rightmost node of its leaf sets. Querying its routing table, node a finds node b, whose identifier matches the longest prefix with the destination key and then forwards the message to that node. Node b repeats the process and finally, the lookup message is answered by node c, which covers the key k. In this case, we say that node c *delivers* the lookup request for key k.

1.2   The Methodology

TLA$^+$ by [6], is a formal specification language based on untyped *Zermelo-Fraenkel* (ZF) set theory with choice for specifying data structures, and on the Temporal Logic of Actions (TLA) for describing system behavior. It is chosen to analyze and verify the correct delivering and routing functionality of Pastry, because it provides a uniform logic framework for specification, model-checking and theorem proving. It fits protocol verification quite nicely, because its concept of actions matches the rule/message-based definition of protocols. In addition,

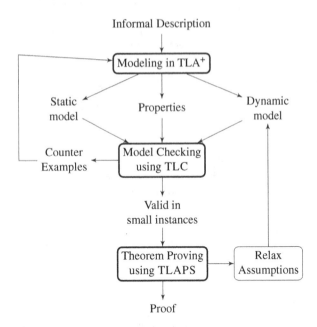

Fig. 2. Verification approach using TLA⁺.

the specification language is straightforward to understand with basic mathematics and classical first-order logic. Furthermore, the convenient toolbox available in [7] includes now both the TLC model checker and the TLAPS proof system.

Fig. 2 illustrates the complete process of this framework which includes modeling, model checking and theorem proving.

Starting with an informal description of Pastry in [3], the first task is to model the requirements of the system using TLA⁺. This paper distinguishes different kinds of TLA⁺ model as *properties* that specify requirements using logic formulas (e.g. *CorrectDelivery*), the *static model* that defines the data structures (e.g. the virtual ring of IDs, the leaf sets etc.), and the *dynamic model* that describes the behavior using actions of TLA⁺.

The challenges here include modeling Pastry on an appropriate level of abstraction, filling in needed details in the formal model that are not contained in the published description of Pastry, and formulating the correctness property of Pastry. These challenges motivate a deeper understanding of the protocol using the model checker TLC.

The model is validated using TLC in an iterative process, which helped to discover unexpected corner cases to improve the model and to ensure that the system has at least some useful executions. For example, accessibility properties are model-checked by checking that the negation is false. To avoid the state explosion problem, only a restricted number of instances are verified using TLC. Upon finding counterexamples, the model is analyzed and reformulated.

Upon successful validation or in the absence of counterexamples after running it for a considerable long time, the model is then verified by TLA$^+$ proofs.

Since the previous publications [11] and [12] have already included the model checking result, we omit it here to save space for illustrating theorem proving details.

The proof of the Pastry join protocol contains an induction part, where invariants need to be found and formulated. Discovering the invariants is the most subtle part of the theorem proving approach. On the one hand, it should be general enough to imply the target property *CorrectDelivery*. On the other hand, it should be specific enough to be provable using itself as induction hypothesis. In order to prove the safety property *CorrectDelivery*, we assume no departure of nodes and that an active node can help at most one node to join at a time, which relaxes the previous assumption we made in [13].

The model checker TLC is applied again to debug the formulation errors or discover invalid hypothetical invariants at an early stage. The invariant is extended during the process of being proved. TLAPS is used to write the proof manually and sometimes to break it down into small enough pieces so that it can be checked automatically using the back-end prover. The final verification result is a TLA$^+$ proof, in which each proof step is automatically verified using TLAPS.

2   Modelling the Concurrent Join Protocol of Pastry

As illustrated in Fig. 2, the formal model of Pastry consists of a static part specifying the underlying data structures and a dynamic part specifying the behaviour of the nodes. Due to the page limit for this paper, the formal description of all the dynamic actions [10] are omitted here.

2.1   Static Model

The static model of Pastry consists of definitions of data structures and operations on them. A data structure is always a boolean value, a natural number, a set, a function or a complex composition of them. An operation on a data structure is always a functional mapping from a given signature of data structures to a returned value, which is again a data structure.

The static model of Pastry remains the same as in [12]. The distance between two nodes on the ring is modeled with clockwise distance $CwDist(x, y)$, which returns how many identifiers lie within the region from node x to y in the clockwise direction. The absolute value $AbsDist(x, y)$ gives the length of the shortest path along the ring from x to y. The routing table has a rather complex data structure, which is used for efficient routing. Since this article focuses on the safety property, details of the routing table are omitted here. The simplified routing table is a set of nodes ($RTable \triangleq [I \rightarrow \text{SUBSET } I]$) and the initial routing table $InitRTable$ is an empty set.

Leaf Set. The leaf set data structure *ls* of a node is modeled as a record (using syntax [*component*1, *component*2]) with three components: *ls.node*, *ls.left* and *ls.right* (a dot is used to access a component of a record in TLA$^+$). The first component contains the identifier of the node maintaining the leaf sets, the other two components are the two leaf sets to either side of the node. The following operations access or manipulate leaf sets. Here we reuse the arithmetic operations (e.g. $\geq$, $\div$) on natural numbers ($I \subseteq \mathbb{N}$).

The operation *AddToLSet*(*delta*, *ls*) adds the set of nodes *d* into left and right sides of the leaf sets *ls*. Due to the space restriction, its complex formal definition is omitted here and can be found in [10].

Definition 1 (Operations on leaf sets ($ls \in LSet, delta \in$ SUBSET I))

$$LSet \triangleq [node \in I, left \in \text{SUBSET } I, right \in \text{SUBSET } I]$$

$$GetLSetContent(ls) \triangleq ls.left \cup ls.right \cup \{ls.node\}$$

$$EmptyLS(i) \triangleq [node \mapsto i, left \mapsto \{\}, right \mapsto \{\}]$$

$$LeftNeighbor(ls) \triangleq \text{ IF } ls.left = \{\} \text{ THEN } ls.node$$
$$\text{ELSE CHOOSE } n \in ls.left : \forall p \in ls.left :$$
$$CwDist(p, ls.node) \geq CwDist(n, ls.node)$$

$$RightNeighbor(ls) \triangleq \text{ IF } ls.right = \{\} \text{ THEN } ls.node$$
$$\text{ELSE CHOOSE } n \in ls.right : \forall q \in ls.right :$$
$$CwDist(ls.node, q) \geq CwDist(ls.node, n)$$

$$LeftCover(ls) \triangleq (ls.node + CwDist(LeftNeighbor(ls), ls.node) \div 2)\%2^M$$

$$RightCover(ls) \triangleq (RightNeighbor(ls) +$$
$$CwDist(ls.node, RightNeighbor(ls)) \div 2 + 1)\%2^M$$

$$Covers(ls, k) \triangleq CwDist(LeftCover(ls), k)$$
$$\leq CwDist(LeftCover(ls), RightCover(ls))$$

Messages. Messages are defined as records consisting of their destinations and the message content: $DMsg \triangleq [destination \in I, mreq \in MReq]$. The message content (*MReq*) consists of different types. The actions in the dynamic model are mainly designed to handle these messages. Therefore, the different message types are formally defined here to provide better understanding of the dynamic models explained later in Section 2.2.

Definition 2 (Message Types)

$$Look \triangleq [type \in \{\text{``Lookup''}\}, node \in I]$$

$$JReq \triangleq [type \in \{\text{``JoinRequest''}\}, rtable \in RTable, node \in I]$$

$$JRpl \triangleq [type \in \{\text{``JoinReply''}\}, rtable \in RTable, lset \in LSet]$$

$$Prb \triangleq [type \in \{\text{``Probe''}\}, node \in I, lset \in LSet, failed \in \text{SUBSET } I)]$$

$$PRpl \triangleq [type \in \{\text{``ProbeReply''}\}, node \in I, lset \in LSet, failed \in \text{SUBSET } I)]$$

$$LReq \triangleq [type \in \{\text{``LeaseRequest''}\}, node \in I]$$

$$LReply \triangleq [type \in \{\text{``LeaseReply''}\}, lset \in LSet, grant \in \{\text{TRUE, FALSE}\}]$$

Statuses. Together with the message types above, a brief introduction of the statuses of a node helps the understanding of the dynamic model.

$$status \in [I \rightarrow \{\text{"ready"}, \text{"ok"}, \text{"waiting"}, \text{"dead"}\}]$$

A node is initially either "ready" or "dead". As soon as a "dead" node sends the "JoinRequest" message, it turns to the status "waiting", which means it is waiting to become "ok". After it has completed its leaf sets and received all the "ProbeReply" messages, it will become "ok". Once it has obtained both leases from its left and right neighbors, it will become "ready". Only "ready" nodes can deliver "Lookup" messages or reply to "JoinRequest" messages.

2.2 Dynamic Model

The overall system specification *Spec* is defined as $Init \wedge \Box[Next]_{vars}$, which is the standard form of TLA$^+$ system specifications. $\Box$ stands for temporal operator *always*. The whole expression requires that all runs start with a state that satisfies the initial condition *Init*, and that every transition either does not change *vars* (defined as the tuple of all state variables) or corresponds to a system transition as defined by *Next*. This form of system specification is sufficient for proving safety properties. Since liveness properties are beyond the verification interest of this paper, no fairness hypotheses are asserted, claiming that certain actions eventually occur.

Definition 3 (Overall Structure of the TLA$^+$ Specification of Pastry)

$$
\begin{aligned}
vars \;\triangleq\; & \langle receivedMsgs, status, lset, probing, failed, rtable, lease, grant, toj \rangle \\
Init \;\triangleq\; & \wedge\; receivedMsgs = \{\} \\
& \wedge\; status = [i \in I \mapsto \text{IF } i \in A \text{ THEN "ready" ELSE "dead"}] \\
& \wedge\; toj = [i \in I \mapsto i] \\
& \wedge\; probing = [i \in I \mapsto \{\}] \\
& \wedge\; failed = [i \in I \mapsto \{\}] \\
& \wedge\; lease = [i \in I \mapsto \text{IF } i \in A \text{ THEN } A \text{ ELSE } \{i\}] \\
& \wedge\; grant = [i \in I \mapsto \text{IF } i \in A \text{ THEN } A \text{ ELSE } \{i\}] \\
& \wedge\; lset = [i \in I \mapsto \text{IF } i \in A \\
& \qquad\qquad\qquad \text{THEN } AddToLSet(A, EmptyLS(i)) \\
& \qquad\qquad\qquad \text{ELSE } EmptyLS(i)] \\
& \wedge\; rtable = [i \in I \mapsto \text{IF } i \in A \\
& \qquad\qquad\qquad \text{THEN } AddToTable(A, InitRTable, i) \\
& \qquad\qquad\qquad \text{ELSE } AddToTable(\{i\}, InitRTable, i)] \\
Next \;\triangleq\; & \exists i, j \in I : \vee\; Join(i, j) \;\vee\; Lookup(i, j) \;\vee\; Deliver(i, j) \\
& \qquad\qquad \vee\; RouteJReq(i, j) \;\vee\; RouteLookup(i, j) \\
& \qquad\qquad \vee\; RecJReq(i) \;\vee\; RecJReply(j) \\
& \qquad\qquad \vee\; RecProbe(i) \;\vee\; RecPReply(j) \\
& \qquad\qquad \vee\; RecLReq(i) \;\vee\; RecLReply(i) \\
& \qquad\qquad \vee\; RequestLease(i) \\
Spec \;\triangleq\; & Init \wedge \Box[Next]_{vars}
\end{aligned}
$$

The variable *receivedMsgs* holds the set of messages in transit. It is assumed in the formal model that messages are never modified when they are on the way to their destination, that is, no message is corrupted.

The other variables hold arrays that assign to every node $i \in I$ its status, leaf sets, routing table, the set of nodes it is currently probing, the set of nodes it has determined to have dropped off the ring (*failed*), the node to which it has sent a join reply and not yet got confirmation if it has become "ready" (*toj*), the nodes from which it has already got the leases (*lease*) and the nodes to which it has granted its leases (*grant*).

The predicate *Init* is defined as a conjunction that initializes all variables. In particular, the model takes a parameter A indicating the set of nodes that are initially "ready".

The next-state relation *Next* is a disjunction of all possible system actions, for all pairs of identifiers $i, j \in I$. Each action is defined as a TLA$^+$ action formula. Due to the page limit, we only show two formal definitions of the actions. The action *Deliver(i, k)* (Definition 4) is referenced in the safety property and formal proof. The action *RecJReq(i)* (Definition 5) is crucial of understanding the improvement of LUPASTRY in allowing only one node to handle join requests to avoid collisions caused by concurrent joins.

The action *Deliver(i, k)* is executable if node i is "ready", if there exists an unhandled "Lookup" message addressed to i, and if j, the identifier of the requested key, falls within the coverage of node i (see Definition 1). Its effect is simply defined as removing the message m from the network, due to the fact that only the execution of the action is interesting, not the answer message that it generates. Each time it receives a message, the node will remove the message from the message pool *receivedMsgs*, so that it will not be received again. The other variables are unchanged.

Definition 4 (Action: *Deliver(i, j)*)

$$Deliver(i, j) \triangleq$$
$$\wedge\ status[i] = \text{``ready''}$$
$$\wedge\ \exists m \in receivedMsgs : \wedge\ m.mreq.type = \text{``Lookup''}$$
$$\wedge\ m.destination = i$$
$$\wedge\ m.mreq.node = j$$
$$\wedge\ Covers(lset[i], j)$$
$$\wedge\ receivedMsgs' = receivedMsgs \setminus \{m\}$$
$$\wedge\ \text{UNCHANGED}\ \langle status, rtable, lset, probing, failed, lease, grant, toj \rangle$$

The actions basically handle the different message types shown in Section 2.1. In action *Lookup(i, j)*, a node sends out a "Lookup" message, which contains only the node j it is looking for. In action *Join(i, j)*, a "JoinRequest" message is sent to node i to join a new node j. Using the same routing algorithm, the "Lookup" and "JoinRequest" messages are routed to the node which covers the key j, through several nodes via execution of *RouteJReq(i, j)* or *RouteLookup(i, j)* actions.

Definition 5 (Action: *RecJReq*(i))

$RecJReq(i) \triangleq$
  $\wedge\ status[i] = \text{"ready"}$
  $\wedge\ toj[i] = i$
  $\wedge\ \exists m \in receivedMsgs :$
   $\wedge\ m.mreq.type = \text{"JoinRequest"}$
   $\wedge\ m.destination = i$
   $\wedge\ Covers(lset[i], m.mreq.node)$
   $\wedge\ toj' = [\text{EXCEPT } ![i] = m.mreq.node]$
   $\wedge\ lset' = [\text{EXCEPT } ![i] = AddToLSet(\{m.mreq.node\}, lset[i])]$
   $\wedge\ receivedMsgs' = (receivedMsgs \setminus \{m\})$
    $\cup \{[destination \mapsto m.mreq.node, [type \mapsto \text{"JoinReply"},$
     $rtable \mapsto m.mreq.rtable, lset \mapsto lset[i]]]\}$
  $\wedge\ \text{UNCHANGED } \langle status, rtable, probing, failed, lease, grant \rangle$

In action *RecJReq*(i) (Definition 5) a "ready" node i covers the joining node in the "JoinRequest" message and has not yet started helping another node to join $(toj[i] = i)$, therefore it replies to the joining node with a "JoinReply" message. It also sets *toj* to be that joining node to prevent other nodes to join through it. This is the mechanism for avoiding collision of coverage caused by concurrent join.

The "Probe" messages are handled in action *RecProbe*(i) by the receivers i. As a reply to the probing message, the node i sends a "ProbeReply" message containing the node replying to the probe (*node*), the replier's leaf sets and a set of *failed* nodes back to the probing node. In the action *RecPReply*(i), the node i adds the sender of the "ProbeReply" message into its own leaf sets. When all awaiting probe messages have been answered, the node becomes "ok". Consequently, it sends out "LeaseRequest" messages to update the leases of its direct left neighbor and right neighbor.

As long as a node is "ok", it can send "LeaseRequest" messages to request leases from its direct neighbors using *RequestLease*(i). In action *RecLReq*(i), the node i replies to the lease request with a "LeaseReply" message containing its own leaf sets, where its own identifier is contained in *lset.node*. Instead of only sending back the node identifier, the leaf sets were designed to provide extra information, which, as in a "Probe" message, may serve to propagate and exchange leaf sets among nodes. If the sender is its direct neighbor, it grants the lease.

In action *RecLReply*(i), the node i updates its lease of the sender of a "LeaseReply" message, if the sender is its direct neighbor. If the node i is of status "ok" and completes leases both of its direct neighbors, then it becomes "ready". If the node i is helping the sender to join the network, it also sets the *toj* to itself allowing it to help other nodes.

The formal model of LuPASTRY actions in TLA$^+$ code can be found in [10].

2.3   The Correctness Properties

Since TLA$^+$ does not have type, state variables should conform to their desired data structures, so that accessing their components will always be successful. For example, *status[i]* should access the state variable *status* of a particular node i and it is supposed to be one of the states, not a node identifier. The correctness of "types" are defined as state property *TypeInvariant* and then proved to be an invariant for the system as shown in Theorem 1.

Property 1 (*TypeInvariant*)

$$
\begin{aligned}
TypeInvariant \triangleq\ &\wedge\ receivedMsgs \in \text{SUBSET } DMsg \\
&\wedge\ status \in [I \rightarrow \{\ \text{"ready"}, \text{"ok"}, \text{"waiting"}, \text{"dead"}\}] \\
&\wedge\ lease \in [I \rightarrow \text{SUBSET } I] \\
&\wedge\ grant \in [I \rightarrow \text{SUBSET } I] \\
&\wedge\ rtable \in [I \rightarrow RTable] \\
&\wedge\ lset \in [I \rightarrow LSet] \wedge\ \forall i \in I : lset[i].node = i \\
&\wedge\ probing \in [I \rightarrow \text{SUBSET } I] \\
&\wedge\ failed \in [I \rightarrow \text{SUBSET } I] \\
&\wedge\ toj \in [I \rightarrow I]
\end{aligned}
$$

Theorem 1 (Type Correctness) $Spec \Rightarrow \Box\, TypeInvariant$

The property *CorrectDelivery* asserts that whenever node i can execute the action $Deliver(i, k)$ for key k then both of the following statements are true:

- The node i has minimal absolute distance from the key k among all the "ready" nodes in the network.
- The node i is the only node that may execute the action $Deliver(i, k)$ for the key k.

Property 2 (*CorrectDelivery*)

$$
\begin{aligned}
CorrectDelivery \triangleq\ &\forall i, k \in I : \\
&\text{ENABLED } Deliver(i, k) \\
&\Rightarrow\ \wedge\ \forall n \in I \setminus \{k\} : status[n] = \text{"ready"} \Rightarrow AbsDist(i, k) \leq AbsDist(n, k) \\
&\quad\ \wedge\ \forall j \in I \setminus \{i\} : \neg\text{ENABLED } Deliver(j, k)
\end{aligned}
$$

Observe that there can be two nodes with minimal distance from k, to either side of the key. Therefore, the asymmetry in the definition of $LeftCover(ls, k)$ and $RightCover(ls, k)$ in Definition 1 is designed to break the tie and ensure that only one node is allowed to deliver. The major verification goal is formalised in Theorem 2, that given the formulas defined for Pastry as *Spec*, it can be entailed that the property *CorrectDelivery* always holds.

Theorem 2 (Correctness of Pastry) $Spec \Rightarrow \Box\, CorrectDelivery$

3   Theorem Proving

Model checking can only provide validation on four nodes. To get a generic verification of the Pastry protocol on arbitrary number of nodes, we need to use a theorem proving approach. Using the TLA$^+$ theorem prover TLAPS, we proved in [12] that the conjunction of *HalfNeighbor* and *NeighborClosest* implies *CorrectDelivery*. The most subtle part left is the induction proof of invariants, which extends these two properties. The proof is based on the **assumption** that there are no departure of nodes and that an active node can help at most one node to join at a time.

3.1   Inductive Proof of Invariant *HalfNeighbor*

The property *HalfNeighbor* (part of Invariant 1) is extended finally to a more complex one: *HalfNeighborExt*, stating that if there is more than one member of ReadyOK on the ring (a node is either "ready" or "ok"), then none of them will have an empty leaf set.

For the special case that there is only one member of ReadyOK k on the ring, the following statements hold:

- k has no neighbor;
- every "waiting" node (waiting to become "ok") knows at most the node k and itself;
- there is no "Probe" message to k;
- there is no "ProbeReply" message or "LeaseReply" message at all;
- the leaf set within a "JoinReply" message can only contain k.

Invariant 1 (*HalfNeighborExt*)

$\lor \forall k \in ReadyOK : RightNeighbor(lset[k]) \neq k \land LeftNeighbor(lset[k]) \neq k$
$\lor \exists k \in ReadyOK :$
    $\land\ ReadyOK = \{k\}$
    $\land\ LeftNeighbor(lset[k]) = k$
    $\land\ RightNeighbor(lset[k]) = k$
    $\land\ \forall \mathbf{w} \in \mathbf{NodesWait} : \mathbf{GetLSetContent(lset[w])} \in \text{SUBSET } \{\mathbf{k, w}\}$
    $\land\ \neg \exists \mathbf{ms} \in \mathbf{receivedMsgs} : \mathbf{ms.mreq.type} = \mathit{"ProbeReply"}$
    $\land\ \neg \exists \mathbf{mk} \in \mathbf{receivedMsgs} : \land\ \mathbf{mk.mreq.type} = \mathit{"Probe"}$
                            $\land\ \mathbf{mk.destination} \neq \mathbf{k}$
    $\land\ \forall \mathbf{mj} \in \mathbf{receivedMsgs} : \mathbf{mj.mreq.type} = \mathit{"JoinReply"}$
                      $\Rightarrow \mathbf{GetLSetContent(mj.mreq.lset)} = \mathbf{k}$
    $\land\ \neg \exists \mathbf{mb} \in \mathbf{receivedMsgs} : \mathbf{mb.mreq.type} = \mathit{"LeaseReply"}$

The formal expression shown in Invariant 1 includes the original property *HalfNeighbor* (the first 5 lines), and its extension (the remaining lines in **bold**).

This invariant is extended during the proof *HalfNeighbor* step by step. Firstly, we check what is missing as prerequisites to prove *HalfNeighbor'* on its inductive proof at each action. Secondly, we strengthen *HalfNeighbor* by adding auxiliary conjunctions in such a way that it provides exactly the prerequisite for the proof. Each time the invariant is extended, the model checker TLC is employed on the Pastry model to help check if the new invariant holds on the model of four nodes. Upon violation of such a model checking approach, the formula derived from the last state of the counterexample is used to reformulate the invariant.

3.2   Proof of *NeighborClosest*

The property *NeighborClosest* states that the left and right neighbors of any "ready" node i lie closer to i than any other "ready" node j.

Property 3 (*NeighborClosest*)

$$NeighborClosest \triangleq \forall i, j \in ReadyNodes :$$
$$i \neq j \Rightarrow \land CwDist(LeftNeighbor(lset[i]), i) \leq CwDist(j, i)$$
$$\land CwDist(i, RightNeighbor(lset[i])) \leq CwDist(i, j)$$

The intuition of searching for the appropriate invariant for proving *NeighborClosest* is backwards symbolic execution. The idea is to find a candidate invariant whose violation trace, if it is not valid, can be shorter, such that the model checker TLC can be used to help discover and improve such an invariant. Based on the assumption that no nodes leave the network and the protocol improvement in LuPASTRY that a "ready" node can handle at most one joining node at a time, the property *NeighborClosest* can be further reduced to the following properties: *IRN* and *NRI* (formally specified in Proerty 4).

The properties *IRN* and *NRI* together subsume the property *NeighborClosest*. The difference is that *NeighborClosest* guarantees that "ready" nodes do not ignore other "ready" nodes between themselves and their neighbors, while *IRN* and *NRI* states that every node does not ignore any "ready" nodes between itself and its neighbor.

Property 4 (*IRN* and *NRI*)

$$IRN \triangleq \forall i \in I, r \in ReadyNodes : i \neq r$$
$$\Rightarrow CwDist(i, RightNeighbor(lset[i])) \leq CwDist(i, r)$$
$$NRI \triangleq \forall i \in I, r \in ReadyNodes : i \neq r$$
$$\Rightarrow CwDist(LeftNeighbor(lset[i]), i) \leq CwDist(r, i)$$

The properties *IRN* and *NRI* state that there cannot be a "ready" node closer to arbitrary node i, than its left and right neighbors. Since these two properties are symmetrical, we only focus on one of them in this paper, *IRN*.

Induction Invariant. Due to the page limit, we only focus on the invariant *IRN* and give intuition of the discovery of the relevant invariants used for proving *IRN*. The formal description and proof of all invariants can be found in full in [10] and are explained intuitively in [9].

Invariant 2 (*InvLuPastry*)

$IRN \land TojNoReady \land SemToj \land TojClosestL \land GrantNeighbor \land GrantHistL \land \dots$

Proof Sketch of the Invariant IRN. The following proof sketch illustrates the discovery and proof of the induction invariant for proving *IRN*, the most interesting and subtle part of the formal verification approach.

Based on the definition of *IRN*, the modification of two variables *lset* and *status* is critical. Regarding the change of leaf sets *lset*, adding nodes into leaf sets preserves the validity of the invariant. Since no action in the new Pastry model removes nodes from leaf sets, the changes of leaf sets always preserve the invariant *IRN*.

Regarding the changes of *status* from "ok" to "ready" in the action *RecLReply(r)*, we construct the negation of *IRN* as shown in Fig. 3: assume that a node *r* is turning from "ok" to "ready" in action *RecLReply(r)* and this node lies exactly between an arbitrary node *i* and its direct right neighbor *n*. The proof is to find the contradiction of this situation.

For this we need an invariant *TojNoReady*: if the leaf sets of some not yet "ready" node *i* is not empty, then there must exist a "ready" node, through which node *i* has joined the network.

$$TojNoReady \triangleq \forall i \in I : i \notin ReadyNodes \land lset[i] \neq EmtyLS(i)$$
$$\Rightarrow \exists r \in ReadyNodes : toj[r] = i$$

Applying *TojNoReady* on the "ok" node *r*, there must be a "ready" node r_2, such that $toj[r_2] = r$. The proof method is to refute the existence of such a node r_2. According to *IRN*, node r_2 cannot be inside the range from *r* to its right neighbor. Hence, 3 cases are possible for the position of node r_2 as shown in Fig. 3.

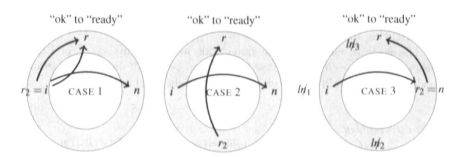

Fig. 3. Case analysis of the node r_2 w.r.t. node *i* and its right neighbor *n*.

CASE 1 : $r_2 = i$. Let us introduce another invariant *SemToj* (the "semantic" of variable *toj*): if a not yet "ready" node *i* has joined through the "ready" node *r*, then node *i* must be *r*'s direct neighbor. We reuse *r*, *i* as binding variables here because we can directly apply the invariant into our sub-goal.

$$SemToj \triangleq \forall r, i \in I : i \notin ReadyNodes \land toj[r] = i \land r \neq i$$
$$\Rightarrow RightNeighbor(lset[r]) = i \lor LeftNeighbor(lset[r]) = i$$

By *SemToj* and our assumption we know that r must be a direct neighbor of r_2.

(1) If r were the right neighbor of r_2, which is now i, then r should be the right neighbor of i, which contradicts with n (see Fig. 3). (2) If r were the left neighbor of r_2, then the left distance (counterclockwise) from i to its left neighbor r is larger than the left distance from i to its right neighbor, which contradicts the definitions of *LeftNeighbor* and *RightNeighbor* in Definition 1. Hence r_2 cannot be i.

CASE 2 : $CwDist(i, RightNeighbor(lset[i])) < CwDist(i, r_2)$. Given that the node r is the direct neighbor of r_2 (shown using *SemToj*), we perform case analysis on the node r. Suppose r is the right neighbor of node r_2 as illustrated in Fig. 3 since the other case can be proved symmetrically.

To refute this possibility, let us analyze the status of node i. If node i were a "ready" node, then this would violate *IRN* for the node r. If not, we need to use invariant *TojNoReady* to construct an arbitraryly positioned "ready" node r_4, through which node i is currently joining. Then we introduce another invariant *TojClosestL*, which states that if node r is joined through some node r_2, then between these two nodes, there exists no further node such as i, which is currently joining through another node r_4. Hence, we can refute the existence of such a node r_4 and get the contradiction to close this case.

$$TojClosestL \overset{\Delta}{=} \forall r_1, r_2, i, k \in I :$$
$$\wedge\ i \neq r_1 \wedge i \neq k \wedge toj[r_1] = i \wedge toj[r_2] = k \wedge r_2 \neq k$$
$$\wedge\ RightNeighbor(lset[r_1]) = i \wedge i \notin \text{ReadyNodes}$$
$$\Rightarrow CwDist(r_1, i) \leq CwDist(k, i)$$

CASE 3 : $r_2 = n$ (n refers to $RightNeighbor(lset[i])$). Here, we make a case analysis on the position of $ln = LeftNeighbor(lset[r])$, and then close all the cases by refuting the existence of such ln.

(i) The node ln cannot be the same node as i (ln_1 in CASE 3 of Fig. 3), because according to *GrantNeighbor* (introduced below), if node ln had granted the node r, then r could not be closer than its right neighbor n.

$$GrantNeighbor \overset{\Delta}{=} \forall k, i \in I : i \neq k \wedge i \in grant[k]$$
$$\Rightarrow CwDist(k, RightNeighbor(lset[k])) \leq CwDist(k, i) \wedge \ldots$$

(ii) The node ln cannot be to the left of i (ln_2 in CASE 3 of Fig. 3). Since the node i cannot be "ready" due to *IRN*, let us use invariant *TojNoReady* to construct a node r_3, through which node i is currently joining. It remains to refute the existence of such a node r_3. The node r_3 cannot be r_2, hence, node r_3 must be the left neighbor of i.

Now we can do case analysis on the position of r_3 as the left neighbor of i. On the one hand, it must lie between i and ln, because if node ln is "ready", it cannot lie between a node i and its left neighbor r_3 by *NRI*. But on the other hand, node r_3 cannot lie between i and ln, because r_3 is "ready" and it should not lie between a node r and its left neighbor ln. Therefore, r_3 can only be equal to node ln.

To force contradiction, the further invariant $GrantHistL$ is needed, which takes the facts above as precondition and derives that r_2 must be closer to i than the other node r. $GrantHistL$ states that if a not yet "ready" node i lies between two other different nodes l and r, and node i is joined through one of the nodes (e.g. l), whereas this node (i.e. l) has granted its lease to the other node (i.e. r), then the direct neighbor of i must be closer to i than the other node (i.e. r). Regarding the last case in Fig. 3, r_2 is not closer to i than r. Hence a contradiction is derived, concluding the proof of this case.

$$GrantHistL \triangleq \forall l, i, r \in I :$$
$$toj[r] = i \wedge i \neq l \wedge l \in grant[l] \wedge i \notin \text{ReadyNodes} \wedge CwDist(l, i) < CwDist(l, r)$$
$$\Rightarrow CwDist(LeftNeighbor(lset[i]), i) \leq CwDist(l, i)$$

(iii) The node ln cannot exist between i and r (ln_3 in CASE 3 of Fig. 3). By IRN, ln cannot be "ready", because it lies between a node i and its right neighbor r_2. Then again by $TojNoReady$, there exists a node r_5, such that $toj[r_5] = LeftNeighbor(lset[r])$. The next step is to make a case analysis of the position of r_5. Because of IRN, it cannot be inside the range $[i, rn(i)]$. Because of $TojClosestL$, r_5 cannot be outside the range of (i, r). Hence, r_5 cannot exist. Hence, node ln cannot lie between i and r.

In conclusion, there is no possible position for such a node ln to exist, which means that there exists no node to grant node r its lease to make it "ready", and therefore, the constructed assumption as violation of IRN is impossible, completing the overall proof.   □

The invariants introduced in this proof are also proved using TLAPS, and further invariants are introduced and proved. The final TLA$^+$ proof for the inductive invariant consists of more than 14,500 lines. Additionally, the type correctness is also proved inductively in about 1,000 lines. These proofs with more than 20,000 lines, corresponding to more than 10,000 proof steps, are all automatically verified using the TLAPS proof manager, which launches different back-end first-order theorem provers or an extension of ISABELLE to find the proof.

4   Conclusion, Related Work and Future Work

This paper represented a formal verification of the Pastry protocol, a fundamental building block of P2P overlay networks. To the best of my knowledge, this is the first formal verification of Pastry, although the application of formal modeling and verification techniques to P2P protocols is not entirely new. For example, Borgström et al. [2] present initial work towards the verification of a distributed hash table in a P2P overlay network in a process calculus setting, but only considered fixed configurations with perfect routing information. As we have seen, the main challenge in verifying Pastry lies in the correct handling of nodes joining the system on the fly.

Chord ([17]) is another virtual ring implementation of DHT. Being described with a more formal specification, it is targeted by many verification approaches, such as [14], [8], [15] and [1]. A recent approach is [18], which uses Alloy to model Chord at a high level of abstraction where operations such as *join* or *stabilize* are considered atomic and non-interfering. Focusing on eventual consistency, she found a flaw in the original description of the algorithm and suggests a repair that may be correct. However, Alloy is not supported by a theorem proving language and tools like TLAPS to formally show an understandable proof of invariants as shown in this paper.

Pastry is a reasonably complicated algorithm that mixes complex data structures, dynamic network protocols, and timed behavior for periodic node updates. LuPastry abstracts from timing aspects, which are mainly important for performance, but otherwise models the algorithm as faithfully as possible. Here a "ready" node adds the joining node as soon as it receives the join request and does not accept any new join request until it gets the confirmation that the current joining node is "ready". In fact, LuPastry has been modified iteratively until the final proof of its invariants. LuPastry is verified against the property *CorrectDelivery* through inductive proof of invariants, under the assumption that no nodes leave the network. The proof serves at the same time as evidence of correctness of the formal model with respect to the verified property *CorrectDelivery* as well as a real world example demonstrating the possibility of using TLAPS for a large scale proof consisting of more than 10,000 proof steps.

Future work will include weaker assumptions to allow some bounded departure of nodes and prove that under particular constraints, the *CorrectDelivery* can still be ensured. Future work may also include formulating liveness properties for proving availability of the system based on our validation approach; generalizing the DHT model based on the static model of LuPastry; and increasing the automation degree of the interactive theorem prover TLAPS based on the similar patterns I have written as part of the formal proof.

Acknowledgments. I would like to thank my PhD supervisors Christoph Weidenbach and Stephan Merz for their support on this research topic and all the thesis and paper reviewers for their valuable comments.

References

1. Bakhshi, R., Gurov, D.: Verification of peer-to-peer algorithms: A case study. Electr. Notes Theor. Comput. Sci. **181**, 35–47 (2007)
2. Borgström, J., Nestmann, U., Onana, L., Gurov, D.: Verifying a structured peer-to-peer overlay network: the static case. In: Priami, C., Quaglia, P. (eds.) GC 2004. LNCS, vol. 3267, pp. 250–265. Springer, Heidelberg (2005)
3. Castro, M., Costa, M., Rowstron, A.I.T.: Performance and dependability of structured peer-to-peer overlays. In: International Conference on Dependable Systems and Networks (DSN 2004), pp. 9–18. IEEE Computer Society, Florence (2004)
4. Haeberlen, A., Hoye, J., Mislove, A., Druschel, P.: Consistent key mapping in structured overlays. Tech. Rep. TR05-456, Rice University, Department of Computer Science, August 2005

5. Hellerstein, J.M.: Toward network data independence. ACM SIGMOD Record **32**(3), 34–40 (2003)
6. Lamport, L.: Specifying Systems, The TLA$^+$ Language and Tools for Hardware and Software Engineers. Addison-Wesley (2002)
7. Lamport, L.: TLA tools (2012). http://www.tlaplus.net/
8. Li, X., Misra, J., Plaxton, C.G.: Active and Concurrent Topology Maintenance. In: Guerraoui, R. (ed.) DISC 2004. LNCS, vol. 3274, pp. 320–334. Springer, Heidelberg (2004)
9. Lu, T.: Formal Verification of the Pastry Protocol. Ph.D. thesis, Universität des Saarlandes, Saarbrücken (2013). urn:nbn:de:bsz:291-scidok-55878
10. Lu, T.: The TLA$^+$ codes for the pastry model (2013). http://tiit.lu/fmPastry/
11. Lu, T., Merz, S., Weidenbach, C.: Model checking the Pastry routing protocol. In: Bendisposto, J., Leuschel, M., Roggenbach, M. (eds.) 10th Intl. Workshop Automatic Verification of Critical Systems (AVOCS), pp. 19–21. Universität Düseldorf, Düsseldorf, Germany (2010)
12. Lu, T., Merz, S., Weidenbach, C.: Towards verification of the pastry protocol using TLA$^+$. In: Bruni, R., Dingel, J. (eds.) FORTE 2011 and FMOODS 2011. LNCS, vol. 6722, pp. 244–258. Springer, Heidelberg (2011)
13. Lu, T., Merz, S., Weidenbach, C.: Formal verification of the pastry protocol using TLA$^+$. 18th International Symposium on Formal Methods (2012)
14. Lynch, N., Stoica, I.: Multichord: A resilient namespace management protocol. MIT CSAIL Technical Report (2004)
15. Risson, J., Robinson, K., Moors, T.: Fault tolerant active rings for structured peer-to-peer overlays. In: The IEEE Conference on Local Computer Networks, 30th Anniversary 2005, pp. 18–25. IEEE (2005)
16. Rowstron, A., Druschel, P.: Pastry: scalable, decentralized object location, and routing for large-scale peer-to-peer systems. In: Guerraoui, R. (ed.) Middleware 2001. LNCS, vol. 2218, p. 329. Springer, Heidelberg (2001)
17. Stoica, I., Morris, R., Karger, D., Kaashoek, M.F., Balakrishnan, H.: Chord: A scalable peer-to-peer lookup service for internet applications. ACM SIGCOMM Computer Communication Review **31**(4), 149–160 (2001). ACM
18. Zave, P.: Using lightweight modeling to understand chord. Computer Communication Review **42**(2), 49–57 (2012)

Formal Modelling and Verification of IEC61499 Function Blocks with Abstract State Machines and SMV - Execution Semantics

Sandeep Patil[1(✉)], Victor Dubinin[2], and Victor Vyatkin[1,3]

[1] Luleå University of Technology, Luleå, Sweden
sandeep.patil@ltu.se, vyatkin@ieee.org
[2] Penza State University, Penza, Russia
victor_n_dubinin@yahoo.com
[3] Aalto University, Espoo, Finland

Abstract. IEC 61499 Standard for Function Blocks Architecture is an executable component model for distributed embedded control system design that combines block-diagrams and state machines. This paper proposes approach to formal modelling of IEC61499 function block execution semantics for popular model checking environment of SMV using Abstract State Machines. An operational semantics of IEC 61499 application with two-stage synchronous execution model is presented using this framework. This paper first introduces the importance of model checking function block applications in different execution semantics. It highlights the uses of formal verification, such as, verifying portability (behavior) of component based control applications across different implementation platforms compliant with the IEC 61499 standard. The formal model is applied on an example IEC 61499 application. The paper compares the verification results of this IEC 61499 application with two-stage synchronous execution model and the same application with cyclic execution model presented in the earlier work. With this comparison, we verify the portability of the IEC61499 applications across different platforms.

Keywords: Formal semantics · Model checking · Formal verification · Abstract state machines · IEC 61499 · Two-stage synchronous execution model

1   Introduction

The IEC 61499 [1, 2] is an international standard that introduces an open reference architecture for distributed control systems, which is an important class of embedded systems with a strong legacy background. The standard is often nicknamed the function block architecture after its main design artifact that is an event driven (and event activated) function block. If one would abstract out unnecessary details, the standard introduces quite an elegant model of distributed application that is a network of function blocks connected via control and data flows. The control flow is modelled using the concept of event that is emitted from an output of one function block and can be received at one or several inputs of other function blocks.

© Springer International Publishing Switzerland 2015
X. Li et al. (Eds.): SETTA 2015, LNCS 9409, pp. 300–315, 2015.
DOI: 10.1007/978-3-319-25942-0_20

Over the past decade, the applicability of the IEC 61499 standard in distributed control systems has been extensively studied in many projects, such as airport baggage handling systems, manufacturing control, mechatronics, building automation systems, machining, process control, and smart grid. These case studies [1] have confirmed many advantages of IEC 61499 over the mainstream PLC technology based on the IEC 61131-3 standard in terms of design and re-design efficiency, and better interoperability and reusability. However, these studies also revealed many pitfalls of the first edition, which are primarily due to the non-exhaustive definition of FB's execution semantics. This, on one hand, gives software vendors sufficient freedom to adapt the IEC 61499 standard into their existing tool frameworks, such as ISaGRAF Workbench. However, on the other hand, different IEC 61499 implementations may not be compatible with one another. Such incompatibility directly results in portability and interoperability issues that are against the standard's original intention. The portability of a function block application A between platforms that comply with execution semantics s_1 and s_2 can be defined as equivalence of the behavior $B(A,s_1)=B(A,s_2)$. However, brute force check of the equivalence can have prohibitive complexity. Instead, one can apply model-checking of A's model under semantic s, $M(A,s)$, against the comprehensive set of requirements R (functional and non-functional, including safety and liveness). Denoting the set of model-checking results as $C(M(A,s),R)$, we define the application A to be portable between semantics s_1 and s_2 if the model-checking gives equivalent results, i.e.:

$$P(A, s_1, s_2) \triangleq C(M(A, s_1), R) = C(M(A, s_2), R)$$

In [3] we introduce a way of modeling function blocks that simplify parameterization of the execution semantics, i.e. generation of model $M(A,s)$ for cyclic semantics s. In this paper we present synchronous semantics case. The modeling is based on the Abstract State Machines (ASM), and SMV is assumed as a tool implementing model-checking $C(M(A,s),R)$. The main modelling approach used in this paper is fully described in [4], the rest of the material presented in this paper is based on the modelling techniques described in [4]. In summary the main contributions of this paper are: (1) An approach to define operational semantics of IEC 61499 function block application on the basis of ASM; (2) ASM-based operational semantics of IEC 61499 application using two-stage synchronous execution model; (3) Mapping Distributed ASM – FB model (DASM-FB) to SMV; (4) Comparing the execution of an IEC 61499 application using two different execution semantics by means of model checking for portability issues.

2   Related Facts

2.1   Function Blocks

In IEC 61499, the basic design construct is called function block (FB). Each FB consists of a graphical event-data interface and a set of executable functional specifications (algorithms), represented as a state machine (in basic FB), or as a network of other FB instances (composite FB), or as a set of services (service interface FB). FBs can be interconnected into a network using event and data connections to specify the entire control application. Execution of an individual FB in the network is triggered by the events it receives. This well-defined event-data interface and the encapsulation of local data and control algorithms make each FB a reusable functional unit of software.

There are several approaches to defining formal models of function blocks like in [5]. In this paper, for the sake of brevity we present only informal examples of function blocks and systems built thereof. For example, the basic FB (BFB) ALU in Fig. 1. (a): is designed to perform arithmetic operations of addition and subtraction, depending on its input events. As seen from Fig. 1. (a): a basic FB is defined by signal interface (left hand side) and also its internal state machine (called Execution Control Chart, or ECC, on the right hand side). The BFB has three algorithms (executed in the ECC states), definition of these is beneath the diagram. It also has an internal variable n initialized to the value 13.

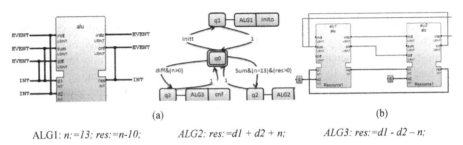

(a)   (b)

ALG1: $n:=13$; $res:=n-10$;   ALG2: $res:=d1 + d2 + n$;   ALG3: $res:=d1 - d2 - n$;

Fig. 1. (a): The basic FB ALU: interface (left), ECC diagram (right), algorithms (bottom row). (b): FB system of two ALUs designed in the ISaGRAF development environment

A function block application is a network of FBs connected by event and data links. As an example, let us consider an application that consists of two ALU function blocks interacting with each other (Fig. 1. (b)). This example, of course, does not comprehensively cover all FB artifacts and is used for illustrative purposes. The application consists of two instances of the arithmetic-logic unit (ALU) BFB type connected in closed-loop (outputs of one BFB are connected to the inputs of other BFB). Following the firing of the *initt* input of *alu*1 (Fig. 1. (b)) (emitted by hardware interface), the application enters an infinite sequence of computations consisting of alternating arithmetic operations - addition and subtraction. Moreover, the input parameters are chosen such that the variables do not change, i.e. when one FB adds a certain number, the second one subtracts it, as a result, the state space of the system is limited. A composite function block (CFB) is defined by a signal interface and internal network of function block instances similar to the application in Fig. 1. (b). The existing execution models of FB systems differ in the disciplines of FB execution scheduling, and the methods of events and data passing between the FBs. For example, in the *cyclic* execution model, each FB in an application is invoked once between the update of environment variables, and its place in the order of invocations is predefined.

In contrast to the cyclic execution models, which is sequential in the nature, *synchronous* execution model is a parallel one. Execution of FBs in the synchronous model is performed in the abstract moments of the discrete time ..., t - 1, t, t + 1, ... At one tick all enabled FBs are executed. In order to avoid the dependency of the result on a FB execution order inside the front of connected FBs, a two-stage scheme with intermediate buffering of output signals has been proposed. At the first stage, all FBs from the front of enabled FBs are executed, but the transfer of output signals to FB-consumers is postponed. At the second stage, delayed signals "come alive" and delivered to the target FBs.

2.2 Abstract State Machines

The Abstract State Machine (ASM) paradigm was introduced by Yuri Gurevich in 1988 [6] with basic definitions presented in [7] by the same author. The ASM methodologies are practical in modeling and analyzing different sizes of systems and have been applied in different research areas such as programing languages [8], hardware and software architectures [9], algorithm verification and network protocols [10]. ASMs have also been successfully used in representing semantics of programming languages such as Prolog, C, C#, and Java. In this research we use ASM (in the form of function change rules) to mathematically represent the rules used for modelling function blocks execution semantics in SMV.

2.3 Formal Modeling of IEC 61499 and Cross-Platform Portability

Formal verification is an act of proving or disproving an algorithm with respect to some specification or property. Model-checking is one such formal verification approach introduced in early 1980s by Clarke and Emerson [11, 12]. Formal modeling of IEC 61499 has more than a decade long history [13, 14]. There are two basic approaches to formal modeling of FB systems using: 1) a direct representation of FB in a language supported by a model-checking tool and 2) modeling of FB using an intermediate formal model and its subsequent translation to a language supported by a tool. The main disadvantage of the works in the first direction, such as [15, 16], is the lack of a systematic approach to constructing models of FB. In particular, there is no comprehensive pass-through formalization of FB models. Methods of constructing them do not reflect the system hierarchy, composite FB, algorithms and execution of FB models.

The most widely reported in the literature are the works representing the second approach. In works [17] a method using net condition/event systems (NCES) as the intermediate representation was proposed and [18, 19] presents a method of modeling NCES in SMV. The main drawbacks of the majority of these works are limitations of model-checkers, insufficient performance or limited support of arithmetic operations. From that perspective, the SMV approach promises some breakthroughs. It should also be noted that the SMV system has been used quite successfully in the industry, e.g. in the verification of the Function Blocks of the IEC 61131-3 standard [20]. Some of the authors of this paper have addressed the portability of FB applications by suggesting semantic-robust design patterns [21] and analyzing the consequences of semantic differences for portability [22]. However, the approach proposed in this paper has the potential for becoming the backend of portability certification based on formal methods.

3   Functional Structure of Operational Model

When defining the FB semantics, two constituent parts should be taken into account:

1) The proper functioning of FB described informally in IEC 61499 standard and 2) functioning of a system which schedules the FB execution on a resource to provide a desired execution model.

Before the development of FB execution semantics, we should evaluate possible variants of functional structural organization of FB formal model as a whole in order to:

1) Identify invariant and changeable parts in order to facilitate the description of a set of FB semantics for different execution models by reusing invariant descriptions; 2) Use the functional structural organization by the implementation of runtime tools.

It should be noted that one can build several variants of functional structural organization of FB semantic models. One of the most convenient cases is based on the hierarchically connected dispatchers (Fig. 2. (a)). In this figure *fb0, fb1, fb11, fb12* are operational models of composite FB or sub-applications; *fb2* is an operational model of basic FB; *d0. d1, d11,* and *d12* are operational models of dispatchers (*Note:* Synonym "scheduler" could be used as well). Model *fb0* can also represent the whole application. Wide arcs represent event and data flow between adjacent levels of FB, and dashed lines stand for the information used in the execution control of FB.

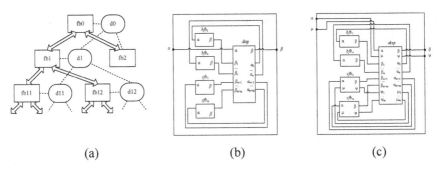

(a)	(b)	(c)

Fig. 2. (a) Functional structural organization of FB semantic model using hierarchically connected dispatchers. Structures of composite FB operational models for cyclic (b) and two-stage synchronous (c) execution models. Here $bfb_1, \ldots, bfb_n$ are basic FB models; $cfb_1, \ldots, cfb_m$ are composite FB models; *disp* is a dispatcher model.

In the two-stage synchronous execution model the first phase performs the sampling of data from the external environment and the execution of component FBs. The second phase carries out the transfer of signals and data between component FBs and issuing of signals and data to the external environment. The sequence of actions in accordance with the two-stage synchronous execution model is as follows (Fig. 2. (c)):

Phase 1 (on start signal α): 1) the transfer of signals from inputs of the composite FB module to input variables of component FBs; 2) start of the first execution phase in all component FBs; 3) waiting for completion of the first execution phase in all component FBs; 4) generating finish signal β.

Phase 2 (on start signal μ): 5) start of the second execution phase in all component composite FBs; 6) waiting for completion of the second execution phase in all component composite FBs; 7) the transfer of signals between component FBs and transmission signals from outputs of component FBs to outputs of the composite FB module; 8) generating finish signal ψ. In the model proposed above, the order of inter-level transmissions in each composite FB can be varied by changing the execution order of the actions at the FB module level. In order to ensure a "correct" signal transmission from the upper level FBs to the lower level FBs and vice-versa, in each module the signal transfer from inputs of composite FB module should be performed first while issuing signals to outputs of composite FB module should be performed at finish of composite FB module execution.

4   Modular formalism for FB operational semantics – Synchronous Execution

In the previous work we have proposed a modification of ASM for modeling FBs system called Distributed ASM – FB model (DASM-FB) [3]. For representation of the formal model of FB systems based on DASM-FB we choose the approach based on SMV modules. In this case, the semantic gap between DASM-FB and SMV model is minimal. Each module of DASM-FB (formal module) can be mapped to SMV module. Both DASM-FB modules and SMV modules work against each other asynchronously, while the rules for changing the functions of DASM-FB module and *next*-operators of SMV module run synchronously. SMV module declaration has the following syntax:

```
MODULE <module name> (<list of formal parameters>)
```

Table 1. below summarizes mapping of DASM-FB to SMV.

Table 1. The correspondence between elements of the formal module and SMV module

DASM-FB	SMV Model
(Formal) module	SMV module
A simple rule for changing the function of variable's values (in the form of one production rule)	*next* statement with the assignment operator
A rule set for changing the function of variable's values	*next* statement with *case* operator
Actual variable	Own variable of SMV module
Variable-representative	Formal parameter of SMV module
Component FB	Variables representing an instance of module of the specified type with *process* (asynchronous) descriptor

Each rule (or set of rules) of the formal module related to changing a variable of a type (for example, event input variables, OSM state, output variables, etc.) can be mapped to SMV statement *next* (with the *case* statement on the right hand side of assignment operator "=") because of *meta-model nature* of DASM-FB. All SMV variables in the *next* statements belong to the same type, like the type of the prototyping variable. The syntax of the *next* statement is as follows:

```
next (<name of variable>): = case
<condition 1 of changing of variable>: <expression 1 for new value>;
...
<condition N of changing of variable> <expression N for new value>;
esac;
```

If at certain conditions it is necessary to preserve the value of a variable, then the following construction should be used in the *case* statement.

```
<condition of conservation of variable>: <name of variable>;
```

Example: `1: < name of variable>;`

Each component FB of the formal model maps to a description (a call) of the corresponding SMV module in the parent SMV module:

```
VAR <name of FB module instance>: process <name of FB module type>
(<parameters of FB module instance>);
```

Note that in this case the keyword *process* defines the execution of the FB module instance as an asynchronous process.

4.1   Definition of Scheme for the Model

In the rest of this paper, we will formally define two state synchronous execution model. A composite function block module (CFBM) for two stage synchronous execution model is defined as follows:

$$M_c^s = (Synt_c, Sem_c^s),$$

where $Synt_c$ is the syntactic part of the definition (same as the cyclic pattern presented in [3]) and $Sem_c^s = (VRT_c^s, T_c^s, D_c^s)$ is the semantic part where the tuple components have the same meaning as the cyclic execution model but different definition as explained below.

Run-time variables are defined as the following tuple:

$$VRT_c^s = (VIB, VOB, FBD^s, \alpha, \beta, \mu, \psi, \omega),$$

Where,

$VIB = \{vib_1, vib_1, ..., vib_{N_{VI}}\}$ is a set of external buffers linked to the input variables, $|VIB| = |VI|, VIB \leftrightarrow VI, Dom(VIB) = N$ (set of integers);

$VOB = \{vob_1, vob_1, ..., vob_{N_{VO}}\}$ is a set of external buffers linked to the output variables, $|VOB| = |VO|, VOB \leftrightarrow VO, Dom(VOB) = N$;

FBD^s
$= \{fbd_1, fbd_2, \ldots, fbd_{N_{FB}}\}$ is a set of additional (semantic) descriptions of component FBs, which are included in the composite FB;

Note: The given set is divided into two subsets: $BFBD^s$ is a set of descriptions of basic component FBs; $CFBD^s$ is a set of descriptions of composite component FBs. $FBD^s = BFBD^s \cup CFBD^s$ and $BFBD^s \cap CFBD^s = \emptyset$.
If $fbd_i \in BFBD^s, fbd_i = (\alpha_i, \beta_i)$ where α_i and β_i are the start and end signals for BFBM. If $fbd_i \in CFBD^s, fbd_i = (\alpha_i, \beta_i, \mu_i, \psi_i)$ where $\alpha_i(\mu_i)$ is a variable of the start of the first (second) phase of execution of ith composite component FB; $\beta_i(\psi_i)$ is a variable of the termination of the first (second) phase of execution of ith composite component FB;

$\alpha(\mu)$ is a variable of the start of the first (second) phase of execution of the module. $Dom(\alpha) = Dom(\mu) = \{true, false\}$;

$\beta(\psi)$ is a variable of the termination of the first (second) phase of execution of the module. $Dom(\beta) = Dom(\psi) = \{true, false\}$;

ω is a condition of the termination of signal transfers in composite FB.

The tuple of transition functions is given below:

$$T_c^s = \left(t_{EI}, \left(t_{EI^i}\right)_{i=\overline{1,N_{FB}}}, \left(t_{EO^i}\right)_{i=\overline{1,N_{FB}}}, t_{EO}, t_{VI}, t_{VOB}\right).$$

It is similar to cyclic execution model, but functions are modified. The function for modification of output event variables t_{EO}, is as below:

$$t_{EO}: [Z_{EI}] \times \left[\bigcup_{i=1}^{N_{FB}} Z_{EO^i}\right] \times [Z_\mu] \times \left[\bigcup_{k=1}^{N_{CFB}} Z_{\psi_k}\right] \to [Z_{EO}]$$

This function sets output event variables of the module as a result of execution of the second phase.

The function of the reset of output event variables of ith component FB is modified by taking into account the conditions of the end of the second phase of FB execution:

$$t_{EO^i}: [Z_{EO^i}] \times \left[\bigcup_{k=1}^{N_{CFB}} Z_{\psi_i}\right] \times [Z_\mu] \to [Z_{EO^i}]$$

The rest remain the same as in cyclic execution model [3].

4.2   Definition of Dynamics of the Model

The rules below are considered for change of functions from tuple T_c^s (when using a scheduler of an intermediate level).

Rule Set 1: Rules for changing the function of values of event input variables of jth component FB:

a) For a case when inside the composite FB, there is at least one composite component FB:

$$\{p_{EI^j}^{C,S,1}[k,j]: Z_\alpha(\alpha) \wedge \bigvee_{\substack{ei_m \in EI, \\ (ei_m.ei_k^j) \in EVConn}} Z_{EI}(ei_m) \vee \bigwedge_{i=1}^{N_{CFB}} Z_{\psi_i}(\psi_i) \wedge$$

$$\vee \bigvee_{\substack{eo_n^x \in EO^x, \\ (eo_n^x.ei_k^j) \in EVConn}} Z_{EO^x}(eo_n^x) \Rightarrow Z_{EI^j}(ei_k^j) \leftarrow true \mid ei_k^j \in EI^j, j = \overline{1, N_{FB}};$$

According to this rule set, an event input variable of a component FB is set to "true" if at least one event input or output variable connected to this event variable is set to "true" as well as there is the start signal for the composite FB.

b) For a case when inside the composite FB only basic component FBs exist:

$$\{ p_{EIj}^{C,S,2}[k,j]: Z_\alpha(\alpha) \wedge \bigvee_{\substack{ei_m \in EI, \\ (ei_m,ei_k^j) \in EVConn}} Z_{EI}(ei_m) \vee Z_\mu(\mu) \wedge$$

$$\bigvee_{\substack{eo_n^x \in EO^x, \\ (eo_n^x,ei_k^i) \in EVConn}} Z_{EO^x}(eo_n^x) \Rightarrow Z_{EIj}(ei_k^j) \leftarrow true \mid ei_k^j \in EI^j, j = \overline{1,N_{FB}}\}.$$

Rule Set 2: Rules for changing the function of values of event output variables are built on the basis of rule $p_{EO}^{C,C,1}$ [3] by adding in it a check of variables β_i and ψ_i since signal transfer to the output is made only at the end of the second phase in all component FBs:

a) For a case when in the composite FB there is at least one composite component FB:

$$\{p_{EO}^{C,S,1}[k]: \bigvee_{\substack{ei_m \in EI, \\ (ei_m,eo_k) \in EVConn}} Z_{EI}(ei_m) \vee \bigvee_{\substack{eo_n^x \in EO^x, \\ (eo_n^x,eo_k) \in EVConn}} Z_{EO^x}(eo_n^x) \wedge$$

$$\wedge_{i=1}^{N_{CFB}} Z_{\psi_i}(\psi_i) \Rightarrow Z_{EO}(eo_k) \leftarrow true \mid eo_k \in EO\};$$

b) For a case when in the composite FB only basic component FBs exist:

$$\{p_{EO}^{C,S,2}[k]: \bigvee_{\substack{ei_m \in EI, \\ (ei_m,eo_k) \in EVConn}} Z_{EI}(ei_m) \vee \bigvee_{\substack{eo_n^x \in EO^x, \\ (eo_n^x,eo_k) \in EVConn}} Z_{EO^x}(eo_n^x) \wedge$$

$$Z_\mu(\mu) \Rightarrow Z_{EO}(eo_k) \leftarrow true \mid eo_k \in EO\}.$$

Since, in our case, the synchronous data sampling is used, all input signals are dropped at the reception of the start signal α. For these purposes, rule $p_{EI}^{C,C,1}$ defined for the cyclic model could be used [3].

Rule Set 3: The reset of output event variables of component FBs is made at the end of the second phase:

a) For a case when in the composite FB there is at least one composite component FB:

$$\{p_{EOi}^{C,S,1}[k,j]: Z_{EOi}(eo_k^j) \wedge \wedge_{i=1}^{N_{CFB}} Z_{\psi_i}(\psi_i) \Rightarrow Z_{EOj}(eo_k^j) \leftarrow false \mid eo_k^j \in$$

$$EO^j, j = \overline{1,N_{FB}}\};$$

b) For a case when in the composite FB only basic component FBs exist:

$$\{p_{EOi}^{C,S,2}[k,j]: Z_{EOi}(eo_k^j) \wedge Z_\mu(\mu) \Rightarrow Z_{EOj}(eo_k^j) \leftarrow false \mid eo_k^j \in EO^j, j = \overline{1,N_{FB}}\}$$

Rule Set 4: The issue of output data is defined by the following rules:

a) For a case when in the composite FB there is at least one composite component FB:

$$\{p_{VOB}^{C,S,1}[m]: \bigwedge_{i=1}^{N_{CFB}} Z_{\psi_i}(\psi_i) \wedge \bigvee_{(eo_k,vob_m)\in OW}(\bigvee_{\substack{ei_j\in EI, \\ (ei_j,eo_k)\in EVConn}} Z_{EI}(ei_j) \vee$$

$$\vee \bigvee_{\substack{eo_n^x\in EO^x, \\ (eo_n^x,eo_k)\in EVConn}} Z_{EO^x}(eo_n^x)) \Rightarrow$$

$$Z_{VOB}(vob_m) \leftarrow Z_{VO}(repr_{VO}(vob_m)) \mid vob_m\in VOB\};$$

b) For a case when in the composite FB only basic component FBs exist:

$$\{p_{VOB}^{C,S,2}[m]: Z_\mu(\mu) \wedge$$

$$\bigvee_{(eo_k,vob_m)\in OW}(\bigvee_{\substack{ei_j\in EI, \\ (ei_j,eo_k)\in EVConn}} Z_{EI}(ei_j) \vee \vee \bigvee_{\substack{eo_n^x\in EO^x, \\ (eo_n^x,eo_k)\in EVConn}} Z_{EO^x}(eo_n^x)) \Rightarrow$$

$$Z_{VOB}(vob_m) \leftarrow Z_{VO}(repr_{VO}(vob_m)) \mid vob_m\in VOB\}.$$

Here, the representative of a variable from set VO defined by function $repr_{VO}$ is used as an argument of function Z_{VO}. The purpose of this substitution is to minimize the number of variables without loss of accuracy.

4.3 Model of the Dispatcher for Synchronous Execution Model

In order to demonstrate various schemes of construction of systems of co-operating FB modules and dispatchers, we will consider a case of implementation of a scheduler for two stage synchronous FB execution model in the form of an *asynchronous* module. It should be noted that the main principles of construction of "synchronous" and "asynchronous" schedulers remain the same. However, in the latter case, it is necessary to watch explicitly, the appearances of some events, for example, the termination of all signals and data transfers in the parent FB.

A dispatcher for the synchronous execution model is defined as tuple:

$$D_C^S = (V_D^S, T_D^S, Z_D^{C,0}),$$

where V_D^S is s set of dispatcher variables; T_D^S is a set of dispatcher transitions functions; $Z_D^{S,0}$ is a set of functions of initial values of the variables.

A set of variables of an intermediate level scheduler for the synchronous execution model is defined by the following tuple:

$$V_D^S = (\alpha, \mu, \beta, \psi, (\alpha_i)_{i=\overline{1,N_{FB}}}, (\mu_i)_{i=\overline{1,N_{CFB}}}, (\beta_i)_{i=\overline{1,N_{FB}}}, (\psi_i)_{i=\overline{1,N_{CFB}}}, \omega),$$

where α and μ are variables of the start of the first and the second phases of execution of the subsystem accordingly (*Note*: the term "subsystem" means "subsystem of FBs". In other words, it represents a composite FB or a sub-application). β and ψ are variables of the termination of the first and the second phases of execution of the subsystem accordingly. $(\alpha_i)_{i=\overline{1,N_{FB}}}, (\mu_i)_{i=\overline{1,N_{CFB}}}$ are sets of variables of the start of the first and the second phases of execution of component FBs accordingly. $(\beta_i)_{i=\overline{1,N_{FB}}}, (\psi_i)_{i=\overline{1,N_{CFB}}}$ are sets of variables of the end of the first and the second phase of execution of component FBs accordingly. ω is a flag of the end of transfers in the parent composite FB. Here N_{FB} is the number of component FBs in a subsystem, N_{CFB} is the number of component composite FBs in a subsystem. For simplicity, we assume that at the enumeration of component FBs in a subsystem, composite component FBs are referred first, and basic component FBs follow second.

Rules of functioning of an intermediate level dispatcher are given below.

Rule Set 5: Rules for resetting variable α and setting variable β accordingly are as follows:

$$p_\alpha^{1,D,S}: \bigwedge_{k=1}^{NFB} Z_{\beta_k}(\beta_k) \Rightarrow Z_\alpha(\alpha) \leftarrow false$$
$$p_\beta^{1,D,S}: \bigwedge_{k=1}^{NFB} Z_{\beta_k}(\beta_k) \Rightarrow Z_\beta(\beta) \leftarrow true$$

According to the given rules, resetting α and setting β are performed when all component FBs included in the subsystem, have completed their execution of the first phase.

Rule Set 6: Rules for resetting variable μ and setting variable ψ are distinguished for the next cases:

a) The subsystem contains one or more composite component FBs:
$$p_\mu^{1,D,S}: \bigwedge_{k=1}^{NCFB} Z_{\psi_k}(\psi_k) \Rightarrow Z_\mu(\mu) \leftarrow false$$
$$p_\psi^{1,D,S}: \bigwedge_{k=1}^{NCFB} Z_{\psi_k}(\psi_k) \wedge Z_\omega(\omega) \Rightarrow Z_\psi(\psi) \leftarrow true$$
b) The subsystem contains only basic component FBs:
$$p_\mu^{2,D,S}: Z_\mu(\mu) \wedge Z_\omega(\omega) \Rightarrow Z_\mu(\mu) \leftarrow false$$
$$p_\psi^{2,D,S}: Z_\mu(\mu) \wedge Z_\omega(\omega) \Rightarrow Z_\psi(\psi) \leftarrow true$$

Rule Set 7:
a) A rule for setting variables $(\alpha_i)_{i=\overline{1,NFB}}$ is represented below:

$$p_{\alpha_i}^{1,D,S}: Z_\alpha(\alpha) \wedge Z_\omega(\omega) \Rightarrow Z_{\alpha_i}(\alpha_i) \leftarrow true$$

According to the given rules, the first phase of execution of ith component FB is started (in the next clock tick) at the presence of signal α of the start of the subsystem as a whole. At that, all signals transfers in the composite FB (from event inputs of this block) should be completed. As it can be seen, all component FBs are started simultaneously. The start of the component FBs will occur correctly under the following conditions: at the presence of ready signals and the data on the inputs. Note that launch of the component FBs is behind by one tick, relative to actions for data sampling and signals transfer from event inputs of the parent composite FB to the inputs of the inner component FBs.

b) A rule for resetting variables $(\beta_i)_{i=\overline{1,NFB}}$ is represented below

$$p_{\beta_i}^{1,D,S}: \bigwedge_{k=1}^{NFB} Z_{\beta_k}(\beta_k) \Rightarrow Z_{\beta_i}(\beta_i) \leftarrow false$$

As it can be seen, variables β_i are dropped simultaneously with setting variable β.

c) A rule for setting variables $(\mu_i)_{i=\overline{1,NCFB}}$ for the launch of the second phase of execution of component FBs is represented below:

$$p_{\mu_i}^{1,D,S}: Z_\mu(\mu) \Rightarrow Z_{\mu_i}(\mu_i) \leftarrow true$$

The given rule is structurally similar to rule $p_{\alpha_i}^{1,D,S}$, but waiting for the end of signal transfers (from inputs) is not required.

d) A rule for resetting variables (ψ_i)$_{i=\overline{1,N_{CFB}}}$ of the termination of the second phase of execution of component FBs is represented below:

$$p_{\psi_i}^{1,D,S}: Z_\omega(\omega) \wedge \bigwedge_{k=1}^{N_{CFB}} Z_{\psi_k}(\psi_k) \Rightarrow Z_{\psi_i}(\psi_i) \leftarrow false$$

The given rule is structurally similar to rule $p_{\beta_i}^{1,D,S}$, but in this case waiting for the end of signal transfers to outputs is required. It should be emphasized, the second phase is defined only for component composite FBs. If there are no composite component FBs in the subsystem, then FB execution of the second phase is reduced only to transfer of signals inside the subsystem.

The difference of a main dispatcher (in other words, a top-level one, denoted as D`) from an intermediate level scheduler is that it is completely independent of other dispatchers and there are no external control signals for handling of FB execution phases. The main dispatcher is defined for FB network of the uppermost level; as a rule, it is an FB network located on a resource.

Completeness of the above rule sets is confirmed by the correct use of the formal notation, a software implementation of FB model in accordance with proposed semantic description [23] and application of these FB models in some R&D projects.

5   Model of the Dispatcher in SMV

For the example shown in Fig. 1. (b), the dispatcher in SMV is given below. To save space it is depicted in a tabular form.

MODULE schedulerSynch(alpha1,alpha2,beta1,beta2,omega)	
ASSIGN	

next(alpha1):= case
  (omega & beta1 & beta2): 1;
  1: alpha1;
esac;
next(alpha2):= case
  (omega & beta1 & beta2): 1;
  1: alpha2;
esac;
	next(beta1):= case
	  (omega & beta1 & beta2): 0;
	  1: beta1;
	esac;
	next(beta2):= case
	  (omega & beta1 & beta2): 0;
	  1: beta2;
	esac;

6   Verification Results

This section presents results of the model checking as applied to the composite block in Fig. 1. (b). For the benefit of comparison, we show the results for both the cyclic execution model [3] and synchronous execution model presented in this paper. Result (A) column shows the cyclic execution model and Result (B) shows the synchronous execution model.

Table 2. CTL Properties and verification results

CTL	Result(A)	Result(B)	CTL	Result(B)	Result(A)
SPEC EF beta1	true	true	SPEC EF (alu1.n=13)	true	true
SPEC EF alpha1	true	true	SPEC EF (alu1.d2=5)	true	true
SPEC EF !initt1	true	true	SPEC EF (alu1.res=3)	true	true
SPEC EF inito1	true	true	SPEC EF (alu1.res=8)	false	false
SPEC EF cnf1	true	true	SPEC EF (alu1.res=18)	true	true
SPEC EF (alu1.S=s0)	true	true	SPEC EF (alu1.res>18)	false	false
SPEC EF (alu1.S=s1)	true	true	SPEC EF (alu2.res>0)	true	true
SPEC EF (alu1.S=s2)	true	true	SPEC EF (res1Buf=3)	false	false
SPEC EF (alu1.Q=q0)	true	true	SPEC EF (res1Buf=18)	true	true
SPEC EF (alu1.Q=q1)	true	true	SPEC EF (res1Buf>0)	true	true
SPEC EF (alu1.Q=q2)	true	true	SPEC AG(EF sub2)	true	true
SPEC EF (alu1.Q=q3)	false	false	SPEC AG(EF (alu1.Q=q2))	true	true
SPEC EF (alu2.Q=q0)	true	true	SPEC AG (EF alpha1)	true	true
SPEC EF (alu2.Q=q1)	true	true	SPEC AG (EF alpha2)	true	true
SPEC EF (alu2.Q=q2)	false	false	SPEC AG (alpha1 -> AF alpha2)	true	true
SPEC EF (alu2.Q=q3)	true	true	SPEC AG (alpha2 -> AF alpha1)	true	true
SPEC EF ((alu1.NI=2) & (alu1.NA=1))			true		true

We can conclude that verification results for both cyclic and synchronous execution models for the given set of properties are same. Table 3. below shows the secondary results related to a better understanding of the synchronous execution model. The results are false, but that is what we want.

Table 3. Specific results for synchronous execution model

CTL	Result
SPEC AG (EF alu1.AbsentsEnabledECTran & alu2.AbsentsEnabledECTran)	false
SPEC EF (AG alu1.AbsentsEnabledECTran & alu2.AbsentsEnabledECTran)	false
SPEC EF (AG alu1.S=s0 & alu2.S=s0)	false
SPEC EF (alu1.S=s1 & alu2.S=s1)	false
SPEC EF (alu1.S=s1 & alu2.S=s2)	false
SPEC EF (alu1.S=s2 & alu2.S=s1)	false

Property *AG(EF sub2) = true* says that the signal on input *sub2* cannot be lost forever and FB *alu2* will be invoked at some point. Property *AG(EF (alu1.Q=q2)) = true* says FB *alu1* can reach state *q2* (adding) always. It means FB *alu1* will be triggered sometime in the future. Properties *EF(AG alu1.AbsentsEnabledECTran & alu2.AbsentsEnabledECTran) = false* and *EF(AG alu1.S=s0 & alu2.S=s0) = false* indicate that FB system is live and there is no deadlock. Properties *EF (alu1.S=s1 & alu2.S=s1) = false* and *EF (alu1.S=s1 & alu2.S=s2) = false* and *EF (alu1.S=s2 & alu2.S=s1) = false* indicate that FB's *alu1* and *alu2* cannot work simultaneously while the synchronous execution model assumes usually the simultaneous execution of FBs. It is due to specificity of the FB system functioning. Here, the two instances of the FB system work alternatively (addition-subtraction-addition-etc.). However the FBs start simultaneously. The simple example such as the one presented in this paper took a maximum of 90 seconds (verify 43 CTL properties) to complete model checking. But as is the case with model checking, with increase in complexity, there is an increase in verification time and state space. Addressing state space explosion problem and verification is not in the scope of this paper and hence would like the reader to refer to [24] that presents some techniques to address these issues specifically targeting the methodology presented in this paper.

7   Conclusion and Future Work

In this paper, we presented a formal model for one of the execution semantics of IEC 61499 Function Blocks based on a "customized" distributed ASM, which is well suited for verification and simulation purposes, using SMV. One can note the following features of our formal notation: 1) the use of state variables and functions of their values in determining the system state; 2) an asynchronous and distributed nature, where one SMV module models one FB module; 3) the presence of shared variables for modules, 4) determinacy of modules; 5) the use of explicit production rules when presenting the ASM programs; 6) a special restriction on the execution of the distributed ASM. This paper explained one of the execution semantics (synchronous). The test results were compared with the those from cyclic execution [3] and we showed that the example system works well in two different environments (tools). In follow up works other semantics (asynchronous and sequential) and their comparison will be covered. This paper presented a simple example, however a more advanced example is presented in [25] that verifies a smart grid system presented in [26].

Acknowledgments. This work was partially supported by the program "Fundamental research and exploratory research involving young researchers" (2015-2017) of the Russian Science Foundation (project number 15-11-10010), and by Luleå Tekniska Universitet, grants 381119, 381940, 381121 and Wallenberg Foundation "Jubileumsanslaget" - Travel grants.

References

1. Vyatkin, V.: IEC 61499 as Enabler of Distributed and Intelligent Automation: State-of-the-Art Review. IEEE Transactions on Industrial Informatics **7**, 768–781 (2011)
2. Function blocks — Part 1: Architecture, IEC Standard 61499-1, Second ed. (2012)
3. Patil, S., Dubinin, V., Pang, C.,Vyatkin, V.: Neutralizing semantic ambiguities of function block architecture by modeling with ASM. In: 9th International Andrei Ershov Memorial Conference, PSI 2014 PeterhofSt. Petersburg, Russia (2014)
4. Patil, S.,Dubinin, V.,yatkin, VV.: Formal verification of IEC61499 function blocks with abstract state machines and smv – modelling. In: The 13th IEEE International Symposium on Parallel and Distributed Processing with Applications (IEEE ISPA-15) Helsinki, Finland (2015)
5. Dubinin, V., Vyatkin, V.: On definition of a formal model for IEC 61499 function blocks. EURASIP Journal on Embedded Systems **2008**, 1–10 (2008)
6. Gurevich, Y.: Logic and the Challenge of Computer Science. Current Trends in Theoretical Computer Science, pp. 1–57 (1988)
7. Gurevich, Y.: Evolving algebras 1993: lipari guide. In: Egon, B. (ed.) Specification and validation methods, pp. 9–36. Oxford University Press, Inc. (1995)
8. Börger, E., Fruja, N.G., Gervasi, V., Stärk, R.F.: A high-level modular definition of the semantics of C#. Theoretical Computer Science **336**, 235–284 (2005)
9. Börger, E., Glässer, U., Muller, W.: A formal definition of an abstract VHDL1993 simulator by EA-machines. In: Kloos, C., Breuer, P. (eds.) Formal Semantics for VHDL, pp. 107–139. Springer, US (1995)
10. Glässer, U., Gurevich, Y., Veanes, M.: High-Level Executable Specification of the Universal Plug and Play Architecture, presented at the HICSS (2002)
11. Emerson, E.A., Clarke, E.: Characterizing correctness properties of parallel programs using fixpoints. In: de Bakker, J.W., van Leeuwen, J. (eds.) ICALP 1980. LNCS, vol. 85. Springer, Heidelberg (1980)
12. Clarke, E.M., Emerson, E.A.: Design and Synthesis of Synchronization Skeletons Using Branching-Time Temporal Logic, presented at the Logic of Programs, Workshop (1982)
13. Hanisch, H.-M., Hirsch, M., Missal, D., Preuße, S., Gerber, C.: One decade of IEC 61499 modeling and verification-results and open issues. In: 13th IFAC Symposium on Information Control Problems in Manufacturing. V.A. Trapeznikov Institute of Control Sciences, Russia (2009)
14. Vyatkin, V., Hanisch, H.M.: Formal modeling and verification in the software engineering framework of IEC 61499: a way to self-verifying systems. In: 2001 Proceedings of 8th IEEE International Conference on Emerging Technologies and Factory Automation, vol. 2, pp. 113–118 (2001)
15. Bonfe, M., Fantuzzi, C.: Design and verification of mechatronic object-oriented models for industrial control systems. In: ETFA '03, IEEE Conference on Emerging Technologies and Factory Automation, vol. 2, pp. 253–260 (2003)
16. Dimitrova, D., Frey, G., Bachkova, I.: Formal approach for modeling and verification of IEC 61499 function blocks. In: Advanced Manufacturing Technologies (AMTECH 2005), Russe, Bulgaria, pp. 731–736 (2005)
17. Patil, S., Bhadra, S., Vyatkin, V.: Closed-loop formal verification framework with non-determinism, configurable by meta-modelling. In: IECON 2011 - 37th Annual Conference on IEEE Industrial Electronics Society, pp. 3770–3775 (2011)

18. Vyatkin, V., Hanisch, H.M.: A modeling approach for verification of IEC1499 function blocks using net condition/event systems. In: 1999 Proceedings of 7th IEEE International Conference on Emerging Technologies and Factory Automation. ETFA '99, vol. 1, pp. 261–270 (1999)
19. Dubinin, V., Hanisch, H.M., Vyatkin, V., Shestakov, S.: Analysis of extended net condition/event systems on the basis of model checking. presented at the Proc. Int. Conf. New Information Technologies and Systems (Originally published in Russian), Penza (2010)
20. Junbeom, Y., Sungdeok, C., Eunkyung, J.: A verification framework for FBD based software in nuclear power plants. In: Software Engineering Conference, 2008. APSEC '08. 15th Asia-Pacific, pp. 385–392 (2008)
21. Dubinin, V.N., Vyatkin, V.: Semantics-Robust Design Patterns for IEC 61499. IEEE Transactions on Industrial Informatics **8**, 279–290 (2012)
22. Patil, S., Yan, J., Vyatkin, V., Pang, C.: On composition of mechatronic components enabled by interoperability and portability provisions of IEC 61499: A case study. In: 2013 IEEE 18th Conference on Emerging Technologies & Factory Automation (ETFA), pp. 1–4 (2013)
23. Drozdov, D.: FB2SMV: IEC 61499 Function blocks XML code to SMV converter (2015). https://github.com/dmitrydrozdov/fb2smv
24. Patil, S., Drozdov, D., Dubinin, V., Vyatkin, V.: Cloud-Based Framework for Practical Model-Checking of Industrial Automation Applications. In: Camarinha-Matos, L.M., Baldissera, T.A., Di Orio, G., Marques, F. (eds.) DoCEIS 2015. IFIP AICT, vol. 450, pp. 73–81. Springer, Heidelberg (2015)
25. Patil, S., Zahabelova, G., Vyatkin, V., McMillin, B.: Towards formal verification of smart grid distributed intelligence: FREEDM case. In: Industrial Electronics Society, IECON 2015 - 41st Annual Conference of the IEEE, Yokohama, Japan (2015)
26. Patil, S., Vyatkin, V., McMillin, B.: Implementation of FREEDM smart grid distributed load balancing using IEC 61499 function blocks. In: Industrial Electronics Society, IECON 2013 - 39th Annual Conference of the IEEE, pp. 8154–8159 (2013)

Author Index

Printed in the United States
By Bookmasters